Sessions with
SINATRA

Library of Congress Cataloging-in-Publication Data

Granata, Charles, L.
    Sessions with Sinatra : Frank Sinatra and the art of recording/
Charles L. Granata.
       p.   cm.
    Includes bibliographical references, discography, and index.
    ISBN 1-55652-356-4
    1. Sinatra, Frank. 1915-1998.   —Criticism and interpretation.
    1. Title.
ML420.S565G73   1999
782.42164'092—dc21

99-27871
CIP

©1999 by Charles L. Granata
All rights reserved
First edition
A Cappella Books
An imprint of Chicago Review Press, Incorporated
814 North Franklin Street
Chicago, Illinois 60610
ISBN 1-55652-356-4
Printed in the United States of America
5 4 3 2

Sessions with
SINATRA

Frank Sinatra and the Art of Recording

CHARLES L. GRANATA

a cappella

For Barbara, Kate, and Alex,

with love

and for Mom and Dad,

who nurtured my love for music, and

encouraged me to follow my dreams.

In memory of Frank Sinatra

1915–1998

Contents

THE CAPITOL YEARS, 1953–1962

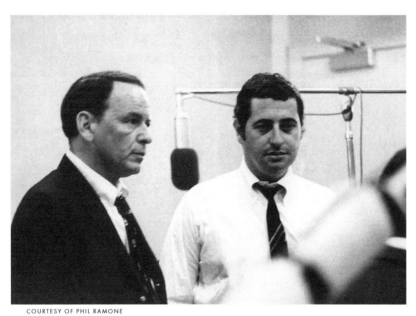

COURTESY OF PHIL RAMONE

Frank Sinatra and Phil Ramone.

Foreword

*F*rank Sinatra has always been a part of my life. From the time I was three, Sinatra always seemed to be the common thread that ran through my musical development. As I grew, I got hip to that finger-poppin' sound of his early Capitol records, and by the end of the 1950s, I knew inside out every disc that he made. When I was in my teens, I would even "conduct" the Billy May band in the same way that kids today play "air guitar."

As I began to think about the process of recording, I knew that Frank Sinatra's albums set the industry standard. When I became an engineer, I studied those album covers that showed him in the studio (like *Sinatra's Swingin' Session!!!* and my favorite, *The Concert Sinatra*), and tried to imitate how the band and the singer were miked. When I finally got the chance to visit a Sinatra session, I looked at every microphone placement and memorized it. The day I realized my dream of engineering a Sinatra session, I was in heaven.

During my career, I've had the good fortune to record and produce artists like Quincy Jones, Billy Joel, Paul Simon, Bob Dylan, Elton John, Barbra Streisand, Tony Bennett, Barry Manilow, and Natalie Cole. But the achievement that I've always been the proudest of is having worked with Frank Sinatra as both an engineer and a producer. When the call came to work with him, there was no question that I had reached the major league. Yet it was never an ego thing, although I must admit, it was an incredible rush for me to realize that I was on the same level with a man who was my hero.

Not everything I learned from Sinatra was specifically technical: the major thing he taught me, and the industry at large, was about professionalism. In fact, everything I know about doing things right I learned from Frank Sinatra.

One night that proved to be a turning point in my career as an engineer was the night Quincy Jones and I went to hear him at The Sands in Las Vegas. We were seated, and as the house lights went down, there came this grandiose announcement: "Ladies and Gentlemen, Francis Albert Sinatra!" Frank walked onstage to begin the first song, opened his mouth and started singing, only to find that his mike was dead. He didn't say a word—he just dropped the mike right on the floor, and walked off. The whole room was as quiet as death. But a couple of minutes later, the announcement was repeated, and he walked back on. You better believe the mike worked this time! He didn't say a word about what had happened during the entire show, but you can bet there was hell to pay backstage afterward. Not from him, incidentally. It came from the people that should have been on top of things right from the start—those that should have known better.

I learned from that experience to always have a back-up: to have two microphones set up, and better than that, to be sure they're tested and re-tested. And I've found that the days that I don't personally check every damned wire myself are the days that things go wrong in the studio.

On my first recording session with Frank, I made sure to double mike it, and he noticed that. I remember he looked at the two mikes, then at me, and asked "Why are you doing that?" I teased him a little bit, then said, "Bill Putnam (one of his favorite engineers in Los Angeles) told me 'Don't

mess up!'" Since I had reached this high a plateau, I prided myself, as I hope anybody would, on not taking any chances.

Everything around him had to be thought out. You'd take all the little details, and then go over them fifty times. I'd ask myself, "What am I going to do in the studio? How do I get everybody to understand that they have to start rolling the tape as soon as we know he's coming down the hall?" I couldn't even imagine any other way of working with Frank. It wasn't that he insisted on it. On the contrary, I would hope that he wasn't even aware of what we were going through in the booth. I wanted him to feel totally free to concentrate only on what was required of him.

There was always an unspoken command that everyone who ever worked with Frank felt: "This is your position in this enterprise, be it musician, engineer, or producer, and I don't expect you to be anything but great." The word "whoops" just wasn't in his vocabulary. He expected the best from everyone. If you approached every day as though a Sinatra session were looming, you'd have a much better attitude about your work, for he simply inspired and brought out the best in you. Actually, you would do even better than your very best. In those two to three hours, there was a level of concentration, of collective excellence, in which everybody in the room was working at the absolute highest peak. The best thing was that, once in a while, when things were really going right, Frank would turn around and just give you a grin. It was the greatest kind of approval you could ever receive—the kind of approval you receive from your parents when they really love you. When you got that look from him, you realized that's what it was all about.

The studio is a great place to be when everything's running smoothly. It's funny, but when everything is tight—when you know what you're doing and operating at your peak—that's when you can cut loose. Once you hit that plane, you can make suggestions, try different things, slow the tempo down or speed it up. You know from experience that this can only happen when everybody is pulling together, when there are no distractions, when you're operating at Frank's own level.

In the studio he demanded total concentration, both of himself and everyone around him. When you get to that place, that sweet spot where everything's "in the pocket," you can even laugh at the rare mistakes that do happen. You don't have to worry that if, for instance, some trumpeter plays a perfect phrase or hits a beautiful high A and somebody else goofed, it can't be done again. You know that if need be, he *can* hit it again—it wasn't a fluke that he was able to do it in the first place. He did it because it's his job, like it is yours as the engineer, to be the best.

Even when he was pushing eighty, Sinatra was operating at a level of excellence that was astonishing. I would be working with the younger artists that were singing with him on the *Duets* albums, and there were specific lines I wanted the other vocalist to sing exactly with him, or perhaps in unison—sometimes maybe an octave away. It was then that they learned that what sounds so easy can be the toughest thing in the world. They'd say, "How the hell did he do that? What did he do? How did he make that happen?"

The energy that flowed between Sinatra and the musicians was something to see. There are always combinations of players who bring to the party, on the first take, something that makes music fabulous. When it came to recording, Frank didn't enter as an individual star. When he came into that room, he was part of an ensemble that was going to make music. The champ was in the ring!

He knew from his days of watching Tommy Dorsey what it meant to have a band play well, and what it took to get the most out of the players. I've seen artists who are aware that the band is there, and they appreciate the musicians, but don't really interact with them—musically or physically—on any level. Even during our last dates together, the string players were coming over with their charts to have Frank autograph them. In my experience, your typical superstar wouldn't want any part of

that, but he would sign autographs and accommodate everybody.

Whatever inspired Frank Sinatra to be the person he was, he mentored for everyone in the world the art of recording, which is what this book is all about.

Through the years we've read a lot about Sinatra. This book is not about the personal side, but the professional part of his life, from a musical point of view. If you have any sort of passion for the music, this book has all of the answers.

Within these pages, Chuck Granata draws on his deep knowledge of both Sinatra's craft and the fine details of the recording process to explain the most important part of Sinatra's legacy: his personal discipline in the recording studio. Reading how the technology evolved around him and how he worked so diligently to use it effectively is fascinating, and highlights all of the major contributions Frank has made to our field. No recording career has ever been chronicled in quite this way.

Then too, no career has the expansive scope of Sinatra's. He embraced all of the music from the big bands to rock, and in doing so, made himself the narrator of the history of popular music.

As I read through it, I asked myself, "If Frank were to pick up this book, what would he think?" I'm sure he would be proud of it and say that it was marvelous. His reaction would probably be much the same as mine: he would start browsing, and begin to remember recording songs that changed the world, and places he recorded in, and people he worked with. For me, that's the important information—the prime stuff!

From 1939 to 1994, Frank Sinatra was the most consistent man, doing the most consistent things in the recording studio, that anyone has ever done.

I think of him every day, and I miss him dearly.

—Phil Ramone
Bedford, New York, April 1999

Introduction

"I adore making records. I'd rather do that than almost anything else."

—Frank Sinatra, 1961

"Frank had the color and the fire and the brains and the imagination. Intellectual background, strangely enough. Artistic sensitivity."

—Nelson Riddle, 1983

Frank Sinatra was a master of the art of recording. His work in the studio set him apart from other gifted vocalists; and performers old and new, vocal and instrumental, emulate his accomplishments there to this day. What did he have that others so admired?

First, Sinatra was above all a musician. His instrument was his voice, and it was a priceless instrument that he worked tirelessly to perfect throughout his long career. Then, Frank Sinatra was directing his own recording sessions and functioning as his own producer years before it became fashionable. From song selection to choice of arranger and orchestral accompaniment, and ultimately, the color of the sound achieved, Sinatra, more than any other pop vocalist, was intimately involved with the creation of his recordings.

PHOTOGRAPH BY KEN VEEDER, COURTESY OF MPTV ARCHIVE

More elusive but equally important, the kinetic energy that Quincy Jones once called "the heat" surrounded the singer. When he entered the studio, the atmosphere suddenly became highly charged. "He had a magical aura about him," said Rosemary Riddle-Accera, the eldest daughter of Sinatra's favorite arranger, Nelson Riddle. "He would come into the room, and you would just be in awe of him."

This book endeavors to re-create the vitality of those moments; to place you, the reader, in the studio with Frank Sinatra to experience the spirit, intensity, and craftsmanship of his recording sessions. At the same time, it traces recording advances that had a direct impact on Frank Sinatra's work in the studio, including the evolution of the microphone, disc recording, magnetic tape, stereo, and digital recording: all critical tools that contributed to his artistic success.

Sinatra's enthusiasm for recording was infectious and motivated those who participated in his sessions to strive for the perfection he demanded of himself. Always exhibiting the highest degree of professionalism and respect for the music and musicians, Sinatra led by example,

inspiring those around him to latch onto the momentum he generated, to reach just a bit higher, to outperform themselves. Each performance bears the imprint of the confident, intelligent artist that he was; his recordings are suffused with the intellectual background and artistic sensitivity that Nelson Riddle spoke of.

Although his singing voice is probably the most recognizable in the world, and dozens of books and articles have been written about the more sensational aspects of his life, few seek to analyze and explain the virtues of Frank Sinatra as a *musician* or *recording artist*. He was an actor, producer, and concert artist, but it is his recordings that express the essence of his genius, guaranteeing his place among the most influential musical figures of the twentieth century.

From his very first session with Harry James in 1939 to the highly successful *Duets* albums of the 1990s, Frank Sinatra presided over more than four hundred recording sessions, resulting in well over a thousand recordings, most of which were released to the public. In 1965, Sinatra explained his interest in recording to CBS News correspondent Walter Cronkite. "I think making records is the great fun of all time, because it's current—it's right there. When you finish a recording, you blink your eye (or your ear, as it may be), and *boom*, the playback's on, and you're listening to what you've done."

From the beginning, Sinatra exhibited a brash confidence that would help propel him to astounding success. As he relaxed between sets with the Tommy Dorsey Orchestra at Hollywood's Palladium Ballroom one evening in the early 1940s, Sinatra remarked to his friend, songwriter Sammy Cahn, "I am going to be the world's greatest singer!" As Cahn later explained, "I looked at him, and said, 'Without a doubt!' He was pleased, and made me repeat what I said. He seemed so intense that there was no way I could dispute what Frank had said."

As he left the bandstand in 1942 to pursue a solo career, Sinatra made a careful assessment of the current music scene, and, realizing there was a place for the romantic musical style he was leaning toward, set out to perfect a musical persona to fit the bill: positioning himself not just as a multi-talented creative artist, but a commercial one as well.

At the same time he embraced the rapidly advancing art and science of sound recording. Throughout his career he utilized the burgeoning technology to his best advantage, devising and mastering techniques that would serve him as he progressed. His half-century tenure as a fixture in the studio encompasses every modern technical innovation in the field of sound recording, and few things have had as profound an effect on Frank Sinatra or our perception of his talent.

Sinatra's interest in the recording process was a logical extension of his desire to control his destiny. The path to greatness, he knew, would be through the piercing vulnerability of his performance. To truly understand the significance of these performances and how they fit into the overall scheme of what Sinatra, from early on, intended for his future, we must first consider how carefully they were planned and executed. Sinatra left little to chance, especially when, for him, singing meant exposing his soul in such a deeply personal way. "If I make a bad record, it hurts me far more than it does the public," he said.

Like Duke Ellington before him, the singer was a perfectionist who understood that a record was *forever*. "You can never do anything in life quite on your own," he once explained. "You don't live on your own little island. I suppose you might be able to write a poem or paint a picture entirely on your own, but I doubt it. I don't think you can even sing a song that way, either. Making a record is as near as you can get to it—although, of course, the arranger and the orchestra play an enormous part. But once you're on a record singing, it's you and you alone. With a record, you're *it*."

As a music enthusiast, I have always been intrigued by the ways the gifted men and women who compose and perform music go about creating their work. Where does their inspiration come from? How do they transfer their ideas to paper and convey it to their collaborators? Why do their recordings sound the way they do?

The answers to these questions as they relate to Frank Sinatra lie within the memory of the people who worked on his recordings, and I have found the recollections and opinions of the scores of participants I befriended in the course of my nine years of research to be warm, insightful, and compelling. His story was *their* story, and it became apparent to me that, without the support of these key players, the music of Frank Sinatra simply wouldn't exist. It is for this reason that I have chosen to rely heavily on the words of these musicians, producers, songwriters, arrangers, and engineers to reconstruct the studio methodology he perfected.

PHOTOGRAPH BY ED THRASHER, COURTESY OF MPTV ARCHIVE

Invaluable to portraying Sinatra as a studio artist are his raw session recordings, from which I have drawn selected excerpts. Having had the opportunity to work on the restoration of his vintage recordings, I was able to gain access to many of the original unedited session discs and tapes containing valuable dialogue that occurred between takes and during breaks in the session. To sit in a modern studio and eavesdrop, fifty years after these moments occurred, is a delightfully eerie experience. In some cases, the conversations are so absorbing and the fidelity so true that you feel as though you are sitting among the musicians in the orchestra. I hope that I have been able to capture and preserve in print what is so fascinating to hear on tape and disc.

Unfortunately, space limitations prohibit me from examining each and every Sinatra recording session or discussing every album he made. Instead, I have presented a representative sampling of historically and developmentally important Sinatra sessions that serve to offer a detailed look at the singer's versatile career.

book, for these are critical subjects that will aid the reader in appreciating the performance and studio situations that arose as Sinatra's career developed.

I have offered some musical critiques as well, at times indulging in an analysis of a particular performance. I hope these will help explain *why* Sinatra's is an art form to be cherished, and what is important to listen for. I have carefully chosen these specific recordings because I felt they captured the essence of Sinatra and his music.

In this regard, the specific recordings suggested in Appendix D, Fifty Songs that Define the Essence of Sinatra, will enhance the reader's understanding of the musical/vocal techniques and sonic qualities described here.

Sinatra's recordings encompass a remarkable range of styles and rhythms. Each of his four main periods offers a distinct musical sound, so that in many respects we hear a different artist with each passing era. This variety transforms his recorded catalog into a vast musical playground, chock-full of nooks and crannies that yield many wonderful surprises for those willing to explore.

While this study generally follows a chronological path, it is organized so that important topics that relate to Frank Sinatra's work in the studio are introduced and explained in a logical fashion. For example, important discussions about Sinatra's voice, his relationships with songwriters, and the importance of the microphone appear early in the

With Nelson Riddle.

It must be stressed that no individual was more or less responsible for abetting Frank Sinatra's success in the recording studio. Those individuals whom the singer worked with brought fresh perspectives to his art, and whether their contributions were small or large, good or bad, Sinatra studied and adopted the portions that fit his needs best.

You will notice that in several sections I have chosen to highlight Sinatra's work with Nelson Riddle. There are two primary reasons for this.

To begin, his work with Nelson Riddle was a critical turning point. Largely by chance, the arranger became a key player at a time when the singer's career hung precariously in the balance, and Nelson unquestionably aided Sinatra's resurrection as a mainstream pop vocalist. Most Sinatraphiles would argue that his finest work, and the style he will ultimately be remembered for, was forged with Nelson Riddle. The

PHOTOGRAPH BY ED THRASHER, COURTESY OF MPTV ARCHIVE

Sinatra-Riddle partnership was musically ideal and illustrates how a symbiotic musical relationship between orchestrator and singer can make a world of difference in what we hear and how we hear it.

Then too, Nelson Riddle not only spoke at great length about his work with Sinatra, but also published an invaluable book explaining his method of arranging. His many articulate interviews, plus the discussions I have had with dozens of his friends, family members, and colleagues, allowed me to study and understand how Riddle worked as a musician, and, more important, how he worked for *Frank Sinatra*.

The most surprising revelation to come from my research was that, despite his fame, Frank Sinatra was a truly modest man when it came to his talent: he was a celebrity who preferred to deflect the credit for his work to others. When speaking of his work, he unfailingly referred to it as a collaborative effort, using the words *we* and *we're* instead of *I* and *I'm*. In doing this, he acknowledged the importance of his musical team and their contributions to the success of the overall performance. Nowhere was his admiration for their talent more apparent than in the recording studio.

In the 1970s, Sinatra told songwriter Ervin Drake that he despised singing his signature song, "My Way," because he felt people might construe it as a self-aggrandizing tribute. "I know it's a very big hit (and I love having big hits), but every time I get up to sing that song I grit my teeth, because no matter what the image may seem to be, I hate boastfulness in others. I hate immodesty, and that's how I feel every time I sing the song."

Because of Sinatra's reluctance to talk about himself, most interviews with the singer are polite but superficial. Frank Sinatra opted instead for musical communication, dropping his guard only behind the microphone, allowing his recordings to serve as the real window to his soul.

This is the story of how he created them.

Recording with trombonist/bandleader Tommy Dorsey, 1941.

PART 1

The Big Band Years, 1937–1942

BEGINNINGS

*A*s he grew older, Frank Sinatra delighted in reminiscing about the big band era. Frequently, in the company of family and friends (especially those connected with "the business"), he would slip into the comfortable role of storyteller and talk about how much he idolized Bing Crosby and what a tough taskmaster Tommy Dorsey was. His unprompted conversation showed that those formative years created fond memories, and his recollections of the period were vivid and full of sentiment. There is little doubt that much of the insight that guided Frank Sinatra over the course of half a century as a musician was based on the practical knowledge he'd gained during his tenure as the featured band vocalist with both Harry James (1939), and Tommy Dorsey (1940–1942).

It was during these years that he befriended many of the talented songwriters, arrangers, and musicians who would weave their way into the fabric of his musical existence, including arranger Axel Stordahl and lyricist Sammy Cahn. He took quickly to songwriters, and it was clear practically from the beginning that he possessed a discriminating taste for top-quality songs and a knack for selecting only those tunes that he instinctively knew fit his style.

His perceptive use of the microphone was born of this era, as was his understanding that a good measure of his craft was his ability to act. When singing, he could manipulate and control his body language to suit the setting of the lyric, which could evoke a certain response from his listening audience.

Much of the singer's musical wisdom stemmed from the day-in, day-out trials and tribulations of a rising band singer. As far back as the early 1940s, Sinatra was crediting Tommy Dorsey with providing the fundamentals that he would adapt to fit his vocal styling, carefully refining his approach to develop a distinct method of phrasing that would become unmistakably his own.

A sharp observer, Frank Sinatra was among the first to realize that the vocalist was quickly supplanting the orchestra as the main attraction in pop music and that he could easily apply his talents to capitalize on the trend. While his arrival signaled the beginning of the end of the big bands, Sinatra was responsible for rescuing the finest components of the swing style, creating a sensational new sound: one that depended on the vocalist to function as the heart of the performance.

While most biographical accounts cite Sinatra's time with Harry James and Tommy Dorsey as being his first real "band" experience, his big band days had really begun much earlier than his first Brunswick recording session, held in New York City on July 13, 1939. While the Brunswick date would be his inaugural *commercial* recording session, it was not his initial foray into a recording studio.

After a stint with a Major Bowes' Amateur Hour touring unit in 1935 (as one of the Hoboken Four, a pickup group assembled by Bowes), he

COURTESY OF MARY MANE AND ROBERT MANDELBAUM

Frank Mane and his orchestra, late 1930s.

fronted a small jazz combo called The Four Sharps. The single extant performance by the group, a Dixieland version of "Exactly Like You," is a *Fred Allen Show* radio aircheck, from May 12, 1937. While Sinatra didn't vocalize with the trio, he continued to kick around Bergen and Hudson counties in New Jersey, where he eventually befriended a young musician named Frank Mane, an alto saxophonist doing freelance solo work wherever he could find it.

Initially, Mane and Sinatra crossed paths at WAAT, a small radio station that sometimes featured live performances broadcast from its studios in Jersey City. Often, after scrounging around the station for work, Sinatra would bum rides from the saxophonist, usually to girlfriend Nancy Barbato's house on Audubon Avenue. (Frank and Nancy met during the summer of 1934; they were married in Jersey City on February 4, 1939.)

Within a short time, Sinatra and Mane were frequenting Bayonne's Sicilian Club, where many musical cronies gathered to compare notes. During one of these nights out, Sinatra learned that Mane was forming a small band for the express purpose of making some recordings.

According to Mane, Sinatra visited the Sicilian Club on the eve of the scheduled recording, where he and his ten-piece band were rehearsing in a back room. Before the group disbanded, Sinatra approached him. "Mind if I come along tomorrow?" he asked. Mane assured him it would be fine, and at the appointed time on March 18, 1939, the band, plus Sinatra, reassembled at Harry Smith's Recording Studio at 2 West 46th Street in Manhattan. Among the musicians in Mane's pickup band was reed player Harry Shuckman, who would later resurface on many of Sinatra's Hollywood recording sessions for Columbia Records, and Don Rigney, a drummer who had served as best man at the Sinatras' wedding.

After three instrumentals had been recorded ("Flight of the Bumblebee"; "Eclipse," a Mane original; and "Girl of My Dreams"), Sinatra approached the sax player, who was bearing the full expense of the session, and asked whether he might record a vocal with the group. With some extra time remaining on the clock, Mane agreed and quickly brought out a stock arrangement of "Our Love," a song based on a melody from Tchaikovsky's *Romeo and Juliet*.

Since Mane desired to record for purely personal reasons (he simply wanted to hear what his arrangements sounded like), and not with the intention of creating commercial discs, only one master record was made of each performance. In all likelihood, neither Frank Sinatra nor any of the other participants received a copy of the recordings they made, and Mane, a fairly modest man, never publicized the recording after Sinatra became famous. This led to a false assumption on the part of well-intentioned historians, who for many years believed that this entry in the Sinatra discography (tagged with an incorrect recording date) was a demonstration or "demo" disc that the singer had made for Nancy Barbato on the eve of their wedding. Only recently, with the "rediscovery" of Frank Mane, have the original recording discs from this session surfaced and the facts been clarified.

"Our Love," then, is Frank Sinatra's very first real recording. (The Hoboken Four performances of "Shine" and "Curse of an Aching Heart" were no more than airchecks of broadcast performances, as opposed to formal studio recordings.) This distinction aside, the song and its performance are quite unusual, as they hint at the direction the polished voice would take. Sinatra's vocal is remarkably relaxed, and fragments of the style that would develop fully in the James and Dorsey periods are readily apparent in his fluid handling of the vocal lines.

Although he didn't know it at the time, Frank Mane (who died in December 1998 at age 94) had given the man who would become one of the greatest entertainers in the world his first real break.

DISCOVERY

*I*n the months before he recorded "Our Love" with Frank Mane, Sinatra had taken a job at a small roadside cafe on Route 9W in Englewood Cliffs, New Jersey. Working as a self-described "singing waiter," he appeared several nights a week as the featured vocalist with Bill Henri and his Headliners. Customarily, radio stations such as WAAT in Jersey City and WNEW in New York would broadcast live from venues such as the Rustic Cabin, which is exactly what happened on the night that Frank Sinatra was discovered there by fledgling bandleader Harry James.

"We would broadcast from the bandstand on WNEW's *Dance Parade* from 11:30 'til midnight," remembers Headliners saxophonist Bert Hall, then known as Harry Zinquist. "Lots of song pluggers would come in to see the bandleaders at the Cabin, 'cause they knew that we were

Frank Sinatra on the bandstand with the Bill Henri Orchestra, The Rustic Cabin, in Englewood Cliffs, New Jersey, circa 1939. (Harry Zinquist is fourth from right.)

broadcasting live on WNEW. One night as we were playing, one of the waiters came up to the bandstand and said to Sinatra, 'Someone wants to see you.' It was trumpeter Harry James, and Sinatra was thrilled!"

It was a warm evening in June 1939 when James, who had left the security of Benny Goodman's band in favor of fronting his own, made the trip to the mountain lodge nestled in the foothills alongside Jersey's Palisades. His attention had been drawn to Sinatra by his wife, singer Louise Tobin, who had tuned in to one of the *Dance Parade* broadcasts. "I heard this boy singer and thought, 'There's a fair singer.' Now, I didn't think he was fantastic—I just thought, 'Well, now that's a good singer.' So I just woke Harry and said, 'Honey, you might want to hear this kid on the radio. The boy singer on this show sounds pretty good.'"

James agreed, and the next evening he visited the Rustic Cabin to hear Sinatra in person. "When he came over to see me, I almost broke his arm so he wouldn't get away, 'cause I was dying to get out of that place," the singer once remembered. Within a day, Sinatra accepted James's offer to join the band.

Jack Palmer, one of James's trumpeters, remembers the first time the musicians met their new vocalist. "Frank was at the theater where we were appearing. After the first show, he went up to Harry's dressing room. Just before the second show, Harry came out and introduced him as the new singer with the band. Frank then joined us at the next date we had, which I believe was in New Haven, Connecticut. I'll never forget how Harry introduced him to the audience. He said, 'Ladies and Gentlemen, this is our new vocalist, and we don't have any arrangements for him as yet. Frank, do you think we can scare something up for you to sing?' Sinatra called out 'Stardust,' which is not the easiest song to sing. Frank gave us the key, and the piano and rhythm section began, and we just tried to get some background to hold it all together."

The band wouldn't have to improvise behind their new vocalist for long, for arranger Andy Gibson immediately went to work on orchestrations that would accommodate Sinatra. As the weeks and months wore on, the repetition of working night after night with a touring band helped him sharpen his skills as both a singer and a showman.

"When he first came to the band, he was almost a novice. . . . He had been working locally, and his exposure was pretty limited. So he acted just like a guy that was inexperienced, on a *national* scale," says Mickey Scrima, the band's drummer. "With Harry, we were playing coast to coast, and it made a big difference. Now Sinatra was being heard on the big radio networks,

where we would broadcast from various hotels and ballrooms around the country. It was experience for a guy who had none: you begin working, and making records for a company like Columbia, and you begin to learn about band setups, and microphones, and things like that."

By early July, the Harry James Orchestra featuring Frank Sinatra was making live appearances at such popular night spots as New York's Roseland Ballroom and Atlantic City's Steel Pier. As they bused from gig to gig, James prepared to enter the studio to make some new recordings for Brunswick Records, a label that had been recently purchased by CBS Radio magnate William S. Paley. Among them would be Sinatra's very first commercial recordings.

THE FIRST RECORDINGS

With Harry James.

*I*n 1928 William S. Paley launched his broadcast empire, the Columbia Broadcasting System (CBS), with the assistance of a number of investors, including the Columbia Phonograph System. Then, in December 1938, CBS entered the record marketplace with its formal acquisition of the American Recording Corporation (ARC). In addition to the Columbia Phonograph System, ARC's holdings included a number of record labels, including Brunswick, Vocalion, Melotone, and Okeh. The resultant conglomeration of recording companies was renamed the Columbia Recording Corporation (CRC). While CRC would primarily function as the radio recording arm of Paley's CBS Radio Network (where programs were recorded and distributed to network affiliates on 16-inch lacquer transcription discs), it soon endeavored to involve itself in commercial recording projects, for which Paley revived the original "Columbia" label name. (This company would later evolve into the one now owned by Sony Music Entertainment, Inc.)

For a short time after the ARC acquisition, CBS continued to issue recordings made by its individual labels, with their original imprints. Since James was under contract to Brunswick, and had been making records for them under his own name since December 1937, his first recording with Sinatra, "From the Bottom of My Heart" and "Melancholy Mood," recorded on July 13, 1939 (Brunswick 8443) was released on that label.

Between the end of 1939 and September 1940, CBS gradually phased out the Brunswick label name and began issuing most of their 10-inch pop 78s (by both the original ARC artists and its own newly contracted Columbia artists) on the now familiar red-and-gold Columbia label. The four James-Sinatra records that followed the Brunswick disc were all issued on the new Columbia label.

Though unrefined, wisps of Sinatra's characteristic vocal style abound in the ten songs he recorded with James. While a more detailed study of Sinatra's vocal powers will be made later, these ten studio recordings, plus the small cache of live radio airchecks, set the stage for a better understanding of what vocal tools Sinatra possessed, and how he set about building upon them to create his unique voice.

Music critic George T. Simon, writing in the September 1939 issue of *Metronome* magazine, provided the singer with his first major review. "Featured throughout are the very pleasing vocals of Frank Sinatra, whose easy phrasing is especially commendable," Simon opined, to the delight of both James and his vocalist.

In the liner notes for Columbia/Legacy's 1994 CD reissue of the complete Sinatra-James recordings, Simon reflected on an incident that prompted him to take special notice of the singer. "It happened more than half a century ago—in

the summer of 1939, to be exact. But to this day, I can still remember Harry James's road manager following me down the steps of New York's Roseland Ballroom, and before I could reach the street calling out, 'Hey, wait a minute, will you? I wanna ask you something—how'd ya like the band?' When I murmured something rather noncommittal (because critics and reviewers don't like being put on the spot in such a clumsy manner), he came right to his point. 'Yeah, but how do you like the new singer?' And then, quite unabashedly, 'The boy wants a good write-up more than anybody I've ever seen. So give him a good write-up, will you, because we want to keep him happy and with the band, and that's the only thing that will make him happy.'" Simon, however, was genuinely impressed by Sinatra's vocal performance. The musicianship that Simon heard that night can be sampled on rare recordings of the band's live dates recently issued on compact disc.

It was "All or Nothing at All," a tune recorded at his third recording session with James (August 31, 1939) that became their greatest hit. While the song wasn't an outstanding seller upon its first release in 1939, it was reissued in 1943 when Sinatra signed with Columbia as a solo artist, and owing to the recording ban that prohibited recordings with instrumental accompaniment, became an overnight sensation.

"It's interesting to listen to that young voice when he first started; the way he attacked that song, and what he did with the breath control and the wonderful phrasing that he used even in those early days," recalls the song's writer, Jack Lawrence. Sinatra admired the song so much he recorded it three more times: as a ballad in 1961 with Don Costa, an up-tempo arrangement with Nelson Riddle in 1966, and a disco version with Joe Beck in 1977. "Later, as he went along he learned a lot more, and added more *interpretation*. But I still prefer that young voice singing it, as opposed to all the other versions he did," Lawrence adds.

Mickey Scrima (in 1999 a spry 83 years young, living in Dallas, and still playing his drums) remembers Sinatra being nervous at his earliest recording sessions. "I won't say he was scared to death, but it was new to him," Scrima recalls. "He was anxious, like everybody else is when we're recording, because if you're not nervous, you don't give a sh—. And besides, Harry had just put the band together and didn't know what the hell it was going to sound like. You can't tell when you're playing in it, but if you record it and play it back you can tell a hell of a lot more about what's going on. So Harry was anxious, too. I remember that, on the playbacks, Frank would sit there and be very critical, saying, 'Oh, I missed that . . .' or 'I should have done this or that . . .' I told him, 'Just cool it; don't dissect the thing.' And we'd do another take, and then he'd say, 'Oh, I like that one better. . . .' Of course, I'd remind him that it wasn't his decision to make: it was Harry's—and that would relax him!"

Jack Palmer remembers Sinatra being confident in the studio, but not cocky. "There is a difference, you know. He seemed to know what he wanted to do. But at that time, we had no idea that history would take the course it did. We just rehearsed for those sides like we rehearsed for everything else; there was nothing special about it in our minds. In terms of doing the recordings, it was pretty easy: we'd go in, they'd balance the brass, then the saxes, then the rhythm, and then the full orchestra. We would usually do a test record, and then we were lucky to get one [take] made!" Scrima vividly recalls that Sinatra was very proud of those initial recordings he made with James. "He did get some copies of those first recordings, some dubs. We would do three or four takes on a tune, and he would ask if he could take one of the ones that wasn't used," he says. "Later, he would play them over and over."

The Sinatra-James sessions, recorded under Columbia's auspices, took place in both New York and Los Angeles. For the Los Angeles dates, Scrima remembers that the CBS radio studios were used. Because there is no documentation confirming the locale for the New York recordings, we must rely on the best guess of Bill Savory, a retired Columbia engineer who was active in the big band recording scene at the time. "Some of the Brunswick and Columbia recordings from 1939 were probably made at World Broadcasting's recording studios, at 550 Fifth Avenue," he believes. "I know that around the same time, Harry recorded 'Daddy' at Liederkranz Hall, because Helen [Ward, Savory's wife] was the vocalist on the date. But the Sinatra-James things don't have the same sound as the recordings that were made at Liederkranz Hall, which leads me to believe that they were done elsewhere, in much smaller studios."

As we will discuss a bit later, the Liederkranz "sound" became a hallmark of Columbia's records, due in large part to the intense, naturally reverberant qualities of the large room. It was actually on James's later recordings that the open, ringing qualities of Liederkranz Hall became apparent; if we listen carefully to the Sinatra-James recordings of 1939, the spaciousness of a typical Liederkranz Hall date just isn't there.

"Back in those days, they used four mikes for the whole band and the vocalist," explains Scrima. "When we recorded, we had one in front of the saxophones (and the brass was behind the saxes), and then they had one in the piano, and one for the rhythm. The vocalists had their own microphone. It was amazing, because the guys that were mixing the stuff were fantastic—they knew what the hell they were doing. They were pioneers."

Scrima believes that one mixing engineer in particular worked tirelessly to help distill the best sound possible from the band's record dates. That young engineer would later resurface as the recording director for many of Sinatra's solo Columbia recordings. "Benny Goodman's band used to make great-sounding records, and the guy that did some of the things for Benny did some of Harry's records, too . . . Morty Palitz. He was a helluva guy! He'd come up and say, 'Hey Mick . . . let's put a pillow in that bass drum, so we can get the thing sounding better. . . . I want you to sound good.' Morty would let you know exactly what was going on: he'd say, 'I can't hear the bass,' or he might tell the brass to keep their horns at a certain level so he could get them all in. And soloists would have to come down and get closer to a microphone, and that all had to be worked out. He never said, 'We *have* to do this,' he'd say, 'Let's try it.' He'd make it simple for you. He knew exactly what he was doing, and back then that was something, because there were very few guys that did what he did. He was an absolute genius as a mixer. Those records are just fantastic as far as the mixing is concerned."

Apart from appearing on the bandstand with Sinatra, Scrima also roomed with the singer and his wife, Nancy, who was then expecting their first child. "We were pretty damned close. I treated Nancy like a sister. We never had an argument, we just enjoyed each others' company. It was tough then, because no one had any money," Scrima remembers. "My dad would have to send us money to eat on, like fifteen or twenty bucks a week, for about a month because we weren't working. We were working two nights a week, and what could you make on two one-nighters? We were all really struggling. . . . eating beans and wieners, which Nancy would cook for us. It was just a fun time. We had a great band, and everyone got along well. Everybody was for each other."

Even though Sinatra had been with Harry James for a scant six months, he was itching to move on to a more established band, where as a featured vocalist he would receive far more attention and wider publicity. "'If Jack Leonard can make it, I won't have any problems,'" Sinatra told Scrima. "I encouraged him to do it. I said, 'Hey, man, all you have to do is sing: you've got the balls, you have a good voice. . . .'"

With his friend's encouragement, the young singer made a bold move that would alter the

course of his life. Sinatra was about to step into the big time as the featured male vocalist with the orchestra of one of the greatest bandleaders in the world: trombonist Tommy Dorsey.

THE DORSEY STYLE

*I*n an April 1965 *Life* magazine article, Sinatra discussed his tenure with the Dorsey band. "In those days, all the struggling singers were trying to get with either Tommy Dorsey or Glenn Miller," he wrote. "Miller's was the hotter of the two [bands], but most fellows I knew, almost to a man, wanted to be with Tommy Dorsey, because he was a better 'showcase.' Miller's was not a 'singer's band,' Tommy's was. He presented a singer in a much more specialized manner. In his arrangements, he avoided as much as he could having the singer stand up after the first chorus, sing the vocal, then sit down and have the orchestra finish. Tommy tried to present the singer as a specialized piece of talent with the band."

When Dorsey came knocking, Sinatra went running. "I didn't know it at the time—I suspected it, but I didn't know—that Tommy had his eye on me. I learned later that he was having a few beefs with his singer, Jack Leonard, and was scouting around for a new boy. With the James band I had cut a record. . . . and the song plugger sent it to Dorsey. He was trying to get Dorsey to record it. Tommy listened to it, all right, but he turned down the song. Instead, he hired me to be his singer! I had been making sixty-five dollars a week with James, and I started with Tommy for a hundred."

Although traces of what would emerge and blossom as Sinatra's unique vocal style are clearly evident as early as the Frank Mane recording, most musicologists and the singer himself credit Dorsey's masterful instrumental phrasing as having a profound effect.

"Tommy didn't work much with me," Sinatra remembered. "He devoted his time to the musicians and arrangements, so that left me on my own to experiment. . . . The thing that influenced me most was the way Tommy played his trombone. He would take a musical phrase and play it all the way through, seemingly without breathing, for eight, ten, maybe *sixteen* bars. How the hell did he do it? I used to sit behind him on the bandstand and watch, trying to see him sneak a breath. But I never saw the bellows move in his back. His jacket didn't even move. I used to edge my chair to the side a little, and peek around to watch him. Finally, after a while, I discovered that he had a 'sneak' pinhole in the corner of his mouth—not an actual pinhole, but a tiny place where he was breathing. In the middle of a phrase, while a tone was still being carried through the trombone, he'd go *shhhhh* and take a quick breath and play another four bars with that breath. Why couldn't a singer do that too? Fascinated, I began listening to other soloists. I bought every Jascha Heifetz record I could find, and listened to him play the violin hour after hour. His constant bowing, where you never heard a break, carried the melody line straight on through, just like Dorsey's trombone.

"It was my idea to make my voice work in the same way as a trombone or violin: not sounding like them—but 'playing' the voice like those instruments. The first thing I needed was extraordinary breath control, which I didn't have. I began swimming every chance I got in public pools—taking laps underwater and thinking song lyrics to myself as I swam, holding my breath. I worked out on the track at the Stevens Institute in Hoboken, running one lap, trotting the next. Pretty soon I had good breath control, but that still wasn't the whole answer. I still had to learn to sneak a breath without being too obvious.

"It was easy for Dorsey to do it through his 'pinhole' while he played the trombone. He could control the inhalation better because the horn's mouthpiece was covering up his mouth. Instead of singing only two bars or four bars of music at a time—like most of the other guys around—I was able to sing six bars, and in some songs eight bars, without taking a visible or audible breath. This gave the melody a flowing, unbroken quality, and *that*—if anything—was what made me sound different. It wasn't the voice alone; in fact, my voice was always a little too high, I thought, and not as good in natural quality as some of the competition."

At the same time, the singer was also thinking of unique ways to present his vocal style. "When I started singing in the mid-1930s, everybody was trying to copy the Crosby style—the casual kind of raspy sound in the throat. Bing was on top, and a bunch of us—Dick Todd, Bob Eberly, Como was coming along, Dean Martin was just starting out—were trying to break in. It occurred to me that maybe the world didn't need *another* Crosby.

"I decide to experiment a little and come up with something different. What I finally hit on was more the bel canto Italian school of singing, without making a point of it. That meant I had to stay in better shape because I had to *sing* more. It was more difficult than Crosby's style, much more difficult."

Nelson Riddle once explained the hallmarks of Sinatra's breath control. "He sings in a 'sustained' manner. He breathes long phrases, and breathes when you'd least expect it, holding over when you'd normally expect him to breathe. He gets the most, dramatically, out of his breathing capabilities by the element of surprise."

While the first few sides Sinatra cut with Dorsey have a slightly shy, tentative air, by their third recording session (March 4, 1940), he seems to have slipped into a comfortable groove, and the song "Say It (Over and Over Again)" emerges as the ideal showcase for his fluid, legato-style phrasing. Here the singer starts to elongate the ends of phrases and reconfigure the tempo of his vocal line within the confines of each measure. Not a word is clipped, and the end of each phrase melts beautifully into the start of the next, as though Sinatra is savoring each and every syllable. This is evident from the very first line:

Saaaay it, over and over again,
o-o-ver and o-ver again,
never stop saying you're miiiiiine . . .
Saaaay it, e-ver and ever so sweet,
eee-ver and e-ver so sweet,
just like an old valentiiine

The gentle way he enunciates the "o" sound in *over* and holds the word "*agaaaaaain*" in the third chorus display his ease in maintaining a languid musical flow through the expressiveness of the vocal line.

If one compares Sinatra's vocals to Dorsey's trombone throughout this recording, it becomes clear that he is indeed trying to mimic what the bandleader was doing instrumentally, as the vocal follows the melodic line exactly. The confidence he was gaining continues in the second song from the March 4 session, "Polka Dots and Moonbeams," on which his voice is almost virginal.

"One of the charms about Frank was that he wasn't like a boy singer in the band," believes Dorsey pianist Joe Bushkin. "This guy was more like a saxophone soloist, or an instrumentalist. That was the feeling we got with Frank, and we loved playing for him."

In addition to the two songs mentioned, a number of Sinatra-Dorsey recordings merit the designation "exceptional," including "I'll Never Smile Again," "The One I Love," "Stardust," "It's Always You," "Without a Song," "East of the Sun," "Violets for Your Furs," "Street of Dreams,"

"Daybreak," "Too Romantic," "Everything Happens to Me," and "I Think of You."

Sinatra worked tirelessly and learned his lessons well. Before long, he realized that his hard work and continued perseverance was beginning to pay off. The greatest dividend he received from the investment was a growing reputation as the vocal model by which all others were being judged.

THE VOICE

Sinatra's friend the late Sylvia Syms once asked, "How does one articulate the excitement of Sinatra? His humor, his humanity, his swinging, his understanding of lyrics that turn them into tone poems with his caress? Sinatra is a violoncello in full bloom. . . . His recordings are ever the mood music to listen to when making love. To watch him in saloons or in concert is to see the art of communication in action."

When discussing Frank Sinatra's vocal style, it is easy to discern the individual components he borrowed from three of his major influences: Bing Crosby, Billie Holiday, and Mabel Mercer.

Crosby, more than anyone, motivated Sinatra to become a singer. By his own admission, Sinatra not only admired the crooner's silky smooth sound, but he also envied the glamour and attention that a singer of Crosby's stature enjoyed. While many have compared Crosby and Sinatra vocally, about the only similarities shared by the pair were their concurrent success as the first true multimedia megastars of the twentieth century. Musically and personally, the two men were as different as night and day.

Crosby, who began his career a decade before Sinatra, has long been considered the quintessential crooner. Working to extend what Rudy Vallee began in the 1920s, he was embraced by the public largely because of the unpretentious, boy-next-door quality of his vocal interpretation. While his singing voice was most pleasant and undeniably unique, it wasn't just his singing that made Crosby famous, or great. It was the intimacy he achieved that gave him credibility and helped make a strong impression on the listening audience.

Bing's range, though, was not near Sinatra's, and his voice possessed a much different timbre. Where Sinatra relied on a solid middle ground and reserved the heights and depths of the scale for dramatic flair, Crosby favored the bass range, which communicated a comfortable, burnished warmth. As a result of the characteristics of his voice, and the way he chose to use it, Crosby was much more proficient than Sinatra at singing in the lower register.

When Crosby did try to sing "up" (to the E to F-sharp range), the physical technique he needed to use limited the strength of his voice, and, more often than not, the results proved that it just wasn't right for him. This is the primary reason that he couldn't "belt" and would rarely stray from the confines of the relaxed, easygoing style he was noted for. Undoubtedly, much of the foundation for Sinatra's soft, round phrasing in the 1940s was inspired by what he admired in Crosby's singing, as evidenced by the Crosby-esque tone of many of his Columbia-era recordings.

Nelson Riddle once compared the two voices. "Crosby's range is from a G to a C. Sinatra probably lacks one tone on the bottom that Crosby has, but he probably surpasses him by as much as four full tones on top. Sinatra has more of a live, intellectual sound, a sort of burning in-

tensity, than Bing Crosby. Sinatra digs into a song, and tries to get *into* it; Crosby has a calculated nonchalance—he tosses off a tune. Sinatra's voice is more 'live' and vibrant and fraught with shadows and coloring than Crosby's voice."

For a pop vocalist, Frank Sinatra's range was impressive. "His practical range was low A-flat to a D, which is about an octave and a quarter," says his longtime pianist Bill Miller. "But his possibilities were low G to high F: almost two octaves. The low G and high F were not 'practical,' and he didn't use them a lot—he would use them once in a while on a tune just to show people that he could do it!"

"Sinatra's is a fairly rangy voice," said Nelson Riddle. "His voice has a very strident, insistent sound in the top register, a smooth lyrical sound in the middle register, and a very tender sound down low. His voice is built on infinite taste, with an overall inflection of sex. He points everything he does from a sexual standpoint."

Music educator Richard Schuller, a vocal music specialist, helps explain the technical characteristics that comprise Sinatra's tonal qualities and the techniques he used for vocal elocution. "Right off the bat, his vocal technique was perfect. The placement of his voice, the way he breathed . . . was absolutely perfect: dead-on. He used his voice the right way, too, so that there wasn't any wear and tear. For instance, the belters' voices go to shreds in a matter of time. Sinatra was able to last as long as he did [vocally] because he had solid technique. Whether he trained his voice to be that way or whether it was just through the grace of God that he had this, his singing was impeccable, *technically*, in terms of vocal production."

Not surprisingly, Sinatra's speaking voice had a typical New Jersey accent. Yet when he sang the accent was virtually undetectable. His diction became precise, his articulation meticulous. "He never garbled, and the words are what I call standard American English," says Richard Schuller.

"In terms of enunciation, the vowels are almost *Italianate* in that they are pure. . . . he didn't slough over the vowels, he didn't make diphthongs when there were none."

Although Sinatra has said he loosely followed the pattern of bel canto singers, his style had few of the true characteristics of the classical style that, translated, means "beautiful singing." "The sound of Sinatra's voice was consistent and smooth. His style was not operatic: it was rooted in the pop music style, and his phrasing was perfect for that," Schuller believes.

The clarity of his diction may have been gleaned from another of Sinatra's favorites, Mabel Mercer, one of the greatest song stylists, whose articulation was militarily precise. Rarely would Mercer round off or "bite" the ends of her words, as Judy Garland often did. Instead, each consonant and syllable would be crisply enunciated, adding to the appeal of her unique phrasing. (Sinatra would make a point of carefully finishing off certain consonants with a sharply articulated ending, especially 'S' and 'T' sounds.)

While Sinatra's superb phrasing is what is usually referred to when evaluating his genius, the *phrasing* turns out to be much more than simply singing the words properly. "I use all the color changes I can get into my voice," Sinatra once said. "The microphone catches the softest tone— a whisper."

"How you pronounce the word colors the sound, which is another method of singing a ballad," Schuller says. "You don't want vowels that are big and spread out. You want to cover them down and caress them, which he could do by how he approached the vowel. Instead of singing it wide open, 'Aaaaahhhhhh . . . ,' for instance, you can cover the vowel down. You can, just by a vocal placement, make the sound come out rounder. Or, a vocalist can spread the sound that he doesn't want, and make it flat. Not flat in the sense of the *pitch*, but flat *sonically*. So when you pronounce the 'A' sound, if it's flat, it sounds like 'Aye.' If it were rounded, it sounds like 'Ah.'

"Within that context, even with a flat 'A,' you can make it less spread. You can drop the jaw and open the throat to get all sorts of different colors. And Sinatra had myriad colors. By comparison, to me, Maureen McGovern has a beautiful voice, but it's colorless in a lot of ways, as opposed to Frank Sinatra, whose singing has a lot of color, in all ranges. And when he goes from top to bottom or bottom to top, it's seamless—you don't hear any breaks between registers. That usually comes with training, but he obviously developed it, through his own sensibilities," says Schuller.

In his book *The Great American Popular Singers*, Henry Pleasants comments that Sinatra "could, and sometimes did, depress the larynx and 'cover,' as classical singers do, to sustain a full, round tone in moving up the scale. On his recording of 'Day by Day' [1961], for example, he gives out with full-voiced, admirably focused E-flats and Fs, and even lands a briefly held but confident A-flat just before the end. His high Fs at the close of 'Ol' Man River' [1963] were also conventionally and successfully 'covered.'"

Often, when a vocalist interprets vowels, the articulation is quite pronounced—almost stark. "Covering" is a technique that singers sometimes use to diffuse the bright sound of a vowel. Pleasants also explains why at times Sinatra consciously avoided "covering," to avoid the artificiality it could add to the vocal sound. "The absence of any impression of art was imperative to his style. . . . he probably wanted to avoid any suggestion of vocal vainglory," he wrote. "He perceived, if I hear him correctly, that the slight evidence of strain audible when these critical pitches are approached openly and lightly, as picked up and amplified by the mike, suggested innocence and sincerity, and, in a song of loneliness or longing, a sense of pain. The way he sings the D on ' . . . *If only she would call . . .* ' in 'Wee Small Hours' [1955] is, as I hear it, a charming example."

Often Sinatra is referred to as a "crooner," like Bing Crosby and Russ Colombo and Rudy

Vallee before him. The crooner hits a note above or below the desired note, and then shifts up or down into that note, producing a distinctive, pleasing warble. Sinatra, however, used a subtler technique known as portamento; in which the vocalist glides gradually from one tone to the next, effecting what amounts to a vocal glissando between notes. Portamento is surely what attracted Sinatra to Heifetz's fluid violin bowing and Dorsey's billowy trombone slides. The circular breathing that Sinatra learned from Dorsey is probably what makes his portamento so completely effective.

Rhythm is another crucial aspect of the Sinatra style. His faultless sense of timing allowed him to toy with the rhythm of a melody, bringing tremendous excitement to his reading of a lyric. Billie Holiday was a master of this technique. "With few exceptions, every major pop singer in the United States during her generation has been touched in some way by her genius," Sinatra once wrote in *Ebony* magazine. "It is Billie Holiday, whom I first heard in 52nd Street clubs in the early 1930s, who was, and still remains, the greatest single musical influence on me."

What he likely appreciated about Holiday was not so much the tonal quality of her voice but the sincerity and expressiveness with which she interpreted a lyric. Like Louis Armstrong, Holiday had an uncanny knack for sensing the proper placement of words and phrases, and she was famous for extending notes well past the confines of a conventional measure, completely rephrasing the rhythm of the melody in the process.

A great deal of Sinatra's flawless handling of syncopation may well have come from his love for Holiday's music. Early in his own career, he realized that robbing time from one note to the next could accentuate the spontaneity or emphasize the urgency of a lyric. This might be planned or spontaneous; regardless of how much he deviated from the original rhythm, it's always made up. He never leaves you hanging.

"The syncopation is affected when you place an accent, or a stress, where you wouldn't normally expect it," explains Richard Schuller. "In 4/4 time, your stress should be on the first beat. If you stress the second beat, you've created what is almost a physical reaction, because it's not where it's supposed to be. Now, the beat always kept going: Sinatra took liberties with the rhythm of the melody, which is *within* the beat. If one were to change the beat itself, the whole thing would fall apart."

Sinatra accomplished this by placing sharp emphasis on certain words in the lyric line. In comparison, Ella Fitzgerald, in her interpretations of songs in her classic "Songbook" series, sticks mainly to the exact rhythmic pattern that the songs were written in. Some songs are written without syncopation, and if vocalists (or instrumentalists) don't add it themselves, the results are pretty staid. (Mr. Schuller reminds me that when Fitzgerald sang some of those songs in her live performances, she often created syncopation where Rodgers and Hart and Cole Porter hadn't planned any.)

As we will see, the arrangers who worked with Frank Sinatra not only wrote intricately textured musical charts for him, they built flexibility into them, allowing him room to work rhythmically. An orchestrator's recognition of these small yet critical details often makes the difference between dull musical backgrounds and ones that crackle with excitement.

When analyzing Sinatra's performance, many critics hypothesize that the characteristic sincerity of his vocal interpretation is a direct expression of his own personal feelings. To some extent this has to be true, for if Sinatra weren't able to understand the emotions he sang about, he would never have been able to communicate them so strikingly.

Producer Mitch Miller, when asked to what degree the vocalist might have drawn on his personal emotion in rendering his work, made an interesting comparison between craftsmanship and emotion. "The ability to bring all of your talent together at a certain moment depends solely on craftsmanship. Emotion never makes you a hit," he says.

"I always tell this to singers: emotion is not something *you* feel—it is something you make the *listener* feel. You have to be very cool, and know what you're doing. You get a little tear in your voice, you put it there if the lyric calls for it. So it's craftsmanship . . . and Sinatra had craftsmanship. It's bulls——t to say that he draws on emotion from his personal life, because what he's drawing is the emotion from *your* personal life, and he's saying it for you."

Miller's assessment makes perfect sense. Anyone who saw a Sinatra concert in person during his last twenty years can attest that whenever he sang it, he rarely failed to turn in a stunningly believable performance of his quintessential torch song, "One for My Baby." Are we to believe that each such performance (and there were thousands over several decades) is tinged with the singer's real sadness? Of course not. It's his ability as an *actor* that allows him to slip in and out of roles that enhance his vocal performance. But he needed to have learned the part.

Of course, on record the singer needed to compensate for the visual effects that played a major role in his stage appearances. When all is said and done, Sinatra's genius, both as a vocalist and in the recording studio, is rooted in his considerable skill as a dramatic actor. The roles for which he garnered critical acclaim—*From Here to Eternity, Suddenly, The Man with the Golden Arm,* and *The Manchurian Candidate*—are convincing examples of the breadth and seriousness of his talent. His ability to intuitively grasp a character's essence and identify the most meaningful elements of a plot helped Sinatra transfer his persuasive on-screen sensitivities to the lyrical interpretation required for his vocal performances.

Ultimately, Sinatra continued a tradition of vocalizing that extended what singers like Peggy Lee and Billie Holiday had begun: a soft, intimate style that drew the listener in. That's the magic of a Sinatra performance—it reels you in, and as the warmth and beauty of the instrumental background flirt with you, the beguiling tonal quality of the voice takes over, and you are mesmerized. "Frank Sinatra is incomparable and irreplaceable," Peggy Lee once said. "His emotional honesty reaches unplumbed depths."

THE SONGS

But the singer's skill as a performer could take him only as far as the song itself could go. From the very beginning of Sinatra's professional career, everything hinged on the song. Sinatra carefully hand-selected his own repertoire both for lyric content and for melody. "They usually say that an artist is as good as his material, and I think that in nine out of ten cases that holds true," Sinatra explained in a 1949 interview with New York disc jockey Jack Ellsworth. "My friends are songwriters," he once told songwriter Ervin Drake. "I don't know what I'd be doing if it weren't for them, because they give me the stuff to sing. I don't write songs!"

Later, when Sinatra felt that he had exhausted the supply of "standard" songs, he implored young songwriters to write better music. "There's nobody writing good songs anymore," he lamented. "I wish some new cat would come along and write something decent for me."

When he discovered composers or lyricists that he particularly liked, he encouraged them and engaged them to work for him whenever he could. It was Sinatra who insisted that the songwriting team of Sammy Cahn and Jule Styne be hired to write the songs for his first major M-G-M extravaganza, *Anchors Aweigh*. When the producers balked, Sinatra told Cahn, "If you're not there Monday, I'm not there Monday."

Frank Sinatra publicly endorsed particular songs during his many personal appearances, where in addition to performing the tune he religiously credited each individual songwriter and arranger from either the stage or from behind the radio microphone. While this became a Sinatra trademark during the concerts of his latter years, it was in fact a practice that he maintained from his earliest personal appearances.

Sinatra's most admiring acknowledgment of a particular tune, however, would be his decision to record it, and, if it was extra-special, re-record it through the years, each time altering the tempo and approach to offer a different perspective. The songs he returned to continually, he turned into classics, such as "All or Nothing at All," and "The Song Is You."

His affinity for Cole Porter's "Night and Day," though, bordered on obsession. Between 1942 (when he chose the song for his first solo recording session) and 1977 (his last official recording of the song), he recorded five unique recordings of the song in ballad, swing, and disco arrangements. (He didn't stop there. At least two completely different arrangements, jazz and solo guitar, were used for live performances.)

Sinatra was among the first solo singers to recognize that individual songs from hit Broadway shows could survive outside the productions they were written for, and his success with several numbers from Rodgers and Hammerstein's *Oklahoma!* in 1943 and *Carousel* in 1945 proved that his hunch was right. Sinatra began to dig deep into the vast reserves of the dormant shows of Cole Porter, Irving Berlin, Rodgers and Hart, and the Gershwins to extract and revitalize songs that, save his intervention, might have remained obscure forever.

But songs came to him in many other ways, too. In the 1940s, he auditioned hundreds of tunes for his multiple weekly radio programs, including the ever popular *Your Hit Parade* and his Vimms Vitamin, Max Factor, and Old Gold programs. Many songs during this period also came to Sinatra via his growing contacts in the music publishing field (he was a partner in Barton Music with Ben Barton, and later parlayed that aspect of his business into several more highly profitable concerns). During the 1950s, he relied on trusted friends like Frank Military (now a senior vice president at Warner-Chappell Music in New York) to screen songs for him. After a day on the movie or television lot Sinatra, Military, and Henry (Hank) Sanicola (Sinatra's sidekick and rehearsal pianist) would kick back in the Sinatra offices on Sunset Boulevard and listen to tunes submitted for publication. The practice in those days was to choose the newer tunes to be recorded and released as singles; the true chestnuts would be saved for inclusion on one of his upcoming theme albums. Later, during the 1960s and 1970s, he would rely on the instincts and suggestions of his favorite producers, primarily Sonny Burke, Jimmy Bowen, and Don Costa, to guide the way.

In another class altogether was Sinatra's "personal" lyricist, the legendary raconteur Sammy Cahn. "I'm considered to have put more words into Frank Sinatra's mouth than any other man," he was fond of saying.

Sinatra recorded eighty-seven Cahn songs: of these, twenty-four of his lyrics were set to the compositions of Jule Styne, forty-three to those of James "Jimmy" Van Heusen. (This tally doesn't consider the dozens of songs Cahn wrote that Sinatra performed on radio, television, and in films, or the "special" lyrics, often parodies, he crafted for both his own songs and those of others).

The Cahn-Styne partnership lasted from 1942 to 1954 and resulted in dozens of tunes that would become Sinatra classics, including "Time After Time," "Guess I'll Hang My Tears Out to Dry," "I Fall in Love Too Easily," "The Brooklyn Bridge," "Let It Snow! Let It Snow! Let It Snow!,"

Rehearsing with Sammy Cahn (standing) and Jule Styne (piano), mid-1940s.

"Can't You Just See Yourself," "The Things We Did Last Summer," "The Christmas Waltz," and "Three Coins in the Fountain." In 1982, the pair reunited to write two songs expressly for Frank Sinatra: "Searching" and "Love Makes Us Whatever We Want to Be."

After Cahn and Styne split in 1954, Van Heusen entered the picture, and with him came a steady stream of standards, all forever associated with Frank Sinatra: "All the Way," "Love and Marriage," "My Kind of Town (Chicago Is)," "High Hopes," "The Tender Trap," "The Second Time Around" and "Call Me Irresponsible" — most of which came from Sinatra films and television specials. Then came a string of songs crafted specifically to open Sinatra's trendsetting concept albums: "Only the Lonely," "When No One Cares," "Come Fly with Me," "Come

Dance with Me," and "Come Waltz with Me" (the latter dropped from the album at the last minute), and album closers such as "The Last Dance" and "It's Nice to Go Trav'ling."

Whenever Cahn was confronted with the inevitable question "Which came first, the music or the lyrics?" he would invariably give one of two tongue-in-cheek answers: "the phone call" or "the check." Given an idea or a melody, this master of words would sit at his typewriter and in short order bang out a perfect set of lyrics. He once described the genesis of the song "Saturday Night (Is the Loneliest Night in the Week)," another Sinatra favorite that was written fairly quickly.

"I was home alone in my apartment in New York, in my pajamas, when my sister called on me," Cahn explained. "She asked, 'Why are you home alone? It's Saturday night!' My reply was that I was in show business, and that for show people, Saturday night was the loneliest night in the week. Then I got thinking . . . that would be a great title for a song. So I called Jule, and within an hour, we had a song. We gave it to Sinatra, and the rest is history!" (Sinatra recorded it at both Columbia and Capitol.)

Cahn more than any other individual understood Sinatra's unconventional response to a songwriter's demonstration of his tune. Although he cherished top-quality songs, the singer wasn't necessarily effusive with praise and could be difficult to read. While few others enjoyed the privilege, Cahn always previewed a new song for Sinatra by singing it to him in person. "My wife once asked me, 'Who came first, you or Sinatra?' I said, 'What kind of question is that? Did he sing the song to me, or did I sing it to him?' She said, 'I guess you came first.'"

"I stand in front of him when I sing him a new song," Cahn once told me. "Sinatra just stands there, his thumb on his lower lip. When I finish, he just nods — that's all. But I wouldn't be standing in front of him unless he nodded!"

The lyricist relished telling this tale. "Jimmy Van Heusen and I wrote 'All the Way' for the picture *The Joker Is Wild*. Van Heusen and I went up to Las Vegas to sing the song for Frank, and my agent came with us. Now, we were told that he would hear the song before breakfast, which really means 4:00 P.M. So four o'clock comes, and we're waiting in the living room of his suite, and Frank comes out of the bedroom looking like all of the Dorian Grays. He just looked at me, and said, 'You—before breakfast? Yuckk!' Van Heusen and I do the song for him, and after I finished the last note, he just turned and said, 'Let's have some orange juice.' We had a wonderful meal, and when we left, my agent was beside herself. 'How could he not like that song?,' she asked. 'He loved it!' I told her. 'He loves them all.' His reaction was always the same."

The duo had a bit of an advantage over other songwriters—Sinatra shared his home with Van Heusen for a while. "Jimmy used to say that he should get more royalties than I do, because he claims that he 'puts the song in Sinatra's head.' When he was around Sinatra with a new song, he would play it over and over again. . . . Sinatra would wake up, and he would be playing the song; Sinatra would be having lunch, he would be playing the song. And I'll tell you this: when Sinatra knows a song, no one sings it better. But, when he *doesn't* know a song, it's another story—he doesn't sing it well. He has to know the song," Cahn said.

THE MICROPHONE

*M*usical influence excepted, the most important benefit of Frank Sinatra's big-band experience was undoubtedly his discovery of the tool that would become his own secret weapon: the microphone, a device that came of age with the singer's rise to vocal power.

If it were not for superior microphones that accurately reproduce the tone and color of sound, it would be hard to enjoy *any* amplified performance or sound recording, vintage or otherwise. A microphone—ideally one capable of capturing a clean, undistorted signal and processing its vibrations into the electrical energy that transmits the sound to the recording machine (be it lacquer disc cutter or tape recorder)—is the crucial first link in the chain that determines the ultimate quality of a recording.

To appreciate the impact of the microphone on Frank Sinatra's work, and on the larger landscape of popular culture, it is essential to trace its evolution from a very primitive communications tool to the ultra high tech instrument that it has become.

The term *microphone* was first used in the first quarter of the 1800s and was derived from the words *micro* ("small") and *phon* ("sound"). The word was originally used by an inventor named Wheatstone to describe a stethoscope-like device he had invented to amplify weak sounds. Wheatstone's idea set the groundwork for the modern microphone, which is simply a sound collector designed to transform acoustic power into electrical power.

Although they are not really related, many of the ideas for the earliest microphones came from the invention of the telephone, which also spawned the development of Thomas Edison's phonograph. In 1861, Philip Reis of Germany constructed and patented the first acoustic telegraph, dubbing it the "telephone." During the 1870s, Alexander Graham Bell experimented with different ways of turning sound waves into electrical impulses.

These efforts culminated in the creation of a device that used a thin membrane diaphragm with a metallic core. The pressure of the sound striking the diaphragm was duplicated by the moving sliver of metal as it interacted with a magnetic field to produce a variable current. An electromagnet placed next to the diaphragm could vibrate it, thereby reproducing the sound through its slight movement as current passed through. By February 1876, Bell and his assistant, Thomas A. Watson, had a prototype that used a battery to provide the electrical current. It is this model they were experimenting with on the fateful evening of March 10, when Bell uttered the immortal words *Watson, come here, I want you!* — the first intelligible sounds to come over a telephone and proof that sound waves could be processed and transmitted electrically.

The same year, Bell introduced a "liquid" microphone at the Centennial Exposition in Philadelphia. This apparatus consisted of a metal wire, only microns thick, placed into a solution of water and sulfuric acid. On the other end of the wire, Bell attached a diaphragm that could be vibrated by voice waves. The vibrations in the water caused a change in the electrical current that was made to flow through the diaphragm, the wire, and the water-acid mixture. Two years later, in 1878, British professor D. E. Hughes invented the first practical microphone, the primitive forerunner of today's instrument. Of course, these early inventions were not so much microphones as they were crude transmitters.

Concurrently, Edison was struggling in his West Orange, New Jersey, laboratory to both improve the telephone transmitter (an assignment he had accepted from Western Electric) and to preserve the electrical impulses generated for later reproduction. Well versed in the various methods of converting sound waves into mechanical movement that could create electrical impulses, Edison experimented with the idea for the "phonograph," basing his work on his earlier invention of an automatic telegraph that used strips of paper marked with Morse code.

Working in the lab one night in July 1877, Edison fashioned an apparatus consisting of a stylus connected to a diaphragm, which was in turn connected to a telephone speaker. As Edison shouted into the speaker, the stylus etched irregular marks (representing the sound waves) onto a strip of paraffin-coated paper running beneath it. When the strip was re-run under the stylus, the shouting could be faintly heard, to the complete amazement of the group assembled there.

Edison and his crew set out to assemble a more refined machine and, in December, unveiled a working phonograph. This improved machine consisted of a cylinder wrapped in tinfoil, which was attached to a long feed screw that could be turned by a hand crank. On one side of the cylinder was a funnel-like mouthpiece connected to a thin metal diaphragm, to which a steel needle (stylus) was attached. Shouting into the mouthpiece caused the diaphragm to vibrate and move the stylus, which etched the sound waves into the tinfoil as the handle was cranked.

On the opposite side of the cylinder was a "playback" mechanism, a stylus and diaphragm that was run back over the etchings made in the foil, which on playback again vibrated the diaphragm, thereby faintly reproducing the original sound. This crude invention fueled massive public interest. When it was demonstrated at the Manhattan offices of *Scientific American* on December 6, 1877, trains full of people arrived to hear their voices reproduced. Even the president of the United States, Rutherford B. Hayes, became interested, wanting to hear for himself the wonders of the "talking machine."

From August 1877 (the official date of Edison's patent for the cylindrical tinfoil phonograph) to September 1887 (when Emile Berliner applied for a patent on his idea for a flat, metal photoengraved recording disc), all phonographic recordings were made on soft wax cylinders. From the end of the cylinder era to the perfection of the flat disc that we know as the 78, many improvements and refinements were made in recording and reproducing discs for home consumption. One of the greatest advances in recording technology occurred in the early 1920s, as the method of recording shifted from *acoustic* to *electrical*. These changes directly affected how artists went about making their records.

Prior to 1919, all sound recordings were acoustic. The performers were grouped around a wide-bell recording "horn," similar to the horn that Little Nipper the dog is cocking his ear to on the Victor "Red Seal" label. Unlike a microphone, which generated electrical current, the horn functioned as an acoustic funnel that concentrated the sound, channeling it to the recording mechanism where it would vibrate the diaphragm and, in turn, the stylus to etch the recording medium. The horn severely limited the scope and quality of the musical sounds that could be reproduced.

Positioning the performers around the horn was an art form unto itself. Since the pickup area around the horn was only a few feet, certain instrumentalists needed to be placed closer to the horn so louder players wouldn't drown them out. As the sound source moved farther away from the horn, the drop in recording volume became dramatic. The early sessions must have been quite a sight, with vocalists scurrying out of the way as instrumental soloists leapt toward the horn! While the early engineers (then called "recorders") balanced and mixed the recording by physically moving the performers around the room to accommodate the position of the recording horn, modern engineers reverse the process by moving the recording microphone around the studio to best suit the placement of the performers.

Although the terms *dynamic range* and *signal-to-noise ratio* would not evolve for another sixty years, they denoted technical factors that early recorders needed to consider. During recording, the wave form inscribed into the wax changed proportionately with the pitch of the sounds. Higher frequency sounds would cause narrow, densely packed waves, while the lower notes caused the stylus to travel longer distances to create longer wave forms. Loud noises forced the stylus deep into the groove and usually de-

COURTESY OF THE UNITED STATES DEPARTMENT OF THE INTERIOR, NATIONAL PARK SERVICE, EDISON NATIONAL HISTORIC SITE

Acoustic recording session, Edison Studios, New York City, circa 1907 to 1912. Note the use of Stroh violins, which featured a minature horn that amplified the comparatively weak sound of the instrument.

stroyed the recording. If a group was placed too close to the horn, making a louder recording, the diaphragm would vibrate rapidly, causing distortion on playback. For these reasons, drums were commonly banned from recording studios, and great care needed to be exercised when a vocalist or instrumental performer reached a loud peak in the performance.

Certain other instruments also wreaked havoc. String instruments were very difficult to record, because the early machines could not reproduce sibilants, or 'S' sounds. To remedy this, the Stroh violin was developed. Attached to it were a sound box and horn, which helped amplify its sound. Usually, piano backs were removed for recording, and the instrument was hoisted into the air to bring it closer to the level of the recording horn. Despite these painstaking efforts, pianists were required to play extra loudly, and even then the instrument sounded tinny upon playback. These inherent problems forced early recorders to be quite selective in what they chose to record for posterity. Whistling records abounded in the 1880s and 1890s, as did recordings featuring the banjo, xylophone, and brass bands—their tonal characteristics were best suited for acoustic recording.

Because they were initially refined for business use, the early talking machines did a remarkable job of reproducing the human voice (especially the deeper male voice). Enrico Caruso, widely hailed as the greatest operatic tenor, was able to make sound recordings, and, for their time, they possess a remarkable clarity and richness of tone. But, as enjoyable and precious as they are, recording technology could not fully capture the fiery color and electrifying overtones that were Caruso's hallmarks. Our perception of Caruso's voice is locked in the boxy, characteristically vintage sound of acoustic records.

Between the early 1920s (when Caruso stopped recording) and the late 1930s (when Frank Sinatra began), recording studios made incredible strides. The recordists of Edison's era developed trial-and-error techniques for manipulating sound, based mostly on the artistic result in individual recordings. By the time Sinatra entered a studio, the balance had shifted toward the scientific, and recording men were fast becoming respected for their ability to function as "painters" of sound. Incoming music and voice was monitored through loudspeakers as the recording was made, offering a much more realistic indication of the balance of sound and the sonic characteristics of the recording room. Musicians still needed to be strategically placed around the microphone to create just the right balance of instruments, but now the emphasis of certain tonal frequencies, reverberation, and microphone placement were all scientific tools that could be used artistically to add texture and substance to the sound of a recording.

Experimentation with electrical recording, where the microphone would replace the acoustic horn, began in both England and America in 1919. Western Electric led the way, and

their process for electrical recording was quickly embraced because it offered better control over recording volume and tone. Microphones enabled recorders to wax performances by larger orchestras, and the sound they got from the instruments was dramatically improved. The increased dynamic range allowed more of the sound of each instrument to be etched into the disc, resulting in a louder, fuller sound.

Recordists continued to utilize many of the skills learned during the trials of acoustic recording. The new Western Electric system still etched the sound signal into a wax record. The operator of the recording machine was required to carefully monitor the cutting, as loud peaks could cause a ruinous jump in the stylus, even after meters were introduced that allowed recorders to monitor the volume level coming into the microphones.

Several procedures instituted in the acoustic era continued into the electrical era, and many of these early practices—the separation of the recording equipment from the room where the performer worked, a "recording" light or bell to indicate that a session was in progress, and special rooms for performers to relax in—are still common in recording studios today.

The heart of most microphones was a relatively noisy carbon transmitter, which had been developed by Emile Berliner and Thomas Edison for telephones. While infinitely better than the acoustic horn, the carbon transmitter mikes lacked the sensitivity to reproduce the full range of voice and music. As early as 1915, though, there had been some experimentation with vacuum tube amplifiers, which would allow the creation of a quieter microphone with improved impedance and output. In 1917, Bell Labs used this technology to make the first modern condenser microphone—a mike with a small built-in amplifier and separate power supply. The instruments were unreliable, and it wasn't until the mid-1920s that improved condenser mikes, made by Western Electric, began to proliferate.

Like all microphones, the new condenser mikes had a diaphragm, but now it was part of a capacitor, or condenser, which was attached to a rear plate with a tiny air space in between. High-voltage current was applied between the plates, and, as the diaphragm moved in response to the sound waves striking it, the energy between it and the rear plate varied, producing a voltage proportional to the sound. The minute energy (capacitance) changes of the microphone required an amplifier to strengthen the current. Early models used a battery for this purpose.

In the late 1920s, a Dr. Olson of RCA's research and development department began building the first *ribbon* microphone. In 1931 the

Rehearsal with the legendary RCA 44 ribbon microphone, circa 1947.

company marketed its first permanent magnet bidirectional ribbon microphone, the RCA 44, the first of the "classic" diamond-shaped microphones that would become associated with the Sinatra of the radio and recording studio throughout the 1940s. A ribbon microphone consists of a thin, stretched duralumin ribbon suspended between the poles of a permanent magnet. While anchored at both ends, the ribbon moves freely back and forth, allowing for sensitive vibrations to be converted to electromagnetic energy. The RCA 44, and its improved successor, the 44B/BX, quickly became the industry standard for high-quality sound.

First, the mike was *bidirectional*, which means it was sensitive to sound coming directly into it from the front and back and not to sounds coming from the sides. This pickup pattern made it particularly effective when recording a vocal or other instrument that needed a degree of isolation. It was also versatile, as performers could be placed on both sides of the microphone face; e.g., a guitarist and bassist facing each other with the microphone between them. Since the mike was bidirectional, it would pick up sound from both players. A 44, or any ribbon microphone for that matter, could be placed directly in front of a sound source, so the desired sound could be captured free of noise or coloration from surrounding instruments, which could affect the quality of the featured instrument by "leaking" sound from other parts of the orchestra into the mike.

Second, the design of the ribbon microphone allowed it to respond easily to the low-pressure sound of treble (high) tones, resulting in exceptional high-frequency response (which translates to a crisp, well-defined sound especially desirable when recording the human voice). With a "flat" sound (uncolored by excessive bass or treble) over the entire frequency range, the RCA 44 mikes reproduced sound with a quality that was at once warm and rich, yet incisive. These fine reproduction characteristics made the 44 a perfect vocal mike, the hands-down choice for preserving the mellowness of Sinatra's voice during this era.

The 44's counterpart, the RCA 77 ribbon microphone, came along in the early 1930s. It was created to fill the growing need for a "directional" microphone—one that could be used in radio broadcast settings to further isolate the sound being reproduced from extraneous noises in the radio (and later TV) studio. The 77 was unique in that adjustable interior vanes allowed an engineer to change the pickup pattern from bidirectional to cardioid to nearly omnidirectional. Retaining many of the same sonic qualities of the 44, the RCA 77, with its familiar capsule shape, joined the 44 as the standard in studios of all types and became closely identified with radio and public speech.

Ribbon microphones, for all of their suitability as an instrument of the radio or recording studio, were not as desirable for rugged exterior conditions, because the ribbon was extremely fragile. Even slight bursts of wind or a person blowing into the mike could tear the ribbon to shreds. Consequently, while the RCA 44 was omnipresent for all of Frank Sinatra's radio and recording sessions, it was absent during his live stage appearances. The less-controlled environment of those performances required a sturdier microphone, and, for in-person performances during the 1940s, the Shure Unidyne Model 55 series and Altec 639B models were the instruments of choice.

Developed in the late 1930s, the familiar Altec "birdcage" microphone was a rugged, reliable directional mike that featured a single element, making it portable and easy to handle. The Shure 55 sported a sleek, modern ribbed design that kept it a mainstay of the industry from the late 1930s to the mid 1960s. These mikes were originally identified with the early rock-and-roll era; today, they are sought after as both working microphones and "props" for modern musicians who wish to add a classic, retro look to their live performances and music videos.

Recording with a Neumann U-47 condenser microphone, Capitol Records, late 1950s.

In 1947, with the audio world poised on the edge of the high-fidelity era, George Neumann introduced his U47, a thick cylindrical microphone that revolutionized hi-fi sound. Neumann set about improving upon the Bell Labs condenser technology of 1917 and by 1928 had developed his first condenser mike, the CMV3 (nicknamed "the bottle"). This instrument was extremely progressive, for it enabled users to use interchangeable heads to vary the directional pickup. One of these capsules, the M7 cardioid, was the one used on the U47. Neumann, by perfecting the condenser microphone, made the potential for lifelike sound a reality. Distributed by Telefunken (thus nicknamed the "Telly" by industry insiders), the U47 was the first condenser microphone able to switch between cardioid and omnidirectional patterns. It was effective for a wide variety of applications, including close vocal and instrumental miking and full area (orchestral) recording.

"When the U47 came along, it was like a bomb went off," says veteran film recording engineer and microphone expert Jim Webb. "Neumann had been experimenting with that technology since the late 1920s, and such remarkable results had never been achieved before. After the U47 hit, everyone was copying it, right down to the size of the tube and the windscreen and everything."

Engineer Bob Fine, then head of recording for Mercury's Living Presence records, was so taken with the ability of the microphone to accurately reproduce sounds over the entire sonic spectrum that he based his innovative process of recording a full symphonic orchestra on a single U47, strategically suspended above the musicians in the recording hall. Mercury further secured the association by prominently featuring photos of the microphone on its record covers; soon other labels—Capitol in particular—followed

Sinatra's exquisite use of the microphone as a stage prop deftly communicated the eroticism of his art.

suit. By 1953, when Frank Sinatra began recording at Capitol Records, the U47 had replaced the RCA 44 as the preferred vocal microphone. The change in technology transformed Sinatra's performance technique.

The microphone was of primary import to Frank Sinatra from his earliest days as a band singer. Building on the foundation laid by Bing Crosby and Billie Holiday, he brought the microphone to its fullest and most creative potential as a logical extension of his voice. "One thing that was tremendously important was learning the use of the microphone," Sinatra said. "Many singers never learned to use one. They never understood, and still don't, that a microphone is their instrument. It's like they were part of an orchestra, but instead of playing a saxophone, they're playing a microphone."

He likely drew this conclusion from the reaction of the largely female audiences to his early stage appearances. He would grasp the tall microphone stand (seemingly for support) and lean into both the mike and the note, physically communicating the dynamic he desired. This simple stage maneuver perfectly accentuated his unique vocal styling, prompting him to observe that "If I did what they call "bending" a note, if I just kind of looped the note, well, they would wail!"

Although other performers of the day followed suit and used the modern microphone to their advantage, none handled it more fluidly or effortlessly. To some singers, it was a barrier between performer and audience; to Sinatra it was a tool that strengthened the intimacy between himself and his listeners—a stage prop. Whether on stage in the 1940s, when the microphone was a birdcage or Unidyne mounted on a tall stand, or in the 1980s, when the cumbersome older mike had been replaced by a handheld cordless model, Sinatra's facile use of this instrument became as important to his musical persona as his fabled breath control.

Of his technique for handling the mike, the singer observed, "The first rule is to use it with great economy. You don't crowd it—you must never jar an audience with it, unless there's a reason to as part of a song—a comedy number or the like. I think you must keep it as subtle as possible. A simple example is popping 'P's and other plosive sounds. They're easy to avoid." His technique reduced the effects of popping and harsh sibilance and also served as a natural dynamic range expander during a recording session. "You must know when to move away from the mike, and when to move back into it. To me, there's no worse sound than when a singer breathes in sharply, and you hear the gasp over the microphone. The whole secret is getting the air in the corner of the mouth, and using the microphone properly."

A quick listen to any of the recordings highlighted in this book will immediately demonstrate the soundness of Sinatra's theory. It was this level of artistic intuition, combined with his careful attention to every last detail, that set Sinatra apart from every other vocalist and make his recordings models worthy of emulation. "When I'm using a microphone [for live appearances], I usually try to have a black one, so that it will melt into my dinner jacket and the audience isn't aware of it," he said. In the April 1965 *Life* article, Sinatra chastised a friend whose talents he greatly admired, citing her lack of proficiency with a stage mike. "Many years ago I found that I could take the mike off the stand and move around with it. That's a boon, and so many singers don't take advantage of it. Ella Fitzgerald, poor girl, still doesn't. They set up a mike for her, and she never touches it. You can't even see her face."

The correlation between the microphone and body movement is critical to a performer. "Singers, in the old days, used to sing deadpan," said Sammy Davis, Jr. "They'd keep their hands in their pockets and stand up there flat-footed and sing. All the singers from Rudy Vallee on did it this way. But Frank used to do things with his hands, and convey the song both lyrically and

PHOTOGRAPH BY SID AVERY, COURTESY MPTV ARCHIVE

The intensity with which Sinatra approached his craft and the use of the recording microphone was effectively captured in the Capitol studios by photographer Sid Avery.

physically to the audience. He'd snap his fingers when he was happy. He'd say it with his hands."

Nelson Riddle said, "Frank's body motion was a clear indication of how he felt when we were recording. Usually, his hands would be outstretched, his feet set apart, his head cocked to one side. That is how he stands at the mike in the large, dramatic moments. Sometimes he puts his left hand in his pocket when he talks to the audience."

British writer Robin Douglas-Home watched Sinatra in the recording studio during the September 1961 dates for the album *Point of No Return* at Capitol. His observation of Sinatra's microphone mannerisms in his book *Sinatra* speak volumes about Sinatra's mastery of microphone technique.

"I saw complete and utter involvement with the song he was singing: involvement so close that one might feel he was in the throes of composing both tune and lyrics as he went along. When he controlled his breathing, he shuddered...almost painfully. Shoulders shook, neck muscles twitched, even his legs seemed to oscillate. His nostrils dilated and his eyes closed dreamily, then opened again as sharp as ever as he watched a soloist, then closed again and his face contorted into a grimace, and his whole frame seemed to be caught up in a paroxysm, quivering all over as he expressed a key note or word, like 'November' in 'September Song.' His mouth, sometimes hardly a centimeter from the microphone, widened into a sort of canine snarl, and he cocked his head now on one side, now on the other, like a puppy listening to the squeak of a toy mouse. He was putting so much into that song, giving so much of himself that it drained my own energy just to watch him—without hearing a note he was singing."

WAX IMPRESSIONS

The three years or so that Sinatra spent traveling with the James and Dorsey orchestras were a prelude to years of voluminous recording activity. Making band records, however, was vastly different from his solo recording sessions. "Every moment was absolutely real," Sinatra said of the hectic pace of the early years. "Driving five hundred miles through the night to the next one-night stand, and having forty minutes to get out of the bus and into the hotel; turn on the shower and the steam, hang up the dinner jacket to allow the wrinkles to come out of it, grab a sandwich, show up on the bandstand, and then...the greeting from the audience was the greatest reward in the world!"

"In those days, we were so busy doing one-nighters that we really didn't have time to rehearse and hash out arrangements for recording sessions, per se," recalls Dorsey alumnus Jo Stafford. "We'd try out new songs and arrangements on the road, and if they went well, we'd get into the studio in New York (or Chicago or Hollywood) and just record the songs that we were doing on our one-nighters. We really didn't *need* to rehearse!" (Pianist Joe Bushkin remembers the exact opposite being true—the band would record a number, then begin adding it to their repertoire as it became popular. It is likely that the procedure occurred both ways.)

The Dorsey-Sinatra sessions for Victor took place at several studios operated by the label at the time. In the 1930s, the label's flagship studio was a converted livery stable located at 155 W. 24th Street in New York City. These studios contained three recording rooms: Studios 1, 2, and 3. Most of the big-band recording sessions were done in Studios 1 and 2, where the New York Sinatra sessions of 1940–1942 took place. In 1940, Studio 3 became the facility's echo chamber.

Victor's Chicago studios were located on Lake Shore Drive; in Hollywood, the studio occupied space above the RCA record plant on Olive Avenue. (The RCA division was responsible for pressing Victor's records.) Each of these studios had equipment setups similar to those in the World Transcription Studios and Liederkranz Hall, the studios that Columbia was using at the time.

During the late 1930s and early 1940s, recording methods were still fairly crude, although they were infinitely better than the acoustic or early electrical recordings of just two decades before. Commonly, only three or four microphones would be placed among the orchestra; vocalists or vocal groups would, of course, have their own dedicated mike. Popular microphones for both recording and stage performances during this period were Western Electric models 630-A (moving coil) and 639 (ribbon) and the classic RCA 44 (ribbon) microphone.

Until late in 1942, most records were made by etching the recording grooves onto a soft, waxy disc (thus the phrase *waxing a record*), then creating a metal-plated master from this soft impression. This resulted in a sturdy but, compared to vinyl, rough-surfaced master disc. It was this metal "part," as it is called in the industry, that would create the stampers from which thick, brittle 78 rpm "shellac" discs could be struck for commercial sale. Since the original wax masters were irreparably altered during the plating process, the metal parts struck from them remain the truest original sources for these early big band recordings, and they are the primary choice (over the 78 rpm discs made from them) as the sound source for modern digital restoration.

There is evidence that some of the Sinatra-James sessions of 1939 may have been recorded on 16-inch lacquer discs, though. In 1997, while making archival transfers of all the Harry James masters in the Columbia vault, Sony Music producer Michael Brooks and engineer Matt Cavaluzzo found one such lacquer disc containing "From the Bottom of My Heart" among the metal parts that comprise the balance of the early recordings. No other lacquers for these sessions have surfaced. Most of the RCA Victor recordings likewise survive only as original metal parts.

To make a master recording on wax, a cake of specially formulated carnauba wax was formed into a disc approximately four inches thick. Carson Taylor, a Capitol Records engineer who worked extensively with wax recording in the early days of his career, describes the process of preparing the blank discs for recording. "We had to shave the wax blocks down so they were absolutely smooth, and then polish them with a diamond stone. When they were ready to be used,

they looked like a mirror: you could see yourself in them, they were so highly polished and shiny. If you had to cut and polish those waxes, they would sometimes break, and since the machine revolved at about 1,800 rpm, it could be very dangerous! One time, I had one break and fly off the wheel, and a piece flew right by my head, and it went right through the building wall that was right next to where I was working."

Once the wax was polished, it would be placed on a Scully recording lathe fitted with a diamond or ruby stylus. "The stylus had to be exactly the right temperature: if it was too cold, the wax would chip, and if it was too warm, you would lose the contour of the groove and you would lose the high frequencies," Taylor explains. When the appropriate conditions were met, the session could begin.

The grooves traced into the soft wax were very fragile. Except in extreme cases (which would more than likely result in irreparable damage), the wax master was never played back. Instead, it was immediately sent out for plating.

Before plating, the disc was coated with silver nitrate. Then the wax impression was given a special high temperature bath, during which it would be coated with a thin layer of copper to ensure conductivity. The original wax master would then be separated from the newly formed plating disc, and this metal disc (actually an unplayable "negative" part containing ridges instead of grooves) became the true master, as it was the first-generation part struck from the wax disc.

The original wax recording disc, having been rendered unusable by the plating process, would be recycled, its surface shaved down and repolished to be used again at another recording session. This could be done until the disc thickness was about one inch, when it would be melted down and combined with other used discs to make new wax blocks.

The metal master was then plated, creating a second metal master. The resulting disc had regular grooves and was known as the "matrix" or "mother" master. It could be played back to check for quality. If any defects were found, a technician, using a microscope and specialized tools, would smooth out rough spots in the groove. Once the corrected disc was approved, it was plated a third time to make the stamper—the metal part that the plant would use to produce the actual 78 rpm shellac discs to be sold at retail.

The manufacture of these records was simple and effective. The stamping press, similar in design to a waffle iron, had a die fitted to hold the metal stamper. A finely powdered compound called shellac was pumped into the press through holes in the side of the machine, which combined with steam to melt the compound, allowing it to flow into the grooves of the stamper. Cold water would then be run through the press. Any excess material around the sides was trimmed, the edges smoothed, and the disc sent to the packaging department.

A side effect of this process, during which at least three metal masters were struck before a record was pressed, was a slight degradation in the shape of the grooves. With each subsequent separation, the grooves became a bit wider, affecting their sonic properties to some degree. When you consider that most 78 rpm discs are really four generations removed from the original session master, it becomes easy to understand why their sonic quality can sometimes be inferior. Furthermore, during World War II, when the chemicals used in the shellac compound were ra-

tioned, many record companies used whatever scrap material they could find to serve as binders and fillers for their 78s. It is for this reason that many of the records pressed during the period are unusually noisy.

After the 33⅓ LP was developed, a quieter vinyl disc replaced the brittle shellac platters. During the 1930s, Union Carbide had developed a vinyl resin called "vinylite," which was compatible with the pressing equipment that made shellac records. In the early 1940s, both Western Electric and RCA were using vinyl ("victrolac") for radio transcriptions, and in 1943 the U.S. government began using a lightweight plastic compound called "formvar" for its "V-discs" (Victory discs), the special recordings sent to American troops stationed overseas.

RCA Victor also issued a number of their Red Seal classical 78s on cherry red vinyl in 1944. The lightweight vinyl disc was the main reason for the superior fidelity of the LP, and, although cassette tapes were extremely popular from the 1970s on, vinyl remained the primary format for recorded music until the dawn of the digital compact disc era (mid-1980s).

As methods of recording and reproducing music improved through the early 1940s, Frank Sinatra became restless and decided it was time for a change. Taking one of the biggest risks of his life, he prepared to leave the comfort and security of Dorsey's band and strike out on his own. Sinatra gambled, and, lucky for us, he won.

Columbia recording session, New York City, October 1947.

PART 2

The Columbia Years, 1943–1952

MAKING THE BREAK

After roughly three years with two fine bands, Frank Sinatra made the decision to try his luck as a solo singer. The proposition was decidedly risky; few singers were making it, as Bing Crosby had a decade earlier, if they were not associated with a dance band. Sinatra knew instinctively, however, that this was the path to follow, and to test the waters he engaged Axel Stordahl, then a trumpeter and house arranger for Tommy Dorsey, to write several arrangements for his first solo session.

On January 19, 1942, Frank Sinatra made his first solo recordings at RCA Victor's Hollywood studio, a date yielding four sides: "The Night We Called It a Day," "The Lamplighter's Serenade," "The Song Is You," and "Night and Day." Since the singer was still obligated to Dorsey, the company required his approval to issue the songs on the Victor label. Dorsey refused, forcing their release on the cheaper Victor subsidiary label Bluebird Records. The sessions were supervised by

Victor's veteranartist and repertoire (A&R) man, Harry Meyerson.

Instrumentation relied mostly on members of the Dorsey band, augmented by four violins, one cello, one oboe, and a harp. There was no percussion used on these recordings. Time was kept by the simple rhythm section of bass, piano, and guitar. From all accounts, Sinatra was mesmerized by the results and spent hours listening to test pressings of the songs. Of the four tunes, three would remain his personal favorites, and he would record them again and again.

While he had begun to rumble about leaving the band as early as September 1941, Sinatra now earnestly sought to sever his ties with Dorsey, who had been irritating him for some time. Skitch Henderson, the pianist on the Bluebird date and a personal friend, vividly remembers the breaking point. "James (Jimmy) Van Heusen and I were roommates and had a house on Rodeo Drive in Los Angeles [Beverly Hills]. The phone rang one night, and it was Frank, saying, 'The Old Man goosed me with his trombone for the last time. I'm leaving the band. . . .' That was when they were at the Circle Theater, and we got Nancy and little Nancy, and got them an apartment."

In 1965, Sinatra recalled the decision to break away. "During the shows we used to let the kids ask questions—they'd ask about my parents and my wife and my kids, and it was obvious that they felt I was the neighborhood boy that had made good. The press helped, too, because they printed stuff from the pro-Crosby group, who were hollering that Sinatra didn't have anything compared to their boy, and my kids would yell back, 'Yes, he has . . .' People began coming to hear for themselves. I began to realize that there must be something to all this commotion. I didn't know exactly what it was, but I figured I had something that must be important. So I decided to try it alone, without a band. What really put the clincher on my decision was when I heard that Bob Eberly was planning to break off from Jimmy Dorsey. Bob was one of the great singers

of all time—he had a good quality, and wonderful intonation. When I heard through the bandstand grapevine that he was striking out on his own, I figured I had to beat him. Nobody had broken the ice since Crosby, and I thought 'Somebody is going to come along and do this any day.' If Eberly got out ahead of me, I'd be in trouble."

In a 1986 conversation with author Sidney Zion at Yale University, Sinatra spoke of his determination. "I was with Tommy almost three years, and then I decided to strike out on my own. And from there on, with God's will and my stick-to-itiveness, I made some kind of stance in my business. Because I believed everything that I was doing was right."

Sinatra didn't allow his lack of formal musical training to impede him. Instead, he thwarted potential criticism by studying with a vocal teacher, with whom he ultimately wrote a short book called *Tips on Popular Singing*.

"Even if I sounded badly, I couldn't tell that, but I knew that eventually, someone would say, 'It's not good enough. Study . . . do something else. Take some lessons.' Which I did, though I didn't study legitimate music—I can't read a single note. I went and found a vocal coach named John Quinlan, who was a wonderful man. He was an opera singer at the Met, became a drunk, and got fired. But he was a great teacher of calisthenics in the throat, so that you didn't tire when you sang. Even today, whether I'm working that night or not, I vocalize every day," Sinatra told Zion.

While Sinatra's time as a serious vocal student was short, he exhibited a natural understanding of music that even the most accomplished classical musicians quickly noticed. He proved to be a quick study and, as if he had a sixth sense, demonstrated unusual proficiency when it came to detecting incorrect notes and sounds within the orchestra.

John Garvey, a violinist who backed Sinatra on some live dates in 1943, shared these recollections with journalist Henry Pleasants. "The musicians were skeptical, until one day at rehearsal, Sinatra and the orchestra were handed a new song. Sinatra just stood there with the lead sheet in one hand, the other cupping his ear, following along silently while the orchestra read through the Axel Stordahl chart. A second time through he sang it in half-voice. The third time through he took over. We all knew then that we had an extraordinarily intuitive musician on our hands."

Sinatra didn't have far to search for a record label willing to sign him. He had sent a set of rough acetate dubs of the Bluebird songs over to Manie Sacks, then head of A&R at Columbia Records, where Sinatra had made his first recordings with Harry James in 1939. The pair quickly became friends. Once Sinatra had a verbal nod from Sacks that he would be welcomed at Columbia, he made the break from Dorsey in September 1942. On December 30, he was billed as the "Special Added Attraction" alongside bandleader Benny Goodman at New York's Paramount Theater. Virtually overnight, the country's newest sensation, Frank Sinatra, teen idol, was born.

Because of a recording ban imposed by musicians' union chief James Petrillo, when Sinatra entered Columbia's New York Studio inside Liederkranz Hall in June 1943, it was sans orchestra, and he began his Columbia career by transcribing a series of a cappella recordings with the Bobby Tucker Singers and Alec Wilder. The ban prohibited him from making a full orchestral recording for another year and a half, so he took the opportunity to do some backfield strategizing. Among his very first decisions was to engage Axel Stordahl as his music director. Fearing he would forever be typecast as a dance band singer, he asked Stordahl to design soft, lush string arrangements that would enhance the romantic image he wished to project. In short order "the Voice" was well on his way to fulfilling the prophecy he had shared a few years earlier with his friend Sammy Cahn—to become the world's greatest singer.

TAKING CHARGE

The Columbia years (1943–1952) found Sinatra experimenting with a wide variety of musical settings, laying a solid foundation for what ten years later would be his greatest period, with Nelson Riddle, Billy May, and Gordon Jenkins. While his band vocal recordings had communicated a warmly nostalgic charm, it wasn't until he signed with Columbia Records that he gained almost complete control over his sessions and was able to shape every facet of the perfection he sought. From the Columbia era on, Sinatra choreographed his own recording

Sinatra supervised every detail at his recording sessions. Here he listens to a playback with (left to right) arranger Axel Stordahl, engineer Harold "Chappie" Chapman, and producer Bill Richards, Hollywood, October 1946 (man in upper left is unidentified).

sessions—a task that most other popular artists, whether through feelings of supremacy or inadequacy, ignorance or apathy, left to others. (In most cases, a record company's A&R representative, or sometimes its recording director, would direct an artist's sessions.)

Although staff recording directors (usually Morty Palitz, Joe Higgins, Bill Richards, and occasionally Manie Sacks) were customarily assigned to work with the singer, he assumed responsibility for and oversaw nearly every detail of his record dates, from song selection to the sonic balances achieved in the studio on the day of recording. While the role of the "record producer" would not fully evolve until the mid-1950s, at the height of the Mitch Miller era, Sinatra pioneered the ways artists were handled and their music recorded for decades to follow. His meticulous supervision and the reputation it fostered quickly turned his recording sessions into unforgettable occasions.

"Quite frankly, I was intimidated," recalls Columbia Records producer George Avakian, who worked on several Sinatra sessions in the 1940s. "Frank would come off the elevator with his bodyguards. Two guards would come off the elevator, they'd look right and left. Then Frank would step out, and two other guys would step out, and they'd look right and left. They looked like five diamonds walking up the hall!" Lest there be any confusion, it must be noted that there was nothing dictatorial or imperial about Sinatra's direction of his recording sessions. Once inside the studio, the atmosphere relaxed, and, from all accounts, Sinatra became just another guy in the band or in the booth.

Unlike other artists who sometimes adopted a prima donna attitude, Sinatra, like his contemporaries Bing Crosby and Nat "King" Cole, placed himself on the same level as the musicians and technicians who aided him. His admiration for the musicians was evident in the loose, good-natured give-and-take that was a hallmark of his recording sessions. Sinatra knew that what went

down in the studio was both a permanent record and a reflection of his aesthetic values. He realized that his livelihood as a popular singer depended on the cooperation of many people, not the least of whom were the musicians who helped make his songs "sing," and the technicians entrusted to preserve them.

Rarely would Sinatra treat any of the players with anything less than the highest regard. This, combined with Sinatra's highly developed musical sense, has prompted most musicians fortunate enough to have worked with him to extol his virtues as a musical ally. In contrast, many of the same top-level professionals have, without solicitation, cited certain other top singers as being preoccupied with their own importance, making them somewhat difficult to work with.

"He had great respect for musicians—all of them," recalls violinist Dave Frisina, who was the first-chair violinist on numerous Sinatra dates at Columbia and continued to be a first call player on the singer's sessions well into the 1980s. "He knew everybody in the orchestra—I suppose he just made it his business to know everyone. He could hear—he was enough of a musician himself to understand when people were playing, if they were really capable musicians."

George Roberts, a veteran of the Stan Kenton band who played a key role in shaping the direction of Sinatra's next musical summit, remembers, "The days I spent working with Frank are, to me, the epitome of everything I had ever dreamed of. He has a charisma, or whatever it is about him, that no one else has." This sentiment has been echoed by dozens of sidemen and technicians who spent years working with Sinatra. While he could become extremely impatient with the time-consuming process of making films and television shows (he was known to bitterly stalk off both film and television stages when the proceedings didn't progress as quickly as he desired), he would willingly spend inordinate amounts of time in the recording studio, interpreting and reinterpreting songs until he was

Having fun as singer Monica Lewis (left) and harpist Elaine Vito, a veteran of dozens of Sinatra's Columbia sessions, look on, circa 1945.

completely satisfied with the results. Sometimes a whole three-hour session would be scrubbed and the recording of the particular song or songs rescheduled for the singer to be sure that it was "just right."

CHARTING THE WAY

The role of the arranger cannot be overemphasized vis à vis the quality and success of Sinatra's music. His instinct for selecting,

song by song, the orchestrator who could custom-tailor the musical settings to communicate exactly the emotion he desired was the heart of Sinatra's genius. His insistence on giving his orchestrators prominent credit on record labels and album jackets resulted in modern pop arrangers being brought to the forefront, where their efforts could be appreciated by the listening public.

While he worked with dozens of talented individuals throughout the sixty years of his career, Sinatra remained loyal to a small group of arrangers who used his boundless musical energy and insight as a springboard for creating not only his orchestrations (which were usually far superior to any they wrote for other singers), but also as the inspiration for their own personal work. "A good arranger is vital, because in a sense, he's a recording secretary," Sinatra told Robin Douglas-Home in a 1961 interview. "I must admit something," he said. "I'd never argue with someone like Nelson [Riddle] on a record date. You respect the arranger. It's his date—he's the leader."

The collaborators Sinatra was drawn to were far more than ordinary arrangers. Axel Stordahl, Nelson Riddle, Billy May, Gordon Jenkins, and Don Costa were, in every way, more composers than orchestrators. "There's a huge distinction between arranging and composing," says composer-musician Joel Friedman. "I could take a piece of music that's already been written, a Bach chorale for example, and arrange it for an orchestra. Then, someone else could come along and use all the same notes, but arrange it their own way. Neither of us is adding anything of our own, yet we each might use different doubling or voices in unison, which will give it a completely different sound."

"An arranger could simply follow the original melody, and maybe expand it a bit, but there's not a lot of imagination being exercised there. What Sinatra's arrangers did was much different: writing is conceiving original melodic patterns, and that's what they were doing. All the intros, and all the minor things that the trumpets and

With his first music director and arranger Axel Stordahl, early 1940s.
The pair brought new meaning to the term "musical collaboration."

"In those days, Axel was writing things that were beautiful. Nobody wrote ballads as pretty as he did until many years later, when Nelson came along. Axel Stordahl really was the 'Daddy' that people began to learn from in the sense of writing orchestrations—he really was the most prolific [arranger] of his time," Sinatra once said. Stordahl's luxurious string arrangements for the singer became synonymous with his suave, romantic image as the premiere crooner of the 1940s.

"Axel was a very good string writer, who wrote with a fine harmonic sense," remembered colleague Paul Weston. "He used to use what we called an 'Axel Ending' on the end of some of the ballads, where he would use a complicated tag where he'd change key a couple of times in the last four bars. Also, Ax and I would write countermelodies for the strings, to be played against the vocal. Most arrangers simply used the strings as 'pads'—few wrote countermelodies against the vocalist." Much of Stordahl's inspiration came from his love of classical music, and strains of Rachmaninoff, Tchaikovsky, and Ravel ring clear in the lush swell of his most lovely arrangements. "A lot of Axel's sound came from the French school of writing, more 'Impressionistic,' using the harp and suspension and major seconds and semi-tones," believes bandleader Skitch Henderson. The Impressionist composers became a constant thread throughout Sinatra's career and would be fully exploited during his later association with Nelson Riddle.

Unfortunately, little has been documented about the details of Sinatra and Stordahl's working procedures. Stordahl's untimely death in 1963 and a rumored dispute between the pair left researchers with just the millions of notes that remain a part of the permanent record. One can surmise, though, that because the two spent such enormous amounts of time in such close musical and personal proximity, it became relatively easy for Stordahl to create the backgrounds Sinatra desired.

trombones are doing to accentuate the melody don't just exist—they're making those things up, even if it was only three notes. That's writing, so they are as much composers as they are arrangers."

Mutual respect and understanding brought Frank Sinatra and Axel Stordahl together in the early 1940s as one of the first true musical partnerships of the pop music era. From the first four solo sides he made for Victor's Bluebird label in January 1942 to the first Capitol Records session in April 1953, it was Stordahl who faithfully served as Sinatra's musical director, creating hundreds of orchestrations and musical cues for his seemingly endless flow of commercial recording sessions, radio programs, personal appearances, Hollywood films, and television shows.

Axel Stordahl's original orchestration for "Put Your Dreams Away," one of Sinatra's favorite theme songs, circa 1945.

ANATOMY OF A RECORDING SESSION

*I*t is difficult for outsiders to appreciate what actually occurs at a recording session. Rarely do we think about the effort that accompanies the creation of a particular song when it is played on the radio or on a record in our homes. Much of the mystery is due to the fact that most recording sessions are closed to the general public. Few people not directly associated with the artist or the recording project are allowed in.

The recording session (or "date") is a highly personal event in which the performing artist is completely vulnerable. During the course of a session, a musician may rehearse difficult passages or make mistakes in lyric or melodic interpretation. Singers may become frustrated and say things not flattering to themselves or their public image. Artists invest every ounce of their being for art's sake, and a perfectionist like Sinatra may be very particular about how the final recording sounds.

Although the Capitol recording sessions of ten years later would differ, during the Columbia years Sinatra's sessions were typically closed. We are able to study and appreciate the Sinatra-Stordahl recordings because they were beautifully recorded and preserved by Columbia Records, reflecting the ideal conditions under which they were made as well as the dramatic improvements in the direct-to-disc recording methods of the early 1940s. In them we see Sinatra creating the pattern for his recording sessions that he followed for the next four decades.

During the 1940s, 1950s, and 1960s, a recording session typically lasted three hours, during which, by contractual obligation, three or four tunes would be completely recorded and mastered. About an hour or so before the start of the session (usually 8:00 P.M. for Sinatra dates—he felt his voice was sufficiently loosened by this time of evening, and it also accommodated his busy daytime film schedule), the musicians would arrive at the studio to lay out their instruments and peruse the evening's orchestrations.

Milt Bernhart, an extraordinary trombonist who came to the Hollywood film and recording studios in the early 1950s following a successful stint with the Stan Kenton band, was a keen observer of the complex behind-the-scenes forces that drove the studio music world in its heyday. As a first-call player for Frank Sinatra's record, film, and TV sessions for over twenty-five years, his insight is invaluable. "We never saw the charts prior to the session," he explains. "But I might show up at the studio early, to see what was there. I wanted to get nervous, I suppose. Most people would say, 'Don't look at it until it's time to start playing,' but I really had to look at the charts, to start thinking about what I was going to do."

Sinatra's role in the sessions began far in advance of the actual date. As we will see later, he developed a ritual where he would first select all the tunes to be recorded and then carefully assist the arranger in sketching out ideas for the orchestrations.

He also prepared physically. "Every day when I'm doing a club date or planning to record,

I try to spend at least an hour at the piano, vocalizing. My standard phrase is 'Let us wander by the bay,' progressing two notes at a time, up the scale and back," he once said. One might wonder how Sinatra's lifelong smoking habit affected his voice and whether it hastened its decline as the years progressed. While he usually cut down dramatically when he knew he was scheduled to record, he rationalized the ravaging effects of smoking on the human voice. "I smoke too much and drink too much, but I've learned that the vocal chords aren't bothered too much by that—they're in a protected part of the body. What does hurt them is overuse: abuse like shouting, and not warming up properly before you sing." (Of course, whether Sinatra realized it or not, smoking did have a deleterious effect on his voice, especially in later years.)

When Sinatra arrived, the assembled cast would begin with a short rehearsal so the engineers could balance the sound. Until the stereo "tape" era (1957), the direct-to-disc and early tape recording method necessitated a perfect balance, or mix, of all the orchestral elements (strings, horns, woodwinds, percussion), plus the vocalist and, occasionally, a choral group.

A properly balanced recording allows the listener to hear each of the instruments clearly as part of the whole orchestra and as standout soloists. It maintains an equilibrium between the volumes of the orchestra and the vocalist. Is the voice too low? Does the orchestra drown it out? Is the vocal too prominent? The orchestra too far in the background? Are the solo instruments heard in the distance instead of up front with clarity and presence? Proper balancing is a direct result of microphone placement and setup of the orchestra in the studio. Each question is pondered on by the mixing engineer, who strategically places microphones around the studio and then auditions each instrumental section, adjusting microphones here and volume levels there, tweaking everything to arrive at just the right blend. Nowadays, years after multitrack tape entered the studios and stereo records have become the accepted standard, individual parts such as the singer's vocal have separate "tracks" or space on the tape, isolated from the orchestra. This isolation facilitates editing or manipulation once the session is over, and engineers can easily rebalance or enhance the sound captured at the live recording session. Recording setups of the 1940s and early 1950s, however, were monophonic—single track, balanced and mixed on the spot, with no opportunity to go back and fix technical or performance errors. Nevertheless, the engineers achieved remarkably well-balanced sound.

"In those days, CBS made their own equipment," says Frank Laico, a retired Columbia engineer who began working sessions in the mid-1940s. "The mixing console had only six positions! So if you had a large orchestra, you had to be careful about how you balanced it. For pop recordings, you had rhythm that had to be heard, so you'd use an RCA 44 microphone (the old diamond-shaped, box-style mike, two-sided) with the bass player on one side and the guitarist on the other. Over the drum kit we might use a single RCA 77, because you couldn't mike individual pieces of the drum setup. You'd use one or two mikes to pick up the brass and woodwinds, and one for the strings. And, of course, your vocalist would have his or her own mike. If we had a vocal group, they couldn't be put on a separate mike, so we'd put them behind the string section and microphone them together, from high up."

The microphones used to record Sinatra's voice in the studio were always chosen with meticulous care. The preferred mike for his vocals during the Columbia years was the RCA 44 ribbon microphone. Noted for its smooth, warm sound and superior reproduction of frequencies in the vocal range, it was a natural for both close instrumental and vocal recording. This is the "old-fashioned" microphone so closely associated with Sinatra's crooner image of the 1940s. "The RCA 44 was a microphone that could be worked

closely, which enhanced the proximity effect of the mike," says microphone expert Jim Webb. "In other words, the closer you got to the microphone, the more bass you would hear. Bing Crosby really took advantage of that and heightened the fullness of his voice by moving in very close to the mike."

The bullet-shaped RCA 77 microphones (as seen on talk shows hosted by David Letterman and Larry King) were also excellent ribbon microphones born of this era. Their frequency pattern and characteristics made them better suited for instrumental work than for vocals, although they worked remarkably well for both.

Once the balance was deemed satisfactory, the orchestra would run down (play through) the song, sans vocal, so that the singer and the musicians could acquaint themselves with the orchestration. This was the point when the arrangement could be modified and errant notes transcribed by the copyist could be corrected. Usually, this run-through would be recorded for the engineers to confirm that their balances were correct.

In the control room, separated from the main recording room by a thick panel of soundproof glass, the recording engineers would adjust the volume on the various microphones placed among the orchestra. This was accomplished with the aid of a simple mixing board or console. The control room, or sometimes a separate area called the cutting room, was where the cutting engineer operated large turntables, which etched the sound from the mixing board into grooves on 16-inch recording "transcription" discs specially coated with a soft plastic lacquer compound.

While earlier recordings had originated on wax, Sinatra's master recordings from 1943 onward were cut at $33\frac{1}{3}$ rpm on optically flat aluminum discs, which offered a much quieter recording and playback surface. For a time during World War II when aluminum was rationed, glass was used as the substrate, and many recording engineers of the era felt it was inferior (in

Columbia engineer Ad Theroux inspects the grooves being etched into a 16-inch lacquer master, the format that supplanted the wax recording process, circa 1943. The cutting lathe was specially developed for Columbia by Ike Rodman.

terms of surface noise) to the aluminum discs. Glass was also far more fragile, and breakage of the original masters was common. The 16-inch lacquer-coated platters, originally developed for the Vitaphone recording process used in early talking pictures, revolutionized the sonic quality of both recording studio and radio recordings and were in many ways the forerunner of the modern "long playing" (LP) record.

While the end result of a session committed to the newer 16-inch masters in the early 1940s was the comparatively noisy shellac 78-rpm disc, the fidelity of the original session lacquers always remained. These have allowed the recent spate of superior CD restorations that reflect the remarkable quality of the original recording sessions. (In the early 1950s, after magnetic recording tape became common in studios, the lacquer discs and cutting turntable were replaced by a tape spool and tape recorder.)

At the sessions, Sinatra used the orchestral run-through time to familiarize himself with the arrangement and plan how to perform the song. Usually he stood just off to the side of the arranger-conductor's podium, singing or humming along softly with the instrumentalists. If any changes were needed, Sinatra suggested them and the arranger and orchestra would work out the details. If satisfied that he was prepared for a real take, Sinatra would give a nod to the arranger, then instruct the booth with a casual "Let's try one." Then and only then would recording commence.

Did Frank Sinatra read music? By his own admission, he did not—at least not in the traditional sense. Sinatra did not play an instrument and never learned to read music per se. His practical experience helped him understand written music, and he learned to "read" a lead sheet by carefully following the patterns and groupings of notes arranged on the page.

On a standard score, the bars that signaled important entry points commonly contained a letter mark, which helped him tremendously. Sinatra made notations directly on the lead sheet during his run-through, which further aided him in articulating concerns about the music as it was being played. Sinatra's practical experience and finely tuned ear also helped him recognize and identify specific notes and distinguish changes in those notes: A from A-sharp, for example.

Unlike today, everything at a 1940s recording session was done in real time. These were live, in-studio performances that offered a freshness and spontaneity that dwindled with the advent of sound-on-sound and multitrack overdub recording in the years to follow. Basically, the musicians were expected to perform these charts, which they were reading for the first time, as though they'd been playing them together for years. But these were the very finest musicians in Hollywood and New York—many from the motion picture studios and the Philharmonic Orchestra or, better still, from the ranks of the Benny Goodman, Glenn Miller, or Tommy Dorsey orchestras or, later, Stan Kenton's band. If anyone did make a mistake, it was back to square one for all involved.

Most of the time, Sinatra's sessions were relaxed because everyone knew their roles. While the musicians and crew had fun and enjoyed their work immensely, the atmosphere in the studio was never less than professional. Some of the greatest laughs came after flubbed takes, especially when Sinatra was poking fun at himself.

On one memorable Columbia date (August 27, 1945), Sinatra was recording "Silent Night." The arrangement set the tone for Sinatra's performance, which is appropriately reverential. The orchestra, playing superbly, is resplendent in the joyous sound of the Christmas season. Suddenly, two-thirds of the way through a beautiful take, Sinatra blows a line. Instead of "sleep in heavenly peace," he recites, "sleep in heavenly sleep." Immediately realizing his error, he breaks the solemnity of the moment. "Son of a b——!" he fumes. "I sang the wrong goddamned words!" The musicians respond with spontaneous laughter. After some good-natured ribbing, the session resumes, a perfect take is made, and everyone is happy.

"BODY AND SOUL": EVOLUTION OF A PERFORMANCE

"Body and Soul" is, without doubt, one of Sinatra's most extraordinary recordings. Long considered the quintessential pop and jazz "standard," it might well (along with "I'm a Fool to Want You") represent the defining moment of the Columbia years. The recording is especially valuable because it comes at a point in his work when Sinatra's voice took on darker hues. He began to inject some pain into the music, as if he were struggling to extract every nuance of emotion from deep within his soul. This somewhat introspective approach to "Body and Soul" brings the complex lyric and melodic subtleties of the song sharply into focus and presages the aching, melancholic mood that would dominate the late Columbia period.

The take-to-take recording session of November 9, 1947, that yielded the song proffers valuable insight into the evolution of a recorded Sinatra performance and a glimpse of the staunchness of his resistance to executive interference. Most striking is the dexterity with which the singer hones his initial rather rough interpretation to a gemlike perfection. The reconstruction of the session is possible through careful audition of the original Columbia session lacquers and through the recollections of arranger George Siravo, who was an observer in the studio.

"Body and Soul" is the first of two tunes to be recorded on the date; the second is the lovely and underrated Paul Madeira and Jimmy Dorsey ballad "I'm Glad There Is You."

Arriving at the Manhattan studio, the orchestra performs a run-through, allowing Sinatra to become comfortable with the pacing of the song and formulate a plan for his vocal approach. This preliminary take, not considered an official attempt, also assisted the engineers with setting the proper balance.

The test gets underway and sounds as one might expect: a bit ragged. In the first few bars of this initial test, featured cornetist Bobby Hackett is heard playing off-mike, the engineers in the control room having inadvertently neglected to switch his microphone on. They quickly correct the oversight, and the crystalline tone of Hackett's horn joins the orchestra. Sinatra begins to work his way through the song as Hackett develops his solos and obbligati. Along the way, both performers hit a number of wrong notes.

As Sinatra sings, he experiments with different ways of enunciating key words, primarily their endings. For example, in the first chorus (1 minute, 41 seconds into the song), he sings:

> *My life a wreck you're makin'* . . .
> [eliminates the 'g,' more informal]
> *You know I'm yours for just the taking* . . .
> [pronounces the "g"]

The take continues, and at the instrumental bridge (2:00), Hackett hits some bad notes. The cornet solo is noticeably different from what it would eventually evolve into on subsequent takes. Then, in the second chorus (at 2:37), Sinatra deviates from the pattern in the first chorus:

> *My life a wreck you're makin'* . . .
> *You know I'm yours for just the takin'* . . .

The song proceeds to the end, and Hackett again plays a different solo from the one that would be issued on the master takes. The final timing of the song is 3 minutes, 18 seconds. The musicians relax as the control room prepares another lacquer disc for the next series of takes.

The first attempt at a real take begins, and shortly into the performance Bobby Hackett blows a note. Nine seconds later, Sinatra stops singing and calls off the orchestra. On the second try, it is obvious that Sinatra is settling in and feeling more comfortable with the song and the orchestration. The tempo has been pulled down (slowed) just a shade, and Frank begins to stretch out a bit, taking just a bit more time to carefully phrase each line. He also becomes deliberate with his diction, carefully articulating the -ing suffixes in the first chorus:

> *I spend my days in longing* . . .
> *And wond'ring why it's me you're*
> *wronging* . . . "

Then, an explosion.

Midway through the song, at the bridge, Hackett blows some critical notes in his solo, which has begun taking on a different melodic slant from the first takes. As Hackett and the orchestra continue to play, Sinatra becomes irritated. "Well, STOP IT!" he testily demands. Stordahl calls the orchestra off, requesting that Hackett (who may have been so engrossed in playing that he didn't realize it) cease playing as well. In the recording room, the volume is abruptly faded down, and the lacquer disc cutter stopped.

The first full take clocks in at 3:23. It is a gorgeous effort—the orchestral introduction is beautiful, Hackett's noodling is heavenly, and Sinatra has again attacked each line with thoughtful deliberation. As with the first few takes, the tempo remains a bit slower. The song concludes with a powerfully emotional crescendo, and the performers are silent as the musical ring in the studio dies down. As they begin to relax, they hear producer Morty Palitz call down from the control room. "Too long," his voice booms over the microphone, and into the studio. "Very nice, Frank, but we'll have to speed it up." To which Sinatra, initially concerned with the emotional impact of the song, replies, "Naw, we can't speed it up—it'll kill the feeling."

"You'll have to do something . . . we can't fit it on," reports engineer Fred Plaut from the booth, referring to the strict time restrictions imposed by the limited groove space of a standard 10-inch 78-rpm single. "You'll have to make a cut—that's the only thing I can think of," says Palitz. This annoys Sinatra, who sarcastically shoots back with the half-statement, half-question, "You mean to tell me a big outfit like Columbia can't put this on a record—it's too long?"

Suddenly, from deep within the orchestra, obscured behind a music stand, a voice defiantly calls out, "We can do it down at Mercury!" Sinatra, his interest piqued, calls back, "Who said that? Stand up, will ya?" With the studio silent, everyone looks around in suspense. Unabashedly, the oboist contracted for the session stands up. It is Mitch Miller, who also functioned as the chief A&R producer at the comparatively smaller Mercury Records. "You serious?" asks Sinatra. "Absolutely! We could do that down at Mercury," says Miller. Sinatra turns to the band. "Take five, fellas," he says, leaving the studio with Stordahl, Plaut, Palitz, and Siravo in tow.

The group shuffles down the hall and reconvenes in Manie Sacks's office. Sacks, who was a vice president at the label, listens carefully to Sinatra's diatribe. "You mean a big f—ing outfit like Columbia can't do what a nickel company like Mercury can do? I don't believe this sh—," he thunders. Plaut, clearly uncomfortable in the crossfire, looks forlornly at Sacks. "I'm sorry,

Manie, I can't tell you anything else. I'm only the engineer. But I can only tell you that what you heard is the truth: Columbia is not capable of doing such things." As the group leaves the office, Sacks—by all accounts the gentlest and most diplomatic of men—glances at Siravo and mutters, "That f—ing Mitch Miller! You take my word: this guy will never set foot again at Columbia Records as long as I'm here!"

The participants, clearly disturbed, return to the studio, where the decision is made to shorten the timing of the recording by eliminating the full orchestral introduction and moving Hackett's introductory solo up front, where it will lend a dramatic flair to the opening strains of the melody. The slower, more emotional tempo that

Columbia recording session, mid-1940s, with A&R head Manie Sacks and conductor Axel Stordahl.

Sinatra demands is maintained. Sinatra turns in a stellar performance. The two master takes drip with heartfelt longing and simple beauty.

On the first, the articulation of each word is perfect, Sinatra sticking with the formal pronunciations of words like *longing* and *wronging*. In the first chorus, he emphasizes the word *you* in the line, "You know I'm yours, for just the taking . . . " by modulating his voice up.

For the second (and final) master take, he loosens up a wee bit, dropping his guard and letting a less formal *wrongin'* take the place of *wronging*.

Then, when he arrives at the appropriate line in the first chorus, he varies the line by deemphasizing the inflection, singing a flat *you*.

The "approved" master clocks in at under 3:18, which leaves everyone, technicians and performers, relatively satisfied.

"Mitch was a good politician," believes George Siravo. "At the time, he was riding the crest of a wave. He was a fine classical oboist and the A&R head at Mercury. As an artist, you had to respect him for that. Because in this instance, even though Mitch was right, Frank realized that you can't have everything your own way and still sing whatever comes to your mind. You have to listen to some people once in a while. [That incident] gave Mitch a little bargaining power." And despite Sacks's order banishing him from Columbia, Miller eventually found his way back to become, as Siravo puts it, "the great white father."

THE COLUMBIA STUDIOS

From the early 1940s, Columbia Records enjoyed a reputation as the top recording concern in the world, with RCA Victor and Decca second and third. For all these studios, their sound was their stock-in-trade—their signature. The legendary "Columbia sound" of the 1940s and very early 1950s was achieved by top-notch engineers working with custom-designed equipment in superb recording facilities—all skillfully coordinated under the watchful eye of Manie Sacks and, later, Columbia Records head Goddard Lieberson.

The CBS/KNX Radio facility at Sunset and Gower in Hollywood was the locale for many of Sinatra's radio programs and Columbia recording sessions in the 1940s.

While at Columbia, Sinatra's recording activity was split almost evenly between New York and Hollywood, depending on his schedule and availability.

In Los Angeles, nearly all of his sessions were held at Columbia's Romaine Street recording studio, the CBS Radio complex at Sunset and Gower (home of station KNX, which also carried Sinatra's weekly radio programs), or the CBS Vine Street Playhouse, located just off Sunset Boulevard. On occasion, Radio Recorders, then the largest independent recording studio in Hollywood, was used.

Since the hub of Columbia's business and recording world was New York City, both the corporate offices and the main recording studios were maintained on the East Coast. The company's research and development department (and its major pressing facility) was located in Bridgeport, Connecticut, so most of the technical direction came from the East Coast as well. For this reason, Columbia's New York studios were considered their flagship facilities, and the company invested a great deal in developing them. Until the late 1950s, the West Coast studios were considered an "annex" and were used mainly to accommodate the artists that lived in the Los Angeles area.

Just as famous concert halls help to define the signature sound of the symphony orchestras that play in them, specific recording studios once played a huge role in defining the highly individual sound of the recordings created by the major record labels. "Columbia's sound became famous largely through Harry James's trumpet recordings at Liederkranz Hall, which had a great

With Axel Stordahl and guitarist Matty Golizio at his first Columbia session with full orchestra, Liederkranz Hall, New York City, November 14, 1944.

echo sound," explains producer George Avakian. "Liederkranz was a large studio in a beautiful building, located at 115 East 58th Street, between Park and Lexington Avenues, and was actually run by the Liederkranz Society. It had very natural sonic properties; it was large and had a lot of old wood."

Howard Scott, a Columbia Records producer who used the room for classical recordings remembers: "Liederkranz Hall was the best recording studio in New York. It was once a German beer hall, and it was a great studio: 100 feet long by 60 feet wide, with 30-foot ceilings. The only problem was that we couldn't have the heat on in the winter because the old radiators snapped and popped!"

Columbia used Liederkranz extensively, along with its own penthouse studio facilities located at 799 Seventh Avenue. It was at these two locations that Frank Sinatra did the bulk of his New York recording from 1943 to 1949. "There were four studios at 799 Seventh Avenue, Studios A, B, C, and D. They recorded Sinatra up there, in Studio B," remembers retired Columbia engineer Bill Savory.

Early in 1948, CBS-TV took over half of the Liederkranz Hall facility and created two television studios. From all accounts, this completely altered the characteristic sound of the original studio, destroying the ambience that had made it a favorite with producers and engineers.

As a solution, Columbia located and purchased a huge Greek Orthodox church located at 30th Street and Third Avenue in Manhattan and turned it into the studio that would become the legendary facility known simply as "30th Street." Many of Sinatra's recordings from 1949 to 1952 were held in the new studio.

"In 1949, Bill Bachman [director of the Columbia Sound Labs], Vin Liebler [head of engineering] and I went looking for a new studio," says Howard Scott. "We found a church at 205 East 30th Street that was not in use. The front part of the church was a radio station—WLIB, I

COURTESY OF SONY MUSIC PHOTO LIBRARY

The former church housing Columbia's 30th Street studio, circa 1949.

COURTESY OF SONY MUSIC PHOTO LIBRARY

The final photograph of the interior of Columbia's historic 30th Street studio, 1981.

believe. Inside, it was just one big room. I know this is when Columbia was about to start using tape, because in the control room there was a small area in the corner where they kept the microphones and such. Right after we bought the building in 1949, they installed mono tape machines in the corner where the microphones used to be stored. For a while, we cut both tape and disc, and then went all tape in the first few months of 1950."

As the primary Columbia recording facility, the 30th Street studio earned a reputation that outlived its sale (and ultimate demise) in the mid-1980s. That success could be directly attributed to the studio's sonics and the thousands of famous recordings that were made there. At first, though, the 30th Street location was avoided by most Columbia staff producers and engineers. Bill Savory, involved in opening the studio, recalls: "Everybody that came in and listened to it said that it was too live. So finally we did something there with Goddard, one of those early Broadway cast albums [*South Pacific*], and he said 'This is just what I want! This is the most flexible place on Earth! You can make it sound like Broadway,

or whatever you want.' After that, it became popular, and they dropped Liederkranz."

Engineer Frank Laico recalls that in 1950 Mitch Miller, relentless in his pursuit of a slick, unique "pop" sound, also fell in love with the studio. "It was a great acoustic room, nearly 100 feet by 100 feet, with very high ceilings. We all got down there to look at it and loved the sound. Mitch walked in and told all the brass in our division, 'There will be nothing done to this room, as long as I'm here. We are going to use it as is.' There were drapes hanging crazily, dust everywhere. It was nothing to be proud of, physically. He wouldn't let them touch the floors, because the first thing they would do is come in and sand the floors!"

The acoustics at 30th Street were outstanding—much better than nearly any other studio anywhere. "The room itself was so beautifully resonant. The sound on those records is something that everyone in the world was trying to duplicate, especially for the strings. We did use echo, too. Mostly for vocals, and sometimes on the strings. We found a room down in the basement that wasn't being used, and used it as an acoustic

Recording at 30th Street with Axel Stordahl and vocal group, circa 1950. The black bottle-shaped microphone suspended from the boom is an Altec M-11, the first modern condenser microphone manufactured in the United States after the war.

echo chamber. It was a very smooth, elongated echo — it was sensational! We would have engineers come from England that used to come in and say, 'God! Tell us how you get that sound, that echo!' and of course, I wouldn't tell them," Laico says proudly.

The words reverb and echo are two of the most misused and misunderstood terms in sound recording. So is the phrase high fidelity, which is often used to describe sound that is true-to-life — as realistic and as possible to being in the concert hall or recording studio.

Of course, a record or compact disc that reproduces exactly what the human ears hear at a live performance would be optimal, but this goal is nearly impossible to attain. One of the most difficult sonic characteristic to translate to a two-dimensional sound recording is that of ambient sound, the acoustic sound of any given room in which a performance (or recording) is made.

To a great extent, the ambient sound of a room is directly related to reverberation — a decay period in which the sound overhangs and

rings. Reverb (or echo) is what provides a good measure of the realism in a sound recording, and because only a limited amount of a recording room's naturally reverberant sound can be captured by a microphone, it became a common practice in the mid-1930s to add extra reverb into the recording mix.

"In the old days, the dead studios resulted in unnatural sounds," said Mitch Miller. "When Toscanini performed in Studio 8H at NBC, the sound was dry and brittle. Then someone decided to use Liederkranz Hall for recording, and the whole conception and appreciation of sound on records changed."

Sound engineers in the 1940s had far less technical equipment at their disposal then today, and when faced with issues such as reverb, they devised unique methods of dealing with the problem. For a time, the men's room became the natural echo chamber at Liederkranz Hall. "Bob Fine had done that with me at Mercury," remembers Mitch Miller. "He was a fabulous engineer. I said, 'Bob, we've got to put a halo around the voice. It sounds like they're singing into a hunk of wool.' So he came up with it in a second. He put a speaker in the bathroom — at Reeves Studio in New York, this was — with a mike hanging there. They sent the signal in there, then took a little bit of the sound that came out of the bathroom speaker, and added it to the original mix."

This method was not without its drawbacks. "There were many stories of recordings being spoiled by someone going to the bathroom," recalls Avakian. "But it always seemed to happen on other people's dates — I don't believe it ever actually happened, but I heard stories like that!" (Actually, the idea of using a bathroom as a reverberation chamber was not new. As early as 1936, Brunswick recording engineers had experimented with placing a microphone inside a toilet to get a close, hollow echo effect.)

The engineers at the 799 Seventh Avenue studios found a somewhat more refined solution. With the studio situated on the top (seventh) floor, the engineers had a back stairwell with seven stories of natural echo at their disposal. Bud Graham, whose primary responsibility was classical recording, explains, "We tried some other things, a narrow room with highly polished surfaces, but it wasn't nearly as good as the stairwell. You see, in the stairwell, frequencies changed — they dissipated and weren't the same all the time. It just had a character that I don't think any of the electronic or digital echoes could ever have." But the finest equipment and best studio space in the world would be worthless without the deft hand of the many skilled and intuitive recording engineers that worked behind the scenes to make recording sessions run. As early as the Edison era, the individuals at the controls were the crucial link in the recording chain, ensuring the success or failure of any particular recording. During the

Columbia era, these individuals working the soundboard were commonly called *mixers*, a term that lasted throughout the 1950s. In the early 1960s, their designation as recording engineers appropriately described the increasing complexities of their craft.

Engineer Carson Taylor once described the philosophy he applied to his work in both pop and classical fields from the 1940s to the 1970s. "There is one thing that distinguishes the mixer of today from the classical mixer of yesterday. Today, the mixer is part of the group, because he produces various effects to make the sounds that the artists want, the sounds that make them distinctive. But that is not true in the classical field. The classical mixer should be virtually transparent. From the conductor and orchestra or whatever artists there are in the studio, to the finished

COURTESY SONY MUSIC PHOTO LIBRARY

This is 799 Seventh Avenue, home of the Columbia Records offices and Penthouse Studios (far right side of building), circa 1950. In the mid-1960s, Phil Ramone renovated the studios and renamed them A&R Recording.

record you play and listen to, there should be no intrusion that is apparent on the part of the engineer. He has to be a truly transparent entity. He controls the mixing so that what the artists want goes onto the tapes, as they want it . . . not as he decides they want it."

Sinatra's producers and technicians approached the task with the utmost respect, and their contributions to his success as a recording artist cannot be praised enough. Their ability to adapt themselves to Sinatra's style and to function as largely uncredited yet dependable supporting players was a primary reason for the superb quality of the final recordings.

During the Columbia years, engineers Fred Plaut and Harold Chapman were largely responsible for transcribing Sinatra's sessions. Their peers, as well as engineers who came to Columbia years afterward, attribute much of the company's reputation for outstanding sonics directly to their efforts. "Chappie's work was unique in the field," believes Sony Music Studios engineer Larry Keyes, himself with Columbia since the 1960s. "When you listen to the recordings that Chappie and Fred Plaut did, you hear every instrument, nothing is blocked out. They had wonderful ears—they were superb engineers."

THE CONCEPT OF ALBUMS

*T*he term *album* originated in the early 1900s, when record companies decided to group 78 rpm records into sets packaged in a photo album-style book. These original albums usually contained four to six brown Kraft paper record sleeves bound between hard cardboard covers and, until at least 1928, were used solely for classical recordings. In 1928, the Royalcraft Album (a twelve-record set) by the English Singers was issued and became the very first nonclassical record set.

By the early 1940s, major American record companies began offering 78 rpm album sets of tunes by their top-selling popular artists. Frank Sinatra's first album was an empty photo-cover album set issued in 1943 by Columbia, which loyal fans could use to store their growing collection of Sinatra records.

Although the term *single* wouldn't really be used until the early 1950s, when RCA developed the 7-inch, 45 rpm disc, most of Frank Sinatra's 78 rpm recordings from 1939 to 1952 (and those of other pop artists as well) were in fact singles—individual discs with one song on each side. Most albums of the era were simply collections of these singles, adorned with colorful, sophisticated artwork that quickly became an integral part of the listening experience.

Then, in March 1946, a Columbia album appeared that was different. Instead of a haphazard collection of singles, it contained a thoughtful musical program; a collection of songs with a musical theme, recorded expressly for the album that bore its name: *The Voice of Frank Sinatra*. This is the very first of Sinatra's "concept" albums.

This album had a purpose. Someone, and it is unclear who, made the decision to have Sinatra and Stordahl record a number similar tunes with orchestrations sharing a unifying spirit.

Advertisements for the album suggest that the marketing department might have originated the concept; whether they accomplished what they originally set out to do is unknown. More important, Sinatra realized that a cohesive musical program would be an extremely effective means of conveying a specific mood and, if presented with care, could make a tremendous artistic and commercial impact.

Columbia released a number of 78 rpm album sets over the next four years: *Songs by Sinatra, Volume One* (1947), *Christmas Songs by*

Sinatra (1948), *Frankly Sentimental* (1949), and *Dedicated to You* (1950). A fifth set, *Sing and Dance with Frank Sinatra*, from 1950 will be discussed in detail later. Of these five sets, three were released simultaneously on 10-inch vinyl LPs, supporting their case for being among the very first Sinatra albums.

"These 'lost' albums are as important to the development of Sinatra's career as any other album," believes Sinatra researcher Tom Rednour. "Most fans discount them as mere collections of old singles, but none of the Columbia 78 sets have been documented as what they really were; albums of new or previously unissued material." (Each of these albums did actually contain both new and old material. The selection of appropriate tunes of similar feel was so smoothly done that the fact is almost unnoticeable.)

For a variety of reasons, the original Columbia albums (these 78 sets and their 10-inch LP counterparts, not the uneven 12-inch LP compilations issued later) were not the commercial successes his Capitol albums would be. But the idea for Sinatra's groundbreaking stream of thematic concept albums, his wave of the future, had been born.

DIVERSITY PERSONIFIED

*O*ne selection from the album *The Voice* epitomizes Frank Sinatra and the romance of the Columbia years. Of the hundreds of ballads he sang in the 1940s, few express his tenderness better than his July 1945 recording of "These Foolish Things" with Axel Stordahl. Backed by a small chamber group (nine pieces, including three strings), the rendition is intimacy personified, seductively melodic, nearly child-like, this is Sinatra at his romantic best: simple, honest, and profound.

Amid the seamless flow of John Mayhew's flute and the delicate tinkling of Mark McIntyre's celeste, Sinatra wraps the lyrics in conviction, infusing them with sweetness and believability. The sensitivity of his faultless interpretation is evident throughout, and his vulnerability is particularly striking when he sings the word *you* in the lines that contain "these foolish things, remind me of you. . . ." Especially moving is the coy inflection he bestows on the phrase *scent of roses* in the line "The smile of Turner, and the scent of roses . . ." just after the violin solo. Here, there is a slight catch in his voice on the first syllable of *roses*, a small touch that renders the performance instantly memorable (the nuance is missing on an alternate take of the recording and is conspicuous by its absence). By the time Sinatra gets to "the waiters whistling, as the last bar closes . . . ," we have images of a scene straight out of *Casablanca* dancing in our heads.

There are dozens of Columbia-era recordings like this, songs that are sentimental without being maudlin, sweet without being saccharine. These are the best Sinatra songs of the era, ones that communicate simple honesty and warmth. "The Nearness of You," "You Go to My Head," "A Ghost of a Chance," "Try a Little Tenderness," "Someone to Watch Over Me," "Why Shouldn't I?," "It Never Entered My Mind," "Mam'selle," and "These Foolish Things" each reflect Sinatra's mastery of the ballad and deserve a place among popular music's greatest treasures.

During the Columbia years, Frank Sinatra was known primarily as a ballad singer. While sweetly romantic orchestrations dominated his musical persona, these formative years also afforded him the opportunity to experiment and grow artistically. People who aren't familiar with the breadth of his Columbia repertoire might be surprised to learn that Sinatra recorded with a gospel group (the Charioteers), an a cappella group (the Bobby Tucker Singers), and small combos (Alvy West and the Little Band and the Page Cavanaugh Trio). He recorded with a Latin bandleader (Xavier Cugat), and had a reunion with a big-band leader (Harry James).

Frank dueted with a bevy of ladies (Dinah Shore, Doris Day, Pearl Bailey, Rosemary Clooney, Jane Russell, Paula Kelly, Dagmar, and Shelly Winters), and nearly a dozen vocal groups (the Jeff Alexander Choir, the Modernaires, the Pastels, the Mitch Miller Singers, the Whippoorwills, Helen Caroll and the Swantones, the Ken Lane Singers, the Double Daters, Four Hits and a Miss, the Ray Charles Singers, and the Pied Pipers). Musically, he left no stone unturned.

Sinatra's flirtation with Cugat provided a pleasant dose of rhumba exotica and is worthy of mention primarily because of an undocumented and unreleased song recorded at the session. While the world at large is well acquainted with the two Sinatra-Cugat tunes cut on May 24, 1945, "Stars in Your Eyes" and "My Shawl," few know that a third song was orchestrated and recorded that day: an obscurity titled "How Long Will It Last?" penned by Max Lief and Joseph Meyer. Originally waxed by Bing Crosby in the 1930s, the song was introduced by Joan Crawford in the film *Possessed*.

It was the last song recorded that day, and a full arrangement had been written. The one extant take is really a run-through, and as a vocal it is incomplete. Both Sinatra and the orchestra sound rough and somewhat off-key. At the bridge, as the strings play tentatively, an obviously pleased Sinatra is heard off-mike. "Very nice . . . I like this arrangement! It's a mother-grabbing arrangement—I like the way it sounds."

Then, at the vocal entrance for the last chorus, he comes back joking instead of singing. "Dee-da-da-da-da-da-dee-da-dum/think we better put this one away/it will take too much time to do it/for today. . . ."

Abruptly he then says, "Get me the hell out of here!" and, as the orchestra completes the song,

he continues joking, reciting one of his oft-used goofy endings: "Ring-dang-bang-dang-pow!" The session ended and the song was forgotten. No master number was assigned, no title written on the disc label, and the recording went undocumented in the Columbia archive until 1993.

A nonvocal project in which Sinatra conducted a full orchestra for a series of Alec Wilder vignettes marked the singer's first attempt to lead an orchestra from the podium instead of the sidelines. Dismayed that Wilder, a friend, could not get the lovely instrumental pieces recorded, Sinatra had a set of radio performances rushed to him and, using the popularity of his name, arranged for the sessions to be held at Liederkranz Hall.

Before the first recording began, Sinatra tapped the podium with his baton and, lest anyone mistake his efforts as self-serving, explained to the assembled musicians that he knew he was not a conductor and was simply asking them to be cooperative in following his lead because he believed in the music and wanted to bring some commercial attention to it. According to sources present, the players were struck with the singer's sincerity and assisted him in a doing a very

COURTESY ARCHIVE PHOTOS

With Alec Wilder at the Sinatra Conducts Alec Wilder session, Liederkranz Hall, New York City, December 1945.

credible job of making the records. "They were among my very favorite instrumental recordings," remembers Milt Bernhart. "When I was traveling with Stan Kenton, I would lay down backstage, in the dark, and just play those Alec Wilder records. They relaxed me and were a joy to listen to because of their tremendous musicality."

In the booth with (left to right) producers George T. Simon and Mitchell Ayres, drummer Buddy Rich, and composer Alec Wilder after recording "Sweet Lorraine" with The Metronome All-Stars, New York City, December 1946.

The album, *Frank Sinatra Conducts Alec Wilder*, attracted the desired attention and remained in the Columbia catalog well into the LP era. Sinatra, an ardent classical music buff, was so taken with conducting that he returned to conduct three instrumental albums: *Tone Poems of Color* (1956); *Frank Sinatra Conducts Music from Pictures and Plays*, (1962); and *What's New?* (1983). He also conducted the orchestra for albums by three of his close friends: Peggy Lee (*The Man I Love*, 1957); Dean Martin (*Sleep Warm*, 1958); and Sylvia Syms (*Syms by Sinatra*, 1982—the last album ever scored by Don Costa).

One of Sinatra's hippest sessions was a December 1946 date with the Metronome All-Stars. This annual ritual, produced by Metronome ed-itor and music critic George T. Simon, placed Sinatra in the company of such gifted jazz giants as Charlie Shavers, Coleman Hawkins, Johnny Hodges, Harry Carney, Lawrence Brown, and Buddy Rich. Accompanying the group for a loose rendition of his own signature tune, "Sweet Lorraine," was pianist Nat "King" Cole. The recording remains one of the highlights of Sinatra's Columbia epoch and one of the earliest indications of the direction his music would eventually take.

IN PURSUIT OF PERFECTION: THE SINGER AS PRODUCER

*T*hroughout his career, the freshness of Sinatra's recordings was due most of all to his continued insistence on the struggle for balanced, natural sound, through the arduous task of performing multiple takes while singing along with the orchestra. While this was a necessity during the disc recording period, he continued the tradition long after the arrival of tape into the studios and well beyond the point when over-dubbing became the accepted practice. Once again, his early training weighed heavily. This method in particular was a holdover from the many nights he spent aiming for an excellent live performance on the bandstand.

In the studio, his almost fanatical obsession with perfection sometimes led onlookers to question whether the singer was truly concerned with the final outcome or just asserting his considerable power. Jazz writer William Gottlieb covered Sinatra's Columbia recording session of October

22, 1947, a date that yielded (among others) the David Raksin-Johnny Mercer classic "Laura" as well as two stunning versions of Cole Porter's "Night and Day" that remained undocumented and unreleased in the Columbia vault for over forty-five years.

"The one thing that stuck out for me about that session was that Sinatra kept interrupting the takes, pointing out mistakes from within the orchestra, which necessitated many retakes," Gottlieb said. "This continual request for retakes meant a lot of overtime, which was very expensive. At this point, Sinatra's career was beginning to wane, and I wondered, 'Does he know what he's doing? Are the mistakes he's hearing really there, or is he trying to show himself and the others that he is still a star?' I asked some friends who were musicians in the orchestra, and they unanimously assured me that he knew—when he found fault that day, he was right. I was relieved."

The two takes of "Laura" reveal subtle but noticeable variations in interpretation; the recording is one of the most haunting and beautiful performances of Sinatra's Columbia years. "Sinatra was once quoted as saying that 'Laura'

COURTESY OF WILLIAM GOTTLIEB

A light-hearted break in the "Laura" session proceedings, Liederkranz Hall, New York City, October 22, 1947.

was his favorite ballad," Raksin told this author. "He nailed the song exactly! He had a way with songs—if he really wanted to do it well, he did it marvelously well. And I was delighted, of course, because in my mind, he was the pre-eminent singer of his day. To have him cite my song as a favorite, and record it more than once, was a real kick!"

Both Stordahl's magnificent orchestration and Sinatra's deadly serious approach to the lyric heighten the sense of mystery, intrigue, and romance that the song is meant to evoke. The recording is a prime example of how the exacting attention Sinatra afforded inflection and intonation pays off in communicating the songwriter's message.

A little-known Sinatra recording date from the singer's transitional phase, surviving on lacquer disc safety copies of a complete Columbia session, allows us to peek inside the studio, leaving little doubt as to exactly who was calling the shots and how unfailingly accurate Sinatra's intuition was.

The first song recorded allows us to focus on Frank's pursuit of sonic excellence; the second is an example of how the entire creative team, headed by Sinatra, diligently worked to perfect a performance.

The recording date is July 10, 1949. As the evening session gets underway at Columbia's cavernous 30th Street Studio, Sinatra, arranger Sy Oliver, and conductor Hugo Winterhalter are auditioning a second instrumental run-through of George Siravo's arrangement of "It All Depends on You." Tonight's date will be jazz-flavored, the orchestra really a big "band"—no strings. Amid the chatter and bustle on the studio floor, the vocalist, listening intently to a passage by the brass section, feels that something is amiss. Even before the session began, there had been problems. For whatever reason (it might have been set in the wrong key), the chart needed some revision, and because Siravo was on the West coast, Winterhalter and Sinatra had asked

Sid Cooper (lead alto player and a gifted writer) to rescore both "It All Depends on You" and "Bye Bye Baby." Oliver is present to execute any last-minute orchestral corrections.

Now, on the actual date, the band has run the chart down, and Sinatra has joined in the second time for a vocal run-through. With the song just a bit too long to fit on one side of the standard 78 rpm disc, the decision is made to cut a raucous tenor sax solo performed at the bridge by sideman Wolfe Tanninbaum. The cut is discussed and executed, and, while Sinatra has already had Winterhalter make some further adjustments in the arrangement, he still senses a deficiency somewhere among the trumpets or trombones.

"I'd like to hear the introduction, with the muted brass," he instructs the conductor. The musicians comply, and the brief section is played for his approval. After hearing the passage, Sinatra carefully instructs both the musicians and the engineers: "I'd like to get that as tight as we can. Trombones: you may have to turn around and face the microphone or something. I'd like to hear the six of you, as a unit," he says. The engineer brings down a microphone with two sides, to help capture the precise tonal quality that Sinatra desires. The section played through again, the singer continues. "Just once more, Hugo, and would you use less volume in the reeds, with the clarinet lead? And would you play it lightly, trumpets and trombones, if you don't mind? I mean *softly*," he emphasizes.

The trombone problem rectified, Sinatra, now in the booth, turns his attention to the rhythm section. He inquires of drummer Terry Snyder: "You got enough pad on the bass drum? It booms a little bit." Then, without the slightest hesitation, he turns to the studio prop men. "Would you put in a small piece of carpet, enough to cover the entire bottom of the drum?" Satisfied, he addresses the pianist. "Say, Johnny Guarneri, would you play something, a figure or something, and have the rhythm fall in? We'd like to get a small balance on it." Guarneri begins

an impromptu riff on the melody, as bassist Herman "Trigger" Alpert, drummer Snyder, and guitarist Al Caiola join in. After a few moments, Sinatra's directions continue. "Bass and guitar: Trig, can you move in about a foot or so, or you can pull the mike out if you wish. And the guitar—also move in a little closer. Just a shade—uh, uh, uh—that's enough."

After thoughtfully surveying the landscape of microphones and cables and instrumentalists he has carefully rearranged, Sinatra has the group play again to check the musicality of his thinking. After another recorded test, Manie Sacks, Sinatra's everpresent aide-de-camp, affirms the changes that Sinatra has made, enthusiastically agreeing, "That's *much* better."

A couple of master takes later, after Sinatra has given his seal of approval to "It All Depends on You," the ensemble moves on to the next tune, "Bye Bye Baby," written by Leo Robin and Sinatra compatriot Jule Styne for a show called Gentlemen Prefer Blondes. His friendship with Styne has given Sinatra an edge: the show isn't scheduled to open until December, and he has scooped everyone by being the first to record any of the songs from the score. (Within a week of this July 10 session, Sinatra would record another song from the show, "Just a Kiss Apart," in New York. Dissatisfied with the results, he re-recorded the song in Hollywood on July 21. Both "Bye Bye Baby" and "Just a Kiss Apart" were released on the same 78 rpm single).

For "Bye Bye Baby," Sinatra will be accompanied by both the band and the Pastels, a lilting four-member vocal combo consisting of David Vogel, Jerry Packer, Naomi Sunshine, and Lillian Clark, wife of arranger Sy Oliver. "I remember that date very specifically, because the studio was dark," remembers Vogel. "Usually the 30th Street studio was brightly lit; this time, it was very dark, except for the small corner where we were working."

Sinatra again steers the proceedings as he coaches and advises the members of the supporting vocal group. As this portion of the session begins, Sinatra and the group have just completed a couple of quick rehearsals of the song, whose tempo producer Sacks has deemed a bit too slow. Amid the shuffling of chairs and music stands and the thumping of microphones being moved as the studio is rearranged to accommodate the vocal ensemble, the singer is heard explaining the finer points of the song's intent and his views on its interpretation to the vocalists. "From my own standpoint, as far as the vocal is concerned, we haven't found the thing that we started to get when we first got on this thing a minute ago. It's an old-fashioned song, it's from a show. . . . It's a new show that's going to open, and it's a song about a dame who's going to Paris. And it's 1920, and it's a real old-fashioned kind of song, and all it should be is just a . . . [snaps his fingers to set the tempo] . . . kind of song."

As the musicians chatter away and settle into their positions, Sinatra polls the brass section. "What kind of mutes do we want to use here?" Pondering his own question, he makes an immediate suggestion. "You want to try your cup

mutes, and stick them in nice and tight?" Surveying the three brass players, he encourages them as one might a championship ballplayer as he leaves the box to pitch a crucial inning. "Put 'em in good and tight, huh?" Then, as if wanting to be triply sure that everyone is on the same page, he quietly asks, "There are cup mutes in the brass for the whole first chorus, right?" This is confirmed as fact.

Guitarist Al Caiola begins to tune up, gently strumming away off-mike, and Sinatra calls for a test. "Let's try it once, just to hear it." A dropped mute clangs to the resilient hardwood floor. Sinatra, quietly addressing the trumpet player, suggests a method for holding the mute tight in the bell of the horn. Manie Sacks, out of the control booth and on the floor of the studio, calls out, "We'll start right at 'A,' Frank, all right?" This is conductor Winterhalter's cue, and he calls the band to attention, issuing the official directive. "Here we go, letter 'A.' " The bass, piano, and brass begin, and Sinatra, off-mike, sings the first few words.

Bye bye baby . . .

Coming closer to the microphone, he picks up the vocal line with:

. . . remember you're my baby . . .

As he utters the phrase, you can almost hear him chuckle, as one of the backup singers, near an open mike, mockingly generates a double lip smack, mimicking a kiss. Sinatra continues, perpetuating and encouraging the relaxed, humorous atmosphere by coyly changing the words of the song:

. . . when they give you the eye.
Although I know that you care,
Won't you write and declare.
That though you're on the loose,
You are still such a square!

Naomi Sunshine, breaking into laughter, muses over Sinatra's funny interpretation. Sinatra, obviously enjoying the response, continues. Sacks, now back up in the control room, breaks in over the studio talk-back mike. "Save it!" he says. Sunshine merrily chides Sinatra. "Don't stop now." There is some dialogue between Sinatra and Sacks; then the take begins.

Sinatra is loose, maintaining the medium tempo he set a few minutes before. About a minute into the take, Sacks' voice booms forth from the booth. "Hold it, Frank—our fault." Sinatra, without missing a beat, quips, "About time you blew one!"—obviously still playing to the giddy girl singer (Sunshine).

Another attempt commences, and this time proceeds to a little over a minute and a half, when it is aborted, this time at Sinatra's request. "Hold it."

Addressing the vocal group, he instructs them. "When you sing that thing, it's not relaxed enough . . . you're anticipating it a little bit. In letter 'E,' the entrance. It should be a little more lazy; hold back on it, I think. Let's try that once,

please," he asks, making an impromptu a cappella vocal pickup:

. . . know that I'll be smiling . . .

Between lines, he calls out, "Letter 'D,' prompting the rhythm section, vocal group and then full band to join in:

Sinatra: With . . . [finds key] . . . with my baby by and by . . .
Pastels: Bye bye baby, so long . . .
Sinatra: Bye bye baby . . .
Pastels: Just you remember that you're my baby, when . . .

After this measure or two, as the group holds over on the word when, Sinatra again halts the proceedings. "Hold it a second. You know what I think is another thing that will help us, Manie? If we can get back just a little bit more toward the first tempo we were doing that you said was a little slow . . . I think we're getting a little fast." The subsequent discussion, more light banter than anything, typifies the good-natured ribbing that set the tone for many of Sinatra's recording sessions.

Sacks: All right, let's try that. We saved about seven seconds.
Sinatra: What's it run now?
Sacks: 2:40. And the last time it was 2:40.
Sinatra: What the hell are we worried about? You put this on a long playing record and you won't see it! *[Elicits laughs from the assembled cast]* True?
Sacks: You're liable to hear it, though!
Sinatra: [Sarcastically] Hey, there's a funny joke!

There are the requisite laughs, and Sacks calls the studio to order. "Quiet! Stand by, quiet please. Hold it—here we go boys." This take is complete, and the producer is pleased. "Wonderful! Wonderful! Wonderful! Everything was wonderful on that," he exclaims. One of the girls, jocularly singing the words to the chorus, compliments Sinatra on his adjustment of the original tempo. "Did I make it, kid, huh?" he asks brightly. "That's sensational!" Sacks proclaims.

Sinatra, zeroing in on the minutest details, feels that improvements can be made, and sets out to sharpen both the vocal and instrumental ending, and a musical discussion between Winterhalter, Oliver, and some musicians ensues.

Then came more failed attempts, each one coming closer to the mark. The group is clearly enjoying themselves, and the merriment continues during a short pause in recording.

> *Sinatra:* I'd like a sip of tea.
> *Sunshine:* I'd like a puff!

The other singers laugh. Sinatra responds;

> *Sinatra:* Well, come with me. You're all
>   under arrest!
> *Sacks:* Hugo, can we hear it starting from
>   'D'? Get on the mikes, will you, kids?
> *Sinatra:* (Jokingly) Just a second, hold it.
>   Don't rush me with the tea! I'll pull a
>   strike on ya—I got four singers with me!
> *Sacks:* No, I don't want to hear you, I
>   wanna hear the group.
> *Sinatra:* Thanks a lot!

As the piano, bass, and guitar noodle, the girls begin an impromptu vocal, their style far more jazz oriented than the arrangement calls for. There is more discussion, and Sinatra and the rhythm section fall in.

The entire aggregation picks up the song, and when they break, Sinatra hones in on the section where the group sings the phrase "I'll be gloomy."

"Don't suppress tonal quality or enunciation," he suggests. "Just keep it soft, but firm when you sing it. 'I'll be gloomy . . . ,' " he sings, softening the sound of the letters *G* and *L* first sylla-

ble of the word *gloomy.* "Round the mouth, so it sounds like a whale," he recommends.

Sacks now wants to hear the very ending with the group. "At the rubato, where the solo is?" Sinatra asks. The ending is repeated, and Sacks, somewhat perplexed, states, "Something happens there!" "Sure, we've got five people singing and an orchestra!," Sinatra shoots back. "But something's wrong with the orchestra . . . something's being left out," Sacks insists.

One of the musicians tells Sacks what the problem is. "We didn't play it that time—we played it down an octave. We're saving it for air time!" he quips. "I want Sy to hear it," Sacks replies, summoning Oliver into the studio. For the umpteenth time, the ending is played, and this time, everything is perfect. "That was all right. As soon as Sy comes in, it's all right!" he muses. More laughter in the studio.

Then, some final directions from the producer. "Listen kids, when you get to the end there, be sure to move in closer, will you please?" he requests. Bugs worked out, the master takes are finally set to begin, and Sacks pounds the gavel. "All right, stand by . . . let's try it. Stand by . . . quiet, please."

After the completed performance, Sinatra issues his assessment.

Sinatra: I don't see anybody going out and getting drunk about that one!

Palitz: It's all right, the group was all right on the end, I thought.

Sacks: Let's try another. [Addressing Terry Snyder] Drums, we're too heavy at the end, my boy.

Sinatra calls for a playback. "May we hear that, please?" Relieved that the finest points of the musical interpretation have been resolved, the artists now set out to polish up individual performances. While it might seem as though the group spent an inordinate amount of time on the details, their efforts have paid off. Excellence comes quickly, and within a few minutes, a couple of takes of the song are made and approved.

For Frank and company, this scenario has been played out session after session, decade after decade. The changes that Sinatra the singer insists on, and the perfection he seeks, all make sense in the final analysis. He didn't need to make heavy-handed demands in the recording studio: he had the admiration and cooperation of those involved long before the session even began. His direction of technicians and musicians and other vocalists is not that of an autocrat: rather, it is the patient, understanding nurturing of an artist who sees the overall picture, one who is not affected by the insecurity that is so common in others of his stature.

Rosemary Clooney, who made three single recordings with Sinatra in the late Columbia period (and later worked with him on television and at Reprise Records), was impressed by his warm treatment of her both before and during the sessions. The two rehearsed at the Hampshire House (near Central Park), where Sinatra and Manie Sacks maintained separate apartments. "Frank was very giving," Clooney says. "He was very un-

Recording with Rosemary Clooney, 1950.

derstanding. I was so anxious to do well, and was just concentrating so much on what I had to do that I didn't even observe anything else, not even him!"

Perhaps pianist Stan Freeman, commenting on Sinatra's professional studio demeanor, said it best. "I only remember him being very aware of what he wanted, and getting it! If he thought a flute or oboe part should be left out of one section, he would say so. He didn't have to take charge, but nominally he was in charge—and everybody knew that. He was always very pleasant, never any tantrums or anything."

Freeman's assessment dispels the myth perpetuated by a number of biographies, which have reported that the Sinatra of the late Columbia period (1951–1952) was so bitter and so difficult to deal with that engineers at his sessions tampered with the controls in the studio in order to damage the sound, thereby discrediting him. From my research, this appears to be absolutely untrue. First, the engineers at Columbia were professionals, and would not have jeopardized the high esteem in which they were held by many artists other than Sinatra. Second, there is no aural evidence to support this assertion: all of the vocalist's Columbia recordings are of uniformly high quality, proved by the proliferation of fine digital restorations made from the master session discs and tapes.

Additionally, working as project director/co-producer of the Columbia Records Sinatra CD reissues, I've listened carefully to all of the original recording session discs and tapes in the Columbia Records vault, and can verify that session dialog and take-to-take recordings indicate that for all of his impending problems, Sinatra never wavered from the professional standards he had set for himself and his colleagues years before. (One engineer who worked with Sinatra ten years after his fallow period felt that at that time, Sinatra could be hard on the engineers. There is no evidence of this occurring during the Columbia era, though).

TRIPLE THREAT: THE CUTTING EDGE OF TECHNOLOGY

*M*any turns in Sinatra's long career seem to coincide with important technical developments, and those of the late 1940s and early 1950s probably had the most profound effect on the singer and the direction his work would take. As Sinatra began his descent from his position as Columbia's premiere vocal artist, the label's research-and-development team was on the cutting edge of technology. Columbia's innovations, in concert with the technical advances brought to the table by other sources, heralded the dawn of the golden age of high fidelity.

Within a two-year span, three separate recording advances that would revolutionize the music industry arrived on the scene: "tracking" (overdubbing), the invention of the vinyl long-playing (LP) record, and the adoption of magnetic recording tape for preserving recordings. Each played an important role in Frank Sinatra's development as a modern recording artist and completely changed the way we hear his music.

SOUND ON SOUND

Although it took years to catch on in the mainstream commercial record industry, overdubbing was not a new idea in the late 1940s. The process had been used as early as the 1930s, when the soundtracks of Hollywood musicals were routinely overdubbed, with great success. In 1941 jazz great Sidney Bechet made the most ambitiously overdubbed recording to date, entering Victor's New York studio to create a disc on which he played six instruments: tenor sax, soprano sax, clarinet, bass, drums, and piano. Problems arose, however, with each successive overdub, and clarity was lost with each new layer of sound.

It was Les Paul, the brilliant artist/inventor/engineer, who perfected the technique, using it to produce a dazzling new sound for his own guitar recordings, which were made in his home garage studio. Paul, a guitarist who tinkered with the technical aspects of recording to devise the most profound revolutions the music industry has ever seen, was the first major pop artist of the "high fidelity" era to take an active role in creating, producing, and engineering his own recordings. His insatiable desire to invent ways to successfully record the progressive musical ideas he dreamed up ended in preserving the thoughts of an entire generation of artists who based their work on the new sonic palette they had at their disposal: The Beach Boys, The Beatles, and Simon and Garfunkel among them. As Mary Alice Shaughnessy points out in her superb biography of the legend, "Generally speaking, performing artists and audio engineers are two distinct species. Musicians often lack the vocabulary to successfully convey their needs to technicians, and vice versa. But Les, fluent in both languages, managed to meld the two disciplines."

Engineer Bill Putnam (who would later play a major role in Sinatra's life) told Shaughnessy, "Les lived and thrived on the gratification of achieving things that were beyond the current state of the art. Nobody was producing the quality of multigenerational disks he was producing

COURTESY OF MICHAEL OCHS ARCHIVES

Musician-engineer Les Paul at the controls in his home studio, 1940s. The drive mechanism of the turntable was fashioned from the flywheel of a Cadillac.

in the mid-forties. And the number of overdubs he was getting—impossible! Considering the fact that he had no formal education as an engineer, his knowledge was absolutely amazing."

Since overdubbing was achieved by copying one disc to another, the problem of dealing with the deteriorating quality from copy to copy was formidable. As Putnam mentions, Les Paul's overdubs were sparklingly clear: of such high quality that they perplexed fellow engineers. Paul was able to produce a high quality overdub because he conducted endless experiments in his studio (ruining some five hundred discs before deeming one suitable for demonstration), and devised ways to compress the frequencies recorded and filter out extraneous noise.

The real secret of his success, though, was the sequence in which he recorded each instrument. His theory was that secondary instruments should be recorded first, so that if they lose something in subsequent copying, this will be far less noticeable than if the clarity or brilliance of a principal instrument's sound were degraded.

The guitarist/engineer would begin by recording drums first, then rhythm guitar, lead guitar, bass, and so on until the last thing recorded was the most important, up-front instrument on the record. "The drums and other rhythm instruments are supposed to be in the background," he once explained. "But the bass player, he's the one who helps set your tempo, so you better have him right up front. And that lead guitar better shine . . . he better be brand new." Paul's method set the standard for multitrack recordings right up into the late analog tape era.

Paul's initial recordings employing the technique are "Lover," on which he overdubbed eight guitar parts, and "Brazil," issued as one Capitol 78 rpm single in February 1948. The record, hailed as an outstanding achievement, pioneered a new sound for the guitarist, and in short order, revolutionized the way sound was recorded.

For vocal/orchestral recordings, Columbia was among the first companies to successfully attempt "tracking," or adding a vocal track to a previously recorded instrumental, to create a composite master. The overdubbing process allowed for greater flexibility when two elements (vocal plus instrumental, for example) needed to be combined for a final recording. The overdubs were accomplished by recording the orchestra on Disc A. Later, the vocalist would come to the studio, and while the engineer played Disc A (the instrumental track) through the studio loudspeakers, the vocalist sang along. In the recording booth, the engineers mixed the feed from the vocalist's microphone with the feed from the instrumental track on Disc A, and the combined signal was fed to a second cutting turntable, which made the "mixed" master: Disc B. (Later, when magnetic tape supplanted lacquer discs, overdubbing was made easier, and facilitated Les Paul's invention of a special multi-track recording head that could record sound-on-sound).

Producer Arthur Shimkin, who directed many recording sessions at both Columbia's studios and at Bob Fine's Manhattan studio, recalls an elaborate process in which several turntables were used to play two or more takes of a song simultaneously. Using the volume controls on the mixer, the engineers could selectively control which take was being fed to the master cutter, thereby editing the original lacquer disc recordings—a tedious and painstaking process.

"We'd have four turntables set up in the control room," he recalls. "They were set up in two rows, with two turntables per row. One turntable would be recording the edited master; the other three would be playing back different takes of a song, which we wanted to extract only certain portions of. We'd start recording on the master turntable, and began playing back the two or three different takes of the song, all on separate turntables. When it came to the point that we wanted to stop one take and insert a piece from another (which was running on the second and third turntables), one engineer would tap the guy in front of him on the shoulder, and he'd pick up

the arm as a third engineer brought up the volume on the disc that contained the section that we wanted to insert. It was a crazy operation! It worked only if you had takes that had the exact same beats, which was usually the case."

Extremely rare for the time, the earliest Sinatra overdubs were done in March 1948, the singer simply dubbing vocals to orchestra tracks recorded the previous December ("It Only Happens When I Dance with You" and "A Fella with an Umbrella"). The decision to use this technique on this first date, as well as on another in December 1948, in which the orchestra was recorded in New York and the vocal in Hollywood ("Once in Love with Amy"), was probably made because of scheduling problems.

THE BIRTH OF THE LP RECORD

Then, in 1948, Columbia Records introduced a new playing medium: the light weight, vinyl "Long Playing" (LP) record.

Whereas previous platters were made of a fragile shellac compound (a comparatively rough surface), and spun at a dizzying seventy-eight revolutions per minute (allowing a typical ten-inch disc to contain little more than three-and-a-half minutes or so of program material), the new LPs were 10-inch discs with a smoother, quieter plastic surface called Vinylite, traveling at a much slower $33\frac{1}{3}$ rpm. In addition to the vastly improved sound quality, the new discs also allowed for far greater playing time. Within a very short time, the ten-inch disc (the standard of the pop music industry from 1949 to 1954) gave way to a twelve-inch platter (initially popular for classical releases), which offered at least twenty minutes of playing time per side.

Attempts to extend the playing time of sound recordings had been made early in the game, as companies strove to increase the approximately two-minute playing time of a typical commercial cylinder or disc. Between 1894 and 1904, a variety of companies including International Zonophone, Pathe, and Victor made unsuccessful attempts to vary both the size and speed of their cylinders and discs.

In 1912, Marathon Records produced some discs that could play as long as sixteen and a half minutes; World Records achieved over twenty minutes. In 1925, Brunswick announced that they had developed an electrically recorded 12-inch disc containing 500 grooves per inch that could store forty minutes of music twenty minutes per side. Both Edison (1926) and Victor (1931) failed with similar products. In addition to technical problems, the buying public just wasn't interested in purchasing the new equipment needed to play the discs.

Much of the technology developed by Vitaphone Corporation, a joint partnership between Warner Brothers and Western Electric, was later adopted for use in sound recording studios. Vitaphone's most famous film, 1927's *The Jazz Singer*, starring Al Jolson, is considered the most important of the first "talking" motion pictures, and the Vitaphone system utilized 16-inch discs, recorded at 33⅓ rpm, to provide the soundtrack. While better systems for film recording supplanted it within a short time, the Vitaphone process became the basis for the 16-inch lacquer disc process that dominated the radio and recording industry throughout the 1940s and very early 1950s.

By 1932, Columbia was manufacturing 12-inch discs, rotating at 33⅓ rpm, for intermission music played in motion picture theaters. The duration of a single side of such a disc was twenty minutes. The speed proved to be well suited to adding sound to motion pictures: a 12-inch disc revolving at 33⅓ rpm could contain just enough sound to cover one reel of film, and the sound quality was quite good. This disc size and speed was ultimately employed by Bill Paley's Colum-

bia Records in 1948 for what would become the modern LP record.

Both George Avakian and Howard Scott (then assistant to Columbia executive Goddard Lieberson) are familiar with the development of the modern LP. According to Avakian, it was Ted Wallerstein (formerly of Brunswick and RCA) who pushed for the development of a workable LP. Familiar with the experimentation at Brunswick in the twenties, Wallerstein believed in the concept of a long playing record, and thought it entirely possible that one day, it would be achieved.

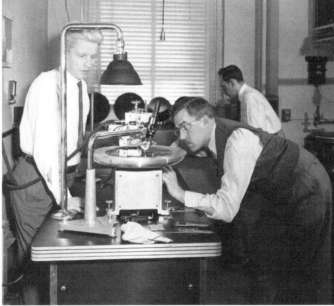

COURTESY OF SONY MUSIC PHOTO LIBRARY

Rene Snepvangers (left) and Howard Chinn at the CBS Research Laboratories, circa 1948.

"Columbia's long playing record worked because it was what we called microgroove, which was developed at the CBS lab by Rene Snepvangers and Howard Chinn, who worked for Peter Goldmark, the Vice President of CBS Research Laboratories. The LP was something they were trying to develop at CBS Labs, simultaneously with color television," Scott recalls.

A priceless reflection: Dr. Peter Goldmark inspects a newly minted LP stamper as Bill Bachman, the engineer who perfected the LP process, looks on.

Goldmark, along with Snepvangers and Chinn, continued to toil at making a long-play record that contained 200 lines per inch (LPI). When they were unsuccessful, Wallerstein moved the research from CBS Labs to Columbia Records, and in 1947 hired William S. Bachman, a research engineer at General Electric, to head the project. Bachman became the Director of the Columbia Records Sound Laboratories in Bridgeport, Connecticut, and with his expert guidance, a disc that held between 250 and 400 grooves per inch was created. The new disc was made of a plastic compound, making it smoother, quieter, and far lighter than a standard shellac disc.

"Jim Hunter devised a way to get the vinyl to flow evenly in a press and not stick to the stam-

pers," remembers Scott. "Bill Savory cut the actual LP masters, using a Westrex cutter and a heated stylus that Bill Bachman had developed. The heated stylus cut the grooves a lot smoother than an unheated stylus, and resulted in less noise. Bill also innovated many other things, such as the variable pitch method, that served to improve the cutting of LPs."

To take advantage of the new medium and exploit their vast back catalogs, most companies, including RCA Victor, Decca, and Capitol, simply transferred copies of their 78 rpm masters to the new LP discs. And, while they may have joined together the individual pieces of a Beethoven symphony that had been previously issued as a cumbersome six-record 12-inch 78 rpm set, the new discs retained all of the scratch and rumble of the originals.

Columbia, predicting the development of a workable LP, had begun to stockpile clean, well-recorded lacquer masters (recorded at 33⅓) as early as 1943. When it came time to reissue their catalog on the early LPs, Columbia did not transfer the recordings from standard 78 pressings or the metal stampers used to create them: it made new, pristine masters from the high-quality safety lacquers it had recorded and stored years before. But the transfer process did not come without difficulty, remembers Howard Scott. "Bill Bachman went down to see Goddard, who headed the Masterworks [classical] department, and said he needed someone who could read a musical score to come up and work with his engineers. So Lieberson sent me up to engineering with Bachman, but at my request I was still on Goddard's payroll so that he could keep an eye on what was going on.

"CBS had sent over these three huge turntables that were operated by photoelectric cells. The turntables were supposed to synchronize with timers. If a side of a 78 rpm record was four minutes and twelve seconds, then the second turntable was supposed to start after four minutes and twelve seconds and carry on with the second side of the record. It never worked because they were belt drive turntables, and belt-driven machines never ran the same way twice: there could be anywhere from a one-half to two second difference. When I got up to engineering, everyone was stuck. They had worked for six years or so with little success, and now Bachman and his team still hadn't solved the problem of how to synchronize the original 78 rpm sides so they could be transferred continuously on to a long-playing master. We needed a simple solution, and that's exactly what Paul Gordon [a Columbia engineer] and I came up with.

"We took a turntable and made a clock on the platter itself. Then, we put a red arrow in the middle of the 16-inch lacquers. You knew where the sides began and ended because you could see them, so I would take the score and mark it where the one side ended and the next side began. Sometimes the sides overlapped: they would often repeat a chord and at times two chords, which made it tricky. But it wasn't as difficult as it sounds, once you got the hang of it."

Scott details the elaborate method by which they accomplished the feat. "If it was three turns of a blank audio to the first note on the next side, I would find a splice point at the end of a side and mark the score accordingly. Then I would signal Paul, who had the needle ready to put down in the groove exactly three turns (measured by the 'clock' markings) before the slice point with the turntable running, and he would let it go. The only thing you had to take into account was the very slight human error factor of my snap to his letting go, yet it worked every time. We could even eliminate the overlapped chords! The problems we had were somewhat troublesome: conductors had a tendency to slow down when they came to the end of a side, or speed up at the beginning of the next side. It was hard to adjust for these changes in tempo that occurred at the original sessions."

In 1976, Wallerstein discussed the subject with Ward Botsford of *High Fidelity* magazine.

"When we were getting ready to move to Seventh Avenue, we were pondering the type of recording equipment to use," he said. "Thinking ahead to the longer record, I insisted that our setup be built so that everything recorded was done at 33⅓ rpm, on 16-inch blanks. This gave Columbia a tremendous advantage over its competitors. When the LP finally appeared, Columbia had masters of good quality going back almost ten years."

Wallerstein also demanded that two lacquer discs be cut for every session: one for the current 78 rpm disc mastering, and one for the future "long-play" archive. These backup safety masters, which existed for virtually all recordings to that point, aided the team in bringing the finest possible sound quality to the new LP masters.

"Ted Wallerstein was very, very bright and he insisted [that] engineering cut double of everything: they had 'A' and 'B' sets of lacquers, and we used the 'B's, which were essentially virgin copies," Scott remembers. (Multiple session lacquers for many of Sinatra's Columbia sessions still exist, and are what help us restore his vintage recordings in the best possible sound today). On June 20, 1948, Columbia Records announced the new format at a demonstration in New York's Waldorf Astoria hotel. By this time, the technical team had increased the playing time from 17 to 22 minutes per side. "I addressed the fifty-odd representatives of the press," Wallerstein recalled. "On one side of me was a stack of conventional 78 rpm records measuring about eight feet in height, and another stack about fifteen inches high of the same recordings on LP. After a short speech, I played one of the 78 rpm records for its full length of about four minutes, when it broke as usual right in the middle of a movement. Then I took the corresponding LP and played it right past that break. The reception was terrific! The critics were convinced that a new era had come to the record business."

Other than those involved in perfecting the product, only one person knew of the impending announcement: RCA's David Sarnoff, and he was not pleased. "Paley had invited him to a demonstration three weeks before," said Scott. "They had plenty of time to move quickly and start doing their own transfers, but they didn't. When Sarnoff heard the demonstration, he was furious and chewed out his entire staff, in front of Paley and Wallerstein. He left in a huff, and of course it was two years before RCA would admit to defeat, and begin making 33⅓ rpm LPs."

Sarnoff's reaction was predictable: since RCA had developed one of the first LPs, it was a serious blow to the company's pride that their main competitor had perfected it, and Sarnoff forbade RCA to adopt the new format for its own recordings. As a rejoinder, RCA quickly developed and marketed a smaller microgroove disc which revolved at 45 rpm touching off a fierce battle in which three different formats and speeds (78, 45, and 33⅓) vied for position. In the end, the LP won out as the primary format for long programming, and the 45 rpm eventually replaced the 78 as the preferred choice for shorter pop singles, forcing RCA to bend and begin producing LPs in 1950.

"Wallerstein was once quoted as saying that he figured that RCA lost 3 million dollars the first year they pushed 45s over LPs," Scott says. "RCA set out to damage the LP as much as possible. In 1962, when I was at RCA, someone finally told me where 45 rpm came from. They apparently took 78 and subtracted 33, which left them with 45, which they went with out of spite.

"One week after the public announcement, on June 28th, they introduced the LP to the entire Columbia distributor and dealer group in Atlantic City. Paul Southard, the vice president of sales, gave a speech during which an LP, Tchaikovsky's *Nutcracker Suite*, was played. Everyone could see the demonstration through a mirror, and at the end of the 22-minute side, the crowd roared! It was a very exciting time at Columbia."

The new long-play format was a boon to consumers and record companies alike. Music lovers could now enjoy more uninterrupted musical programming and it sounded better because the coarse shellac surface of the comparatively crude 78s had been eliminated. The recording labels, looking to boost sales and regenerate interest in records, began to reissue the performances in their back catalogs, now enhanced for the new format.

George Avakian, long considered a pioneer in the field of 78 rpm jazz album set reissues, elaborates on the marketing of the new LP. "It was the summer of 1947, and we didn't have anybody specifically in charge of popular albums at the time, because that it was essentially a singles [78 rpm] market and the demand for pop albums was quite small. Ted Wallerstein told me that he wanted to create a pop album department, and that I was to run it. He asked me to start thinking in terms of more albums but he didn't tell me why," Avakian says.

"In the fall, Wallerstein came into my office again, and shut the door. He said, 'Now, I've got to tell you something about these albums. We're hoping to have a long-playing record very soon.' He very emphatically said, 'You can't tell anyone—not even your wife.' After outlining the plan, Wallerstein told me that if it succeeded, I'd be busier than ever, and that I should continue to put together pop albums, and also start looking at the pop singles catalog to see what eight-song packages could be assembled from it, should this long-playing record became a reality."

Avakian's first series of ten-inch pop LPs were released in the summer of 1948. "By July 1, we had one hundred titles out," he recalls. "I purposely made Columbia's very first pop LP (#6001) a Frank Sinatra disc, because he was the best selling and most important pop artist we had at that time." Avakian's choice was a reissue of Sinatra's classic 78 album set from 1945, *The Voice of Frank Sinatra*, which hit the market as a 10-inch LP on June 28, 1948. "Making pop LPs was much easier than making the classical reissues, as Howard Scott had to do, because I didn't have to worry about synchronization," he says. "All I had to do was select eight songs that made sense when put together, and they could be assembled quite easily. Howard had to blend all the classical sides together in a very exacting way."

THE MAGIC OF TAPE

Crossing paths with the new LP technology was an ingenious method of storing sound for playback and distribution. Beginning as early as 1948, new sessions at some of the labels were being recorded not on lacquer disc, but on magnetic recording tape, a medium that had been tinkered with experimentally since the mid-1930s. The musician responsible for bringing tape into the studios was Sinatra's friend, crooner Bing Crosby, an early financial backer of the new technology.

By 1940, Crosby's annual income was estimated at nearly $750,000, the bulk of which came from his appearance fees in motion pictures, on radio and records, and from some very lucrative investments in music publishing, racetracks, and real estate. Although his NBC Kraft Music Hall show was top-rated, by 1946 the singer wished to stop performing it live, and began to investigate the possibility of recording it on 16-inch lacquer transcription discs, the standard practice for preserving radio programs for time-delay. While the standard lacquer discs preserved the music with excellent fidelity, the difficulties involved with editing (disc-to-disc rerecording) were a concern, particularly for radio programming, and the discs themselves were fragile. While lacquer disc mastering was well suited for the controlled environment of the recording studio, it was fast becoming clear that for radio, a more rugged, reliable recording and playback method was needed.

When Crosby talked with network officials about the possibility of prerecording, he met with resistance. Both the network (NBC) and song-writing union (ASCAP) insisted on maintaining the union-enforced tradition of "live" radio broadcasts. Rumors about the reasons why Crosby wished to prerecord have abounded for decades, many revolving around his desire to have more free time to play golf. While prerecording would afford him a more flexible schedule, in reality, Crosby simply wanted greater control over the timing and quality of his program.

While NBC would not relent, ABC was willing to accommodate Crosby's desire to prerecord his program, and upped the ante by offering him a staggering $30,000 per week budget (including his salary of $7,500) to produce one radio program, to be sponsored by Philco. To sweeten the deal, Crosby also negotiated to receive an extra $40,000 from several hundred independent radio stations, in return for the rights to broadcast the show, which would be provided on 16-inch lacquer discs. To top things off, the singer's own production company, Bing Crosby Enterprises, produced the show, enabling him a broad measure of control over content, guests, creative presentation, and other technical details, including what format the program would be preserved on.

COURTESY AMPEX CORPORATION

Jack Mullin (right) demonstrates a new tape machine for Ampex executive Alexander Poniatoff.

In mid-1947, Alexander Poniatoff, head of the Ampex Corporation, saw a demonstration of the 1935 German "Magnetophone," brought back from Radio Frankfurt by recording engineer Jack Mullin. The machine, built by BASF and AEG, utilized a 1/2-inch ribbon of plastic tape, coated with iron oxide, wound onto large reels, as its recording medium. Each reel enabled a recordist to preserve twenty minutes of uninterrupted, high quality sound. Mullin, quickly sizing up the amazing potential of this great machine, also carted fifty bulky reels of tape back from overseas. Upon witnessing the capabilities of the prototype, and convinced that the recorder could become an integral part of radio and studio recording, Poniatoff immediately set his research and development engineers to work on building an improved version of the German recorder.

A year later, in June 1947, Murdo MacKenzie, one of Bing's associates at Bing Crosby Enterprises, also saw Mullin's demonstration, and by August, Crosby had hired Mullin and his machine to begin using tape to record his radio program. For Crosby, the ease with which the recordings could be edited was of primary importance. By using tape, the singer could record extra material, then edit the program to fit the precise time constraints. "In that way, we could take out jokes or gags, or situations that didn't play well, and finish with only the 'prime meat' of the show—the solid stuff that played big. We could also take out songs that didn't sound good. It gave us a chance to try a recording of the songs in the afternoon, without an audience, and then another one in front of the studio audience. We'd dub the one that came off best into the final program," Crosby said in his autobiography.

In 1976, Mullin reminisced about some of the traditional radio and TV techniques that stemmed from these experiments with the new tape recorders. "One time, Bob Burns, the hillbilly comic, was on the show, and he threw in a few of his folksy farm stories, which were not in Bill Morrow's script. Today they wouldn't seem 'off-color,' but things were different in radio then. They got enormous laughs, which just went on and on! We couldn't use the jokes, but Bill asked us to save the laughs. A couple of weeks later, he had a show that wasn't very funny, and he insisted that we put in the salvaged laughs. Thus, the laugh track was born."

A savvy investor, Crosby put money into Ampex Corporation, encouraging them to produce more machines. In 1948, the second season of Crosby's *Philco Hour* was taped with the new Ampex Model 200 tape machine that had debuted in April; the magnetic tape was the newly formulated Scotch 111 from the Minnesota Mining and Manufacturing Company (3M), featuring an improved acetate base.

Crosby used every opportunity to promote the new machines, and in his 1950 film *Mr. Music*, he is seen warbling into one of the new

COURTESY OF AMPEX CORPORATION

Singer Bing Crosby, a financial backer of early tape technology, encouraged friends in the industry to embrace the new medium. Here he poses with a portable Ampex machine, early 1950s.

Ampex recorders. He also encouraged his colleagues to utilize the emerging technology.

The ease of editing the magnetic tape (which was accomplished by physically cutting out the unwanted portion with a razor blade, and then "splicing" the remaining sections of recording tape together) was just one of its merits. Magnetic tape preserves sound by sending an electromagnetic current through a recording head, over which the tape passes. As it runs over the head, the current passing through the head arranges the microscopic magnetic particles impregnated on the tape in certain patterns. Unless another magnetic field disturbs those patterns, they are permanently stored for later playback.

While disc recording involved a cruder physical process (the grooves were cut into the lacquer, and each successive playback eroded a minute portion of the sonic information), tape eliminated the scratches, crackles, and other anomalies that are inherent with the disc recording system. Tape was also more durable and less susceptible to damage than recording session masters made on disc. (Magnetic tape presented its own problems, however, primarily tape "hiss" caused by the tape running over the heads.)

Perhaps most important was tape's ability to translate to a recording a much broader frequency range, which resulted in sharp, clear sounding records. By mid-1950, most of the major recording studios had adopted magnetic tape as their primary recording method.

SINATRA SWINGS!

For Frank Sinatra, the benefits of these technical breakthroughs were brought to fruition in April 1950 with the creation of the 10-inch Columbia concept LP *Sing and Dance with Frank Sinatra*, an album that was conceived and recorded solely with the new Long Play technology.

Where the earlier Columbia 78 album sets contained tunes with a common theme, they usually contained selections recorded over a period of several years. With the exception of one tune, each song on this album was waxed specifically for it. Far more important than its obscurity might lead one to believe, the *Sing and Dance* album was the first major Sinatra recording to use overdubbing, which was easily facilitated by the new, high-fidelity recording tape.

Unlike Sinatra's 1948 experimentations, the overdubbing for *Sing and Dance* was not chosen to accommodate busy schedules: it was born of necessity, because at the time the singer was vexed by some exasperating vocal problems. "When we came to do those records, Frank's voice was in terrible shape," recalls Mitch Miller, the producer of the sessions. "His voice was very fragile. It was great, but it was fragile. He would be in the booth, and he'd sing a beautiful phrase, and then on the next phrase, his voice would go. But you couldn't edit! There were a lot of musicians involved, so to save the session, I just shut off his microphone, and got good background (orchestra) tracks. Didn't even tell him! Then, after it was over, I got him. I said, 'When your voice is back . . .' We'd come in crazy hours, midnight, whatever—the doors were locked so no union representative could come in. You see, I could have been kicked out of the Musicians Union because tracking was not allowed. And that whole album is tracked!"

Not merely a technical milestone, *Sing and Dance with Frank Sinatra* survives as a crucial piece of Sinatra's musical puzzle, especially noteworthy for the cohesiveness of its rhythmic orchestrations, provided by the relatively obscure arranger George Siravo. Once the idea (whether the conception of Miller, Sinatra, or both) became firmly planted in the singer's musical head, the entire *Sing and Dance* package (conceptually, thematically, and musically) provided the rock-solid foundation from which Sinatra, in his initial work with Nelson Riddle, could spring. As his first consciously developed thematic "tempo" album, these were, in the words of Sinatra historian and biographer Will Friedwald, "the recordings that proved Sinatra really could swing."

"Sinatra was time-conscious," says drummer Johnny Blowers. "Working with Frank is like working with a great, swinging horn." Solid takes of "It All Depends on You," "Should I," "You Do Something to Me," "Lover," "When You're Smiling," "It's Only a Paper Moon," "My Blue Heaven," and "The Continental" placed Sinatra smack-dab in the middle of a rhythmic arena that he was obviously gravitating toward, and many of these tunes would work their way into his stage repertoire, which at the time was being more or less directed by Siravo. (Sinatra reprised seven of the eight songs from this album for *Sinatra's Swingin' Session!!!*, recorded in 1960 with Nelson Riddle.)

George Siravo describes the genesis of the seminal recording. "I had gained the confidence of Mitch Miller and Percy Faith. They used to send Percy to run the booth, and I'd run everything else. I just had the librarian and the copyist bring in all the music—Frank didn't even pick the tunes. I picked the tunes, I picked the keys, I wrote the arrangements . . . he didn't even know what the hell he was going to sing! We made tracks—he didn't have to know what was going on. Most of the time, he was in the studio, live with the band—this was an exception," he noted.

This hands-off approach was unusual for Sinatra, but is understandable in light of the stresses and preoccupations of his personal life at the time. Mitch Miller has said that the concept for *Sing and Dance* was his, and that since Sinatra had been performing some of these songs in his nightclub repertoire, it made sense to include them on the album. Since Siravo was involved in assisting him with scoring the tempo numbers for those live appearances, the singer may have felt comfortable giving him wider latitude, given his many personal distractions. Siravo also points out that the idea for Sinatra to move in different directions and concentrate on snappier material, was not new at all. "Frank always had a feeling for finger-snapping things—he loved those things. He had that finger-snappin' feeling from the first day that I met him, so it wasn't a new, innovative thing. Occasionally, a guy like Mitch Miller would plant the seed, and sometimes he'd listen to them . . . most of the time he would follow his own intuition."

While Stordahl may not have been adept at creating rhythm charts, he frequently turned to orchestrators who had a knack for writing the best in the business, often Siravo or Heinie Beau. "I never got the chance to do ballads with Sinatra, because Ax was his man," remembers Siravo. "I used to do all the rhythm and jazz things. When Sinatra was doing his radio shows, they did a lot of up-tempo things, and I used to fly from Hollywood to New York. Back and forth, back and forth . . . Christ, I was writing on the plane all the time!" he said. "I'd put the sh— in my lap, and everybody would crowd around and ask, 'How do you write those things? What do they mean? You've got nothin'—not even a harmonica or a tuning fork!'"

Although Siravo never became a familiar name among the general listening public, he was well respected within professional music circles. His work on Sinatra's *Vimms Vitamins* radio show of the early 1940s led to a steadier gig "ghosting" largely uncredited tempo arrangements for Stordahl, and eventually, the assignment for the complete, eight-song *Sing and Dance* LP, for which he was given full credit. Concurrent with his work on the 1950 album, Siravo helped plan and orchestrate Sinatra's many nightclub performances, and his *Light-Up Time* radio program as well. The Sinatra charts, as well as the instrumentals he recorded around the same time for a ten-inch Columbia album titled *Dance Date with Siravo*, demonstrate his distinctive style, which sounds much like a blend of a refined society orchestra, dance band, and jazz combo.

"I learned how to write transparently, and I have to give a whole bunch of credit for that to Ray Heindorf," Siravo explained. Heindorf, the longtime music director at Warner Brothers studios, was also a fellow clarinetist. "Ray said to me, 'You've got to forget about vertical writing—that went out with High Button Shoes.' This was when people were still writing vertically, like the Glenn Miller sound. With vertical writing, the notes happen 'upstairs' in the melody, and under each note, it's like a telephone pole.

"The top of the pole is the melody, the second one under each melodic note is a harmonic note, and that's the way you write. So, you have five reeds, four saxes and a clarinet on top, but underneath it is four notes that make the harmony. But Ray told me, 'You've got to think horizontally: left to right. Don't think about chords any more.' Holy sh—, what that did to my life! I started to weave music, like baskets or a rug, or like a three-way conversation where one guy says something, and we all go back and forth. You add something . . . you echo . . . you weave something in and around what everybody says. That's the way I wrote for strings—from left to right," he said. "Axel also wrote with great transparency. It has a beautiful sound. You can see it, too: in other words, if you look at a score, the 'blacker' it looks, the more depressed a lay person would be. The denser it looks, the worse it will sound.

"Gus Levene once asked me, 'What do you find the most difficult thing to put on the score sheet?' Before I came up with the answer, he said 'A well-placed rest—where nobody plays.' When you write an arrangement for Frank, he doesn't know where you're gonna put the punctuations in the music. When you do a date, sometimes the singer will say, 'Hey, that figure is in my way . . . you gotta take it out, it's in my way.' But Frank would never say that. He would always use what the arranger put in there to his benefit. He'd de-

tour: he would postpone singing in there [at that spot], he would back off. He'd say, 'F— it. I won't sing there—I'll wait till the riff passes, then I'll do it.' When he sang, he reminded me of what it's like when you go out in the rain, and its just started, and there are only a few drops and you can duck between the drops to keep dry. To me, Frank was singing between the drops.

"First, a great voice alone is not sufficient to be a winner. There are other ingredients that must accompany the great voice, otherwise there will never be any success achieved . . . These are the things that are needed to reach the plateau of a winner. First, you need sensitivity, and to learn how to use the voice to portray an emotion. Second, you have to have a cultivated ear. If you weren't born with one, you have to cultivate an ear for singing in tune.

"Then, you need to know what the hell you're singing! This is where a lot of singers screw up: they go to a date, and they're holding a microphone, yet they still don't know what the hell they're singing—they're so in love with their voice that they don't realize what the words mean. That's where Frank was a genius! He knows lyrics—he has a great feeling for lyrics. He's telling a story, but he's doing it musically with his voice. Sinatra's the original! He really is, because he's got the rare combination of voice and showmanship . . . everybody copied him— even the way he unknots the tie. Now, anybody's best shot is to be themselves; the more yourself you can be like, the more individual you'll be. Nobody else can copy you without being you— the original has got the edge."

Maintaining his originality was foremost in Sinatra's mind in 1951, the lowest point in his life. Pop music trends were changing, and there was little interest in the sweet, pensive vocals that reminded many of the turmoil of the war years. Intense personal problems forced the singer's emotional hand, and he eventually found himself without his beautiful wife, Ava Gardner, familial stability, and, on the professional side, a movie or television deal. At Columbia Records, Sinatra floundered to gain solid ground against recently installed artist and repertoire director Mitch Miller's controversial approach that would, depending upon one's perspective, revolutionize or bastardize pop music.

DOWNWARD SPIRAL: THE MITCH MILLER INFLUENCE

COURTESY OF CHARLOTTE AND TONI JANAK

Unguarded moment: engineer Tony Janak caught Frank Sinatra and Mitch Miller reflecting on a playback in Columbia's New York studios, circa 1950. Within a short time, the tranquility of this scene from early in their relationship would be forever shattered.

*H*ow will musical history ultimately judge Mitch Miller's contributions? If money and commercial success are the measure, Miller should be canonized for creating a new genre that spawned the careers of dozens of pop artists of the 1950s, including Tony Bennett, Rosemary Clooney, Johnnie Ray, and Guy Mitchell. Does their early work, almost entirely based on novelty tunes, even begin to approach the exceedingly high standards of the recordings that Sinatra produced at Columbia between 1943 and 1950? Certainly not. If the benchmark is musical quality, Miller could well be damned in the court of popular opinion.

But in 1950, Miller was the undisputed king of a new breed of record-label A&R producers, and the hundreds of thousands of records that were shipped monthly from Columbia (many of which became million-copy sellers—in itself remarkable at that time) pumped a staggering amount of adrenaline and cash into the record industry. "I took over as A&R Director in February of 1950," Miller recalled. "Columbia came from number four to number one in two years. We had eight of the 'Top Ten' bestsellers in the country some weeks!" he adds proudly.

The enormous success of the label under Miller's guidance earned him the respect of the CBS executives, as well as a tremendous measure of power that, combined with his penchant for control, could be intimidating for an artist. "I know for a fact that Mitch wanted things his way, and in certain instances, it worked," recalled Rosemary Clooney. "After he finished recording something, he could call the Sales Department and say, 'Ship three hundred thousand on consignment.' I mean, he had that kind of juice." When it came to convincing Clooney to record her first major hit, "Come-On-a-My-House," Miller was at first persuasive, then demanding. "He was very sure about what was going to happen. You know, I found fault with it, saying, 'I think I should do "Tenderly,"' and he said, 'I think you should do this.' And then it got to the point of, 'You are going to do this. You've got to do this.' I went along with whatever Mitch wanted to do, which created a very good relationship as far as getting the records out there, because of the very control that he had. If he can call the sales department and say 'Send them out,' then he can really do you a favor along the way."

While Clooney acceded to Miller's pressure, her colleague Tony Bennett, who had joined the label in 1951, was less willing to do so. He agreed to record some numbers Miller insisted on, with the proviso that he be allowed to concurrently make records of better songs that utilized the jazz backings that he favored.

"If I'm going to do a song, I don't want to do a bad song—I don't care how much money it makes. Because if you do a bad song, you're stuck with it," Bennett said. "Mitch was a very strange guy. He was the finest oboe player in America, he was one of the greatest classical musicians that ever lived. But he had a hunger for a lot of money. He was just sitting there playing great music with Toscanini and Alec Wilder and people like that, and all of a sudden, he said, 'I'm not just going to be a sideman. I wanna make more money than any of these guys.' Even though he's frowned upon, and a lot of people look at him like he took a wrong turn in the music business, he was the first producer. He taught everybody how to be a producer. Today, everybody has to have his cigar and beard. Mitch invented that—he was the first guy with that, and he made sure that he made as much money as any artist. Years ago, there were no producers; there were just music men in charge of A&R. Today it's hard to find a guy who even knows music," said Bennett.

Indications that Sinatra was displeased—almost embarrassed—at what Miller was attempting to do came as early as 1950, when he granted an interview to Atlantic City radio personality (and former Harry James band member) Ben Heller. Publicly, the singer groused about his dismal sales figures, directly blaming Miller by claiming that he was "forced" to record inferior songs. Much of Sinatra's attitude toward the Mitch Miller's influence at Columbia can be

gleaned from the tone of their conversation about Sinatra's latest recordings.

> *Sinatra:* We've got a new one that's moving pretty good called, you'll excuse the expression, "Goodnight, Irene."
> *Heller:* Hey, that's a nice tune.
> *Sinatra:* You wanna bet? [pauses] Naw, it's really cute.
> *Heller:* You oughta do a lotta songs like that.
> *Sinatra:* Don't hold your breath!

Miller describes a planned 1951 session that Sinatra aborted before even entering the studio. "I had two songs, 'The Roving Kind,' and 'My Heart Cries for You,' that I thought would be good for Frank to sing. So I had the arrangements made. Frank was on his way to see Ava in Spain, or Africa . . . I don't know where he was going. But he was coming in to New York first, and I met him, Ben Barton, and Hank Sanicola at La-Guardia airport, when they arrived at 7:30 in the morning. We came to the studio right away, and I played these two songs for them. Frank looked at Sanicola, then he looked at Barton and Sanicola, and said, 'I'm not going to do any of that crap.' I had musicians hired, I had the chorus hired . . . the session was supposed to be that night because he was going away the next morning. So, to save the thing, I got a hold of Al Cernick [who, under Miller, became Guy Mitchell], and I spent all day with him, rehearsing these two songs. We did them that night, and both sides were Number One! And, I daresay, if Sinatra had done them, I don't think they would have been hits—[even] if he did them perfectly. Because the prejudice against him personally at that time, wrongly, was outrageous," Miller said.

Part of the reason for the singer's refusal to defer to Miller is outlined in an article appearing in the September 24, 1956, edition of the *Philadelphia Inquirer*—a full four years after his separation with Columbia. In the article, which reports on CBS's testimony before the House Judiciary subcommittee investigating the broadcast industry, Sinatra alleges favoritism between Miller and certain publishing concerns. Sinatra felt that the CBS empire, which included Columbia Records and the powerful CBS Radio Network, took advantage of their position as both a recording and broadcasting entity, and pushed songs that would have maximum financial benefit for both the company and, in turn, Mitch Miller. Journalist Merrill Panitt quotes the singer (who provided a statement to the Congressional committee via telegram) as saying, "Before Mr. Miller's arrival at Columbia Records, I found myself enjoying a freedom of selection of material; a freedom which I may modestly say resulted in a modicum of success for me. Suddenly, Mr. Miller, by design or coincidence, began to present many, many inferior songs, all curiously bearing the BMI label."

From its formation in 1914, ASCAP (the American Society of Composers, Authors, and Publishers) controlled all music licensing. Then in 1940 a consortium of broadcasters began BMI (Broadcast Music Inc.) to go head-to-head with ASCAP. To this day, the primary role of both BMI and ASCAP is to collect fees from broadcasters for musical performances, and distribute it to the composers and publishers. One of the ironies of the singer's complaint about Miller's preference for BMI songs, and his hint of some sort of collusion between the broadcast giant and BMI, is that Sinatra himself at the time owned separate ASCAP and BMI firms, which published many of the songs he sang, and from which he collected both performing and publishing royalties.

"Before Mr. Miller's advent on the scene, I had a successful recording career, which quickly went into a decline," Sinatra maintained. "Rather than continue a frustrating battle, I chose to take my talents elsewhere. It is now a matter of record that since I have associated with Capitol Records, a company free of broadcasting affiliations, my career is again financially, creatively, and artisti-

cally healthy." Statistics suggest that Sinatra's potshot at Miller, CBS, and BMI was unjustified. During the Miller era at Columbia, the singer recorded a meager five BMI songs, and fifty-two ASCAP controlled numbers. By comparison, in his first three years at Capitol, he waxed a total of eleven BMI tunes, twice as many as during a similar stretch at Columbia—including his first major hit at the new label, "Young at Heart."

In his own defense, Miller vehemently denies trying to sabotage Sinatra, and scoffs at the singer's assertion that he was "forced" to sing bad material. "Start with this premise: nobody brings Sinatra in the studio to do things that he doesn't want to do. I don't care who it is," Miller said. "A lot of the critics said, 'Well, what's Sinatra doing?' So, Sinatra turned it on, and said I'd 'forced' him to do bad songs. Nobody could force Sinatra to do bad songs, or to do a song he didn't want to do. Imagine pulling Sinatra in by the ear and saying, 'You sing this.' Right! He [Sinatra] had the right to okay any record's release. There was a clause in his contract that gave him forty-eight hours to approve any master for release. If he didn't want a particular song released, he could have killed it by invoking that clause."

While Miller bore the brunt of Sinatra's wrath, as well as the lion's share of blame for the downward spiral of his career, the producer was fair in his assessment of the public's perception of Sinatra during this fallow period. "People don't understand the psychology of what happened. When he started this thing with Ava, and was running around . . . it was a different climate in those days. Ingrid Bergman had a child out of wedlock. Today, everybody in Hollywood has a child out of wedlock, and they brag about it. In those days, she was banned from movies in America. Sinatra, with his public behavior with Ava, and leaving his wife, had the priests saying, 'Don't tell the kids. Don't buy his records.'"

However Miller chooses to rationalize Sinatra's behavior, and his own role in what has become one of the most controversial and legendary stories in the music industry, the fact remains that Sinatra's jibes stuck in his craw and caused him a great deal of anguish. Once the *Philadelphia Inquirer* article ran, Miller seized the opportunity to vindicate himself, and quickly made photocopies of the story, which, along with a handwritten personal note scrawled on its side, were distributed to friends in the business. "Hi Fellas—a lot of you have asked me so many questions about this episode, that I am taking the liberty of sending you this clipping from the Philadelphia Inquirer—Yours, Mitch."

Economics, more than anything else, turned out to be a critical snag in the complicated relationship between Sinatra and Columbia Records. Miller's explanation of a special financial arrangement between the singer and the label helps clarify a very confusing series of events that ultimately led to his severance as a Columbia Records artist.

"Sinatra had to pay the IRS a big fee for back taxes," Miller recalled. "He went to Manie Sacks, and Sacks loaned him an advance against royalties. Then Sacks left to go to RCA Victor. In the meantime, I came to Columbia, and Ted Wallerstein, who was then president, said, 'Mitch, we've got to make this money back, so get him the best things [to record].' Of course, that was my whole point! I made 'Azure Te,' and 'Birth of the Blues,' and 'Why Try to Change Me Now,' which were fabulous records. He was singing great, as you can hear. But you couldn't give them away at the time. So when it came time for his renewal, Columbia just didn't want to re-sign him. And even Manie Sacks wouldn't sign him at RCA! Columbia said, 'No more,' and I had to abide by that. He had lost his M-G-M contract, he had lost his television show. He had burned all his bridges behind him. I was only working with him on his records—I had nothing to do with the television show, or his films, although he tried to say I ruined his career.

"We all have weaknesses, we all have craziness in our lives. Frank could never face the fact that he was responsible for any failure he had. I always called him the sorest winner I ever met.

"After he left Columbia Records, he pleaded with Columbia Pictures to do *From Here to Eternity*. They didn't want him, they thought he would be a detriment to the picture. By getting stomped to death in that movie, he did like a 'public penance' for all of it," Miller believes. "You chart it: from the day that movie came out, his records began to sell. [That Columbia] stuff was never publicized. And then the public's attitude changed, and it helped. Once he left the company, we repackaged the old stuff, and not only did we get back the $250,000 advance, but he made God knows how many hundreds of thousands of dollars in royalties more, after that."

At the core of many of their disputes was the simple fact that Miller and Sinatra were cut from similar cloth: both were immensely talented yet fiercely independent, and headstrong to a fault. "The problem was that Frank didn't go about voicing his complaints the right way," Arthur Shimkin, the founder and President of Bell Records and an associate of Miller, speculates. "If he had gone to Mitch and sat down with him one-on-one, and simply said, 'Mitch, this is what I feel that I do best,' Mitch would have listened. Instead, Sinatra told him, 'Stay the f— out of my studio.' The irony of it is that when I asked Mitch what he thought about Sinatra, he said, 'He's the most talented singer in history.'"

One of the complexities of the relationship that surely added to the tension was that while Miller was responsible for launching the careers of many artists from their start, he inherited Sinatra after the singer had spent nearly seven astoundingly successful years at Columbia, accustomed to being the center of attention and having his own way. In all likelihood, it was painful for Sinatra to be caught in such a terrible rut, unable to regain lost momentum while others around him were being nurtured by Miller, skyrocketing to fame on the coattails of music that repulsed him.

Paul Weston, then West Coast A&R Director for Columbia, remembered one embarrassing and humiliating incident that occurred during the singer's penultimate session for the label on June 3, 1952. "They came out here, and it was the only time I was on a session. I was the producer of the session, but Mitch was out [in the studio] running around. We were recording some horrible song ['Tennessee Newsboy'], and Speedy West, the guitarist, was known for making the guitar sound like a chicken. Frank sang the vocal, and Mitch rushed out into the studio, and everybody thought he was going to congratulate Frank for getting through, because he did it well. Instead, he rushed right past Frank, and embraced Speedy West, because he'd made a good chicken noise on the guitar. Frank was disgusted. . . ."

Weston was well aware of Miller's penchant for encouraging artists to record lesser quality songs, because his wife, Jo Stafford, experienced the same pressure. "You can't believe the crap that he had Jo record, tunes like 'Underneath the Overpass,' stuff that just died. He would be very persuasive, and the artist didn't have much choice. They'd say, 'This is a piece of crap,' and Mitch would say, 'Oh, it's gonna be a hit,' so they'd do it."

"I thought he [Mitch] was arrogant," says Johnny Blowers. "You couldn't tell him anything. Frank gave Mitch strict orders: 'You don't tell the guys what to do from the control room. Tell me or Axel, and we will tell the guys.' Now, I guess Mitch didn't hear him very well, because he would forget about that, and next thing you know he's telling the band 'Do this' and 'Do that.' This annoyed Frank to no end."

One point of contention was Miller's legendary penchant for taking on the role of engineer, adjusting levels and such himself in the control room. "With Frank and Axel, you corrected mistakes; you made your own dynamics," Blowers explains. "Frank didn't want you turning dials. 'Leave the damn dials alone—the musicians do that.' But Mitch did, and then all of a sudden one day Frank had as much as he could stand. Quietly, he looked in the control room, pointed his finger, and said, 'Mitch—out.' When Mitch didn't move, Sinatra turned to Hank Sanicola. 'Henry, move him.' To Mitch, he said, 'Don't you ever come in the studio when I'm recording again.'"

Tempest in a teapot: Sinatra's contempt for Mitch Miller is readily apparent in this 1952 session photo, in which he seems poised to lunge over the music stand in frustration. Miller, who produced the session, is in front of Sinatra, out of the camera's range.

The point of no return for Sinatra and Miller occurred on May 10, 1951, when Frank was paired with the busty comedienne Dagmar for the most degrading song of his career, the infamous "Mama Will Bark." An exercise in absurdity, the tune features Sinatra crooning to the accompaniment of a howling dog, recreated in the studio by imitator Donald Bain.

"We made that record as a shot in the dark," Mitch Miller recalled. "This song came in, and I thought, 'Try this novelty number, because they aren't buying the great records—try something.' He was at The Paramount Theater, working with Dagmar, so since they were onstage together, I figured, 'Why not?' I even tried to insure the success of 'Mama Will Bark' by backing it with a great song—'I'm a Fool to Want You.' People don't understand this . . . there was nothing inferior [about what Frank Sinatra was recording at the time] except 'Mama Will Bark,' but he keeps coming back to that," Miller says.

Truth be told, the year that culminated with the ill-fated "Bark" was a good one, repertoire-wise, for Sinatra, proving the accuracy of Miller's observations. From the June 1950 "Goodnight, Irene" session to the May 1951 date that produced the nefarious canine classic, he waxed twenty-six tunes, including such remarkable recordings as "April in Paris," "Neverthe-less," "I Guess I'll Have to Dream the Rest," "Let It Snow, Let It Snow, Let It Snow," "I Am Loved," "Hello Young Lovers," "We Kiss in a Shadow," "I'm a Fool to Want You," and "Love Me," the theme of his CBS-TV variety show. Among the lesser-known but equally gorgeous tunes recorded during this eleven-month period were "If Only She'd Looked My Way," "Remember Me in Your Dreams," "Take My Love," "Faithful," and a second duet session with Rosemary Clooney that yielded "Love Means Love" and "Cherry Pies Ought to Be You."

The wistful "April in Paris" demonstrates Sinatra and Stordahl's ability to bring a sense of drama to the music, through the dynamics of the musical arrangement and carefully controlled vocal execution. (Sinatra himself must have known that this version of "April in Paris" approached perfection, for he mimics its vocal lines virtually note for note in the 1957 re-recording with Billy May—in itself, a masterpiece).

Sinatra's original recording of "I Could Write a Book," from January of 1952, can be viewed as a vocal turning point. The depth of his tonal quality, punctuated and intensified by his razor-sharp diction, is luxurious and satisfying, a true precursor to his subsequent work with Nelson Riddle and Gordon Jenkins. It is with this recording (and several others from the months just preceding this session) that we begin to hear the subtleties that would later surface as full-blown trademarks of Sinatra's silky, smooth baritone style, including a marked deepening of his vocal timbre and a penchant for a stunningly effective long-phrased glide culminating in a seemingly effortless key change at the song's end.

One of the most interesting tunes from Sinatra's underappreciated late-Columbia period is "My Girl," from February 6, 1952. Here we find him bending notes and using the suppleness of his voice in new ways; for example, the buttery smooth dip he applies to the words *when* and *night* in the line "when the night is cold." The whole feel of this recording, from Sinatra's over-

Late Columbia session, Hollywood, February 1952.

all vocal execution to the ambient sound of the recording itself, is virtually the same as on his recording of "I'm Walking Behind You" from his first Capitol session on April 2, 1953. Of course, Axel Stordahl's presence unified the two dates, but when the recordings are played back to back, the similarities are so pervasive that if you didn't know otherwise, you'd believe they were recorded at the same session.

Two tunes in Sinatra's Columbia catalog define his transition from the Sinatra of the late Columbia period (1951–52) to the artistically reborn Sinatra of the Capitol years (1953). Almost ignored at the time, his brash, gritty recording of "The Birth of the Blues," and his dramatically contrasting, stark and desolate rendition of "I'm a Fool to Want You" indicate the real strength of

his voice, sharply dispelling the myth that he had lost his vocal edge, and point up the direction he envisioned for his future.

"The Birth of the Blues" receives a confident, snarly interpretation that proves Sinatra had strength and endurance, and moreover, the fortitude to stand up for what he believed in. One cannot help but think that this was Frank's way of flipping Mitch Miller the proverbial "bird" as he left through the backstage door, and speaks directly to where the singer would be, a year later, with Nelson Riddle.

Although the oft-repeated story about Sinatra leaving the recording studio in tears after singing "I'm a Fool to Want You" on the March 27, 1951, session may be apocryphal (he in fact either remained in or subsequently returned to the studio to record one other song, "Love Me", and those present do not recall such a melodramatic reaction), this dramatic performance was no doubt influenced by the singer's deep personal turmoil.

So gripping a performance is this, replete with fragments of the singer's carefully guarded reserve of personal anguish, that it vies for position as the single most devastating recording he ever made. The precision with which Sinatra controls his vibrato on these late Columbia efforts is remarkable, and his vocal dexterity is compellingly displayed in the sotto voce ending of "I'm a Fool to Want You." Here he drops his voice to a near whisper to sing, "Take me back, I love you . . . pity me, I need you . . . ," injecting a neat little dose of portamento on the word need. The ending then builds feverishly until Sinatra's voice becomes one with the soaring choir that brings the song to an intense climax.

It is clear from performances like this that Sinatra knew exactly where he wanted to go musically, and exactly how to get there. The late Columbia recordings prove that while he was struggling to reorganize his personal life, he was also growing by leaps and bounds artistically. If given the chance, he would certainly have salvaged the tattered remnants of his final year at Columbia, more than likely with one of the label's house arrangers like Percy Faith.

Mitch Miller and the powers that be at Columbia didn't share his vision, though, and the near-decade-long tenure that began with such sensational promise ended on a subdued note. For his final recording for the label on September 17, 1952, Sinatra swallowed his pride and entered the 30th Street studio with Percy Faith to preserve his ironically glum farewell statement, Cy Coleman's "Why Try to Change Me Now." After the master take, Miller is heard over the booth's speaker saying, resignedly, "That's it, Frank."

Compounding the damaging effects of nearly every professional wall caving in on him

was the fact that as Frank prepared to leave Columbia, his friend and musical partner, Axel Stordahl, stood poised to move on as well. No doubt he figured that when Sinatra went down, he would be out of a job as well. His decision to depart for the East Coast as Frank was settling on the West Coast distressed the singer, and when Stordahl hinted that he might take advantage of an offer to work as the music director for the Eddie Fisher television show, based in New York, Sinatra gave him an ultimatum. When Stordahl took the Fisher position, the friendship was severed, and as far as anyone connected to the pair remembers, they didn't speak for nearly ten years.

Not everyone in the music business agreed with Columbia that Sinatra was washed up. "I met Hank Sanicola through a friend who worked at Barton Music," recalls Arthur Shimkin. "Sinatra had left Columbia, and in 1952 I made him an offer to come and record for Bell. The deal was pretty good, too: $48,000 for twelve sides. We would pay for the date, and the setup was that for every song that Sinatra picked to record, Bell would choose one. I met with Frank once to discuss the offer, at the Hotel 14, behind the Copa. He looked at me, and remarked rather wryly, 'You wouldn't pick something that would make me unhappy, would ya?' I told him, 'For every song we select, there'll be three alternates from which to choose. You will make the choice.' He smiled and said, 'Okay.'

Professionally and psychologically important as the offer was for Sinatra at that moment, the singer's nemesis ended up nixing it for him. "I also started Golden Records, which was a children's record company that was underwritten by Simon & Schuster," Shimkin continues. "My Music Director at Golden Records was Mitch Miller, whom I had hired in 1947. My boss at Schuster, Jim Jacobson, was very close to Mitch, and when Jim approached him and inquired about Sinatra's viability as an artist, Mitch flatly replied, 'f— him. He's a has-been.' Well, that's all Jim had to hear. He wasn't investing $48,000 in what Miller called a 'has-been.' I disagreed—I thought Frank could make it again."

Sinatra never forgave Miller, rebuffing the former A&R director's repeated attempts to patch things up. "A bit later," Miller recalls, "I had a radio program on CBS, an interview show. I'd go out to Las Vegas and do a lot of interviews, and I got to know Joe E. Lewis. So, this one time, I see him in the lobby of the Sands at about two or three in the morning. He said, 'Look, Mitch. Frank is with Jack Entratter (who managed the Sands). Come on over and say hello.' I said, 'No, I'm not interested.' Now, Joe's a little loaded, and he grabs me. So, we go over, and Joe says, 'I brought Mitch over. Why don't you shake hands?' And Frank, who was half-loaded himself, said, 'Get lost, creep.'

When interviewed in the early 1990s, Miller (for all the negative things Sinatra has said about him) seemed quite objective about the singer's years at Columbia, agreeing that while it was dif-ficult to work with him, he always believed that "Sinatra was an incredible talent." He seemed to bear no grudges. In the few years since, though, Miller has changed his tune.

Upon Sinatra's death in May 1998, when Miller was quizzed by a British television pro-ducer about his involvement with the singer, he flew into what the TV producer described as a near tirade, ranting that "Sinatra was a pain in the ass who gave me nothing but troubles." He said he "couldn't understand what all the fuss was about, and why Sinatra was getting all this atten-tion now that he is dead. He was washed up—in a few years this music will be forgotten."

A music industry friend of Miller's reports that his questions evoked a similar response. Af-ter listening to a lengthy diatribe about how dif-ficult Sinatra was to work with, the friend posed a question: "But Mitch, Sinatra was a great tal-ent. Wasn't it all worth it?" Miller's simple reply was a reflective "Yeah, it was."

Recording at the Capitol Records studios, Hollywood, April 1953.

PART 3

The Capitol Years, 1953–1962

*H*OLLYWOOD: NEW CAPITOL RECORDS SPLENDID. "The record situation is upped considerably this week but not with any thanks to the Big Three. They are so busy with occupational jitters . . . that they've paid very little attention to the business of making and selling records. The same is not true on the coast. There, Johnny Mercer, Glenn Wallichs of the famed Music City store at Sunset and Vine, and Buddy DeSylva, production chief for Paramount, have organized a new record company, with labels printed as Capitol Records. . . ." (Mike Levin in *Down Beat*, July 15, 1942)

The idea for the new record label was born of frustration. Songwriter Johnny Mercer had befriended music merchant Glenn Wallichs, and the two began comparing notes regarding the sorry state of affairs in the record business. Mercer, fast becoming one of the top tunesmiths in the country, felt that artists were routinely given short shrift by the labels that recorded them, and that they were rarely presented at their best. Wallichs, whose Music City was a rapidly growing record retailer, was disturbed by the merchandising and distribution policies of the three major labels: Columbia, RCA, and Decca. Since he was looking to expand his small custom recording service, the pair began mulling over the idea of starting their own company.

Within a short time, Mercer enlisted the assistance of songwriter Buddy "B.G." DeSylva, who he hoped could provide the cash they would need to get started. A luncheon meeting at Lucey's Restaurant in Hollywood clinched the deal, with DeSylva putting up a total of $25,000 to launch the label. Mercer, in describing the company's beginnings, said, "Buddy had always been smart and lucky, and could 'smell' money better than a divining rod. He was too busy to actively participate, but he put $10,000 in the bank, and later added $15,000 to get us started. . . . We only spent $15,000 of the original $25,000 advance, and were never in trouble from that day on."

Ginger, Mercer's wife, came up with the name "Capitol." "We were sitting in Chasen's one night at dinner, trying to decide on a name," Mercer once said. "I had tried to clear Liberty from Liberty Music Shops in New York City, but they were reluctant to let us have it, and seemed steamed at the suggestion. Gosh knows how many [names] we had been through. Victory was popular at the time, but it was mighty close to Victor. Then, Ginger came up with Capitol. Well, it certainly seemed solid enough, and dignified. And when Glenn came up with the four stars around the dome, that was it."

Reviewer Mike Levin, in the *Down Beat* article that heralded the June arrival of the first batch of Capitol releases, lauded the tiny label's product. "Their first records are excellent. Surface noise and record materials are far better than the general output. The choice [of songs] is good, with the obvious concession to commercialism.

What gets me, though, is that with everybody else in the business pulling in the shutters, these guys are setting sail full of drive and confidence that they can make a go of it."

Despite the widespread optimism, the small West Coast label that dared to stand up against its three major competitors was almost knocked off the block within months of its birth, primarily due to the limit on shellac available for record production imposed by the War Production Board in April of 1942, and the industry-wide recording ban enacted in August, which prohibited the recording of any songs that used an instrumental group. Dave Dexter, a veteran executive with the company, later spoke of the grim future the company faced. "With the union's ban on recording and the frustrating shortage of shellac, Capitol's chances for survival were estimated at one hundred to one," he said.

The recording ban ended up working in their favor. "When James Petrillo [head of the musician's union] slapped his ban on all recordings shortly after our first release, we again thought we were licked," said Wallichs. "But it turned out to be our biggest piece of good fortune. Before the ban went into effect, we worked night and day, turning out such tunes as 'Cow Cow Boogie,' and 'G.I. Jive.' When those tunes became popular, we were the only company that had recorded them, and dealers from all over the country began buying them from us."

The company struggled along, and by 1948 had sales of nearly $18 million, compared to the almost $200,000 it took in during its first year of operation. Among the label's many hits for the year were four that had extended positions in the number one slot: Peggy Lee's "Mañana," Pee Wee Hunt's "Twelfth Street Rag," Margaret Whiting's "A Tree in a Meadow," and Nat Cole's "Nature Boy."

Everyone, from studio janitor to graphic artist to Glenn Wallichs (vice president), felt that Capitol was a family, and the philosophy was that there was room for any idea that was valid, either artistically or commercially. The late Mike Maitland, a Capitol staffer who later went on to executive positions at Warner Brothers and MCA, once wrote that "The secret to Capitol's success in the 1940s was that the staff was unencumbered by old ways of thinking. The prevalent moods were, 'What if?' and 'Why not?' rather than 'But . . .' and 'Well, seven years ago . . .' If the idea made sense, it went into effect immediately. And that meant right now: not next Friday, not after it cleared legal, not after it went through the accounting department or the board of directors."

As the label's success snowballed, its artist roster swelled, and by the end of the 1940s it boasted some of the top names in the music business: Peggy Lee, Jo Stafford, Les Paul and Mary Ford, Margaret Whiting, Benny Goodman, and the undisputed "king" of the jazz world, Nat Cole.

By 1948, the studios had begun recording on magnetic tape, and in 1949, Capitol became the first label to release records in all three speeds: 78, 45, and 33⅓, a move that *Billboard* applauded in an editorial titled "Three Speeds Ahead!" Endorsing the growing label, the industry bible acknowledged the important trends that Capitol was setting: "The water has now burst the dam. Let's hope the flow strengthens as companies other than Capitol find the courage and resources to follow the lead of the West Coast major." The growth of the company over the next four years, and its nurturing, familial atmosphere, would make Capitol a warm, inviting place for a singer like Frank Sinatra to call home. They welcomed him with open arms.

COURTESY OF MICHAEL OCHS ARCHIVES

Sinatra's transformation from the ballad singer of the 1940s to the swinging sophisticate of the 1950s was effectively communicated through personal, musical, and sartorial changes.

SINATRA IN HOLLYWOOD

The transition from Columbia to Capitol, between June 1952 and April 1953, involved a complex series of creative and personal changes for Sinatra, and culminated in a complete revitalization. After shedding some personal baggage and shifting his base of operation entirely to the West Coast, the singer emerged with a completely new look, attitude, and sound. Gone were the floppy bow ties and slicked hair of yesteryear; in were stylish cravats of the finest silk and pattern, and a snap-brimmed hat that communicated a jaunty, sophisticated style. No mere props, these tasteful choices breathed freshness into his image, and consequently, his work. A brand-new Sinatra had emerged, and every inch of this transformation is reflected in his enthusiastic approach to the two main crafts he concentrated on: acting and singing.

Alan Livingston, then vice president of A&R at Capitol, was responsible for signing Sinatra to the label. "Sinatra had hit bottom, and I mean bottom. He couldn't get a record contract, and he literally, at that point, could not get a booking in a nightclub. It was that bad—he was broke, and in a terrible state of mind. I received a call from Sam Weisbord, at the William Morris Agency, who told me that they'd signed Sinatra, and asked if I'd be interested in signing him. I said, 'Sure! His talent is still there . . .' And that's how he came to Capitol."

Eventually, the success would come; it was not without painstaking effort, though. "I announced that we [Capitol] had signed Sinatra at our national convention in Colorado," remembers Livingston. "There must have been a couple of hundred guys there . . . and the whole room went, 'Unnhhoooo . . .' My answer to them was ' . . . I only know talent, and Frank is the best singer in the world. There's nobody that can touch him.'"

Thus in a short time Sinatra found himself three thousand miles and a cultural world away from Manhattan, comfortably ensconced in Capitol's Melrose Avenue recording studios (the former KHJ Radio studio), which from April 2, 1953, to January 16, 1956, would be the locale for the recordings that marked one of the greatest comebacks in entertainment history. It was here that he made some of the most appealing and recognizable recordings of his career.

While Sinatra demonstrated to Livingston that he was still a viable artistic asset whose talent would propel him to unparalleled heights in the entertainment business, there were several tangential factors that aided the vocalist in his virtually instantaneous rebirth.

In the early 1950s, the Hollywood music scene was about as far removed from the New York scene as one could imagine. As the epicenter of the film industry, Hollywood had seen a massive immigration of artists during the 1930s and 1940s, when the region was still relatively un-derdeveloped. This influx was critical in later establishing Hollywood as a haven for the artistic community.

"Los Angeles in the 1930s and 1940s was probably very similar, in terms of musical and artistic feeling, to what Paris must have been like in the 1920s," observes conductor Leonard Slatkin, music director of the National Symphony Orchestra. "In the 1930s, you had a convergence of artists who had come to California for many reasons. You had composers: some of who came to California for health reasons, and some who had come to escape various tyrannies. Stravinsky was there, Rachmaninoff was there . . . you found great artists and writers there—it was an incredible time. But unfortunately, at that time the whole city never embraced the artistic culture; it was always felt to be very much on the fringe, and it was never taken seriously. Only the film industry established itself as the main occupation in L.A."

Where New York was the acknowledged home to the jazz scene, Hollywood attracted the more avant-garde and classical musicians, who quickly found lucrative work in the studio orchestras at M-G-M, 20th Century Fox, Paramount, and Warner Brothers. Because of the volume of steady work on the West Coast, many musicians aspired to become part of the Hollywood studio system, and maintained their interest in classical music as a sideline.

Slatkin, whose parents, Eleanor and Felix, were major contributors to both film and popular music, recently commented on the correlation between classical and film music. "I don't find the juxtaposition of so-called concert [classical] music and film music at all at odds with each other. I believe John Williams said that essentially, film music was to the second half of this century what opera had been to all the centuries before. Film music almost took over that role: scripted music, moving a story along. Almost all of the composers of the 1930s and 1940s who operated in the big film studios came from serious classical backgrounds: Korngold, Max Steiner, Dimitri Tiomkin, Miklas Rozsa . . . they had impeccable credentials in terms of their compositional backgrounds. They chose to use those skills in the motion picture industry, because it was lucrative, and it was a very good outlet for these creative talents. And remember: we also had a problem in that musical styles had changed dramatically in this century, and for the neo-romantics as it were, there was not so much a place for them in concert life, and they became enamored of expressing themselves through the motion picture industry."

The motion picture music system was firmly rooted in tradition until the early 1950s, when, concurrent with Sinatra's move to Capitol, new jazz forms were taking hold. Many of the jazz musicians who had ridden out the end of the big band era found work in the post-band groups such as the Stan Kenton Orchestra, whose style blended elements of both the big band and modern jazz idioms. In these top bands were some of the most proficient young players to emerge in years; not quite old enough for the era of Tommy Dorsey and Glenn Miller (the early 1940s), but certainly interested enough to adopt the feel, if not the essence, of the big band style—men like Frank Rossolino, Conrad Gozzo, George Roberts, and Milt Bernhart.

When the popularity of the post-band era groups waned, the most logical place for these superior improvisers was the Hollywood film stdios. But in the beginning, the studio establishment resisted accepting them into their ranks. While these fabulous players were increasingly involved in their own recording dates and as key players on the sessions of pop vocalists such as Sinatra, it wasn't until 1954 that they began to carve a niche for themselves in the film studio market.

"I had gotten off the road with Kenton's orchestra in 1953, and a bunch of us were new in town," recalls Milt Bernhart. "Among us were some very fine players who had a reputation,

COURTESY OF MILT BERNHART

Milt Bernhart (right) with British bandleader Vic Lewis, late 1940s.

which meant nothing out here in Hollywood. I had drawn a straw: should I go to New York, or L.A.? I had no real reason to go to either place— no roots there at all. It seemed to me that Los Angeles was where television was going to start to develop, and I was looking for work. So I came to Hollywood. For the first six or eight months, I didn't get a job. Then, I got a gig working at The Lighthouse in Hermosa Beach, with Howard Rumsey's Lighthouse All-Stars. It was me, Shorty Rogers, Shelly Manne, Bud Shank, Jimmy Giuffre, Bud Cooper. . . . It was our only job for quite a while, about a year. I don't think we were making a hundred a week! Studio work just wasn't there."

An interesting twist of fate, and the 1954 intervention of an unlikely supporter, Marlon

Brando, broke the dam that eventually forced the admission of the jazz players into the studio orchestras.

"Brando, who was working on the film *The Wild One*, was sitting in a room at Columbia Pictures one day, when the discussion of music came up," Bernhart recounts. "They asked him, 'Who do you want to score the picture?' Then, the producers offered the services of some very good people: Dimitri Tiomkin, George Duning, Victor Young. Marlon simply listened, and said, 'Listen—I bought a record yesterday, a jazz record, and I think this guy is great. You have to hear this stuff; I want him to do my score.' 'Who is it?' they asked. Brando snapped his fingers, and said to an underling, 'Get the album.' It turned out to be a Capitol album that Shorty Rogers had made: I was on it, Shelly [Manne] was on it . . . and Brando had bought it! He told them, 'This is what I want.'"

"Well, Columbia Pictures was scared to death! The music department, which was under Morris Stoloff, was afraid of young jazz players. The consensus was, 'They're all dope fiends.' That was the legend. But they really had no reason not to believe in us. The old-fashioned New Orleans Dixieland players certainly didn't read much music, and there were a lot of drinkers in that group, so they were convinced that these be-boppers were the same way. There were a lot of junkies among the be-bop musicians, but not everyone was into drugs. There were a lot of good musicians there—good readers, too. We wouldn't have been with guys like Kenton if we couldn't read! And Kenton was also very particular about how you behaved and looked on the bandstand."

"The studio people tried to dissuade Brando, telling him that 'The musicians are unreliable . . . they won't show up . . . they can't read music . . . they'll be out of their element.' They used these arguments to try to keep us off the picture, but Brando insisted on having us," the trombonist says. "So, they dispatched some studio people—

executives—to The Lighthouse, to check us out. They came every night for a week, dressed like hippies, trying to fit in: these guys had their hair combed over their eyes . . . wearing tattered clothes . . . they looked ridiculous! But they watched every move we made."

"Now, as luck would have it, we weren't 'faking it' at The Lighthouse. Shorty wrote things, and he came in every night with new stuff, so we'd be kept interested. It was a big attraction down there—it made West Coast jazz, and I felt very fortunate to have been there with those guys! Finally, after a week of watching, the studio people were convinced that we were all right. They approached Shorty, told him who they were (as if we didn't know), and we got the job. This was the first time for jazz musicians in a motion picture studio. It had a tremendous effect: Elmer Bernstein's score for the Sinatra picture *The Man With the Golden Arm* came directly off of that. And the doors opened for me overnight—I was in! Suddenly, I was getting calls like I couldn't believe. Of course, it affected our record dates. It didn't occur to me until much later, but Stan Kenton was very solid at Capitol, and Voyle Gilmore, their A&R man, had been doing all of Kenton's recording dates. Stan knew all of us; word had been passed down, and that's how we got started working at Capitol."

By 1952, Capitol's recordings by the likes of Nat Cole, Margaret Whiting, Stan Kenton, Peggy Lee, Jo Stafford, and Les Paul and Mary Ford were making a deep impression on the pop music industry. Although the ten-year-old company was enjoying an increasingly respectable reputation, it was still the smallest of the major labels, and the only nationally competitive one based in Los Angeles. Yet, despite its youth, the company was attracting top-flight artists. From the bold logo and gorgeous album covers to the unequaled richness of the sound of the records, Capitol was everything a record label strove to be: chic, cool, artsy, hip. As Milt Bernhart wryly observed, "At that time, Capitol Records *was* Hollywood."

Soon, Sinatra would discover that going there was the single greatest move of his career.

FRANK MEETS NELSON

Sinatra thrust himself into the Capitol era with passionate energy. By 1954, with an Academy Award for Best Supporting Actor in *From Here to Eternity* under his belt, he was free to concentrate on revamping his image and re-establishing his position as the world's premiere pop vocalist. He used each opportunity to its best advantage, coming to the game prepared to play, knowing it had to be hard and fast. As with all things Sinatra, the hookup with Capitol turned out to be downright electrifying—half the current, in this case, supplied by the young, talented arranger Nelson Riddle.

Riddle began his orchestrating career with lessons from the great jazz arranger Bill Finegan, then worked as a trombonist and staff arranger for Charlie Spivak and Tommy Dorsey. Eventually he landed in California, where he studyied with Italian composer Mario Castelnuovo-Tedesco. By 1950, he was the main "house" arranger at Capitol, ghosting uncredited Nat Cole charts for Les Baxter (among others).

"It was Voyle [Gilmore], then laying out Sinatra's recordings, who undoubtedly suggested that there should be a couple of Jimmy Lunceford-type backgrounds made for him," says Bernhart. "He thought that the Lunceford two-beat style would be nice, since Sinatra hadn't done much of that at Columbia, where it was mostly lush string arrangements. They [Capitol] wanted to be sure that the arrangements were right—that he could sing with them. That's where Nelson came into the picture. Who had heard of us? Who was Nelson Riddle? As for Frank, there wasn't any reason to believe that he could really handle the jazz phrasing correctly, because most of what he'd been doing was so square. I wasn't convinced that he was going to be able to sing jazz style: I didn't know him that way at all! So I was one of the most surprised people in the world. Of course, his timing was impeccable—all he needed was the right place to do it."

Even though Nelson Riddle came with an admirable list of recording credits (including "Mona Lisa" and "Unforgettable" for Cole) Sinatra was, at first, reluctant to work with him. Bill Miller, the singer's new pianist, heard Sinatra's criticisms. "Frank had to be sold on Nelson. On the first or second album, he said, 'Pshew, we gotta be careful of him.' Nelson, with his harmonics, had the polytones: G over A, A over G . . . all that kind of stuff. I said, 'Hey, Frank—it's different. It's working . . .' But Frank was unsure. He'd say, 'Well, that's good. We'll see. Let's see what happens next time.' It developed, it really developed."

"We were going to do pop songs as they came in," recalls Alan Livingston. "And I said, 'Do yourself a favor. Work with Nelson Riddle.' We were all very high on Nelson, he was marvelous! He knew how to back a singer, and make them sound great, and I wanted Frank to have the benefit of that. But Frank said, 'Oh, Alan . . . I've worked with Axel Stordahl for practically my whole career.' He insisted on Axel, and I said, 'Fine.' We made the first Capitol date with Axel, and nothing happened—nor did I expect it to happen," Livingston remembers.

"I'm Walking Behind You," from the first Capitol session of April 2, 1953, did not make the splash that everyone thought it would. Two other songs, "Don't Make a Beggar of Me" and a Billy May composition called "Lean Baby" (orchestrated for Stordahl by Heinie Beau), were pleasant, but unremarkable. The most impressive tune from the session, Johnny Mercer and Rube

PHOTOGRAPH BY KEN VEEDER, COURTESY OF MPTV ARCHIVE

Recording "Lean Baby" with Stordahl at the first Capitol session, Melrose Avenue, KHJ Studio, April 2, 1953.

Bloom's "Day In, Day Out," remained, undocumented and unreleased, in the Capitol vault for nearly thirty-five years.

Twenty-eight days later, on April 30, the principals reconvened at the Melrose Avenue studio for their second outing. For this session, Livingston had done some fast behind-the-scenes work that was equal to the best sidewalk con game in history. Instead of bringing Sinatra to Nelson, he brought Nelson to Sinatra. "I was determined to get Frank together with Nelson Riddle," explains Livingston. Riddle clearly remembered how things came together. "I heard that they put Frank with Billy May, but that Billy was out of town with his band, doing live dates down south. So I went in, and did two sides like Billy May would do 'em ['I Love You' and 'South of the Border'], and two sides like I would do 'em ['I've

Got the World on a String' and 'Don't Worry 'bout Me']."

According to Capitol/EMI producer Alan Dell, everything jelled at the April 30 session. "Frank came in, and saw a strange man on the podium, and said, 'Who's this?' I said, 'He's just conducting the band—we've got Billy May's arrangements.' They went into 'I've Got the World on a String' and he said, 'Hey, who wrote that?' and I said 'This guy—Nelson Riddle.' Frank said 'Beautiful!' and from that, the partnership started," Dell recalled.

It quickly became apparent that Riddle, of all the arrangers the singer had worked with, complemented Sinatra's talents better than anyone else. While in the years to follow Sinatra would rely on Stordahl and Gordon Jenkins for pensive orchestrations that spoke tenderly of love and youth and spring, and on Billy May to sound all the whistles and bells with his full-steam-ahead tempo charts, it was Nelson Riddle and his unflappable temperament that provided an even keel.

With the bold cymbal splash and brass-section stinger opening of the explosive "I've Got the World on a String," the tone was set. It was obvious that the pair was of one musical mind, and that their perspectives would quickly meld into some incredibly tight, polished performances. Riddle, a quiet, unassuming man, suddenly became sought after by dozens of other vocalists, eager to have him duplicate the Sinatra-Riddle "sound" for their own recordings—perhaps the greatest endorsement of the success of their partnership.

COURTESY OF ROSEMARY RIDDLE-ACERRA

(Left to right) Bass trombonist George Roberts, Nelson Riddle, and Christopher Riddle.

THE TEAM

While Riddle had mainly stuck to string-oriented arrangements for his earliest work with Nat Cole (primarily scoring his ballad sessions), he quickly expanded his horizons and began to feature his own favored instrument in his charts for Sinatra. Bass trombonist George Roberts recalls the birth of Riddle's signature style. "I was over his house an awful lot, and we would talk about a lot of things. He said he needed 'identification.' I told him I thought he should use flute, Harmon mute trumpet [tastefully provided by Harry "Sweets" Edison], bass trombone and strings . . . and do something with that combination, which he did. And that was where his 'identification' came from!"

"In planning *Songs for Swingin' Lovers*, Frank commented on 'sustained strings' as part of the background to be used," Riddle once wrote. "Perhaps unconsciously my ear recalled some of the fine arrangements Sy Oliver had written for Tommy Dorsey, using sustained strings, but also employing rhythmic fills by brass and saxes to generate excitement. The strings, by observing crescendos in the right places, add to the pace and tension of such writing without getting in the way. It was a further embroidery on the basic idea to add the bass trombone, plus the unmistakably insinuating fills of Sweets's Harmon-muted trumpet."

Riddle may have been attracted to Roberts's ideas because his own instrument had been the trombone. "I always said that I felt bass trombone was as melodic a horn as any horn there is, and it should be written as a melodic horn," Roberts says. "I thought, 'Wouldn't it be neat to play bass trombone and pretend, within reason, that I'm Urbie Green playing down an octave, and play pretty melodies and things like that?' That's the way it started, really, because I liked Urbie so much. Urbie noticed it, and once said to me, 'God, that's sensational! You're the only guy that plays that like a trombone.' Nelson said to me, 'You must have the heart of an elephant!' but then he wound up writing bass trombone melodically, and I'll be damned if it didn't work for him. He was the only one doing that at the time."

Roberts's melodic solos on "Makin' Whoopee" (*Songs for Swingin' Lovers*, 1956) and "How Deep Is the Ocean?" (*Nice 'n Easy*, 1960) persuasively demonstrate their thinking. "The little jazz piece in the middle of 'Makin' Whoopee' was the first time I had ever played a jazz thing like that, and I was petrified, because I was going to be 'exposed' in the middle of Frank's record. Nelson gave me the part, and I brought it home, and my wife played the piano, and we went over and over it . . . I wanted it to be a really good thing! I was very nervous about that: anytime I had any kind of exposure, especially with someone like Frank, I was paranoid—you know, very excited. Frank so intimidated me, in the sense of style, and the way he sang things, that it almost dictated what I wanted to do as far as playing on bass trombone," Roberts maintains.

On the touching ballad "How Deep Is the Ocean?" the bass trombonist plays as though he were a second vocalist. "I listened to Frank for so long, that I really did want to play my instrument the way he sang," Roberts says. "One of the most important things to me was, and still is to this day, to make the bass trombone important; in a sense, being a vocalist on the horn. I want to have the same kind of charisma that Frank has—what a style that is! That's classy stuff. . . ."

In Harry "Sweets" Edison, Riddle found the musical wit that, for his arrangements, would be the icing on the cake. "Harry has a wonderful sense of humor, both as a musician and as a person," Riddle once commented. "The humor, in a musical sense, is in his head."

In an interview with Stanley Dance, Edison spoke of his work with Riddle and Sinatra. "I met Nelson Riddle in the early 1950s, and in those

Sketch of George Roberts's bass trombone solo on "How Deep Is the Ocean," from Nice 'n Easy, 1960.

days, I was reluctant to go into the studios because when you play studio music and jazz music, it's a different ballgame. [With] jazz, you're on your own when you're out there playing . . . you're playing what you were born to do. I wasn't equipped to do studio work. My reading wasn't that fast," Edison said.

"When you're in the studio, your eyesight has to be good, you have to watch for direction, you have to blend with other musicians. There's so much you have to learn. The fellows [in the studios] were trained to play in studios: guys like Manny Klein, Mickey Mangano, Conrad Gozzo, Conti Candoli, Ray Linn . . . those guys were trained musicians, and I owe a lot of my success in the studios to them because of the experience I had playing with them. Nelson Riddle was the most patient man I've ever been with. I would get to a date a half-hour before, and he took time to show me how things would go. I'd tell Manny Klein, 'Look, this is not "One O'Clock Jump" we're playing. This is something that you're going to have to teach me to play.' And they were absolutely fantastic. I had so much fun playing with Sinatra. It was a compliment to me for him to request me all the time."

So comfortable was Riddle with Edison that he abstained from writing any musical parts out for him; rather, the trumpeter was set apart from the horn section and given his own microphone, and free rein to enhance the mix, wherever and whenever he felt it appropriate. While Edison provided textural support, functioning almost as a rhythm player, the actual rhythm section also helped in shaping the Riddle sound and giving it dimension.

"Many times, there would be little tags at the end of songs, like little bass figures, or percussive accents. Those initially came from Joe Comfort (bass), and Alvin Stoller (drums): they were their own thoughts and contributions to what we were doing. They were very, very effective, and also contributed to the overall humor of the records," Riddle said.

"Joe Comfort had a cuteness about him," remembers guitarist Al Viola. "After the sessions, they'd listen to the playbacks. I was so fascinated by the beautiful harmonies that Nelson wrote that I'd stick around. One night, we were listening to some playbacks, and Nelson looked at Comfort. 'You know what, Little Joe?' he said. 'I write something, and I don't have any idea for an ending, and you do your own thing.' Then he looked at me and Willie Schwartz, and said, 'He does it better than me writing it!' Nelson made sure Joe Comfort did all the dates."

"Joe played that way anyway, with whoever he played with," says reed player Buddy Collette. "Some bass players are pretty straightforward—they play very basically. Joe kept doing those fills on these dates, and Nelson figured that if Joe played that way, he could write that way."

The bass and drum combination that Riddle refers to is especially audible on the tails of the songs on the 1960 album *Sinatra's Swingin' Session!!!* Comfort's neat little bass licks, in concert with Stoller's cymbal accents and afterbeats, lend a whimsical touch to the already happy feel of the arrangements.

The Sinatra-Riddle and Sinatra-May dates owe a great deal to the spontaneity and rhythmic accuracy of the band's drummers, who Sinatra

has acknowledged were critical players on his team. Much of the energy and propulsion of the recordings from this period are generated by Stoller and Irv Cottler, the two mainstays of the Sinatra rhythm section from the early 1950s onward. Both were strongly influenced by Buddy Rich.

"It was an entirely different style, sort of a Jimmy Lunceford two-beat thing," said Stoller, describing his remarkably loose percussive accompaniment. "Drum-wise, with Nelson, the charts were not very exciting . . . there was no meat there. I took it upon myself to make it that way—I would use what was on the chart, and try to be creative with it. I like brushes—they've become a lost art. And I used a regular drum set—as far as the 15 tom-toms and 18 cymbals [of today] go, they weren't my bag. I used a good top cymbal with a pair of hi-hats. Although they were set up, I probably never hit a tom-tom in my life! I usually played on a fairly tight snare drum, to get a sharp sound, which is what those charts really require. I did everything I could when I worked for Frank—I played my heart out. I loved him, and I wanted to make it come off the best it could."

Irv Cottler began playing with Sinatra in late 1955, on the first session for *Songs for Swingin' Lovers*. "I sent Irv to sub for me when my Dad was sick in New York," Alvin Stoller remembered. "When I didn't travel, Irv jumped in because he wanted the job. He was not a technician, but he was well studied. He had his own style. He liked to say that we were the only two drummers of our kind around."

Where Stoller was noted for a looser, big-band beat, Irv Cottler's playing was distinguished by a rock-steady, solid beat that never flagged. "Irv kept that heavy beat that Frank wanted, and he really set it down—he took charge," believes percussionist Frank Flynn. "Boy, when he got behind a band, it was going his way!"

"Irv had a metronomic mind as far as knowing where the beat was," says percussionist Emil

Richards, who recorded and toured with Sinatra and Cottler. "Frank always depended on him. Frank would go into a song, and just bring his hand down, and Irv would take up the tempo. And Irv was right, every time! He would lock into a tempo that he knew Frank wanted, and he wouldn't let go. I don't think there's another drummer that could do what Irv did, as far as knowing the tempo that was gonna make it really cook for Frank."

Cottler was an acerbic individual who had little patience for anyone who even hinted at telling him what to play or how to play it. This caused dissension within Sinatra's touring band of the 1970s and 1980s. "We would do a live show, and the dancers would come in and say, 'Faster! faster! I want it faster!' and Irv would say, 'You tell me where you want it, and I'll put it there and I'll keep it there, but don't tell me to play faster or slower,'" Richards remembers.

Binding the musical team together was pianist Bill Miller. Sinatra had discovered him playing in the lounge of the Desert Inn in Las Vegas in 1951 and had been impressed with his style. He hired him, and after Miller played the last few Columbia Records dates and did nightclub appearances with Sinatra, he followed him to Capitol Records.

In a sense, Miller became to Sinatra in the fifties what Stordahl had been to him in the forties. Although Sinatra was relying more and more on Riddle as his musical stenographer and arranger, the relationship wasn't exclusive, as the Sinatra-Stordahl partnership had been. Instead, Miller became the common thread, rehearsing with Sinatra and working as a close assistant on sessions, no matter who was arranging and conducting.

Miller, more than any other musical figure in Sinatra's life, understood him and the way he worked. Except for a brief falling out in the late 1970s, Miller remained Sinatra's pianist and musical confidant from 1951 to the singer's death in 1998. The superiority of his playing, and the sub-

tle way that he was able to weave his own personal style into that of Sinatra, are credits to this unassuming genius. "Bill was the best pianist," says Emil Richards. "There's no one that can play saloon piano like he does."

Being so close to Sinatra put Miller in the direct line of fire when things weren't going right. "Bill took a lot of flak, always, from Frank," Richards observes. "But his way of getting Frank back would be if he asked for a key, and Miller would hit just one note, Boop, and that would be it—he wouldn't give him any more. He'd just give him the dinkiest little note, as if he were saying, 'Come on, b——, find it! You've had it over me all this time, now I got you!'"

Though the singer had already had a profound impact upon the world of popular music, it took an inventive arranger like Nelson Riddle to provide the musical support Sinatra needed to carry him to a new level of performance. The style that Riddle developed for Frank Sinatra went far beyond what he was doing for Nat Cole, both conceptually and musically. While Riddle's orchestrations for Cole are beautiful, they are bland in comparison to the intricate textures and rhythms he created for Sinatra. But then Cole was far less involved in the minutiae of his recordings and did not spark the arranger's imagination as Sinatra had. "Frank undoubtedly brought out my best work," Riddle told Robin Douglas-Home. "He's stimulating to work with. You have to be right on mettle all the time. The man himself somehow draws everything out of you."

By December 1953, Sinatra had recorded a surefire hit, "Young at Heart," and the future that only a year before had made him virtually suicidal was looking much better. The astonishing richness of high fidelity tape and improved microphone design brought Sinatra's razor sharp diction and fabled phrasing front and center for anyone and everyone to hear. The greater playing time and crystalline sound of the LP allowed the singer, in partnership with Riddle, to fully realize his vision for the thematic concept album—

audibly clear in his first two Capitol 10-inchers, *Songs for Young Lovers* and *Swing Easy*. Sinatra, as well as his essential forum, had arrived.

While his Columbia years bespeak versatility, Sinatra's peak years with Capitol Records reflect quality. Virtually every song the singer recorded at Capitol is a model of perfection, and nowhere is his deft hand more apparent than in the meticulous care he lavished upon his individually crafted theme albums.

Both *Young Lovers* (1953) and *Swing Easy* (1954) were created with the intimacy of small group settings in mind: the former featuring the Hollywood String Quartet plus rhythm and two saxophones performing arrangements by George Siravo; the latter a stringless fourteen-piece brass-and-wind band interpreting new Riddle charts. Each exemplified the fresh sound that was fast becoming associated with the "new" Sinatra; the choice of songs was superb, the arrangements sublime.

Songs for Young Lovers, whose cover was the first to feature Sinatra with his signature lamppost, featured heartfelt ballads such as "My Funny Valentine," "Little Girl Blue," "The Girl Next Door," and "Violets for Your Furs." Although he went uncredited, the album actually relied on the stage arrangements that George Siravo had done for Sinatra. Of the eight orchestrations, Riddle created only one. Clarinetist Mahlon Clark vividly remembered the recording session. "The charts were the ones they had been using on the road," he said. "They were tattered . . . the only one that was new was 'Like Someone in Love.'"

Swing Easy, though, was Nelson's work and reflected his love for the jazz idiom. Many buoyant recordings that stayed with Sinatra for years were born of this album, including "All of Me," "I Get a Kick Out of You," and "Just One of Those Things."

Their next long-play effort, *Wee Small Hours* (1955), was issued on two 10-inch discs (eight songs each); shortly thereafter, they were com-

PHOTOGRAPH BY KEN VEEDER, COURTESY OF MPTV ARCHIVE

Recording "Ill Wind" for the Wee Small Hours *album, 1955.*

bined to create one 12-inch album, and from that point on, 12-inchers were the rule.

This album was really the first concept album to make a single persuasive statement: the program was extended, and the melancholy mood is completely exploited through small group arrangements of "Ill Wind," "Glad to Be Unhappy," "Mood Indigo," "I Get Along Without You Very Well," and the evocative title track, "In the Wee Small Hours of the Morning," a new song written by Dave Mann and Bob Hilliard.

"Bob and I had written the song and happened to be in New York en route to visit a publisher. As we were walking along the street, Bob said, 'Hey, there's Sinatra and Nelson Riddle.' Sure enough, they were walking ahead of us, so we called out to them, and showed them the song. Frank liked it, and asked, 'Is this published yet? We'll use it on the album we're doing right now,'" Mann explained. Since the title begged for it, Capitol requisitioned an artist's rendering of Sinatra, 3 A.M., slouched against . . . you guessed it, a lamppost.

This album may well represent Sinatra's vocal zenith. "What Is This Thing Called Love?" for example, is imbued with the most expressive vocal shading possible. If just one Sinatra ballad album could define both him and an era, I'd choose this as the most likely candidate.

A MUSICAL MARRIAGE

When planning a recording, Sinatra would sit down and make the tune selections himself, then work out the order of the program, carefully controlling its pacing and flow. "First, I decide on the mood for an album, and perhaps pick a title," Sinatra says, describing his routine. "Or sometimes it might be that I had the title, and then picked the mood to fit it. But it's most important that there should be a strong creative idea for the whole package. Like *Only the Lonely*, or *No One Cares*, for instance. Then I get a short list of maybe sixty possible songs, and out of these I pick twelve to record. Next comes the pacing of the album, which is vitally important. I put the titles of the songs on twelve bits of paper, and juggle them around like a jigsaw puzzle until the album is telling a complete story, lyric-wise. For example, the album is in the mood of 'No One Cares'—track one. Why does no one care? Because there's 'A Cottage for Sale'—track two. And so on, until the last track . . . the end of the episode," Sinatra concludes.

Once the songs were chosen, Sinatra selected the arranger best suited for the particular theme.

"Once we choose the songs that will be in a particular album, I'll sit with Bill Miller, my pianist, and find the proper key. Then I will meet with the orchestrator, and give him my thoughts on what I feel the background should be, from either eight measures to eight measures, or four measures to four measures. Should we use woodwinds, or brass, or strings behind the vocal? We discuss it, then I'll ask, 'How wrong am I?' More than likely, he'll say 'You're about 60 percent all right . . . but let me explain how I think it should be done.' Usually, we wind up doing it the way the arranger feels it should be done, because he understands more than I do about it."

Miller, as the singer's primary accompanist and de facto music director, worked closely with both Sinatra and the arranger to insure that the singer's ideas were expressed in the orchestration that awaited him on the day of recording. "I would say that Frank was very accurate in his musical ideas," says Miller of the planning sessions. "Once we picked the keys and sketched out the ideas, it was then up to the arrangers to do their best, and most of them did."

Sinatra spent more time discussing ideas for recording sessions with Nelson Riddle than with anyone else. Riddle, because of his association

COURTESY OF ARCHIVE PHOTOS

Rehearsing with Bill Miller.

with Sinatra from the early years of the Capitol era, was as much responsible for the development of the "concept album" format as anyone.

His and Sinatra's intense pre-studio planning shaped the character of each album as much as the actual sessions themselves.

According to Sinatra, Nelson Riddle was the ultimate musical secretary. "Nelson is the greatest arranger in the world, a very clever musician," Sinatra told Robin Douglas-Home. "He's like a tranquilizer—calm, slightly aloof. There's a great depth somehow to the music he creates. And he's got a sort of stenographer's brain. If I say to him at a planning meeting, 'Make the eighth bar sound like Brahms,' he'll make a cryptic little note on the side of some scrappy music sheet, and, sure enough, when we come to the session, the eighth bar will be Brahms. If I say, 'Make like Puccini,' Nelson will make exactly the same little note, and that eighth bar will be Puccini all right, and the roof will lift off!"

Sinatra's request for classical strains was a natural extension of his fondness for the genre. Among the composers he enjoyed most were Puccini and the Impressionist masters. His all-time favorite, though, was Ralph Vaughan Williams, who he would often listen to late in the evening, on his rare off hours. "He was really interested in good music," recalls Billy May. "We went to the symphony a couple of times with him and his wife, and he astounded me. One night, he was telling me how much he liked Glier, who is more or less an obscure Russian composer who was a contemporary of Rimsky-Korsakov. But Sinatra knew a lot about it."

Riddle, in discussing Sinatra's keen awareness of the classical figures he knew would be of value in particular settings, described to Douglas-Home how he fulfilled the singer's wishes. "There's a song called 'To Love and Be Loved,' and [that was] one song he wanted a Puccini sound behind him on. Well, anybody with half a thorough musical knowledge would immediately know what that was. But I had to go to

COURTESY OF ROSEMARY RIDDLE-ACERRA

Nelson Riddle.

the library and open a Puccini score, because I had studiously avoided operatic music . . . I found that what he meant by a 'Puccini sound' was that the melody is doubled in octaves in the orchestra—and that is what he wanted."

"Frank and I both have, I think, the same musical aim," Riddle once said. "We know what we're each doing with a song—what we want the song to say. Frank would have very definite ideas about the general treatment, particularly about the pace of the record. He'd sketch out something brief, like 'Start with a bass figure, build up second time through and then fade out at the end.' That's possibly all he would say. Sometimes, he'd follow this up with a phone call at three in the morning with some other extra little idea. But after that, he wouldn't hear my arrangements until the recording session."

The strategizing could become tedious. Shortly before his death, Riddle spoke at great length about the pre-session meetings with Sinatra. "In those days, twelve or more songs comprised an album. Frank would start with the most agonizingly specific comments on the first few tunes, often referring to classical compositions for examples of what he expected to hear in the orchestration. This hot, precise, demanding pace would continue for an hour or two, perhaps through the first four or five songs. Then, as if he too were beginning to feel the strain, he would start to slack off. The comments would grow less specific, and perhaps a tune or so later, he would say, simply, 'Do what you think is best.' My headache would start to subside, my pulse return to normal, and another Sinatra-Riddle album would be launched."

Riddle once described his systematic approach to scoring a Sinatra record: "In working out arrangements for Frank, I suppose I stuck to two main rules. First, find the peak of the song and build the whole arrangement to that peak, pacing it as he paces himself vocally. Second, when he's moving, get the hell out of the way. When he's doing nothing, move in fast and establish something. After all, what arranger in the world would try to fight against Sinatra's voice? Give the singer room to breathe. When the singer rests, then there's a chance to write a fill that might be heard.

"Most of our best numbers were in what I call the tempo of the heartbeat. That's the tempo that strikes people easiest because, without their knowing it, they are moving to that pace all their waking hours. Music to me is sex—it's all tied up somehow, and the rhythm of sex is the heartbeat. I usually try to avoid scoring a song with a climax at the end. Better to build about two-thirds of the way through, and then fade to a surprise ending. More subtle. I don't really like to finish by blowing and beating in top gear."

Christopher Riddle, Nelson's son and a fellow trombonist, recalls a heated argument between his parents, in which his mother accused Nelson of having only two things on his mind: music and sex. "The next day, I asked my father about it. He looked at me with a twinkle in his eye, and said, 'After all, what else is there?' Music and sex. That was like a window into the man's insides—that was him."

The quiet, dry-witted Riddle was occasionally plagued by a feeling of inadequacy. Even as he enjoyed a reputation as one of the most sought-after arrangers in history, he privately stewed, feeling he'd been cheated out of true success. "Nelson really thought that he should have accomplished more on the order of Henry Mancini," says Milt Bernhart. "Nelson composed, but he didn't have the huge hits that Mancini had. I think that affected his outlook some."

One of the driving forces motivating the arranger in the early years was his first wife and mother of his children, Doreen. "My Mom and Dad were just a real powerful combination in those early years," explains Rosemary Riddle-Acerra. "I know that my Mom wanted so much for my Dad, and encouraged him to be certain places, and make the connections that he did. She was such a powerful part of that." After twenty-three years of marriage, though, the pair split. "They really had such a strong relationship, and when you struggle so much for success together, it unifies you. Then, when the success is reached, sometimes there's not a lot of glue to keep the relationship stuck together when there are other things eating away at it."

"I think his music was a strong outlet for my Dad's sense of humor. Julie Andrews used to call him 'Eeyore,' because she always felt he had this sadness, this somberness about him. But his music was a whimsical kind of way for him to communicate his humor. He would almost hold back, in terms of dealing with people, and blowing his own horn. But music was a safe outlet for all this, and it was where he felt safe. Through his music, he could communicate the freedom he didn't have in relationships, or in real life."

Riddle worked quickly, and usually—because of the demand for his work on records, in films, and on television—under tremendous pressure. A beautiful, glass-enclosed gazebo of Oriental design (located behind his home at 3853 Carbon Canyon Road) with a million-dollar view of the Malibu surf served as the setting for Riddle's painstaking orchestrations of the some of the best-loved recordings in the history of popular music.

"Dad was very businesslike about his work," says Chris Riddle. "His pencils, Eberhard-Faber Blackwing #602s, were laid out, and he always had an electric pencil sharpener at hand. He was very organized. He had stacks of long score paper, which a special place over on Highland would make up for him, with his name printed at the bottom. There was a Steinway out there, and a record player. . . . He had this table that was like an artist's table, that he liked to work at. The gazebo was a big room, enclosed with thick plate glass windows, and the view of the ocean was framed by eucalyptus trees—it was gorgeous!"

As a child, Rosemary would watch her father work as she played in the garden. "That's a strong memory for me," she says. "I would see him jotting down the notes on that long, yellow manuscript paper. . . . He loved the Pacific Ocean—he was a daily swimmer for years there. The fact that the ocean was right there was an intense connection for him, that kind of solitude was important for him. During the crazier times, when he was really deadlining it, he would work late into the night."

"My rather long-winded treatise of vocal lines and lyrics, and transposition all comes to life if I develop the habit of 'sketching' before I score," Riddle noted. "In the busy days at Capitol Records, I was hard-pressed to find time to write the arrangement itself, let alone sketch first . . . I considered it laborious, and, in a way, repetitive.

Sometimes I sit at the piano to find what I'm looking for—sometimes I can hear it."

"The best things that you get are the ones you don't need to fiddle for. Sometimes you can fill them out by using the piano, but as far as melodies or introductions are concerned, the ones that you hear in your head seem to have the most continuity and are the most appropriate for whatever you're doing. It all starts from there. When you're stuck trying to find something on the piano, it's a lot of wasted time, and the danger is that you won't have the fresh spontaneous sound that it would jumping out of your head. But, I work from the piano, which is a form of a crutch. In truth, I can really hear the instruments in my head. I almost do as well if I have a table near the piano, where I can look at the keys. To look at them gives me the feel of it. And yes, you can hear the orchestra."

Although an arranger would be provided with a lead sheet, or perhaps a demo recording of a particular song, it was necessary to be resourceful when orchestrating the instrumental bed, especially if the song was popular and had already taken on an identity for listeners. Riddle avoided repetition and "familiar" music lines in favor of his own clever melodies and counter-melodies.

"I would do that for several reasons," he explained. "You have the first say in an arrangement, because most singers require an introduction, so you have the first say as far as setting the mood. If you can find something within that introduction that has mileage in it, you can use it in certain breaks in the melody later on. That keeps it interesting. Also, it gives the overall orchestration a subtle cohesiveness which nevertheless is felt, so it seems to be a particular arrangement written especially for this song, whatever the song is. It keeps you occupied, it keeps you interested in what you do. Even so, when you are writing under pressure and have to move fast for whatever reason, you tend to reach toward tricks that are tried and true. They can either ruin your work because of the triteness, or they can add to your signature," he said.

Sinatra understood and appreciated Riddle's genius. "Though Frank never really learned how to read music, much less play an instrument, he is a man attracted to all the arts, especially classical music. When writing arrangements for him, I could often indulge myself in flights of neo-classical imagery, especially in introductions and endings. If he feels I have caught the right mood in the introduction I have written, he is quick to acknowledge it."

Riddle was a master at creating inspired musical fills that floated buoyantly atop a soft bed of feathery-light sustained strings, deftly arranged to contrast with Sinatra's vocal lines. His charts are packed with complex rhythms and subtle melodic motifs which, bit by bit, create a strong underpinning that expertly accentuates and supports a vocal line. Comfortable with nearly any tempo or style, Riddle had a knack for painting backdrops that were richly layered in texture and tone, cushioned enough to allow plenty of room for Sinatra to toy with the rhythm of the lyric, yet distinct enough melodically to stand on their own. His orchestrations were infused with fine gradations of color and strong, purposeful instrumentation.

"Many of the effects and colors I used are obtained by superimposing one instrument on another, or one section over another section," Riddle wrote in his book on arranging. For example, he often paired alto flute with English horn. "The effect achieved is quite unusual, since it combines the 'honeyed' roundness of the English horn with the velvety softness of the flute." He also favored the alto flute-muted horn combination. "Four alto flutes and four muted horns are an exquisite sound: soft, yet full, with the quality of cool, veiled mystery." Many of the swing arrangements he made for Sinatra used a blend of four trombones against a baritone saxophone: "It has a richness and appeal that provides welcome relief from five saxes and four trombones playing as a section."

A session of "active listening," where the listener tunes out the most apparent melodic/vocal line and focuses on the underlying sub-melodies and rhythms, helps to show how Riddle achieved his musical surprises. Often he would fold contrapuntal rhythms and snippets of the primary melody into the framework of the chart, which, when skillfully blended into the whole of the arrangement, become almost invisible behind the vocalist and primary instrumental lines. Individual instruments from within a particular section (woodwinds, for example) are first voiced individually, their melodic phrases then repeated and stacked together to achieve a thick underlying base that provides body and strength to the overall melodic structure.

"In a sense, arranging is a similar exercise to 'Theme and Variation,'" Riddle said. "The arranger is given the basic melody, and his ingenuity and skill combine to form an arrangement of the melody. He can slide any number of different backgrounds and treatments under this original melody, as long as he does not hide it or disfigure it with inappropriate or uncomfortable harmonies. Passing tones are used to give a feeling of flowing motion; these passing tones should be most active when the melody is least active."

Two such accomplished musicians as Riddle and Sinatra needed a little time to adjust to each other. Milt Bernhart once recounted a record date shortly after Sinatra and Riddle began working together. "They were going to do an album, so we came into Capitol, and I remember clearly that the first arrangement was for 'Wrap Your Troubles in Dreams.' It was just a jazz band: brass, sax, rhythm—no strings. Sinatra was at his lead sheet—I don't think we'd even made a take yet. He was running the song over, and suddenly stopped—cold. And the band stopped. Frank said. 'Give them a break.' He crooked his finger at Nelson, and they walked out of the studio. I recognized that the arrangement hadn't gone over at all. Most of the guys began to play poker; I don't know why, but I followed them, and watched them in the smaller studio, from the hallway."

"Nelson was standing frozen, and Frank was doing all the talking. His hands were moving, but he was not angry . . . he seemed to be telling him something of great importance. He was gesticulating, his hands going up and down and sideways. He was describing music, and singing! When we came back, the date was over. And I was positive that I knew what Frank was telling him— it was about the arrangement! I could tell it was very busy. Too busy. There was no room for the singer. If they had taken away the singer, it would have made a great instrumental. The voicings for saxophone were Duke Ellington. Everything about the way the band played was like Duke Ellington, in fact. I was surprised, because at that point, I didn't know much about how Nelson Riddle wrote, but I could tell then who his idol was. Would you know that now, even? That he was influenced by Ellington? He stopped—he may have stopped right then, on the spot. At that point, Nelson had a lot of technique as an arranger, but

he had to be told to take it easy when writing for a singer. And he was told! Frank was giving him a lesson: a lesson in writing for a singer. A lesson in writing for Frank Sinatra."

Buddy Colette, one of Hollywood's finest reed and woodwind players, began working with Riddle at the same time Sinatra joined Capitol. "Nelson really had the knack, he knew what Sinatra wanted. He wrote differently for Frank than he did for Nat Cole. He found Frank's groove. Nat could swing no matter what. Sinatra liked to swing, but you could see that his body would need something—he needed a little kick. He'd be popping his fingers and asking, 'Can we get the brass to kick a little here?' He was always looking for that, and it was easy for Nels once he knew what the swing patterns were, and as long as he just stayed out of the way and got those little fills. A lot of people, depending upon how they sing, may not need the fills. But Frank sometimes clipped the words, and what Nelson was doing with the band was perfect for that: he bounced off of the phrases. Frank was a swinging type singer, and this was a whole different artform that they were creating."

PHOTOGRAPH BY KEN VEEDER, COURTESY OF MPTV ARCHIVE

PHOTOGRAPH BY KEN VEEDER, COURTESY OF MPTV ARCHIVE

DYNAMIC DUO

*D*uring the Capitol period Sinatra began to take more noticeable liberties with the rhythm and timing of his vocal lines. "I've always believed that the written word is first, always first," Sinatra once said. "Not belittling the music behind me, it's really only a curtain . . . you must look at the lyric, and understand it. Find out where you want to accent something, where you want to use a soft tone. The word actually dictates to you in a song—it really tells you what it needs. I figure speech is the same way. Syncopation in music is important, of course, particularly if it's a rhythm song. It can't be 'one-two-three-four/one-two-three-four,' because it becomes stodgy. So, syncopation enters the scene, and it's 'one-two,' then maybe a little delay, and then 'three,' and then another longer delay, and then 'four.' It all has to do with delivery."

The "heartbeat" meter previously described by Riddle, in combination with Sinatra's just-ahead-of or just-behind-the-beat syncopation, is the crux of their musicianship, and the most important element of the singer's post-war signature. The 1956 versions of "Night and Day," "Oh! Look at Me Now," and "From This Moment On" (among dozens of other examples) reveal powerful sexual overtones, stunningly achieved through the mounting tension and release of Sinatra's beat-teasing vocal lines.

A recording that neatly demonstrates Riddle's skill as a crack tempo arranger and Sinatra's brilliance as a syncopational improviser is "River, Stay 'Way From My Door," from April 1960. While the song itself lacks the sophistication and urbanity of "I've Got You Under My Skin," it has more raw firepower: where "Skin" cooks under the tightest of control, "River" is wide open. This is prime Sinatra, playing fast and loose. The performance is pure hard-driven swing.

The chart begins with a gentle but decisive tempo, which it maintains throughout the first part of the song. From chorus to chorus, though, intensity builds as the brass section soars, climaxing at so fierce a level that on the last chorus, the drummer sounds as if he is standing on the balls of his feet, battering the skins of his kit, punctuating every beat in exact ¼ time, with deliberate, pounding force. By the song's end, Sinatra, sparring with the band, sounds like he's lunging at the microphone, as if to shout in admonishment, "Yeaahhh . . . There. Take *that!*" It is one of the few times that the singer pushed his microphone to its technical limit. The strain on the instrument is clearly audible at the end, when he sings the line "don't you start breaking my heart/river, stay away from the door . . . " amid the frenzied climax of the orchestra. (The singer was obviously taxing himself as well; his final emphasis on the word *heart*, just before the out-chorus, sounds as though he's nearly run out of breath.)

The listener's excitement and anticipation of a big, fat, wailing ending rises with the tempo, which seems to build and build. In fact, though, the pacing of the song hasn't changed a bit. While it appears as though the song has modulated from a medium-slow to a fast tempo, it never once wavers from the prescribed "heartbeat" meter.

Riddle crafts the musical dynamics so adroitly that the illusion of a change in tempo becomes an integral part of the performance. While most of Sinatra's tunes of the era climaxed two-thirds of the way through, the most dramatic impact here occurs at the song's ending, when Riddle suddenly drops the orchestra way down, and then, in concert with Sinatra's vocal, executes a gradual, controlled crescendo, the orchestra quickly returning to full volume, and holding it to the finish.

The arranger, in his textbook *Arranged by Nelson Riddle*, described the importance of building dynamics into the orchestration: "Dynamic shadings are a vital part of presenting music effectively. Some of the most effective crescendos I ever incorporated into my arrangements were not achieved by writing dynamic markings or exhorting an orchestra to observe my flailing arm motions. They were accomplished by gradually adding orchestral weight until the desired peak was reached. The same can be said for diminuendo, in which case the orchestra is progressively thinned out until a *ppp* (very piano, or softly) is accomplished. True dynamics [changes in loudness] in an orchestra are achieved beautifully and naturally by a combination of orchestral textures and lines. When 'peaks and valleys' occur under these conditions, they sound so logical and effortless as to appear perfectly natural, which they are." Nothing makes an orchestration as attractive as the contrasts achieved by close attention to sensible dynamics.

"Frank accentuated my awareness of dynamics by exhibiting his own sensitivity in that direction. It's one thing to indicate by dynamic markings (*p*, *mp*, *mf*, and so forth), how you want to have the orchestra play your music. It's quite another to induce a group of blasé, battle-scarred musicians to observe those markings and play accordingly. I would try, by word and gesture, to get them to play correctly, but if, after a few times through, the orchestra still had not observed the proper dynamics, Frank would suddenly turn and draw from them the most exquisite shadings, using the most effective means yet discovered: sheer intimidation!"

Jazz guitarist George Van Eps, inventor of the seven-string guitar, was one of the hundreds of top-flight players who were impressed with

PHOTOGRAPH BY BOB WILLOUGHBY, COURTESY OF MPTV ARCHIVE

Sinatra's sensitivity toward the musicians when it came to instrumental interpretation at recording sessions. "We were recording 'Last Night When We Were Young' for the *In the Wee Small Hours* album," Van Eps recalls. "The coda was mainly strings and horns—very low key—and there was a very short guitar solo in the mid-guitar range, which is the baritone range. The phrase was a total of six notes, written as quarter and eighth notes. We rehearsed the arrangement, and Frank sang along with it. When we were finished, Frank noted that there was something wrong with the coda. So he came over to me very slowly (he had to carefully climb over other musicians), and he just said 'I'm gonna tell Nelson that the guitar solo should be played slower, but I wanted to tell you first so you can prepare for it.' Then he went back to the podium, and told Nelson that he'd like the guitar solo to be played much slower. Frank had respect for Nelson—he didn't go over his head. He asked him first, but he warned me also, which is fair at both ends. So Nelson called over to me, 'George, we're going to slow the solo way down. You take your time with it, and then I'll follow you.' So I played the solo in half-time; it was much more relaxed, very laid back. That was good musicianship, and it was Frank's idea. Frank was loaded with things like that."

"'Last Night When We Were Young' was a particularly difficult recording," Nelson Riddle once told radio personality Jonathan Schwartz. "I think we did about thirty takes—partly my fault. I learned a lot from Frank about conducting for a vocalist . . . but I was still very much in the learning process then. He was extremely patient with me, and we went through it thirty times. Not all my fault, but at least half. And, in those days, he had voice to burn, obviously."

"With Nelson's arrangements, you wouldn't need to use any amplification of the guitar at the sessions," explains Van Eps. "For Sinatra dates, I used a 'Gretsch George Van Eps' model seven-string guitar. It's a better rhythm instrument, and rhythm doesn't sound the same on an electric guitar. He also had a different way of writing for guitar: I did two albums with Axel Stordahl, and Axel used the guitar more as the primary instrument in the rhythm section. The guitar didn't take the place of the drums—but it added a tonality or sonority to the sound of the rhythm section where the guitar is played gently. Nelson had the same respect for the sound of the rhythm section, except that very often Nelson would double the guitar with the cello, which created a very subtle sound, because the cellos outnumbered the guitar. There were always two or three violoncellos in Nelson's orchestra, and one guitar doesn't have a chance! But it added a temper to the tone which was slightly different. That was the type of thing that made Nelson very individual."

John Palladino, the Capitol mixing engineer who worked all of Sinatra's Melrose Avenue dates, points out that an arranger who understood the technical side of recording could keep things flowing smoothly on a record date. "Nelson understood recording, so if you told him, 'I can't control this . . . ,' he would know exactly how to correct it within the orchestration. Nelson had it down pat, so that by the time of the session, it was completely worked out. He would have already made arrangements that considered the technical pitfalls of recording."

In his textbook, the arranger cautions students on the importance of understanding how various instruments will sound in different acoustic settings. "The violin has a tendency to 'thin out' as it climbs, which means that the upper notes, to be effective, must be reserved for the large string section. To write a C above high C for the violins of a six-violin section is quite foolish since the note, even if played in tune by all six, is thin and ineffective. Such heights should be reserved for sections including at least eight violins, more if possible. If you are writing an arrangement for a recording session, a skillful engineer can place the string mike in a position that will ensure a warm, intense C above high C, even though the violins may number as few as the eight I mentioned."

The situation changes when the performance takes place in a less controlled environment (a TV studio or outdoors, for example), and in these instances, the appropriate adjustments to the orchestration would be made.

Sinatra too was mindful of such details. He had learned that strings sound better when played in a sharp key, and thereafter insisted that his string parts be scored accordingly. "Strings sound more brilliant in sharp keys," explains Bill Miller. "If there was a choice between playing strings in B-flat as opposed to B-natural, the B-natural would be better sounding."

While Sinatra was notorious for his opposition to doing repeated takes on a movie set (he felt it robbed the scene of freshness and believability), in the recording studio, he would spend whatever time was necessary to arrive at what he felt was his finest effort. "With Sinatra, it was unusual that he would have to go past four or five takes," says Milt Bernhart. "But I remember he was being careful, very careful, at that time. This man had instinct. He knew what was going to be important."

It took twenty-two takes of Cole Porter's "I've Got You Under My Skin" to satisfy the singer. Sublimely erotic, this recording is the turning point in the Sinatra-Riddle epoch, the pivot on which all future Sinatra efforts would hinge. Ironically, it almost never came to pass, as it was added to the list of tunes for the *Songs for Swingin' Lovers* album shortly before the session at which it was recorded. In the forty-plus years since its waxing, the recording has become one of the most studied and admired Sinatra performances of all time.

"When we ran the arrangement down the first time, the band played it like they had played it many times before, and when they were through, they applauded Nelson, probably because somebody knew that he wrote it in a hurry," recalls Bill Miller. In speaking with Jonathan Schwartz, Riddle recalled the circumstances. "I was living in Malibu, and it was apparently done under pressure, because I had to stay up quite late to finish it."

To breathe new life into the tune, Riddle enlisted bass trombonist George Roberts to help him devise an intriguing musical passage that would lead up to the song's "bridge," the instrumental middle of a song that all the tension builds to before releasing. "Nelson called me up, and said, 'Frank wants a long crescendo for the middle of "Skin." Do you know any Afro-Cuban rhythmical patterns . . .?' And I said, 'Well, why don't you steal the rhythmic pattern out of Stan Kenton's "23 Degrees North, 82 Degrees West?" He said, 'How does it go?' And I gave him the beginning trombone lines, the Afro-Cuban-sounding thing, which he developed into the 'bop-bop/bom-bom/bom-bom-bom-ba-bop' crescendo that led up to the trombone solo."

"I left the best stuff I played on the first five takes," believes Bernhart, the man responsible for the blistering trombone solo that absolutely blew the top off the record. "It was a spontaneous solo.

COURTESY OF MILT BERNHART

Sketch of Milt Bernhart's trombone solo on "I've Got You Under My Skin" from Songs for Swingin' Lovers, 1956.

As with many of Nelson's charts where there was room for a solo, there were chord symbols sketched out in the chart—but nothing was written out." "Frank kept saying, 'Let's do another.' This was unusual for Sinatra! I was about ready to collapse—I was running out of gas! Then, toward the tenth take or so, someone in the booth said, 'We didn't get enough bass . . . could we get the trombone nearer to a microphone?' I mean, what had they been doing? There was a mike there for the brass, up on a very high riser. 'Can you get up to that one?' they asked. And I said, 'Well, no—I'm not that tall.' So they went looking for a box, and I don't know where he found one, but none other than Frank Sinatra went and got a box, and brought it over for me to stand on!

"After the session, I was packing up, Frank stuck his head out of the booth, and said, 'Why don't you come in the booth and listen to it?' So I did—and there was a chick in there, a pretty blond, and she was positively beaming. He said to me, 'Listen!' That was special! You know, it never really went past that. He never has been much for slathering around empty praise. He just doesn't throw it around very easily. If you weren't able to play like that, then why would they have called you? You knew that you were there—we all were there—at Frank's behest. Rarely, if ever, would he directly point something out in the studio."

On one session, Bernhart recalls, French horn player Vince DeRosa executed an extremely difficult musical passage. "We came in to do a date on the next night, and Frank said something to the band like 'I wish you guys could have heard Vince DeRosa last night,' and then, typically Sinatra, he added, 'I could have hit him in the mouth!' We all knew what he meant—he had loved it! And believe me, he reserved comments like that only for special occasions. You see, it was very hard for him to say, 'It was the greatest thing I ever heard . . . ,' But that's Sinatra. He could sing with the grace of a poet, but when he's talking to you, it's Jersey!"

Songs for Swingin' Lovers and its follow-up, *A Swingin' Affair!* (both from 1956) brought the Sinatra-Riddle style to its zenith and remain the defining moments of the Capitol era. Replete with cream-of-the-crop standards, each retains an irresistible swing feel. More importantly, they solidify Sinatra's image as a "swinger," from both a musical and visual standpoint.

"Sinatra was influenced a lot by Sammy Davis," believes Buddy Collette. "A lot! Sinatra was intrigued 'cause Sammy could swing anybody to death. Sammy was very influential as far as clipping the notes, popping the fingers, and making sure the thing had a groove. I know that from the early 1950s when I started working with

Frank, to ten or fifteen years later, he was a different Sinatra in the way he approached a song."

THE HOTTEST TICKET IN TOWN

The anticipation of Sinatra's record dates would often lead the top musicians in Hollywood to cancel other film, television, and recording engagements to accommodate his schedule. Sometimes they'd even break the law to get there on time.

"Harry Edison showed up at a Sinatra date once with a policeman on each arm," Nelson Riddle remembered. "He'd run several red lights, and the cops nailed him. When they asked, 'What's all the speed, Mr. Edison?' he said, 'I'm on my way to a Sinatra recording date.' 'Sure you are.' So Harry said, 'All right, come with me, and I'll show you.' And the three of them marched into the recording session, and there was Frank and everyone else. So they released him, laughed, and walked away!"

As with many other highly creative individuals, life in the recording studio with Frank Sinatra could at times be trying. Nelson Riddle once confided to George Roberts, "There's only one person in this world I'm afraid of. Not physically—but afraid of nonetheless. It's Frank, because you can't tell what he's going to do. One minute he'll be fine, but he can change very fast," he said. Roberts vividly recalls their conversation. "Nelson told me the reason he was so paranoid when we went to do a Sinatra date was because he (Nelson) wanted a performance the first time.

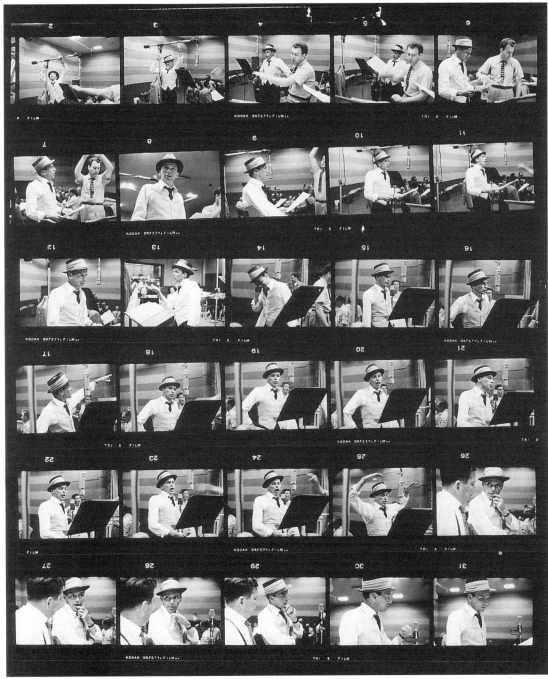

In the studio, Sinatra is like a caged rabbit, relentlessly pushing for perfection. Whether adjusting the mike stand, directing the orchestra, or singing his heart out, he afforded unprecedented attention to the proceedings at hand.

He said, 'I want it right—now.' He didn't want to give Frank the chance to say, 'I don't like the chart.' Nelson really did feel a lot of pressure."

Publicly Riddle offered these observations. "At a Sinatra session, the air was usually loaded with electricity. The thoughts that raced through my head were hardly ones to calm the nerves. On the contrary, questions such as 'Will he like the arrangements?' and 'Is the tempo comfortable for him?' were soon answered. If he didn't make any reference to the arrangement, chances are it was acceptable. And as far as the tempo was concerned, he often set that with a crisp snap of his fingers, or a characteristic hunching of the shoulders."

"Frank contributed a lot to the orchestral part of his own records, just by leveling a hostile stare at the musicians, with those magnetic blue eyes! The point of this action was to make me, or any other conductor, feel at that exact moment as if he had two left feet, three ears, and one eye. But it was a positive factor that found its way into the record. And that, I ruefully admit, is what counts."

"We knew when the 'Old Man' was pushing us," says Al Viola. "If we didn't play, he'd look around and say, 'Push it!' or he'd make a statement like, 'Don't lay back.'"

Alvin Stoller remembered one of the few studio sessions at which Sinatra became irritated as he struggled to create a musical sound for which he had a mental blueprint. "We didn't quite hit it off, this one time," he recalled. "Frank had an idea—he wanted something [percussively] that I didn't want to do, and I said, 'No, I'm not gonna do that, it's not me—it doesn't fit.' The rhythm section was too conflicting . . . one part was playing it a certain way, kind of old-fashioned, and he wanted one microphone set up with the guitar, bass, and drums sitting all around it, to get a certain sound—and it wasn't working. He suddenly had this strange kick he was on . . . we could go in like we always did in Studio A at Capitol, and set up and record, and he didn't like it. So, we'd

have to tear the studio down, and move everything over to the next room, and see if that would make him happy. They did everything they could to make him happy—they were kind of afraid of him. But he's like Tommy [Dorsey]—very demanding. In a sense, he knew what would 'show him off' best [musically], and they would tear everything down and accommodate him. But he had proven himself to Capitol, and that had a lot to do with it."

Ray Breem, a Los Angeles radio talk-show host and music enthusiast, was at the final session for the *Come Fly with Me* album, in October of 1957. "Stereo was just coming into play for recording," he remembers. "And Sinatra did a couple of takes of the song 'Brazil.' Now, after the second take, he grabs his jacket, and starts to walk out the door. But the engineers had a problem—possibly a balance problem—and they told him from the booth that they'd like to get another take to be safe. And he refused! And they went back and forth for a few minutes, the producer, Sinatra and the engineers, and he finally sputtered and said 'Whatever you've got is all you're gonna get 'cause I'm leaving!' and he was out the door. They never got another take, as far as I know."

"Frank had the right attitude," says Buddy Collette. "There were times when he couldn't pull it off . . . maybe he'd been hanging out too much. But he knew right away! He also knew when something was right. Sometimes he'd be doing two or three tunes on the date, and on the last tune he'd do one take, and as soon as he finished say, 'Good night—I'll see ya!' He had somewhere to go. And we'd be like, 'Should he hear the take?' But you see, he didn't have to hear it: he knew that was the take, like a guy throwing a basket with his back turned. There were times when he knew that he had it, and he didn't have to listen. We'd all be baffled, and we would have to listen . . . but if he said, 'That's it,' you wouldn't hear a bad note in there."

The critical and financial success of his Capitol recordings definitely afforded Sinatra certain luxuries. George Van Eps remembers an evening in February 1955, as the musicians and technicians assembled for one of the 1955's *In the Wee Small Hours* recording sessions. "We were to record with a quartet that evening [Van Eps, guitar; Bill Miller, piano; Phil Stephens, bass; and Alvin Stoller, drums]. Now picture this: Sinatra comes in, and he's got a felt hat on the back of his head, which was his trademark at the time. We were all set. Frank sang a few notes, stopped, then said, 'Good Night, fellas . . . I'll see you tomorrow night.' Walked out the door! We all got paid. Sinatra left because he felt he didn't have the right sound, his voice was not good that night. He came back the next night, and it was perfect. He was very picky about what he did."

Few recording companies would bear the expense of a full orchestral session that was thrown away because the vocalist showed up and then decided he wasn't up for the play. For Sinatra, however, they made an exception.

In 1956, the Los Angeles Musician's Local 247 scale was $41.25 for each musician for a three-hour session, as well as for the contractor, who was responsible for scheduling each of the players. The conductor earned $82.50 (double scale) for a three-hour session, and an arranger on the order of Nelson Riddle received approximately $525 per orchestration. The copyist, who methodically wrote out each individual instrumental part on score paper, was paid $303.70. If the session went into overtime, the musicians received double the union scale for the entire session. Using these figures as a guide, an average Frank Sinatra date in 1956 featuring a 35-piece orchestra with no overtime would cost approximately $4,000 in musician's fees, plus whatever costs the record company expended in overhead such as producer salaries, studio time, materials, engineering, security—at least another $1,500 per night. (Sinatra's advance in 1956 was 10 percent; at $3,000 per song, the singer received a $300 advance, of which $30 was taken by his agent as commission.)

During the 1940s and 1950s, labels routinely employed "house" producers: A&R men whose function was to direct the recording careers of the artists signed to the label. Usually, the producer would find appropriate material for each of his artists and bring it to their attention. When a recording date was scheduled, it was the producer's responsibility to coordinate and supervise the session: booking studio time, notifying the arranger, making sure the contractor had the required musicians on call. At the session, he would direct the proceedings, working with the artist and engineering staff to achieve the best recorded performance possible, making suggestions and asking for retakes when necessary. Later, the producer would make reference cuts for artist review, and ultimately approve the final master. Unlike Sinatra, many artists relinquished creative control to their producer, whose word was considered gospel.

With producer Voyle Gilmore, April 1953.

Sinatra enjoyed the service of three staff producers while at Capitol: Voyle Gilmore, Dave Cavanaugh, and Dave Dexter. These A&R men had even less of a real hand in "producing" than had Palitz, Higgins, Richards, and Sacks at Columbia.

Gilmore, from all accounts a gentle and knowledgeable recording director, basically just helped keep things running smoothly. The paternal producer worked well with Sinatra, yet he was not the first choice when the singer joined the label in 1953. Originally, Dexter was slated, but because he had written an unkind review of a Sinatra performance in a music publication years before, the singer vetoed him. Sinatra and Dexter never saw eye to eye. Cavanaugh, who began to take over the direction of Sinatra sessions in the late 1950s, was a musician involved in all facets of the recording industry: player, arranger, producer. Although Sinatra still controlled the proceedings, he viewed Cavanaugh as a friendly ally.

MY BUDDY

*W*hile there is no doubt the singer held the musicians who performed so dependably for him in high esteem, he rarely socialized with them outside of the studio setting. Even though he seemed quite at ease with them, Sinatra's personal relationships with musicians were complex. On the one hand, he respected and appreciated their talents and understood their importance to his career. On the other hand, there must have been some subconscious desire on his part to keep them at arm's length, perhaps to insure that they would remain

in awe of him. Maybe Sinatra feared that the old adage, "Familiarity breeds contempt," might just come back at some point to bite him. With few exceptions, chumminess with his supporting players was usually limited to his graciousness and cordiality in the performance setting.

"Once in a while, he did invite the musicians over to the Villa Capri restaurant after a record date. Even there he almost never made the rounds of the room, staying at his table in the back. We would approach him and say 'thanks,' and he'd beam, and that was that," remembers Milt Bernhart. Chris Riddle, then a youngster, remembers being with his dad and carousing with Sinatra and friends after a studio session. "Sometimes, after the [Sinatra] dates were over, they'd pile into their cars, and run over to the Villa Capri. If Patsy [D'Amore, the owner] was in bed, Frank would call him and tell him, 'Go down and open the place up!' They'd have a party, to kind of celebrate the fact that they'd just done classic stuff, the likes of which would never be recorded again, I suppose. One night, I got Frank to give me a ride over [to the restaurant] in his new car, a Dual Ghia."

On occasion, after a special session, Sinatra might throw an "in-studio" party for the technicians and the members of the orchestra. "After he finished A Jolly Christmas in July of 1957, he threw a huge Christmas party for everyone," recalls Sinatra pal Frank Military. "It was incredible—catered food, drinks, everything. It was really something to see—Christmas in July! Everyone appreciated it. . . .Those were very special days. Frank had an office down the hall from Danny Kaye, and every night, there'd be some sort of party going on there—Sammy [Cahn] and Jule [Styne] would drop by; all kinds of stars would be coming in and out. It was absolutely amazing."

Milt Bernhart recollects a gathering of musicians that took place in the mid 1950s at Sinatra's home off Coldwater Canyon. "We entered the house, and sitting in the outer room were three or four very important Hollywood people: Lauren Bacall, Adolph Green, Bill and Edie Goetz. In the main living room were some musicians: me, Murray McEachern . . . about twenty of us. I felt a bit funny, because Frank spent several hours with us, completely ignoring his other guests! And they were terribly aware of it, because one by one, they left. But this was his day with us, and I got the feeling that he enjoyed it—that it gave him a kick, making them wait. Only Sinatra would do that! At one point, we were on the patio, and he was going from person to person, asking them, 'What can I get you?' And I said to him, 'I can't believe this is happening. I may wake up!' He enjoyed that, and said, 'Why? What's the matter? Whaddya mean?' 'Well,' I said. 'You didn't have to do any of this.' He chuckled, and said, 'Don't tell me what I didn't have to do!'"

Buddy Collette remembers another evening at Sinatra's home, where the celebrity guests included Robert Mitchum. "I knew that Frank liked me, because he had given an interview to *Melody Maker* magazine in London one time, and he named six jazz people he liked, and I was one of them. . . . During dinner that night at his home, he played my album *Calm, Cool and Collette* all during dinner. Another time, we were on a plane going somewhere, and Frank had a portable record player with him. I was sitting behind him, and he was playing a 45, which happened to be a song that I wrote called 'Monorail.' I heard it, and I looked over to see whose record it was. Frank said, 'I know what you're doing!' and he picked the thing up and walked away. He had a good sense of humor."

Sinatra's keen memory for names and faces was legendary. Chris Griffin, one of the key brass players on many New York Columbia sessions, told Sinatra biographer Will Friedwald a funny story about the singer's recall, in which the singer remembered him years after their last session together. "He spotted me sitting there at a rehearsal one day, and said, 'Hi Chris!' I couldn't believe that he not only recognized me, but remembered my name. Later, Frank remarked to the other guys, 'Isn't it nice that Chris remembered me after all these years?' "

Buddy Collette also enjoyed special recognition. "Everybody would be waiting for him; he'd come in to the session, and look around the room. He had this look where if he smiled, he would brighten up a room. Inevitably, he'd happen to see me. Now, I wouldn't be trying to wave or anything, and he'd say 'Hi Bud!' The other guys would say, 'Why does he speak to you?' I told them 'I don't know!' You see, I was one of those guys that never tried to push my weight around, or even say 'Hi Frank, remember me . . . ' Sometimes he'd be having trouble with his voice, and when he went into the booth to listen to the take, he would joke with me. 'Bud,' he'd say. 'I may need a reed, so get me one out!' At the *L.A. Is My Lady* session [1984]. I said, 'Frank, if you need a reed, I got plenty!' He just smiled," Collette remembers.

Eleanor Slatkin, who, along with her husband Felix, shared considerable social time with the singer, remembered "Frank was an unbelievable host. We were having dinner at his home one evening, and he had a gallery of paintings facing the dining room table—it was like a hallway. And I looked up, and said, 'Oh my God—that clown is absolutely incredible!' I went bananas over this painting, which he had done himself. When we left, it was in my car—he gave it to me! I have loved it for over forty years. Another night, Frank came to our house for dinner, and I couldn't get my sons to go to bed—you know, they were so excited. So Frank went upstairs, and sang to Leonard and Fred, and put them to sleep. And they have never, ever forgotten it—they simply adored Frank."

Leonard Slatkin, then a youngster, recalls: "As Frank began to work more and more with my parents, he began to develop a very striking friendship with them, and as a family, I remember several trips we took to Frank's home in Palm Springs, just to spend weekends with him, and for our families to be together. It was very exciting, but you know, as a young person, it just didn't seem to be that different. Sinatra had been over to our house several times, we'd been over to his house . . . it never occurred to me that he was a 'larger-than-life' figure! He was just always 'Frank,' and I think sometimes even 'Uncle Frank.'

"Frank Sinatra loved young people. He couldn't have been nicer to my parents, and to us, and all the people we saw him with. And, yes—we had always heard that there were dark sides of Sinatra, but frankly, I never saw them. He was always gracious and generous. There were occasions after my dad died where I wrote Frank with the idea that perhaps we could collaborate on a project in St. Louis, and he always answered himself—it never came through his attorneys. He always answered them personally, and on a couple of occasions, he called just to chat," the conductor says.

Sinatra was among the first to call at the Slatkin home upon Felix's unexpected death in 1963, at age forty-seven.

"I wasn't dealing with it well," Eleanor recalled. "Frank set up a session at Goldwyn, *The Concert Sinatra* sessions. I wasn't really up to playing, but he said, 'I won't play unless you agree to do the album.' He was trying to get me back, because I was nowhere. And finally, I said, 'Okay,' and I broke down completely. He was responsible for getting me back in the business. He had principle, and he stood for what he believed in, whether you liked it or not. If he was a friend, he was a friend."

Says Leonard, "My father was an alcoholic, he smoked three packs of cigarettes a day, and he was overweight. So he had three strikes against him. When he died, I was the one who tried to keep calm in the family. My mom, I think, was confused by my father's death—she didn't know what to make of it. They'd had a rocky marriage; somehow, they'd always stayed together, but it had its problems. And Sinatra kept saying, 'Any-

thing I can do for you . . . but no matter what, you're my cellist.' And so he tried to bring her back, as a form of therapy (not that my mother needed it—she was a very, very strong woman), but perhaps to make her realize that friends and colleagues supported you in both ways, that they were not people who were going to abandon you, although some did. But Sinatra didn't. For some of them, all of a sudden my father wasn't there, and my mother was just a cellist . . . but Frank never felt that way. She was a friend first, who happened to be a cellist. I think he liked the idea that my mother would be a constant in his life as well."

Perhaps more lasting than the personal relationships Sinatra struck up with his musicians was his support of their efforts to integrate the Los Angeles musicians' unions, which until the mid-1950s were segregated: the black musicians' union housed in the downtown area, the whites' in Hollywood.

"When I first came to town, there weren't many black guys sitting with us," remembers Milt Bernhart. "Certainly, in every nightclub and recording studio, the musicians were integrated. But the Hollywood film and television industries were very racist. People like Sinatra were very unhappy about that, and when Frank had a record date, he bent over backwards to try and find black musicians who could play the music. That was the problem—demands were demands. Certain music required good players, the best players, regardless of color. That was an uphill battle: there never were enough black players who could walk into a studio and sight-read the music and play it."

Several exceptional African American musicians, though, fought to preserve the rights of all, and began the groundswell that resulted in the union merger. "Buddy Collette, Benny Carter, and Red Callender were three of the top black players that demanded to be there," recalls Al Viola. "They said, 'I can play it. Why shouldn't I be there?' Buddy was an excellent musician. He played flute and was a great reader. He broke the barrier when Nelson Riddle hired him for Sinatra dates. Nelson was one of the first arrangers to begin doing that. Some of us, Milt [Bernhart], me and a bunch of other musicians that we called 'The Guild' fought to get the black musicians into our union. Those guys were readily accepted by us: as long as you had talent, no one looked at how you dressed or how you walked or what the color of your skin was. You were a musician! That's all that mattered. Frank was proud of the fact that he insisted on having an integrated orchestra . . . he was all for that, and he was very happy when the unions came together."

The Capitol Studios: 5515 Melrose Avenue

By the mid-1950s, Sinatra's recording sessions were celebrated occasions among Hollywood's elite. While few outsiders had been admitted to Sinatra's Columbia recording sessions, the atmosphere was markedly relaxed after his move to Hollywood and Capitol Records.

"There was always a crowd at those Sinatra sessions on Melrose," says Bernhart. "They should have charged admission! Because the studio had been a radio theater, it had an auditorium. And the place was packed to the back. You weren't just playing a record date, you were playing a performance. They took a great chance on the people applauding, because they could get caught up in the thing, and ruin a take . . . but believe me, they were sitting on the edge. And it was an "in" crowd: movie stars, disc jockeys. It was big, big . . . It was hard to get in, you had to be invited. But they'd fill the damned place!"

One of the few songwriters to attend Sinatra sessions was close friend Sammy Cahn, who was always considered part of the singer's "in" crowd. "One night he was recording a song I wrote called 'The Tender Trap,'" Cahn told me. "KHJ Studios . . . Melrose Avenue . . . Nelson Riddle's arrangement . . . and Sinatra sings the song. And he gets to the end, and sings, 'You fell in love and love . . . [sings the second love flat] . . . is the tender trap.' Beautiful! Except the last line should have been sung 'You fell in love and luuuuuuvvvvve is the tender trap.' The word love should have been way up high. So I went over, and I said, 'Frank, why didn't you sing it like this?' Then, I demonstrate it for him. He looks at me funny, and says, 'That's a high F.' I looked back at him, and said, 'And you're Frank Sinatra!' He looked at me again, called the orchestra back, and it's on the record. Now, this is the point of the whole story: Frank Sinatra would have sung that F even if he didn't have it!"

The surviving session outtakes show Sinatra coaching for the reed and percussion sections. He is very direct in telling them and producer Voyle Gilmore what he expects to hear.

The take begins, and after a half minute of playing, Sinatra cuts the band off with a sharp clap of his hands.

> *Sinatra*: Don't change the interpretation of it, but don't blow it so loud. The saxes are thundering after that!
> *Gilmore*: Is that right after the trombones?
> *Sinatra*: Yeah! Can't you hear 'em? I could hear 'em if I were over at NBC!
> *Gilmore*: Yeah, they're pretty good in there.
> *Sinatra*: (Addressing drummer Max Albright) And Max, try to hide after you whack that bass drum. Whack! Whack the hell out of it!

Sinatra choregraphed every note of every session he presided over; tightening here, cutting there . . . it all contributed to the punch and sparkle of the final, polished take.

"Working with Frank was different than other artists," retired Capitol engineer John Palladino remembers. "He had the entire band under his control, and he was so completely professional about his approach and his use of microphones, that it really amazed me."

As he had been at Columbia, Sinatra remained very involved in the entire recording system, and could only have admired the incredible sound that Capitol's engineers were attaining. The original tape masters vividly bring every vocal and instrumental nuance and texture to life. "We were the very first to go to tape," says Alan Livingston, speaking of the transition from disc to tape recording in the late 1940s. "On top of that, we prided ourselves on our sound, and in our use of pure vinyl for our pressings. I believe Decca was using sand, or some type of recycled material in the vinyl for their records, and they had the worst quality in the world."

COURTESY OF JOHN PALLADINO

The Capitol studios (formerly KHJ Radio) at 5515 Melrose Avenue, Los Angeles, circa 1949.

Prior to 1949, Capitol leased session time at several small studios in the Hollywood area, recording primarily at C. P. McGregor Studios on Western Avenue and then Radio Recorders on Santa Monica Boulevard. In 1949, the company bought the building that formerly housed KHJ Radio Studios, located at 5515 Melrose Avenue. This structure was tucked away at the very end of the busy boulevard, just a stone's throw from the gate of the Paramount Pictures lot. Fronting the building was Nickodell's bar (a favorite among the classical and jazz musicians who made their daily rounds through the studio doors); across the street was Lucey's restaurant, which Sinatra would occasionally visit after wrapping up a session.

According to John Palladino, a mixer whose skills have been lauded by nearly all of his former colleagues, the KHJ/Melrose studio had excellent acoustics. "Studio A was on the upper story and was the original radio theater with audience and stage facilities. Downstairs there were two smaller studios and the control room. For a long time, Studio C was the key studio and was perfect for smaller groups. I distinctly remember recording some of Sinatra's albums, like *In the Wee Small Hours,* in Studio C. The dance band recordings with Nelson and Billy May were done in Studio A, which was better suited for larger orchestras."

While the three major labels (Columbia, RCA Victor, and Decca) each perfected a signature sound for their recordings, it was the smaller Capitol Records that bested them all, coming closest to achieving true "high fidelity." The Capitol recordings of the era are, in a word, sumptuous: the perfect balance of clear, sweet treble and deep, rich bass, tempered with a characteristically mellow set of mid-range tones. They create warmly silken sound that, even on the earliest monophonic recordings, is exceptionally clear.

"The whole secret of Capitol's sound, and something that was given a great deal of attention, was the use of acoustic echo chambers," says Palladino. "We were very, very lucky to have people that spent the time and money to develop the chambers. In the early days of mixing, it was a 'hands off' style: you had only a few microphones, and you'd try to position the musicians in a room that was acoustically good, like Liederkranz Hall. But we wanted to have control over the sound in a physically limited situation, like a small studio. The only way we could do that was to concentrate on proper equalization, use of the best mikes, and developing the best echo chambers."

From the time that Capitol began recording at Radio Recorders through the Melrose Avenue era, the chambers were placed on the roof of the building. In order to create a realistic sonic portrait, the engineers manipulated the reverb and controlled the amount that was used on each individual microphone.

"Capitol was known to be a progressive company, and the manufacturers knew this," explains

COURTESY OF JOHN PALLADINO

Control booth in the Melrose Avenue studio, circa 1949. Note the early mixing board (left) and tape machine (right). Capitol was among the first companies to embrace the new tape-recording technology.

Palladino. "We'd get the newest and best microphones, speakers, and tape machines, but the boards (mixing consoles) were really simple, basically one step up from a radio board! Capitol designed the consoles, which were twelve position boards with rotary pots. There was basic EQ available on ten of the twelve channels, and I mean basic—two positions for high frequencies, two for low. At that point, on Melrose, we were using the Ampex 200 tape machine, running at 30 ips [inches per second—the speed of the tape passing through the machine. Faster speeds produce greater sonic accuracy]."

"Everything was monophonic at Capitol until late 1957, when we began recording most things in stereo, although we were doing some experimental stereo recording early in the game on Melrose," he recalls.

The acetate-based (and later, polyester-based) tape stock, which has held up remarkably well in the intervening decades, was usually Scotch 111 or a similar formulation manufactured by Audiotape. So good were the setup and balance and the final tape recording, that it is hard to believe the current CD remasters were made from session tapes that are more than forty years old. "The tape at that time was not a high-output type, so we were very careful about setting levels, and riding the gain, so that we didn't get too much noise. Those early tape machines could introduce a lot of noise, so we tried to get the best signal-to-noise ratio possible, to minimize it," the engineer explains.

One of the outstanding characteristics of the early Capitol recordings, when compared with the Sinatra recordings on previous labels, is the fullness of the singer's voice. The timbre and tone of Sinatra's voice was captured with a fairly new, ultra-sensitive condenser/tube microphone, the Neumann U47, which almost immediately became an essential part of any studio's complement of microphones. "The U47 was a good choice for a vocalist, because it had a fine cardioid (heart-shaped) pickup pattern, and gave nice direction, for isolation," Palladino explains. "On Frank's vocals, I would cut him off at 8 or 10 Khz, otherwise, we'd have to deal with (high frequency) sibilance, which the tape machines didn't handle very well."

Microphone expert Jim Webb, an engineer who worked on dozens of Hollywood films, feels the U47 had a unique sound. "It was transparent, but the microphone sound had some coloration—a good coloration. For instance, there might be some slight darkening of the color in the woodwinds. But those are very subjective opinions."

Palladino details his studio setup for a typical Sinatra dance band session at the Melrose studio: "At a session, every microphone would be placed to its best advantage; each mike had a certain characteristic, so we would utilize the proper mike to get the best sound. The RCA 44, with a bit of EQ, was a hard microphone to beat. . . . For a typical mono session, I'd use a 44 split on reeds, placed low (around 18 inches off the floor) to get that nice, 'fat' sax sound. Then, off the side of this mike, I'd use another 44, or a Neumann U47 for the trombones. Now, above the trombones were the trumpets, which were picked up by the trombone mike, but I'd still give them their own mike as well. The piano would be miked (I favored the 44 for piano); the drums would have one RCA 77 over the top of the kit, and for the acoustic bass, I'd either use a 639, or an Altec contact mike that could be strapped to the bass. The guitar got its own mike as well. Miking strings along with so much rhythm and brass could be a problem, because the sound of the strings just got overwhelmed by the other instruments. Of course, at that point, we couldn't record them separately and cut them in later, so we just dealt with it."

As at his live concerts, Frank would be out in front of the band, close to the rhythm section. For most of the monophonic sessions, it was unnecessary to shield him from the rest of the orchestra, as any spillover of sound into his vocal microphone would be folded into the mix with

no unpleasant sonic results. When stereo and three-track recording came in, instrumental leakage into the vocal microphone required a separation between the singer and the orchestra. "Frank always preferred to be on the stage with the band," says Palladino. "He wanted eye contact with everyone, he charged the musicians— that's what made his sessions so special. Usually, I kept him right there, with the band, but sometimes we'd use a small isolation screen."

"Frank always wanted to sing live with the band," remembered Harry Edison. "Nowadays, you put the voice on tape, and the musicians come in and play . . . that's not the business to me. The older singers want the band where they can hear it: where they can get with everybody, get the feeling. There's a certain feeling you get from the musicians when you're all together than when you're sitting in the studio by yourself with earphones on. I just don't know how a person can get the feeling that way."

Many factors dictated how the engineers prepared the studio and set about achieving optimal recording balances. "When we were recording the *Songs for Swingin' Lovers* album, we had so many musicians on the stage in Studio A at KHJ that I put Frank down below on the floor, which is maybe four feet down from the main stage to get better isolation, and it worked out fine," Palladino explains. "Some of the best recordings I remember making were Billy May's dance band records, which we recorded the same way. I think it was a matter of space, because that studio had the stage, and you could blow the band over the top of the room, and the kickback wouldn't come until a bit later. That simple process produced great sound! It was much harder to accomplish when we went up to Vine Street, because without the open space on top, the sound would just slap right back at you."

In the control booth, tape machines whirred away. At the time, it was the standard operating procedure to run one tape machine as the master recorder, and at least one machine as a

COURTESY OF AMPEX CORPORATION

Engineer John Kraus operates a bank of Ampex 300 tape machines in the recording room at the Capitol studios, Los Angeles, circa mid-1950s.

COURTESY OF MICHAEL OCHS ARCHIVES

Crouching in front of a studio monitor speaker, Sinatra studies a playback.

backup. When Capitol began experimenting with stereo recording, at least one (and sometimes two) additional recorders would be run to tape the sessions in stereo.

After what was deemed to be the best take had been recorded, Sinatra would request a "playback," at which time he issued his approval or disapproval of the selection as a final master. "The playbacks were very important to Frank," engineer Hugh Davies explains. "It gave him the chance to relax, and he got the admiration of everyone around him. He listened very intently. If we had some editing to do, we'd do it right then, after the playback, with him in the booth."

Then Frank and his producer decided which take would be used, and this was noted on the control booth copy of the chart. Fred Grimes, a producer who supervised the tape editing department, described how the original session tapes were transformed into the album master tape, commonly called the "assembly" master:

"We receive a set of session reels and a copy of the booth chart that listed the takes selected for inclusion on the album. We would then remove the appropriate takes from the session reel, with the audible 'slates' included [the producer announcing 'Master E17650, Take 2' etc.], and make a reference disc for Voyle [Gilmore] or Frank or whoever needed to hear it. Once we had the okay, we would cut out the identifying slate announcements and make the album master tape in whatever order the songs were to be in.

In most cases, it would be unusual not to do some editing of different takes. Although in most cases, Frank had probably decided, 'Okay, use Take Four,' there might be a small problem: someone dropping something in the studio, or a chair noise, for example. That's when we might go in, when Frank didn't know about it, and just edit in the two bars that were needed to eliminate the noise. I remember doing that on 'Moonlight in Vermont.'"

If the song was to be released as a single, it would be cut off the session reel and added to what was called, in Capitol vernacular, a "phonoreel," an amalgamated reel containing all the label's singles (not just Sinatra's), in sequential recording order.

Contrary to popular belief, it was unusual for the engineers to let the tape machines roll for the entire session: once the take was over, the recorders were routinely stopped until the ensemble was prepared to start the next attempt. This didn't always happen, however, and extant tapes containing longer pieces of the chatter and rehearsals that occurred between takes have been critical tools for historians studying an artist's working habits. Outtakes, including complete alternate takes (like the first four or five takes of "Skin" described earlier by Milt Bernhart), are likely lost forever—victims of the "cutting room" floor. "Once we cut the approved take from the session reels, the outtakes were generally put in the disposal bucket. They weren't discarded until we got the signal that the assembled master was acceptable, and approved. Then the outtakes were scrapped," Grimes says.

But what about the two or three backup reels that existed as safety copies? "They were held until everything on the assembled master was approved and then they were scrapped too," he explains. "Of course, if something especially funny happened in the studio, or if there was a glaring error by a musician who should not have made the mistake, then that might be saved aside. But it became a question of space. Where would

you store all that stuff? We only made one assembly master from one set of original session reels. The rest were just held in case the first set was damaged in some way. Then the safeties were disposed of."

Preliminary research at the Capitol vaults indicates that Grimes's recollections are accurate: there are virtually no full session reels for the mono sessions, and only some full session reels for the stereo sessions. In contrast, Lee Herschberg at Warner/Reprise reports that their label has all of the original session tapes, outtakes included, for most of their Sinatra recordings. One Reprise-era engineer, who has since passed away, would commonly make "private" reels of the raw sessions for his own personal archive, and it is copies of these tapes that have circulated among hardcore Sinatra enthusiasts for more than twenty years. Little extraneous session material has ever leaked out of Capitol, and even less from Columbia, where the lacquer discs contain far less session chatter than Sinatra's later tape masters.

THE CAPITOL STUDIOS: HOLLYWOOD AND VINE

By 1954, Capitol Records was bursting its seams—the office space above Wallichs's Music City and the Melrose Avenue studio was just too small. So Capitol began plans to build a new studio office complex, and in 1955, broke ground for what would be called the Capitol "Tower," strategically located at the corner of Hollywood and Vine Streets in Hollywood, just steps away from Sunset Boulevard and the Hollywood Walk of Fame.

The Capitol "Tower" at Hollywood and Vine streets, Hollywood.

Sinatra poses with Welton Beckett's architectural model of the Capitol Tower Studio/Office Building, circa 1954.

Designed by architect Welton Beckett, the Capitol building's unique cylindrical shape replicates a stack of records, complete with a "needle" on top (the building's spire, which contains a blinking red light that spells out "Hollywood" in Morse code). Especially striking when lit up at night, the structure remains one of the most recognizable and historically unique landmarks in Hollywood. "Capitol had bought that lot, and we hired Beckett," remembers former Capitol President Alan Livingston. "He [Beckett] said, 'I have always wanted to build a round building, and this is the time to do it.'"

When the building was completed, an elaborate inaugural was planned, and on February 22, 1956, Frank Sinatra, arguably Capitol's most popular artist, was invited to preside over the very first recording session in the new studios. This time, however, he traded his tonsils for a conductor's baton, leading a full symphony orchestra in a series of musical vignettes composed by the day's top composer-orchestrators, for an album simply titled *Tone Poems of Color*.

"I'm really a frustrated conductor," Sinatra once told Nelson Riddle. For this special record-

ing, he engaged a series of top composers and arrangers to orchestrate miniature tone poems that reflected specific colors. Not surprisingly, both the concept and the music are solid, as one would expect with people like Nelson Riddle, Andre Previn, Jeff Alexander, Victor Young, Gordon Jenkins, Alec Wilder, and Elmer Bernstein involved.

In addition to the full *Tone Poems of Color* album, Capitol issued a special, narrated, 7-inch EP called *The Capitol Record: A Souvenir of the Capitol Tower* to commemorate the premiere session and the new facility.

The transition from Melrose Avenue to Vine Street was not without incident. While the new Tower studios were designed to duplicate the acoustics of the Melrose studios, they couldn't possibly be the same. "The sound at Melrose was so good, it took us about a year to work things out so everyone was happy, including Sinatra," Palladino recalls. Nelson Riddle remarked, "Most of our finest Capitol records were not made in the round building—they were made at Melrose. They had immense trouble with those new

A view from the control room: Sinatra conducts a full orchestra for the inauguration of Studio A in the new Capitol Tower, 1956.

standing there around the room, and when we started playing, it was like, THUD! It was just dead as hell—like the problems with Studio 8H in the Toscanini days. The engineers fixed it on the board, so it sounded okay on the recording... but in the room, it was awful."

The engineering staff tinkered with the acoustics within the room, adding splays and experimenting with different wall coverings. Most of the adjustment, though, was made outside the building.

As on Melrose Avenue, much of the sound quality at the Capitol Tower was directly related to reverberation. "On Hollywood and Vine, the echo chambers are buried about fifteen feet below the ground, under the parking lot," Palladino says. "They were carefully designed—very highly developed. There are four wedge-shaped chambers, made of hard cement, each eight to ten feet

studios when they were first built. We always joked, and said that the building actually was a hell of an office building, but nowhere where one would want to record music! Later on, they more or less fixed it, but it wasn't until millions of dollars later that they got it right."

The sonic shortcomings of the new studio were obvious from the first official recording session for *Tone Poems.* "The problem was, these were the first sounds made in the main recording studio, Studio A, in that building. We went in there, and the first sounds that we made were just appalling, because the balance in the room was all off," remembers Mitchell Lurie, principal clarinetist on the date. "It was just terrible! All of the different arrangers were

A break in recording Tone Poems of Color. *Cellist Eleanor Slatkin (right) once recalled the exact moment this photo was taken: "Frank asked me what I thought of the playback, and I said, 'I think it sounds like sh—! As the word came out, I heard the click of the camera as the photographer snapped the picture. I could get away with it—he just laughed!"*

The first recording session in the Capitol Tower studios: Frank Sinatra conducts a 56-piece symphonic orchestra.

One of the Editing Rooms, where recorded magnetic tapes are prepared for final processing. Below, a Recording Room, where music on tape is transferred to master discs.

THE RECORDING STUDIOS

Ultra-modern recording and engineering facilities occupy the Tower's rectangular base. The three studios are the first to be designed exclusively for phonograph recording. Each studio "floats" on a layer of asphalt-impregnated cork, to insulate it from external vibration. Zig-zag wall panels and movable reflecting surfaces—birchwood on one side and Fiberglas on the other—provide complete and variable acoustical control.

At left, James Bayless, Vice President in charge of Manufacturing and Engineering, flanked by Capitol engineers, inspects underground Reverberation Chambers during construction. These unique shock-mounted chambers are used by sound technicians to provide, with complete naturalness, any degree or quality of "room tone" desired in recording.

COURTESY OF JOHN PALLADINO

This promotional brochure from 1956 illustrates and explains the attributes of the new Vine Street facility, including the echo chambers.

high. Humidity became a problem with the underground chambers, so different epoxy paints were tried until the sound was perfected. The microphones used underground were the very best. Most of the time, we'd print the reverb directly to tape at the sessions: for mono, we'd use one chamber. For stereo it would be two chambers and two mikes."

Everything used by Capitol was judiciously selected and hand built, including the speakers installed inside the echo chambers: a pair of Altec "Voice Theater" speakers, with selected L-85s on top, and JBL energizer amps and shelving circuits. The microphones were Altec 21-B tube condenser mikes—two per chamber.

"For a long time, we'd rent out time for people to use the echo chambers," Davies remembers. "People just wanted to come in to add our special sound to the mix of their records." The world-renowned echo chambers, still in use at Capitol today, are especially helpful when the

studio's engineers are remixing and restoring multi-track tapes made at the facility more than forty years ago. (Sadly, the original tube microphones and speaker configuration have been changed, which has significantly diminished the characteristic warm Capitol sound).

Three studios—A, B, and C—comprise the bulk of the Tower's ground floor. Studios A and B played host to vocalists who dominated pop music throughout the 1950s and early 1960s: Sinatra, Nat Cole, Judy Garland, Dean Martin, and Peggy Lee were all signed to the label and recorded there. The facility was also a prime jazz recording venue, with Benny Goodman, Harry James, and Duke Ellington embarking on updated "hi-fi" rerecordings, joining the undisputed "king" of Capitol jazz, Stan Kenton, in the Capitol catalog. Many of Norman Granz's Verve recordings, including some classic jam sessions and the early *Ella Fitzgerald Songbooks*, were made there as well. (Studio C was used for small-group sessions, jingles, voice-overs, commercials, and some radio transcription recording and editing.)

Studio A underwent major restoration in the early 1990s: the room was stripped to the concrete walls, and the control room was completely updated with state-of-the-art digital equipment. Many who knew the virtues of the original room believe that the sound is inferior, and certainly completely different.

In Sinatra's favorite room, Studio B, virtually nothing has been touched since he left the label in 1962. The striated, wood-paneled walls are the very same, and the simple metal stools the singer loved still dot the floor. Moreover, much of the original analog recording equipment is still in place, offering a retro look, feel, and sound to new recording projects. "The performance area in Studio B has not been touched," explains current Studio Director Michael Frondelli. "Frank is the 'Godfather' around here. Other artists come here to record because they understand the studio's history and want to be a part of it. It's like the 'voodoo' is in this place."

MODEL OF PERFECTION: *CLOSE TO YOU*

*C*lose to You, the first vocal album Sinatra recorded in the Vine Street studio, is a superb example of an album's evolution, and of how each element contributes to the overall success of the final recording.

In early 1956, inspired by the semi-classical overtones of Nelson Riddle's ballad orchestrations and the intimacy of the small group settings

COURTESY OF FRED ZLOTKIN

The Hollywood String Quartet (left to right) Felix Slatkin, Paul C. Shure, Alvin Dinkin, and Eleanor Slatkin.

he'd crafted for *In the Wee Small Hours*, Sinatra engaged Riddle to orchestrate a series of tunes to be recorded with the Hollywood String Quartet (HSQ), a superior group comprising four of his most reliable session musicians: Felix Slatkin (violin), Paul C. Shure (violin), Alvin Dinkin (viola), and Eleanor Slatkin (cello). All were Hollywood film studio players, who fulfilled their passion for classical repertory by playing together in their offtime. "In 1939, I became the first cellist at Warner Brothers," recalled Eleanor Slatkin. "Felix and I married, then formed the Quartet. The original group was Felix, Joachim Chassman, Paul Robyn, and me. Then Felix went into the army in 1941, and there went the Quartet! When he came out of the service in 1945, Felix continued as concertmaster at Twentieth Century Fox, and we started the Quartet again."

The 1945 group replaced Chassman with Paul C. Shure (at that time assistant concertmaster at Fox, he is the sole surviving member of the Quartet). During the next nine years, the group gained widespread recognition. "We were the most famous American quartet—the first ever, in fact, to be invited to the Edinburgh Festival," Shure recalled. "We went at it 'hammer and tongs,' and rehearsed almost every day, creating a fine quartet that became world famous more on the strength of its recordings than anything else." The original vinyl pressings of their LPs are highly prized collectibles today.

Far from a stuffy ensemble dedicated solely to "longhair" music, the four were busy session musicians who contributed to every aspect of the Hollywood music scene. "We were affiliated with Capitol and had an agreement to do all the commercial records to make money, because we certainly didn't make money from the Quartet!" Eleanor maintains. "Early rock-and-roll, jazz, and pop albums; TV and film scores . . . we did it all," says Shure.

"The advantage of being a studio musician was that you were under contract, and like a symphony orchestra musician, you worked approximately twenty-two to twenty-four hours a week, and had a great deal of free time to pursue other interests. Hence, my parents were able to not only have a decent living by working in the studios, but it provided them with a means to establish one of the great quartets of our time," explains Leonard Slatkin.

"Outside of the fact that each person in his own right was an extremely capable instrumentalist was the flexibility that we had. We could play all different styles of music, without having to reach for it. Eleanor was a damned good commercial player—she had a real sense for the style of commercial music," Shure says. "Curiously, even though we were extremely active in the Hollywood scene, the name 'Hollywood String Quartet' had nothing to do with 'Hollywood' music. We all happened to be from Hollywood, and no one ever had a quartet from there that made anything of themselves. So, we said, 'Why not?' Instead of 'The Los Angeles String Quartet,' we'll call ourselves 'The Hollywood String Quartet.'"

Listening to the quartet's recordings of works by Ravel, Schubert, Beethoven, Borodin, and Schoenberg (among many others), one immediately understands what attracted Sinatra, and why he found the notion of recording with the group so appealing. The four principals created a sound that had a luxuriant glow. "In the Quartet, we made room for each other technically and soloistically—but the blend of sound was the main thing. You either have it or you don't; it's a product of instinct and hard work—50 percent of each, really," Shure observes. "We were like a family for many years. Eleanor was a wonderful player—she had the most beautifully rich, warm sound and absolutely perfect intonation. Felix had a great sense of timing and a sense for phrasing a long phrase. In a quartet, all four people have to be of the same caliber, or it doesn't work. . . . You draw the sound by your ability: the kind of vibrato you use, the way you apply pressure to the bow . . . these are all very subtle techniques in string playing. I have no guilt or false pride when I say we had four wonderful players."

Leonard Slatkin explained the importance of similar music "training," which differs from country to country and ultimately affects the player's technique and the resultant sound of the ensemble. "I think when musicians get together, many times the question of 'backgrounds' never comes up, and you have disparate kinds of chamber music institutions: people from a French school mixed with someone from a Russian school mixed with someone from a German school." "With the Hollywood String Quartet, you had four people who basically had the same kind of training, four people who were more or less of the same age group and who approached music in almost identical ways. The manner in which they played and practiced individually was quite different. My father, for instance, hardly ever practiced. He could just pick up a violin after three or four weeks off (if he had such a thing), and produce an extraordinary Tchaikovsky concerto. My mother always resented that he didn't have to work so hard; she had to practice like a dog, about four or five hours a day."

By 1954, the original violist, Paul Robyn, had left to pursue family interests, and his substitute was another Fox Studio colleague, Alvin Dinkin. Throughout the group's various incarnations, Felix Slatkin was the glue that held it together. "Felix was a wonderful violinist, and probably, to some degree, a frustrated man. I think he would have loved to have had a conducting career," remembered Shure. (Slatkin had in fact studied conducting, under Fritz Reiner of the Chicago Symphony Orchestra. Apart from the Quartet, Slatkin conducted numerous albums of orchestral music for the Hollywood Bowl Orchestra and for Liberty Records.)

In Slatkin, Sinatra found a kindred spirit, as the violinist's immaculate playing paralleled what Sinatra sought to achieve with his voice; serious listeners will note many similarities when comparing Sinatra's and Slatkin's individual approaches to musical interpretation. One hallmark of the HSQ was its long, smooth phrasing, which was accomplished through controlled bowing techniques; Sinatra utilized breath control to realize the same effect. Likewise, where Felix would frequently add a slight upward portamento to a critical note and neatly strike an emotional chord, the singer would often inflect a note upward or downward or seamlessly glide from one key to another.

"My parents would talk to Frank very often about their own technique," said Leonard Slatkin. "He asked them questions. 'What is that when you take the bow and you just kind of move it up and play several notes at a time? How do you do that?' he'd ask. He was fascinated by this, and my parents would say, 'But Frank, we want to be able to imitate your voice!' I think that was a part of Sinatra's relationship with his musicians: there was a give-and-take, and everyone was interested in how each other produced what they did. Sinatra was always asking for advice to improve his singing, and they were always asking for advice on how to improve their phrasing vis-à-vis being more vocal in the way they played."

"The concertmaster was responsible for instituting a mutuality of expression," explains violinist Marshall Sosson, a close friend of both Slatkin and Sinatra. "The first chair violinist was the concertmaster, and he would set the bowing and keep the entire section working together. It was more important in the symphonic world; less so on these pop dates."

Slatkin was concertmaster for most of Sinatra's dates at Capitol and Reprise until his death in 1963, providing many of the piercing romantic violin solos that add color and dimension to Sinatra's finest ballads.

"Felix was always there for Frank," Eleanor remembered. "If he had a session elsewhere, he would cancel it and go to Frank's date. He really enjoyed Sinatra—but we all did. It was just sheer pleasure. Frank did, on many occasions, look to Felix for [musical] approval. Other people may not have been aware of it, but I was. And Felix *loved* it. He was flattered because he "idolized the man for what he was contributing." Sinatra was so excited by the way they played, the style, and sense of improvisation that they brought to the music, and he began to form a friendship with them," said Leonard Slatkin. "From that point on, my father served as not just the leader [concertmaster], but sometimes as contractor when there were disputes with other musicians."

Sinatra's appreciation for the classical genre enhanced not only his understanding of music, but his personal relationships with its musicians. While both Slatkins had begun performing at Sinatra sessions during the Columbia era, it wasn't until the Capitol period that their friendship blossomed. "We became very close friends and spent many weekends at his home in Palm Springs," recalled Eleanor Slatkin. "As you know, he has a tremendous collection of classical records, and every time we were at his house, he had classical music playing . . . and a lot of opera too. He is very knowledgeable, and of course, he knew many of the artists. He fell in love with the Quartet . . . we saw a lot of him in those days, between recordings and socially, and he said, 'You know, I think it would be a terrific idea to do an album with a string quartet, . . . ' and so came *Close to You*. Everything you did with Frank was Frank's idea."

Although panned by critics upon its release, the album's magnificence was not lost on the musical cognoscenti. "My wife and I have been married for fifty-five years, and she is a fine, classically trained pianist, yet we have both been fans of everything Frank ever did," says clarinetist Mitchell Lurie, who accompanied the Quartet on several tracks. "Not many people believe that as classical musicians, we're interested in listening to the 'other side.' That's just not true. We listen to this album often and we just wait for the next tune, and the next one, and so on—as if we were hearing it for the very first time." Lurie, like Slatkin, studied at Curtis in Philadelphia, and was a protégé of conductor Fritz Reiner. He was a principal clarinetist with both the Chicago and Pittsburgh Symphony Orchestras, and occasionally with the Hollywood String Quartet.

From a thematic standpoint, of all the Sinatra LPs of his "golden" era, *Close to You* comes closest to perfection. The twelve tracks, as they appeared on the original LP (Capitol W789) poignantly convey the album's tale of lost love: "Close to You," "P.S. I Love You," "Love Locked Out," "Everything Happens to Me," "It's Easy to Remember," "Don't Like Goodbyes," "With Every Breath I Take," "Blame It on My Youth," "It Could Happen to You," "I've Had My Moments," "I Couldn't Sleep a Wink Last Night," and "The End of a Love Affair."

Like a three-act play, the album centered around three main songs and themes. Scene one: "With Every Breath I Take"—the confessional; scene two: "Blame It on My Youth"—the act of contrition; and scene three: "It Could Happen to You"—the admonishment.

Lasting a mere three minutes and forty-one seconds, Sinatra's reading of the Leo Robin-Ralph Rainger gem "With Every Breath I Take"

is the epitome of finesse and should be required listening for anyone aspiring to sing a note of popular music. Riddle's elegiac touch provides first a trace of melodic support for the vocal, via Felix's violin and Julye's finely strummed harp. The nakedness of the barely whispered vocal against the simplicity of the orchestration brings each muted color into focus.

These songs sound so natural within this demure setting that it's nearly impossible to imagine them any other way—a more grandiose orchestral setting would destroy their bittersweet fragility. When sung by equally gifted vocalists, the songs just don't seem to communicate the same sincerity as Sinatra's *Close to You*.

The concept for this album was extremely progressive by the standards of its day. Where many operatic singers made successful transitions to the commercial pop side of the business, it was rare for a vocalist as firmly rooted in pop and jazz as Sinatra to venture over the classical. Even more unusual was the willingness of a pop arranger to cross it.

"It's the most stunning thing that Nelson Riddle ever did," believes Paul Shure. "Using the string sound as a basis rather than a pad or an enhancement really was a turnaround for Nelson. String quartet writing is the hardest thing to do, because everything is so open. With a larger orchestra, you have a big palette to work with, and there are all kinds of things going on. You can use the orchestra to overcome melodic deficiencies, by using riffs and doing things with the woodwinds or brass over a string pad and get away with it. When you're writing for four, six, or eight instruments, it's another story."

"I always like a big string section," Riddle once told British music historian and writer Stan Britt. "It's been hard for me to get used to chamber music and enjoy it. Not because of the orchestral colors, because they're rather sparse in chamber music; very often, chamber music is written for a string quartet. My original interest in writing arrangements came because of orchestral colors. I became fascinated with the harmonies and the various effects you could achieve with single instruments or groups of instruments of varying colors. Therefore, I'm always fascinated by large groups, and I find that small groups are more demanding in a way because you have less to work with. Now, *Close to You* utilized a string quartet…[but] when you're given an assignment, you don't sit there and quarrel about it."

As a young observer, Leonard Slatkin remembers that Riddle visited the Slatkin home many times during the planning of *Close to You.* "He was consulting with the Quartet day and night, just to make sure it was all done right. A lot of the things you hear in the album itself, and many other albums, is the result of input from other musicians," he said. Two classical composers whose influence can be clearly heard in his orchestrations for this album are the Impressionists Debussy and Ravel. Riddle's predilection for these composers began when he was a child. "I received a gift of an old-fashioned windup Victrola from my aunt Dorothy," he once recalled. "With it came a few recordings, among them a huge Victor Red Seal disc with 'Reflets dans L'eau' on one side and 'La Cathedrale Engloutie' on the other—two Debussy piano compositions peformed by Jan Paderewski. I probably blunted a bushel of cactus needles exploiting the wonders of those two treasures."

"He talked about Ravel and Debussy at home. He was so connected with the Impressionists," says Rosemary Riddle-Acerra. "I remember going to the symphony with Dad, and he was so based in the classics. He was quite friendly with Leonard Bernstein for a while, and Bernstein wanted to work with him on his conducting. He felt that he had a real sense of the music."

In describing the foundations of string writing to Britt, Riddle made the following points: "In order to get the full sound of the strings, string writing has to be developed from an almost 'clas-sical' precept. To be able to balance X number of violins and violas, I believe that the rate is four violins = three violas = two celli. Because naturally, as the instrument descends (as it gets lower in pitch), the sound is thicker and more penetrating. You start with that. Then, you study string writing in general: what register the strings cut through best—where they are effective, where they are ineffective. All this evolves from listening to music, from studying scores, from being at sessions and listening to picture scores, and so on. Or from talking to violinists. That all sounds very calculated, and it was, and it's how I approached string writing. Also, through the classics— through Debussy and Ravel. Ravel, of course, was a marvelous orchestrator, from top to bottom."

"Nelson was influenced by those composers, and Villa-Lobos as well," maintains Paul Shure. "He delved into the work of the Impressionist composers and tried to draw from the qualities and tonal palettes of that school of music, rather than from the Classical or Romantic school . . . it was quite a departure, and you can hear the early Impressionist composers in the feeling of the voice with the intimate (yet very beautiful) writing he did for the small combinations on this record."

A movement of nineteenth-century French painting dominated by artists such as Monet and Renoir, Impressionism also carried over to music, where its primary proponent was Claude Debussy. The French composer was among the first to express mood and atmosphere through pure tonal color, as opposed to traditional melody and harmony, in the process using new harmonies and scales that created room for new tonal possibilities. Essentially, the Impressionist style is evocative, "as vague and intangible as the changing lights of day, and the subtle noises of the rain and wind." Debussy was an influence upon Ravel, as well as Delius, Respighi, de Falla, Milhaud, and Dukas. Ravel is particularly important, as he is considered to be the father of modern orchestration, which is probably why so many arrangers look to his work for inspiration and guidance.

Close to You shows Impressionist influence, yet it is pure Riddle. "Nelson had his own sound, which was (even for the time) unusual because he might put one chord against another, the way that he does at the end of certain songs, or the sound of the three or four flutes that he has going on when the strings play. They're all typical Nelson Riddle gestures," explains Leonard Slatkin. Harp, via one of his signature glissandos or as a more prominent accent instrument, is also characteristic of a Nelson Riddle arrangement. While never lost in even the most raucous uptempo charts, harp creates an even more spectacular effect in this, most intimate of settings.

Select accent instruments (clarinet, oboe, muted trumpet, flute), offset the formal sound of the Quartet without spoiling its integrity. "My guess is that adding the individual instruments to the Quartet was Felix's idea, because he always chose those of us that played with his group," says

Nelson Riddle's original score for "Close to You," 1956.

Mitchell Lurie. The supplemental instrumentation adds texture, and emphasizes certain moods. On "The End of a Love Affair," for example, the dark color of the oboe helps convey the loneliness Sinatra sings of; on "It's Easy to Remember," Lurie's clarinet provides an interesting contrast to the underlying string bed. A beguiling flute solo by Harry Klee is heard on the charming "Wait Til You See Her"—a recording that was excluded from the original vinyl album.

Segments of the original session outtakes reveal the sensitive care lavished on the album. The title track, "Close to You," had been one of Sinatra's favorite songs from the time he published it with Ben Barton and introduced it in 1943 (it was his very first Columbia recording, done a cappella with the Bobby Tucker Singers). Riddle's knack for writing lines against both the vocal and the individual instruments is amply displayed here. For this, the album opener, Sinatra wished to create a subdued yet dramatic atmosphere, as the following dialog between him, Riddle, and harpist Kathryn Julye reveals:

> *Sinatra:* The downbeats with the tremolo, the strings and the vibe: is that on the same downbeat?
> *Riddle:* The downbeat of seven, Kathryn. Are you playing octaves there?
> *Julye:* I did—I played a couple of octaves.
> *Riddle:* Just give me one note.
> *Sinatra:* Just be real definite on those downbeats.

It is the loveliest arrangement of the entire recording. Accenting the solo violin opening are the tightly controlled harp and vibe parts, which then give way to the vocal entrance and the full quartet, firmly supported by a gently plunked, rich acoustic bass. The violins answer Sinatra's vocal lines in counterpoint, while in similar fashion the viola and cello pleadingly answer the violins. At the bridge, the string instruments play off each other in a call-and-response manner. After

a gently syncopated harp accent, the violins "sing" the main part, while the viola and cello "answer" in the form of counter lines (in bold):

> *Violins:* Close to you . . .
> *Viola and cello:* **Close to you, oh I'm so close to you . . .**
> *Violins:* I will always stay . . .
> *Viola and cello:* **Close to you, I'll stay so close to you . . .**
> *Violins:* Can't you see . . .

Then, as the pitch is taken up an octave:

> *Viola and cello:* **Close to you, oh I'm so close to you . . .**
> *Violins:* You're my happiness . . .
> *Viola and cello:* **Close to you, I'll stay so close to you . . .**

The melody is constantly enhanced and reinforced not just by the vocalist, but by the individual instrumentalists as well—resulting in a fine cohesion of harmony and melody that strengthens the song's structure and increases its tension and drama.

Invaluable to the overall warmth of an orchestra's musical sound is the quality of the instruments. Nowhere is this more apparent than with string instruments, where lineage is as crucial as the player's training and technique. "A great instrument, being played on and cared for, will mellow and sound better as time goes on," explains Paul Shure. "The age of the instrument certainly affects what you hear, and that's the beauty of old Italian instruments. Keep in mind that the wood [maple and spruce] these instruments are made of was probably fifty or a hundred years old before the instrument was made. A good bow is even harder to find, and certainly affects the sound it draws. You can use two different bows on the same fiddle and get a completely different sound. The great bow makers' bows just draw a better sound . . . their knowledge of balance and the way they cut the bow is a fine art."

For his Hollywood String Quartet performances, Felix Slatkin played a Guadagnini (1784) and a Guarnerius Del Gesu (circa 1730); Paul Shure chose an Andreas Guarnerius (circa 1691—stolen from the violinist in 1957) and a Vuillaume (1860); Eleanor Slatkin's cello was also a Andreas Guarnerius (1689); Alvin Dinkin's viola was an Albani (1711). Felix's Guarnerius Del Gesu was purchased from the estate of the late violinist Albert Spalding; it was the exact model that Jascha Heifetz played for most of his life. "It is the same caliber instrument as a Stradivarius,

except it has a little more power," explains Marshall Sosson.

These rare instruments are as costly as the finest works of art. In 1988, for example, a violin made in 1743 by Joseph Guarnerius Del Gesu sold for $915,200; the highest price paid at auction for a violin was $1.7 million in 1990 for a 1720 "Mendelssohn" model Stradivarius. A Stradivarius cello (circa 1698), known as "The Cholmondeley," garnered $1.2 million at auction in 1988.

Close to You belongs among the most artistic and most cherished recordings of the twentieth century. "My mother and father were about

PHOTOGRAPH BY SID AVERY, COURTESY OF MPTV ARCHIVE

as proud of *Close to You* as they were of any of the albums they made of Beethoven or Brahms, because here was the preeminent popular musician of the time, having faith and confidence in doing something different. It wasn't a big seller in terms of Sinatra albums, but it was one of the most respected by everyone. I think my parents always felt that they had to do a good job and always be proud of it, because Sinatra went out on a limb for them," says Leonard Slatkin.

"It was a labor of love," concludes Paul Shure. "It was a joy to record. Frank was absolutely enthralled with the whole project, and what Nelson came up with just blew his mind! We had no idea what we were getting into in the beginning . . . we just got together with these songs, and as one came to another and Frank started singing, we all got caught up in it, and by the time we were finished, we were celebrating. We knew that artistically, we had something very good. We didn't know what was going to happen with it, but we sure knew there was something great there as far as the artistic endeavor was concerned. It was very satisfying."

There is a funny postscript to the creation of *Close to You*. As early as 1956, with the acrimony of the late Columbia period just four years behind him, Frank was once again disenchanted with the bureaucracies of the record industry, feeling that the labels were being run by marketing people who rarely paid attention to the quality of the music they sponsored and promoted.

To prove the point, the singer selected the inane (and hysterically funny) "There's a Flaw in my Flue," written by James Van Heusen and Johnny Burke, and went to the trouble of having Riddle score it with the same integrity as the rest of the songs on the *Close to You* LP. In the studio, Sinatra and the quartet rehearsed and recorded the tune, and at Sinatra's behest, producer Voyle Gilmore included it on the test pressings of the album that were distributed to Capitol executives. One can only imagine what the group, sitting in their ivory tower, were thinking as, from

the shimmering strings, delicate harp, and mellifluous oboe, these lyrics emerged:

> *I used to sit by my fireplace*
> *And dream about you*
> *But now that won't do*
> *There's a flaw in my flue*
> *Your lovely face in my fireplace*
> *Was all that I saw*
> *But now it won't draw*
> *Cause my flue has a flaw*
> *From every beautiful ember*
> *A memory arose*
> *Now I try to remember*
> *And smoke gets in my nose*
> *It's not as sweet by the unit heat*
> *To dream about you*
> *So darling, adieu—*
> *There's a flaw in my flue*

The joke almost backfired, as Sinatra's hunch that "no one was listening" was dead-on. The powers approved the album, "Flaw in my Flue" and all, and had the prankster himself not taken them to task, it might have ended up on the commercial pressings. The song remained an oddity in the Sinatra discography until about fifteen years later, when the story behind its creation was divulged and the song was then officially released.

FROM MONO TO STEREO

*U*ntil mid- to late 1957, almost all of the record industry's recording sessions were monaural, or monophonic, transmitted by a single channel. Listening to a monophonic recording is somewhat like listening to a performance with just one ear. Monophonic recordings lack a certain depth, as well as a clearly defined spatial perception. That does not mean, however, that mono recordings are inferior: the thousands of extremely fine recordings made prior to the invention of stereo sound testify to the ultra-high quality that could be achieved with mono recordings. They can be as clear and as distinctive (and, in some cases, superior) to a true stereo recording.

Comparing sound to sight, monophonic sound is like having no peripheral vision. With a monophonic recording, an engineer has a fairly narrow sonic "soundstage" to work with. Within that limited landscape, he must condense the color and texture of every instrument of the orchestra, assuring that each sound is naturally balanced against the others. Since the instrumental or spatial balance of a monophonic recording was set at the session, engineers were meticulous about how they miked the orchestra and paid close attention to the overall quality of sound. Once multi-track stereo came into play, some engineers became lax, adopting a "we can fix it later" mentality, which caused the quality of some early stereo recordings to suffer.

Stereophonic sound approximates the way humans hear. The idea that binaural human hearing could be imitated by two separate (right and left) microphones was first introduced by Alan D. Blumlein, who theorized that stereo sound would work because the brain compares the intensities of incoming sounds and contrasts the input received by each ear. The brain senses and evaluates the arrival time from the right and left sound sources, the reverberation, and the intensity of the sound and can then determine the direction and distance of the sound almost instantly.

As with the microphone, experimentation with binaural sound came well before the invention of the phonograph. It was Alexander Graham Bell who first used the term "stereophonic phenomena," around 1880.

The first transmission of a live performance in "stereo" took place in France in 1881, when inventor Clement Ader placed ten transmitters (microphones) in pairs on the edge of the stage at the Paris Opera and linked them by wire to the Palais de l'Industrie, site of the Electrical Exhibition. At the Exhibition, visitors could pick up two telephone receivers and enjoy the live performance. So impressive was the demonstration that the December 3, 1881, issue of *Scientific American* translated an article that appeared in the French publication, *L'Electricien*. "Everyone who has been fortunate enough to hear the telephones at the Palais de l'Industrie has remarked that, in listening with both ears at the two telephones, the sound takes on a special character of relief and localization which a single receiver cannot produce. . . . "

In terms of application to sound recording, real work did not begin until the late 1920s, when W. Bartlett Jones patented his idea for putting discrete sound signals in either adjacent grooves of a phonograph disc, or on the opposite sides of a record. Synchronization of the two required styli was a major problem, and the most impressive (and accidental) application of this general idea were two recordings made by Duke Ellington on February 3 and 9, 1932.

The Ellington sessions (two medleys) took place at Victor Record's New York studios, the engineers using two turntables to make separate transcriptions of the session. The recording was issued on 78 rpm disc. Years later, an astute Ellington historian noticed that a second pressing of the same record sounded different. When the two 78 pressings were synchronized, it became clear that while they were the very same take, the discs had been struck from alternative masters.

For this session, the recording engineers had set up a second set of microphones, their signal being fed to a separate cutting lathe, which resulted in a unique wax master (of the same performance) being cut. Since the mike placement for the two cutting lathes differed, each microphone setup (and thus, the two records) offered a different perspective of the orchestra, and when synched, sounded very much like a true stereo soundstage. Close audition of the recordings, now released in stereo on CD, reveals such skillful instrument placement that one can't help but believe that this was a successful stereo "test."

In truth, the 1932 Ellington "stereo" sides are as much serendipity as not. Apparently, RCA had been using Western Electric's electrical recording process and disliked paying royalties to the company. In an attempt to eliminate the Western Electric system, RCA began to develop its own electrical recording process, and for these Ellington recordings, one master was cut using the Western Electric system, one with the new RCA system. (The comparisons proved that the Western Electric system was superior, and RCA continued to refine its process, which supplanted the Western Electric process in 1934.)

Using the Blumlein theory, which had been patented in 1931, EMI made some experimental recordings at their Abbey Road Studios in London in 1933. Research continued, and later in that year, Arthur Charles Keller and a team of engineers from Bell Telephone Labs demonstrated "auditory perspective" at the Century of Progress Exposition in Chicago, via stereo recordings made of Leopold Stokowski conducting the Philadelphia Orchestra. Discs from both these early sessions survive, and the stereo imaging is surprisingly good.

The film industry, always progressive and flush with cash, helped prove stereo sound feasible. Walt Disney's *Fantasia*, recorded in 1939 by RCA with seven separate channels, demonstrated the wonders of the stereophonic process. Within a short time, many film companies were recording on separate channels. Today realistically restored "stereo" CDs are routinely created for soundtracks of musicals of the 1940s and 1950s by mixing individual channels (made from varying locations on the soundstage) that were miked

and recorded on separate session discs and tapes. (These discrete microphone setups around the stage were called "angles," indicating that the separate recordings were made to capture the individual performer's placement on the soundstage.)

For the record industry, the problem of styli placement and a workable method of cutting separate channels into the grooves of a traditional disc master seemed to be the biggest problem with the stereo idea. After magnetic tape recorders were introduced into the recording studios, the idea was revived in earnest by a few of the major record companies, primarily RCA Victor (in the United States) and Decca (in Europe), and was first used only for classical recording sessions.

The late Jack Pfeiffer, the legendary producer responsible for directing RCA Victor's "Living Stereo" recording sessions, once described, for journalist Susan Elliott, the tape machines used for his earliest stereo recording: "The RCA engineers had made their own tape machines . . . we now call them the Tinkertoys! They had small 7-inch reels, and they ran at 30 ips, so you could only get seven and a half minutes per reel. Anything that went on for any length of time had to be overlapped. We used to do that on some of the early Toscanini recordings and then had to splice them together. Generally, we ran two machines on everything. If a piece was more than seven and a half minutes long, we would stop one machine, change the reel, start that up, then stop the other machine, change the reel, and then start that one up, and so on."

"By 1950, we had machines [the RCA RT-11] with 16-inch reels, so we could record up to 130 minutes of music at 30 ips. These were mostly used for assembling LP masters and Toscanini broadcasts. Then, around '52 or '53, Ampex came out with some good 15 ips machines: the heads were better, the electronics . . . even the mechanical aspects were better. Torque was more consistent, there was little wow or flutter, and you

COURTESY OF JAMES LUM/ESTATE OF JACK PFEIFFER

Legendary RCA Red Seal producer Jack Pfeiffer directs a stereo session, mid-1950s.

could record a whole LP side (about twenty-three minutes) with the 2,400-foot reels."

RCA, under Pfeiffer's urging, continued to be the new format's greatest proponent. "In 1953, RCA had two-track professional equipment and were designing a console to accept multiple inputs," he said. "The engineers felt that three microphone input channels for each track were sufficient and incorporated provisions for splitting a microphone signal between the two. I was so enthusiastic that I pressed for every opportunity to experiment with live orchestras. The first was on October 6, 1953, with Leopold Stokowski and his Symphony Orchestra in Webster Hall, New York City. Nothing remains of the two-track results of that session, but in December [1953], Pierre Monteux with members of the Boston Symphony Orchestra were in Manhattan Center for recording of excerpts of Delibes's *Coppélia*. The equipment was only partially set up, because engineers were actively engaged in getting a

commercial monaural recording. But some takes were recorded stereophonically with a two-microphone setup. It was so promising that I argued that all orchestral sessions should have a double crew, one for commercial monaural recording and the other for stereo experimentation."

The first full-fledged stereo recording session committed to tape was made by Pfeiffer on February 21 and 22, 1954, in Boston's Symphony Hall, and the producer had vivid recollections of the excitement generated by the performances and the recordings made of them. "The first such setup was used for Charles Munch and the Boston Symphony's recording of Berlioz's *Damnation of Faust*. Since there were soloists, we used three microphones, splitting the center one between the left and right tracks. The 'Ride to Hell' section was so impressive, I used it on a demonstration tape that I later played for everyone who would sit still for it. This demo tape was lost, but a fragment of the famous 'Ride' was saved from another take."

Pfeiffer, along with engineer Leslie Chase, approached the initial stereo recording setups very simply. On their earliest stereo sessions, they used two widely spaced condenser mikes (Neumann M-50s). "Stokowski had always been such a pioneer in sound experimentation, and we set up a double recording system for his sessions of the Beethoven *Pastorale* on March 18, 1954," Pfeiffer recalled. "Manhattan Center in New York City has a high ambient reverberation level, and to get more presence, we tried a third microphone. But Stokowski had a strange orchestral setup: strings all on his left, woodwinds right, brass in back of the woodwinds, percussion center-rear. Even though the results were interesting, the unconventional orchestral setup precluded considering it later for a stereophonic release."

In time, the producer was able to convince RCA executives that stereo was worth the time and effort they were spending it. "With the BSO, CSO, and Stokowski, we began to feel more confident in our judgment concerning the ideal ratio of direct to reverberant sound. To me, this ratio was the determining factor in giving the listener a sense of reality in a recording. But I felt that more different recording sessions were needed to develop the proper technique," he recalled.

At roughly the same time, it became apparent that stereo was adaptable and desirable for popular recordings as well. Pfeiffer remembered the push to introduce stereo to the pop side of the business. "[During the summer of 1954,] Arthur Fiedler and the Boston Pops had a series of sessions: some were recorded in stereo, some not. By this time, the results we had obtained were impressing the pop producers, and pressure was on the engineering department to work on popular sessions. There was only a limited amount of stereo equipment to go around, though. The pop people felt, and rightly so, that stereo would get a great publicity push and larger internal support if it could be shown to be effective with popular music. The big band era was going strong, and stereo was the logical medium to dramatize their sound."

Mercury's Bob Fine had been recording binaurally with the Ampex model 350-2 tape recorder, and he sought to have Ampex modify its ubiquitous Model 300 to accommodate the preferred half-inch tape and three separate recording tracks. By 1956, Ampex was promoting such a machine, and record companies began to re-design their mixing consoles to allow for more input channels. Increasingly, the mixing engineers were abandoning monitoring in mono in favor of stereophonic monitoring in the control rooms. "The artists loved it, although some were a little confused," Jack Pfeiffer remembered. "I set up a stereo playback for Vladimir Horowitz, and he stared at the two speakers and complained, 'But . . . the piano comes from the center where there is no speaker!' And Heifetz called this new technology 'hystereo' to register his contempt for it."

By the time Westrex developed the 45/45 head for cutting a stereo groove into an LP lacquer master, RCA Victor had a growing collection of stereo recordings by the classical superstars of the day and began transferring them to the new stereo format. "Everyone involved sat down, scratched their collective heads, and asked, 'What shall we call this new sound?' Finally, our public relations people took the hint from all of us who were claiming that it represented a lifelike experience, and settled on 'living stereo,'" Pfeiffer concluded.

Over at Capitol, the records were dubbed "full dimensional stereo," and the company emphasized the concept of full-frequency reproduction by redesigning its LP label, which now sported a vivid ring containing every color in the spectrum around its edges, implying that Capitol's records were ablaze with all of the tonal color that the sonic spectrum had to offer. Indeed, Capitol had much to be proud of, and the symbolism of the new label was reflected in the superior sonics of the records themselves.

While Capitol's engineering department had experimented with stereo recording as early as 1954 (at the Melrose Avenue studio), it wasn't embraced for pop recording until late in 1957. Carson Taylor was one of the engineers who was responsible for transcribing the early stereo sessions and recalls here the trepidation that accompanied the transition to the new format: "I had gotten into doing the stereo recordings, because some of the fellows did not want to. One night, when I'd just finished a stereo mix at the studio, a vice president of Capitol (whose name I can't remember) backed me up against the wall and lectured me for about thirty-five or forty minutes on the folly of wasting my time, because stereo was just an idea, a fad . . . and that it would never work. Of course, it went in one ear and out the other with me, because I didn't believe that! That was probably around 1956. There was a lot of opposition in the beginning, mostly from the dyed-in-the-wool hard-core mono producers and mixers that did not want to change. . . . On the other side were the more modern ones who were very interested in stereo, and believed it had a future."

Taylor described his approach to the initial stereo recording sessions at Capitol. "I ran a separate set of mikes for stereo, and I mixed them in a different room than the mono mixer, because at that time, mono was still the 'king.' But there were two separate boards, two separate rooms, and two different mike setups. For the stereo setups, I used mostly Neumann U67s; then, we got some newer Neumann mikes, and I tried those. I was a great one for trying out the new mikes . . . a lot of the fellas didn't want to depart from what they were used to, but I liked to use the new ones to see if they were any good. And in so many cases, they became the standard microphones that we would use. The 67 has a peak up in the top end, and the newer Neumanns just sounded warmer.

"To record the orchestra, we used three microphones in a triangle, which was a metal triangle on which they were mounted and hung high above the musicians. There was one mike on each corner in the rear, and the third microphone was in the front. The triangle itself was probably about three feet on each side; it was an equilateral triangle. That went on for a while, but it had quite a few flaws in it. There was a lot of experimentation and struggling: some of it worked, some of it did not. Whatever was done, we had to be careful of phase shifting, because it would affect the mono mix, which at the time was still of primary importance. If you split the vocal mike equally to both sides, you ended up with part of it out of phase. I heard results at that time where when you combined them to mono, the vocalist disappeared!"

John Palladino explains, "The control rooms were initially set up for mono, but for a time we ran both stereo and mono recorders at the sessions." "The big question was, How do you produce your stereo records? Do you make a separate mono recording, or mix to mono right off the stereo? What is stereo? There was always an argument between the purist approach to stereo and the practical approach. Stereo sound could simply be sound coming out of two speakers, or it could be a true duplication of the sound of the room, in which case you'd try for a fairly straightforward setup. It was up to the engineer to determine the most effective use of microphone placement and balance."

When stereo began to gain momentum, Ampex followed the suggestion of a few engineers who had been conducting serious experiments with tape and stereo recording and, in the mid-1950s, introduced a three-track tape machine. The three-track machine allowed for greater flexibility in recording and mixing: the orchestra could easily be recorded on the first two tracks, and the vocalist on the third. Each track was "isolated," and using the mixing console, mixing engineers could blend and manipulate the three channels in a variety of ways: they could make certain parts of the orchestra louder or softer, or they could even eliminate the vocal by turning down the volume completely on the third track. They could also drop the orchestra out altogether, and listen to the vocal only. The three-track system made dubbing vocals to pre-recorded orchestral parts a breeze—far simpler and more cost effective than it had been with lacquer disc recording.

Years earlier, though, Les Paul had set out to devise a way to squeeze more layers of music onto magnetic recording tape by overdubbing the same way he overdubbed with multiple lacquer transcription discs. The audio advantages of tape would give him an ultimately cleaner sounding recording; he recorded a guitar solo on one tape recorder, then played a new guitar part while simultaneously recording both parts on a second tape machine.

To eliminate the need for two separate Ampex machines, Paul approached Jack Mullin, and within hours, the pair had come up with the idea of adding a second playback head to the existing recorder. By re-recording and adding new material to the basic tracks, Paul achieved his goal. Adding a second recorder added even more flexibility, as the tracks could be "bounced" back and forth between each machine, allowing for infinite layering.

In 1951, as most of the major record companies were just getting their feet wet with recording tape, Paul was working feverishly in his home studio, using his modified Ampex recorder to overdub guitar and vocals an unprecedented twelve times to record a hit version of "How High the Moon" with wife Mary Ford. Later, further refinements based upon Paul's idea led to the four, eight, sixteen, twenty-four, and forty-eight track recorders of the analog era, opening a whole new world of technology to the artist and producer.

By April 1957, Capitol was making a firm commitment to the stereo format, and Sinatra's first two stereo albums—*Where Are You?*, recorded in April and May; *Come Fly with Me*, in October—found him experimenting with two great arrangers who would form the balance of his core orchestrating team: Gordon Jenkins and Billy May.

WITH GORDON JENKINS

*S*inatra found a haunting melancholy in the arrangements of Gordon Jenkins, whose style, like the compositions and orchestrations of the film composer Bernard Herrmann, relied heavily on sheets of sound created almost solely from the string section of the orchestra. Where Herrmann preferred the darker

tones of the lower strings (cello and double bass, for example), Jenkins favored the higher, sweeter tones of the violin and viola. To this, he added the barest whisper of minor-key woodwinds, horns and soft (mallet) percussion, lending the songs the poignant back-alley, late-night color of Lonely Street. "With Gordon Jenkins, it's all so beautifully simple that, to me, it's like being back in the womb," Sinatra observed.

He once told radio personality Sid Mark that "Gordon was a man who was always open to suggestions, but he was one man that I felt I could almost leave alone—just let him work by himself. I think he was probably the most sensitive man about orchestrations . . . you can hear it in his music.

"I used to call him 'Lefty,' because he had a very good left-handed [golf] swing. But also, it

PHOTOGRAPH BY SID AVERY, COURTESY OF MPTV ARCHIVE

With Gordon Jenkins, 1957.

was confusing to me when I first started to work with him, because when you're used to looking at a conductor in front of you on a podium, waving his right hand, and suddenly, you're looking for the beat and he's on the other hand . . . it was confusing for the first couple of dates, but it worked out in the end."

Jenkins and Sinatra's first two albums, *Where Are You?* (1957) and *No One Cares* (1959), both have the silken texture of Jenkins's writing, yet they are as different as night and day. *Where Are You?* has a sweeter sound, relying more heavily on the upper registers of the violins and violas to create a pensive wistfulness. With *No One Cares*, the mood is decidedly darker, for here the arranger has orchestrated the entire string ensemble to emphasize the lower registers, and has added more percussion and deep woodwinds to accent the lyrics foreboding sorrow.

"When Frank sang with Gordon, it was a whole different Sinatra," believes Buddy Collette. "He could always pull it off, and it was good. As much as they were great, he didn't want to always do all Nelson things, so his work with Gordon was a contrast. He thought he needed a different type of sound, and sometimes those albums go to different people. You still have your main fans, who'd say, 'I like him better with Nelson . . . ,' and you might say, 'Oh, but I love this Gordon Jenkins thing . . . the material they're using is so soft and bedroomish . . . ' Sinatra was intrigued by the way Gordon set up his chords."

Jenkins once explained the care he lavished on an orchestration: "I can make an arrangement in two-and-a-half or three hours if I had to, but I prefer to have four days, because it gives me the chance to fool with it, and then go back and look at it again to change a note or chord if I think it needs it. Just little things. I know nobody's going to notice it, but if you don't have them right, then the whole thing isn't going to be right. An instrumental takes you much more time than the vocal, because in the vocal your main goal is already established: it's gonna be the baritone, or

the girl, or whatever. But when you have to write a long instrumental with eight brass, and all the strings too, then it takes hours."

In a radio special hosted by Wink Martindale, Jenkins said of Frank Sinatra: "I don't know him well at all—I doubt if anybody does. I might be his favorite arranger for some things, for what he calls 'wood songs.' Songs like 'Laura' or 'Lonely Town,' where he wants to set up a feeling like in the *September of My Years* album. Frank is withdrawn. He's the charmer of all time when he's right . . . when he feels like being charming. Nobody comes close to him. But, when he quit laughing, you're not any closer to him than you were before."

The arranger obviously understood Sinatra's drive for perfection. "You talk about high standards—he's the inventor," Jenkins said. "The scrapes he's gotten into, and the bad publicity he's gotten, is only because he expected more of people than they ever delivered. If he hires you to do something, he expects it to be the absolute world's best. Whether it's cutting the grass or playing the piano, he never questions how much money you want: he pays whatever you want, really, but he expects it to be absolutely perfect. And it depresses him when it isn't."

Jenkins went on to compare the studio methodology of several top artists, including Sinatra. "I never heard Nat Cole make a recording that I thought he should have done over. Frank might have been tired, or he had a date, and he didn't want to do one again. I'd ask him to do it again, and he'd say, 'No.' With Judy [Garland], I'd just lock the door of the studio, and make her do it again. But if Frank wants to go home, he generally goes home. During recording sessions with Sinatra, a magic takes place . . . between Frank and myself. It's as close as you're gonna get without being opposite sexes! I like to have him right in front of me, and I just never take my eyes off him, so it's kind of a hard thing to describe. But there's a definite mental connection between the two of you when it's going down well . . . he lets loose—he's all over the place when he's going—he doesn't hold anything back. It's in his personal life that he holds back.

"The excitement of working with him is following him, because he likes to wander around . . . he doesn't necessarily do a song the way he rehearsed it. So I never take my eyes off of him, I wouldn't dare. You just never let up for a minute. If you take your eyes off of him, or relax, he'll leave you. He'll stop in the middle of a bar, and talk to somebody, and then you have to figure out where he's gonna start again, or whether he's gonna start at the beginning. He generally might give you a little hint, but he might not: he'd just assume you'd be there!"

On a personal note, Jenkins, like Nelson Riddle and Billy May, found that keeping a polite distance was the best policy. "We have never had a cross word," he said. "We never had any fights—ever. I stay away from him as much as I can when we're not working. It's a temptation to hang around him, 'cause he has so much to offer, but I figure that we've gotten along fine by not being

buddies, so when we get through at night, if he goes out the left door, I go out the right. I think it's worked out fine."

WITH BILLY MAY

With Billy May, Sinatra rarely involved himself with pre-session particulars. "He's easy to work with, as far as I'm concerned," says May. "All we did was figure out the tunes. We might get to a session, and he'd say 'Let's try this a little differently,' and then we'd try it at a completely different tempo, and usually, it worked very well."

In his interview with Robin Douglas-Home, Sinatra spoke of his fondness for May's work. "Recording with Billy May is like having a cold shower, or a cold bucket of water thrown in your face. Nelson will come to the session with all the arrangements carefully and neatly worked out beforehand. But with Billy, you sometimes don't get the copies of the next number until you've finished the one before—he'll have been scribbling away in some office in the studio right up until the start of the session! Billy works best under pressure. He also handles the band quite differently than Nelson or Gordon: with Billy, there he'll be in his old pants and a sweatshirt, and he'll stop them and he'll say, 'Hey cats, this bar sixteen. You gotta oompah-de-da-da-ch-Ow. OK? Let's go then . . .'

PHOTOGRAPH BY KEN VEEDER, COURTESY OF MPTV ARCHIVE

With Billy May, late 1950s.

And the band will GO! Billy is *driving*," Sinatra emphasized.

"Billy wrote with meat," said Alvin Stoller. "I don't think that Nelson really knew how to write for the drums . . . I would use what he had, and try to be really creative and make it come off. Billy was just the opposite. He had meat on it, and I knew automatically what I was gonna do. You see, the figures just lay there for a drummer, and when they're good figures and the chart is great, you automatically feel it, and play it. I love Billy, himself and his writing. He's never once in forty-five years said one word to me in terms of playing . . . never suggested anything, never said, 'leave that out.'"

Stoller, who worked his entire life as a band drummer, coming came from virtually the same school as May, is a keen observer of all things cool, and might be considered a biased witness if called to testify on May's behalf in the court of history. But it was not just the jazz guys that dug what Sinatra and May were doing with the hightest stuff: even a seasoned classical professional like Eleanor Slatkin could be hep to their jive. She once said that May could inspire musicians in a way that Riddle never could. "Billy May, who to me is one of the greats of all time, had a way of making an orchestra play . . . he inspired you. I liked all the sessions, whether they were ballads or swing. I couldn't differentiate, because the swing sessions were so incredibly orchestrated."

"Billy would try things," says Buddy Collette. "He might put in little songs, start a little melody and work that through the whole chorus, and Frank would like that because it was different. Billy May was very inventive . . . he'd be putting the song into the background and voicing it, which would work against the chords. He could get away with it, where Nelson stuck to doing those little rhythmic things, like the tags that Joe Comfort played."

While stories proliferate of May's legendary last minute mad dash into the studio, score paper and pencil in hand, poised to complete the last chart set for that evening's session, Eleanor Slatkin remembers that it never affected the quality of his work. "Billy was the most meticulous of arrangers, and God knows, I saw enough scores! He was certainly not a person who dressed to the nines or anything like that . . . he was just carefree, very casual. But not when it came to music. When you looked at one of his charts, it was if it were printed. When it came to anything having to do with music, he was a perfectionist."

Leonard Slatkin, a sharp sideline observer at the sessions, recalled that "Billy was capable of making immediate adjustments, right at a session. He didn't have to think about it—he was so natural. Nelson had to work; with Billy, it just rattled off the top of his head. He might say something like, 'Flutes, I made a mistake there. I need the alto flute playing G-natural . . . here I need this . . . ,' and so on. And it's not as if he just looked at the score and decided on the spot. It was as if he were saying, 'This is what I really intended, so let's try it, fellas.' He was just so natural about it. In that respect, he was a little like Henry Mancini. I was always surprised that Sinatra never got together with Mancini. It would have made an ideal combination and would have been the logical step after he finished his work with Billy May."

"Billy is a very gregarious person, and when you talk to him, you know that right away—he's right on," said Eleanor. "With the orchestra, he has a way of telling them how he wants something played. One time in particular, he was trying to get something in the brass section, and he couldn't get it right. He was trying out some different things, and he says, 'Hey guys, I want it to sound like this: hit it, and then let it cool.' And they understood immediately from that expression. That's the way Billy was. He is a dream of a human being."

I recently asked Billy May where an arranger gets his musical ideas. He laughed and said, "It's a good question, and one I've often asked myself. There are a lot of variables there, and you have to take them all into consideration. You can figure out what you're going to do, the plot of it, more or less. Some melodies suggest things to you, and for others, you just have to figure something out! Or, you'll listen to it, and it will remind you of another tune, and that will remind you of a good record you heard of that tune, and then you can think along those lines. It's all derivative, I guess. If you're hired by Frank Sinatra, you know you've got to do a passable job, and you can't 'fluff it off.' On the other hand, if you've got a far out idea, you'd better talk it over with him before you go to the trouble of writing it all down. That's happened a couple of times, and he bought it."

From his perspective as an arranger, May observed firsthand Sinatra's insistence on using whatever instrumentation it took to accomplish the results, regardless of cost. "When you hired the band, all the record companies used to say, 'Use as few men as possible,' because they didn't want you to spend too much money. But with Sinatra, you'd ask 'How many strings shall we get, Frank?' and he'd say, 'Fill up the outfield!' He knew, as we all knew, the more the better, especially with strings."

May's habit of imbibing at the sessions added to the unconventional atmosphere. "Like Nelson, Billy was not a great conductor," recalls Leonard Slatkin. "He had a habit which really did bother people: he would drink while he was doing the sessions. He would have maybe a fifth of scotch sitting there, and I remember one musician joking that Billy could down about a half of it between the third and fourth beat, while he was conducting! Seemed not to affect him very much, and he was one of those musicians that was always consistent. He knew what he wanted, he was well liked, and he seemed to be great friends with everybody. Nelson distanced himself a bit, but Billy was much more outgoing and friendly toward the musicians." (For the record, May quit drinking in 1964; he had seen his close friend and musical colleague Conrad Gozzo die from alcoholism.)

"Frank was pretty hip about what was going on with a band. He can look around in the band, and pretty much tell if it's a happy band, or if there's some bulls—t going on," May observed. When discussing the pure fun that most of the participants recall about their sessions with him and Sinatra, May said, "I figured, 'What the hell.' If you're going to go in and do it, what the hell is the use of doing anything unless you're having fun with it? I try to make it that way. I feel we're lucky to be able to be musicians, and be professional about it."

The arranger's comment to me at the end of one casual conversation probably sums up his feeling best: "I feel privileged and fortunate to have worked with two of the greatest musicians in the world, people I truly admire: Glenn Miller and Frank Sinatra."

Come Fly with Me is one of the jauntiest Sinatra albums of the period, the Billy May follow-up to Riddle's masterful *Swingin' Lovers* and *Swingin' Affair!* The title tune, written by Cahn and Van Heusen expressly for the project, is a lofty affair that is the perfect vehicle for Sinatra's languid, breathy vocals, so evocative of the feeling of flight.

Frank Flynn vividly remembers the afternoon of October 8, 1957, just before the session that yielded the title track. "I was on staff at CBS, and Billy and I were doing a half-hour radio show with Stan Freeberg. On the afternoon of that session, we had a four o'clock rehearsal for the radio show. Billy said, 'Geez, I still have to write two arrangements for the date tonight.' Remember: this was four in the afternoon, and the session is just a few hours away! Between four and eight o'clock, Billy wrote two charts, and one of them was 'Come Fly with Me.' He was an absolute genius."

The percussionist also remembers Sinatra's contribution to the orchestration on one song, "On the Road to Mandalay." "Billy had written the arrangement so that when we got to the line that says, ' . . . And the dawn comes up like thunder,' I would hit this huge gong as a punctuation.

Frank Sinatra's original vocal lead sheet for "April in Paris" from the Come Fly with Me sessions, 1957.

Then the arrangement would continue for about another half a chorus. Well, after the first run-through (which I don't believe was taped), we were doing the take, and Frank decided that after the gong, we would just cut it there. He wouldn't come back in—it'd just be left hanging there. And it made sense, musically—it worked just as well as if we'd gone on."

In 1957, when *Come Fly with Me* was recorded, Sinatra had been a major artist for more than a decade. Those who worked with him noted that his voice was showing new qualities.

In a 1955 *Time* interview, Nelson Riddle commented, "His voice is more interesting now: he has separated his voice into different colors, in different registers. Years ago, his voice was more even, and now it is divided into at least three in-

teresting ranges: low, middle, and high. [He's] probing more deeply into his songs than he used to. That may be due to the ten years he's put on, and the things he's gone through."

Two tunes from *Come Fly with Me* stand out as examples of Sinatra's breath control, legato-style phrasing, and especially the vocal maturity that Nelson Riddle spoke of: "April in Paris" and "Moonlight in Vermont." Both also highlight Billy May's rarely noted ability to write for strings.

In "April in Paris," the arranger sets the tone with a sweeping instrumental introduction. A throbbing string crescendo opens the song, and with the first downbeat—when the cymbal crashes and the low woodwinds attack—a counter-rhythm, working against the syncopation of Sinatra's vocal line, is established.

Pay careful attention to the way the instrumental and vocal lines play off each other: the first orchestral downbeat comes just before Sinatra's vocal line begins. The tension of the building orchestra mounts, quickly climaxes, and half a beat later, Sinatra's vocal comes in against a sweeping sea of suspended strings. Then the strings, voiced melodically, begin building again, heightening our anticipation of another climax.

In the next line, the reverse happens: the strings complete their syncopated crescendo and resolve on a downbeat that comes half a beat before Sinatra's vocal ends. This technique is very effective in maintaining a high level of drama.

Listen closely to the precision with which Sinatra opens and closes off his syllables, especially those that come at the ends of lines. Note the distinct enunciation of the ending of the word face in the first line, as Sinatra holds the second "face" and pronounces the "s" sound in a way that's sharp and articulate, but not overdone.

In the second line, the shading and color that others have spoken of is heard especially in his inflection of "heart," "sing," "warm," and "embrace": Sinatra's control throughout is exacting, his vocal; sharp, articulate, and clean.

Behind the vocal, May follows Sinatra with similarly phrased instrumental lines that augment and support the lyric. The orchestration is so simple that the singer's every vocal characteristic can be discerned.

The chorus demonstrates the singer's breath control, most apparent in the transitions that take him from line to line. Between the first and second lines of the chorus, he holds the word "trees," seamlessly blending it into the word "April" with no audible trace of breath and the most controlled vibrato imaginable.

Again, note the crisp deliberateness of the endings on the "s" words, like "Paris," "chestnuts," and "tables." (On "trees," he covers the "s" sound a bit within the slide from word to word.) Sinatra's voice blooms with color, especially on the words and phrases he holds over like "trees"

and "reprise." The latter word melds ever so smoothly into the "I" in the following line. But this time, Sinatra adds a bit of melancholic inflection to the word *reprise*.

The fourth and fifth line of the chorus are replete with lovely inflective tones. Sinatra emphatically ends the word embrace with a sharp, focused "s," and then begins a smooth downward spiral on the word "till," which he melds directly into the "April" of the final line of the song.

On "Moonlight in Vermont," we hear the same gradations of color and tone, and more of Sinatra's fluid legato style. On this tune, he chooses an airy, relaxed approach, and May's picturesque orchestration is sentimentally plush. Particularly noteworthy is the way Sinatra, using the harmonic changes in the orchestration to their best advantage, imparts a half-step key change as he glides from the word lovely to the word evening in the second chorus. The transition is silky smooth, the simple maneuver heightening the listener's anticipation at a critical point in the performance.

The ballad orchestrations for *Come Fly with Me* leave us wishing that Sinatra and May had done more of this. They did, but unfortunately, not for twenty-two years.

MELANCHOLY SERENADES: ONLY THE LONELY

*I*n 1958, to complement the highbrow *Close to You*, Sinatra and Nelson Riddle set out to create what each would cite as the finest example of their work, *Only the Lonely*.

While the orchestrations for *Close to You* express the intimacy of a chamber-music setting, for *Only the Lonely* the arranger chose to unfurl his musical canvas, painting aching portraits of loneliness on an expansive landscape sparingly dotted with musical colors and textures. Against a somber backdrop of understated strings speak judicious traces of instruments like French horn, oboe, flute, clarinet, bassoon, and trombone, and the barest wisp of a rhythm section. Semi-classical in feel, each four-minute tune is a short story of gloom and despair transformed into a cry for sympathy.

"As an arranger, it has always been a joy to me to occasionally have the opportunity of shaking off the confines of a sax section and its derivative doubles, and to contemplate the luxury of a full woodwind section with all the misty, velvety sounds that issue from such a group if properly used," Riddle once wrote. "In *Only the Lonely*, I had the advantage of such a group, within a larger still combination of other instruments. Since that time, I have, whenever appropriate, turned to this setup to enrich and beautify an arrangement. The combination employs the 'classic' series of pairings: two flutes, two oboes, two clarinets, and two bassoons."

"A contributing factor to the mood of the album was the fact that my mother had died earlier that month," Riddle explained to disc jockey Jonathan Schwartz. "She was in Sinai Hospital with terminal cancer. I think the somber circumstances of one's mother dying contributed to the darker colors of the album. And, I had also lost a daughter three months earlier—a little girl. So, if I can attach events like that to music, perhaps *Only the Lonely* was the result."

With so much tragedy surrounding the arranger, it was amazing that he could even function, let alone consider scoring an album for Frank Sinatra. "I'd be painting the house during the daytime," he said. "I find it's good therapy for any arranger to paint his house because arrangers work in small jerky motions to write notes, and painting a house requires long, sweeping motions. For me, it was therapy."

The sessions for *Only the Lonely* are remarkable in that instead of the album being recorded over three successive nights (as was the custom), there were four sessions spread over a month and a half. A number of circumstances forced this unusual arrangement. On May 5, 1958, recording commenced in Studio A at the Capitol Tower. The date yielded three songs slated for the final album: "Guess I'll Hang My Tears Out to Dry," "Ebb Tide," and "Angel Eyes." Unhappy with the results, Sinatra deemed the recordings unacceptable. (The tunes would be re-recorded at subsequent sessions.)

Al Viola, Sinatra's steady guitarist, was in the studio and recalls that particular session. "I got a call from Manie Klein, who was the contractor, to do all of the *Only the Lonely* dates. When I arrived on the first date, George Van Eps was also there. George had a certain guitar style, and he was called to play the verse on 'Guess I'll Hang My Tears Out to Dry.' I was playing rhythm guitar.

"So we began to make a take. Nelson wrote the chart in the key of B, and he had written a pedal point of low F-sharp for the guitar. Now, what happens when you have to reach for that low F-sharp on the guitar is that it interferes with your movement to the other chord progressions . . . what makes it difficult is that you hear your fingers moving. So, they went for a take on the song, and there was silence after it was finished. Frank said, 'That's fine.'

"Then, someone in the booth said, 'Frank, we need another one, because of the verse.' They never played it back, and Frank just said, 'All right.' He was very sympathetic, knowing that there was something wrong with the guitar in the verse, and that it wasn't him. So they did another take, and that was it. I myself was hearing something that wasn't quite right [in the guitar part]—there were no mistakes there, but it was just hard for George to play as written, with that low F-sharp pedal point."

The next scheduled session for the album was May 29. "I was on another recording date in the afternoon, and the Sinatra session was supposed to start at 8:00 P.M.," Viola recalls.

"I got a call from the Kleins through my service. 'They want you to bring your gut string guitar tonight.' Now, I didn't have it with me—and it's already 6:00 P.M., and I can't get home! But I knew a salesman down at Music City on Sunset and Vine, so I went down and borrowed the best gut string they had. I get to the studio, and I begin looking at the parts from Vern Yocum, the copyist. And I see 'Guess I'll Hang My Tears Out to Dry.' I call over to Bill [Miller]: 'Bill, is he gonna do this again?' Bill says, 'Yeah—don't worry about it. So you do it! Is it hard?' And I explained to Bill about the F-sharp and all that . . . it's like stepping on eggs, because it's just Frank and the guitar there."

Viola, a consummate professional, used his ingenuity to get around the problem. "I had some training in classical guitar, and I could play 'fin-ger' style—no pick. This is how George Van Eps was playing, but he was using a rhythm guitar—I was using a gut string. So when I saw that F-sharp bustin' my ass, I did what classical guitar players sometimes do: I raised the low E to an F-sharp. This meant my right thumb could hit the F-sharp without me fingering the F-sharp, which gave me the pedal point and the ability to move around on the guitar! And that's what you hear on the record: you hear an F-sharp, but it's open. And there is no 'F-sharp' on the guitar! It's always an E. On that tune, I raised it to an F-sharp pedal point, and it's ringing out—it sustains—because it's not fingered. That's how I got away with it. We did one take, and Frank looked at me and said, 'Yeah, Dago! That was clean!' It had

PHOTOGRAPH BY SID AVERY, COURTESY OF MPTV ARCHIVE

Frank Sinatra surveys the orchestra at the sessions for Only the Lonely, May 1958. Guitarist Al Viola is at the far right.

COURTESY OF AL VIOLA

Sketch of Al Viola's gut-string guitar solo on "Guess I'll Hang My Tears Out to Dry" from Only the Lonely (1958).

been the F-sharp that was screwing everything up—it was too hard to maneuver and achieve the way Nelson had written it. I was scared sh—less, but I did it."

"Nowadays, a guitar player would say, 'How come this is in the key of B, the guitar is playing an F-sharp, and it's ringing out?' And, you know, Frank hadn't said anything to Van Eps, because everybody loved him. George was trying to do something that Nelson had messed up. Nelson really didn't know too much about the guitar—he knew a lot about horns and strings. He called me to do the Julie Andrews Show, and when I used to look at the guitar parts, he'd have eight notes on a stem . . . and there are only six notes on a guitar! So I'd figure out what he meant—what he wanted. But this particular song was very touchy, yet it came out fine," Viola concludes.

When Viola redid "Tears," Nelson Riddle wasn't even in the studio. "I was booked to do a

PHOTOGRAPH BY SID AVERY, COURTESY OF MPTV ARCHIVE

Frank Sinatra sings while Felix Slatkin conducts Only the Lonely.

tour of Canada with Nat Cole that summer and had hoped that maybe we could finish the album before I left," the arranger said. "I wrote all of the arrangements, but Felix Slatkin conducted the session."

Eleanor Slatkin distinctly recalled the singer expressing his pleasure with Slatkin's conducting and the outcome of the session. "We went out for a bite to eat afterwards, and Frank, right in front of Felix, said, 'This is the marriage of a dream.' But then, Felix was a conductor. That's the difference—he turned every phrase to fit Frank. You have to be a conductor to do that—that the others couldn't do."

Most arrangers, by default, lead the orchestra for their recording sessions. Since conducting is a study unto itself, many orchestrators are not truly accomplished conductors, although their skill is sufficient to the needs of most pop recordings. Nelson had studied conducting with both Slatkin and violinist Victor Bay, but he wasn't a pro.

Warren "Champ" Webb, a fine woodwind player and personal friend, describes Riddle's conducting method. "Nelson was a superb conductor in this sense: he looked awkward—his hand-eye coordination was not the greatest in the world—but he listened to us. Whether we were doing a film or record date, we'd say, 'Just give us one in every bar—that's all we need.' Then he'd become very relaxed, and he'd be able to conduct."

Pressured by the loss of the songs recorded at the May fifth session (this delayed finishing the album), Sinatra completed seven full songs at the Slatkin-conducted session of May 29, more than double the normal yield for a standard three-hour session. An eighth song planned for inclusion on the album, the haunting Billy Strayhorn classic "Lush Life," was attempted and ultimately left incomplete—possibly owing to the fatigue of such a long session.

While "Lush Life" is beautiful and well suited to interpretation by a vocalist with the dramatic flair of Frank Sinatra, it doesn't really fit into the overall scheme of *Only the Lonely*. Part of the reason is an awkward, out-of-meter piano introduction that evokes images of a honky-tonk piano bar, blatantly out of character for the album's otherwise low-key atmosphere. The intro lacks the finesse and subdued sophistication so evident in the piano intro to "One for My Baby," the record's quintessential saloon song. Extant session tapes shed some light on what transpired in the studio and why Sinatra abandoned the song after three partial takes:

From the booth: "Master 19257, Take One." Bill Miller begins the piano intro, and after ten seconds, the take is halted. The tape is again slated: "Master 19257, Take Two." The piano introduction is completed, and a simple swell of strings spiral down, giving way to a harp glissando and Sinatra's entrance at the verse. "I used to visit all the very gay places/those come what may places/where one relaxes on the axis of the wheel of life. . . ."

Sinatra cuts the take. "Once more," he asks, vocalizing through the first few lines off-mike to get a sense of the timing. On the third take, which runs a little over two minutes, Sinatra gets through the verse and tentatively approaches the chorus. "Life is lonely/again, and only last year/everything seemed. . . ."

"Hold it!" he calls. "It's not only tough enough with the way it is . . . but he's got some slides in there!" Mockingly, Sinatra begins to joke, exaggerating his mannerisms. "Ooohh, yeah! Well, Ahhhhh . . . " From the booth comes the suggestion to put the song aside, and try "Sleep Warm." "Yeah, all righty now . . . ," Sinatra continues. "Put it aside for a minute," someone (possibly Slatkin) says, and Sinatra sarcastically retorts, "Put it aside for about a year!"

Moments later, "Lush Life" is forgotten, and Sinatra turns in a searingly plaintive version of "Willow Weep for Me."

On "Lush Life," Nelson Riddle commented, "It's a rather complicated song, and I think Frank would have been momentarily put off by all the changes that had to go on. He could not have but admired the song, and that's why he included it in the list. But when he got down to singing it, it was another matter; not that he couldn't have sung it with ease, and beautifully, if he had tried a couple more times. But it takes a lot of concentration to do seven songs in one session, and by that time he might have gotten a little tired."

Warren Webb's graceful oboe and English horn playing provided much of the interesting textural color on the album. "Those arrangements are the finest things that Nelson ever did," Webb believes. "He had unlimited resources—almost sixty or seventy players. We had a complete symphonic woodwind section: two flutes, two oboes, two clarinets, two bass clarinets, two bassoons, four horns, four trumpets, and four trombones. For this album, Nelson wrote the woodwinds exactly the same way that he would write for the strings; I had never heard that—it was the first time he'd done it. He had never had that big a section before! In the early days, Nelson would rely on me and Harry Klee, who would be the only two woodwinds on date after date. But Nelson would write in such a way that we sounded like a full woodwind section! Here, he had a complete section, and he had wanted to have something like that for so long."

Webb looks upon "What's New?" recorded at the third session (June 24) as a prime example of the album's clever woodwind composition. "Ray Simms plays the melody, and Tommy Pederson played the jazz figure underneath him. Ray embellished the melody a little bit, and I wondered if Nelson wrote everything that he played, or if he just gave Tommy and Ray some indication on the chart. It was so unobtrusive, and it was unusual to have two trombones playing, with one accompanying the other with a little rhythmic figure underneath a sweeping ballad like that—particularly on a tune like this," he says.

Also rehearsed at the June 24 session was the Sinatra showstopper: "One for My Baby," which the singer had originally recorded for Columbia in 1947. Unaware that the tape would be saved, Sinatra made a take of the song with Bill Miller's piano accompaniment. Two days later, at the final session for the album, the song would be re-recorded as rehearsed, with the addition of the full orchestra. When the forgotten rehearsal tape was found in the Capitol vaults in 1990 and issued on compact disc, it became clear that the song is most effective when performed most simply.

Sinatra once shared with author Robin Douglas-Home the intimate atmosphere that permeated the studio when he made the master recording of "One for My Baby." "We ended *Only the Lonely* with that song, and something happened then that I've never seen before or since at a recording session. I'd always sung that song before in clubs with just my pianist Bill Miller backing me, a single spotlight on my face and cigarette, and the rest of the room in complete darkness. At this session, the word had somehow got around, and there were about sixty or seventy people there: Capitol employees and their friends, people off the street . . . anyone. Dave Cavanaugh was the A&R man, and he knew how I sang it in clubs, and he switched out all the lights—bar the spot on me. The atmosphere in that studio was exactly like a club. Dave said, 'Roll 'em,' there was one take, and that was that. The only time I've known it to happen like that."

Two more gems followed *Only the Lonely*: the infectious, rip-roaring *Come Dance with Me*, another Billy May jumper (recorded in 1958); and the ultra-melancholy *No One Cares*, with Jenkins (waxed in 1959). Both extend the contrasting attitudes begun with their predecessors, *Where Are You?* and *Come Fly with Me*. *Come Dance with Me* garnered tremendous critical attention. The album reached number two and maintained a place on the Billboard charts for 140 weeks. It also brought home three Grammys: Album of the Year, Best Male Vocal Performance, and Best Arrangements.

SEASON OF DISCONTENT

*I*n spring of 1960, Frank Sinatra and Nelson Riddle began working on a collection of ballads for an album that was tentatively titled *The Nearness of You*. Far more optimistic in spirit than *Only the Lonely* or *No One Cares*, the selection of tunes—all classic American popular standards—was matchless, and especially noteworthy since each of the twelve were re-recordings of songs the singer had sung at Columbia in the 1940s and early 1950s.

Realizing the importance of the songs and the value of Sinatra's updated interpretations, Riddle arranged many of the tunes to feature short instrumental solos. These simple vignettes brought freshness to the remakes and highlighted the capabilities of some of Sinatra's most cherished musical friends: Bill Miller (piano—"I've Got a Crush on You"), Plas Johnson (tenor sax—"Nevertheless" and "That Old Feeling"), Harry Klee (flute—"Fools Rush In"), George Roberts (bass trombone—"How Deep Is the Ocean?"), Carroll Lewis (trumpet—"She's Funny That Way") and Felix Slatkin (violin—"Try a Little Tenderness" and "Mam'selle").

Sessions for the album were held over three nights in the first week of March. Sinatra was in exquisite voice and completed four songs at each session.

In the days that followed, the decision was made to drop "The Nearness of You" and replace it with a snappier song that could succeed as both the title track and a commercially viable single. The substitute tune, "Nice 'n Easy" (written by Lew Spence, Marilyn Keith, and Alan Bergman) was recorded one month later, and although its comparatively bright tempo upset the thematic balance of the album, it served the purpose. So, *The Nearness of You* became *Nice 'n Easy*.

"Lew had a relationship with Sinatra's publisher, who said he needed a title song for this album of ballads, so we came up with 'Nice 'n Easy,'" Bergman explained. "Marilyn and I were in the control room when he recorded it, and Frank really liked it. It was the first time we had met him, and we were really in awe of what was going on."

The session tapes for the song are among the most interesting of all the singer's outtakes. Sinatra's demeanor during this session is playful—occasionally bawdy.

After the customary run-through, the first full take of "Nice 'n Easy" begins, and although Sinatra falls into the gentle tempo with ease, the performance is marred by some flat notes and tentative syncopation. When he reaches the ending, he stumbles over a word, throwing the timing off. "Ah, ya dirty mother!" he quips. "That quarter rest is murder!"

Between attempts, Sinatra jokes with producer Dave Cavanaugh and the songwriters in the booth. "The jury said one more," he announces after one take, alluding to the awestruck composers standing in the control room. Further on in the proceedings, when asked for another take, his response is humorous. "You better get me while you can!" he retorts, feigning drunkenness.

Later, after a partial take is aborted, Cavanaugh immediately rolls the tape, verbally slating the upcoming take. Sinatra, unsure of what the problem was, interrupts. "Whoa, whoa, wait—time! What's the matter? Notes? Clams?" When the producer affirms this, Sinatra defends his errors: "Whaddya expect, I don't know the song!"

The takes progress, and after twelve tries, the decision to combine the complete vocal performance from take eleven and the ending from take twelve is made.

Sinatra, knowing that they'd have to "hook" the listener with a memorable close, paid careful attention to the ending. It was his idea to adopt the "one more time/one more once" reprise from Count Basie's famous recording of "April in Paris." "The tag was a big surprise, and his doing it twice delighted us," Bergman remembers. Especially fascinating is how Sinatra works to find the proper wording and rhythmic cadence for the half-spoken, half-sung tag.

On the released record, the reprise and tag play out like this:

> *Nice 'n easy does it,*
> *nice 'n easy does it,*
> *nice 'n easy does it every time*
> (spoken) *like the man says one more*
> *time . . .*
> *Nice 'n easy does it,*
> *nice 'n easy does it,*
> *nice 'n easy does it every time*

On the familiar record, the song then ends with a seven-note acoustic bass fill and one Sinatra finger snap on the last beat.

What happened to the reprise in the takes before the final master is another story! During the first eight takes, Sinatra adds a *second* spoken tag to finish off the record. Here is a sampling of his ribald "alternate" tags that didn't make it to the final cut:

"Just put your hand on it, baby, that's all" (take one), "Slowly, baby" (take eight), and "Isn't that better, baby?" (take nine).

Though out of context on this soft, dim-the-lights-style album, "Nice 'n Easy" is a sprightly romp that emphasizes the carefree bacheloresque image that Sinatra cultivated at this stage of his life, and it remains one of his most memorable hits. The real prizes—the twelve ballads from the *The Nearness of You* sessions—are like a satchel of gold nuggets.

Enhancing the appeal of the performances is the album's superb sonics, perhaps the best of all Sinatra's records. The expertly balanced stereo mix is full of well-defined textures and tones. The bass is deep, solid, and satisfying; the top end sweet and clear. The rich mellowness of the vocals is enveloped in the warm bloom of the satiny-smooth string section, a lustrous backdrop for the contrasting soloists.

While he appeared to be the master of congeniality on the April 1960 session tapes for "Nice 'n Easy," Sinatra was feeling an increasing disdain for Capitol and the executives on the top floor of the Tower.

For years (since the "Flaw in My Flue" incident of 1956) he had felt the label was focusing more on the marketing and less on the creative aspects of making records. The executives controlled every move he made. The adventurer in him found this stifling. Using his stature as one of the label's most profitable artists as leverage, he requested that Capitol create an imprint label for him: he would control it creatively, and they would promote it through their powerful distribution system. His suggestion fell on deaf ears.

In late 1960, the singer issued an ultimatum to the company's executives. "Capitol had loaned him $250,000 against future royalties," recalls Alan Livingston. "It was no tremendous risk—Frank paid it back very quickly, because he was earning so much. When he had paid it back, he went to Glen Wallichs, and said, 'I want my own label, and here's the deal. . . .' And it wasn't that the deal was so terrible—it was just totally contrary to everything going on in the record business then. So Glen said, 'If I give it to you, Frank, I've got to give it to Nat Cole, and so-and-so . . . you're disrupting our whole business!' So Glen turned him down, and Frank went off in a huff and said, 'Screw you. I won't record

anymore—you can't make me sing.' Sinatra didn't sing, avoiding the Capitol studios for seven months (from September of 1960 until March of 1961).

Before storming away on his self-imposed exile, Sinatra had recorded what is one of the shortest, yet probably the gassiest of all the Sinatra-Riddle efforts, the gut pounding *Sinatra's Swingin' Session!!!* Armed with a slew of standards (including "My Blue Heaven," "It All Depends on You," "It's Only a Paper Moon," and "Always"), the singer entered Studio A, and without so much as a run-through, immediately requested that Nelson increase the tempo on each of the arrangements. Whether he was thumbing his nose at the Capitol brass or whether he just wanted to finish the album in record time may never be known, but it had a profound effect on the album's overall excitement.

Except for the beguiling "September in the Rain" and "Blue Moon," most of the tunes are taken at breakneck speed, adding mightily to the

The highly-charged atmosphere is palpable in this studio overview from the Sinatra's Swingin' Session!!! recording date.

electricity that makes the barely thirty-minute collection irresistible. Especially appealing are two outstanding sax solos by rhythm and blues legend Plas Johnson: on the driving "My Blue Heaven" he turns in a set of rollicking, gritty licks; on "Blue Moon" the mood is bluesy and soulful. This album reveals how Riddle, when writing for Sinatra, assiduously avoided the stereotypical musical figures he relied on with other singers. The devilishly sexy "I Concentrate on You," for instance, is one of the few times he featured bongo drums in the Sinatra rhythm section—something he did quite frequently when orchestrating for Judy Garland.

Like Nice 'n Easy before it, *Sinatra's Swingin' Session!!!* had excellent sound: the stereo balance is perfect; the band, bold, bright and snappy. The recording's most outstanding sonic characteristic is its lifelike ambient sound, preserved due to thoughtful microphone placement and sensitive use of reverb.

"Presence" is the whole feel of a recording: how close or distant it sounds, the balance and contrast of the instruments, and how much of the recording room's natural acoustics have been retained. Here, the smallest details, such as Comfort's bass line tags and the small cymbal accents, are clean and clear, and Sinatra's vocal is close, warm, and sharp, especially in "September in the Rain," "I Concentrate on You," and "My Blue Heaven." On the latter, note the tight, close feel of the bass-drum kick and cymbal splash that close the song.

Sinatra's feud with Capitol lasted just over half a year, focusing primarily on Alan Livingston, the very man who had made Sinatra's comeback possible. "I had left Capitol [during Sinatra's hiatus]; when I came back, he had not made one record," says Livingston. "I thought, 'Let me see what I can do.' So I picked up the phone, and I called Frank, and said, 'Frank—I'm back at Capitol now.' He said, 'I know.' I said, 'Well, why don't you and I sit down and see if we can't work things out?' Now, I won't say the four

letter words he used on me, but he said, 'I'm going to tear down that Capitol Tower . . . to hell with you!'"

Ultimately, the impasse was worked out and a deal struck whereby Sinatra would record two more albums and one single for Capitol, while concurrently recording and releasing albums and singles for his own newly formed label, Reprise Records.

MANIC DEPRESSION: COME SWING WITH ME AND POINT OF NO RETURN

While the control and ownership of record and imprint labels by artists is common today (and is, in fact, a point of negotiation in contract discussions with the world's top recording artists), Frank Sinatra was the first to insist on it.

According to Sinatra, he named the label Reprise Records (in music reprise means to recapitulate or repeat the main theme) because these would be records "to play and play again." More likely, the name was a play on the word *reprisal*, prompting some to call the imprint "Revenge Records." Reprise was a label where the executives concerned themselves with the artistic first, and the financial details second. It was the first to allow artists to maintain full creative control over their product, and to retain the financial rights to them as well. Sinatra was now free to pursue whatever musical whim caught his fancy—a luxury he extended to any artist willing to take a risk and sign with a new label.

However, the label floundered for a period during its infancy, crippled by fiercely planned competition from Capitol. Ultimately, Jack Warner stepped in and purchased the company from Sinatra for three million dollars in 1963 (Sinatra retained a one-third share in the new Warner-Reprise).

"As soon as Frank started Reprise, we [Capitol] began to exploit our whole Sinatra catalog, because we weren't going to have him anymore," said Livingston. "We had so much Sinatra product on the market that Reprise couldn't get off the ground! After a couple of years, Reprise was practically out of business, and when Warner Brothers bought it, they put Mo Ostin in charge, and they began to have some success. They did quite well as a Warner Brothers label."

This is a virtual repeat of what happened when Sinatra left Columbia Records in 1952. At that time, Columbia had hurriedly assembled a group of uneven LP collections culled from the 1940's singles, in order to compete with Sinatra's new, snappier concept albums at Capitol. In retaliation, Sinatra began to re-record many of his best songs from the Columbia years at Capitol, a tactic he would repeat when he left Capitol to form Reprise.

Though they were recorded under forced contractual obligation, the two Capitol albums *Come Swing with Me* and *Point of No Return*, of March and September 1961, show no sign of this. *Come Swing with Me* is a jubilant listening experience. Instrumentally, May's band is in rare form, fueled by the highest octane available. Of the singer, Nancy Sinatra once remarked that you can actually hear Frank smile on a record. If that is true, on these sessions, he was grinning from ear to ear.

For this, his third album with Sinatra, Billy May fashioned some of the most clever orchestrations ever to grace a vocal record. Instead of using his often-imitated sax section, May eliminated it and opted for a big, bright brass band. "I got the feeling that the people at Capitol wanted me to copy what I'd done on an album prior to that called *Billy May's Big Fat Brass*. They'd liked that album, and that's where they got the idea of using the brass band," he recently said.

Because the stereo spread would be highlighted, May approached the scoring of the album differently than he would a standard big band session. "Around that time, they started talking about using the stereo ping-pong effect, so that's why we divided the band in half, to try and accomplish that. But I couldn't use too much of that in the band, because my primary purpose was backing Sinatra. We used two complete brass sections with ten guys in each section, and set them up on two sides of the studio to deliberately get that separation." What results is the most animated musical conversation imaginable.

Devoid of the exaggerated tricks that were common on stereo "showcase" records of the day (the ultra-mod "Stereo Action" Esquivel records from RCA come to mind), the unique concept and unusual instrumentation worked, primarily because of the care May had used when laying out the arrangements. Each of the individual groups, set up to the right and left of the singer, comprised four trumpets, three trombones, two French horns, and one bass trombone. Making a rare appearance on a Sinatra record, a tuba rounded out the brass instruments. Folded into the mix was one standard rhythm section (piano, bass, drums, and guitar), glockenspiel, and harp.

Owing (in part) to the decisive placement of the principal players on the studio floor, *Come Swing with Me* is one of the few albums of its era that demonstrates the dazzle of well-recorded stereo. The driving momentum of the performances simply adds to the happy topography of the album.

Of its twelve songs, seven are re-recordings of tunes Sinatra had recorded at Victor and Columbia: "Day by Day," "Almost Like Being in Love," "Five Minutes More," "On the Sunny Side of the Street," "That Old Black Magic," and "Lover." Of these, only "Five Minutes More" and

"Lover" bear any resemblance to their forebears; the balance enjoy fresh perspectives. New recordings of "Sentimental Journey" (taken at a sensuous ballad tempo), "Yes Indeed," "Don't Take Your Love from Me," "Paper Doll," and "I've Heard That Song Before" round out the older favorites.

Assisting Billy May with the orchestrations was arranger Heinie Beau, who charted five of the twelve songs on the record. Beau often worked closely with May, duplicating his style under the orchestrator's close supervision.

The top tune on the album happens to be the shortest, but Sinatra, May, and Beau prove that quality, not quantity is what counts, packing tons of witty music into the scant two minutes of Lerner and Lowe's "Almost Like Being in Love." Within these two ultra-rhythmic minutes, dozens of small but integral bits of melody fly by, the orchestration built as carefully and intricately as a six-story house of cards. Body and richness is provided by the tuba and dual bass trombones (both positioned solidly to the left side) and the rhythm section (confined to the right side of the soundstage). Brass ensembles split the difference, expertly layered to provide texture to the ebullient arrangement.

Kicking things off are two emphatic snare drum beats, which give way to the brass section trading a few sharply attacked, slurred crescendos. Under the brass fireworks, the tuba is voiced to play the same melody, while the French horns form a light bed, sustaining a simple, long-lined countermelody against it. After Sinatra's vocal entrance, the joyously plucked bass and loosely articulated cymbal accents keep the entire ensemble moving buoyantly along. Behind and around the vocal, sharp melodic punches continue from the brass section.

"There are at least three different things going on within the orchestration," explains composer-musician Joel Friedman. "Obviously, there's the whole vocal part. Then, there's the rhythm section, with its little melodic ornaments.

But the most interesting part is the French horn melody that's meandering through its own slow, little world. The horn melody there is of its own rhythm, and if you heard it alone, you would never assume that it would go in that kind of song. It doesn't sound as it was written so much with the original melody in mind; rather, it moves differently. It follows the melody in a way harmonically, though: it's in key, and follows the chord changes. At some points, it even harmonizes the melody a little bit."

Friedman describes how notes within a chord help to harmonize a melody: "If you're playing a note that's in a chord, and the melody is also a note from that chord (but they're two different notes), then basically, you're harmonizing that melody. Doing this definitely enhances the melody . . . it moves with the melody, while at the same time preserving its own little form. Strings will very often perform this function: there'll be a string patch of a chord, and then it will change. As it's approaching the next chord, it might do a little step up to it in some of the notes, to prepare you for the chord a little bit."

The driving musical accompaniment challenges Sinatra to stay on his toes; toward the end, he effortlessly glides into a quick key change during the word way, taking it up a step to heighten the interest.

For *Point of No Return*, the mood in the studio was quite different from that for *Come Swing with Me*. Aside from the vexing business problems with Capitol, Sinatra was forced to confront personal issues regarding his long-lost friendship with arranger Axel Stordahl, who was chosen to aid the singer on his last classic Capitol album.

Trombonist Milt Bernhart counts it among his favorite Sinatra recordings, despite the difficulties that accompanied its creation. "Dave Cavanaugh had thought it would be a nice touch to have Stordahl do the last album. By this time, Sinatra was having some difficulties with the record company, and the strain between them showed in the studio. Capitol didn't have a chip on their shoulder: Sinatra did. Capitol did everything possible to make him comfortable, but he showed up an hour and a half late for each session—something he never did before. It gave Axel some extra time to rehearse, though, and when Frank came in, everything was ready to go.

"When he did come in, Sinatra was all business," Bernhart says. "The usual audience was there and he walked in with his entourage and went right up to the microphone, and said, 'What's up?' Didn't really even address Stordahl [who was seriously ill at the time]. On most of the tunes, he did only one, maybe two takes, with no run-throughs. At one point, Dave Cavanaugh (the producer) asked him for another take on a song, because something had gone wrong in the booth. Sinatra refused. The lead sheet was already on the floor. He said, 'Nope. Next tune.' When Cavanaugh tried to cajole him into doing another take, Sinatra just glared at him, picked up the lead sheet, and tore it into about twenty pieces. 'Didn't you hear me?' he asked. 'Next number!'"

That Sinatra still harbored a grudge against Stordahl was obvious from the tension in the studio on these sessions. This was something that Bernhart had learned about firsthand years before. "It had occurred on the day that all the musicians were visiting his home," Bernhart says. "I had always loved the arrangement that Axel did for Sinatra's "The Night We Called It a Day" from 1942. When we were talking, I thought I would make a big hit with him, and I told him how much that recording had meant to me. Frank just kind of looked at me, and asked, 'Have you heard the one I just made with Gordon Jenkins?' I hadn't, and he was very intent on having me hear it, so we went to his big hi-fi setup, and he played it for me—he stood and watched as I listened!"

"Musically, it wasn't the same—it was lemonade! I was never a big fan of Gordon Jenkins, and this didn't have nearly the same feeling as the Stordahl arrangement. I didn't say so to

Frank, but I am sure that he knew by my expression. He's very perceptive that way. But when he looked at me, that's when I knew, and I knew it right away. Something was up between him and Axel. Bill Miller had told me that Frank had practically disowned him, after the Eddie Fisher TV thing. Unfortunately, Axel turned his back on him, and Frank never forgave him for that."

Robin Douglas-Home attended the sessions of September 11 and 12, 1961, the evenings on which the album was recorded. He viewed the proceedings from a much different perspective than Milt Bernhart. He wrote, "The only moment that the atmosphere got tense was when the man in the control room said he wanted to re-record an improvised passage on the piano by Bill Miller, put in at Sinatra's suggestion. 'Why?' asked Sinatra. 'I don't like it,' a voice boomed through the speakers. 'Well, I do. Next tune,' answered Sinatra. And that was that."

Douglas-Home describes Sinatra's final moments in Studio A, a place he would not revisit for more than thirty years. "At 11:45, the last playback came to a final chord. There was a moment of silence which, after the tremendous volume of noise, gave one the strange feeling of being left suspended in mid-air. Then, the orchestra started clapping. Sinatra turned away, pretending to be unaware of the applause, and occupied himself by busily buttoning his shirt and straightening his tie. He eventually raised an arm and said, 'Thank you, fellers,' and walked toward the door. There was a disorderly shout of, 'Night, Frank,' then the scores were folded, the instruments packed away, and in no time at all, the studio was empty and quiet."

Listening to the album song by song, and understanding the stressful conditions under which it was recorded, one can easily distinguish between the "true" Sinatra and the lackadaisical, intractable singer that merely showed up because he had to. Albums are not usually sequenced in the order in which the songs were recorded, and the songs that Sinatra had invested real effort in are mixed with the ones he might as well been phoning in.

The moving "When the World Was Young" is easily worth the price of the album. The simplicity of his whimsically musical narration, coupled with the poignancy of his singing, proves his effectiveness as both an actor and storyteller.

Sprinkled in among the lesser renditions of "September Song," "A Million Dreams Ago," and "These Foolish Things" are superb renditions of "Memories of You," "As Time Goes By," "I'll Remember April," and "There Will Never Be Another You." The remaining songs are perfunctory run-throughs which, when compared to the flawlessness of his earlier Capitol recordings, fall far short of the mark. One telltale sign is a couple of clearly audible edits, including a glaring one at the end of "These Foolish Things," in which the final word, "you" in the line " . . . these foolish things remind me of you," is obviously cut in from a different take. That these were allowed to slip by indicates how fully Sinatra had divorced himself from Capitol.

Rubbing salt in a sore wound, the company insisted that Sinatra provide them with one additional single, as specified in their contract. Averse to even setting foot in the Capitol studios, Sinatra fulfilled his obligation by turning in a remote, affect-less reading of the Harold Arlen-Ted Koehler classic, "I Got a Right to Sing the Blues," recorded at the end of a Reprise session at United Recording on March 6, 1962. (The song selection was both ironic and contradictory: Sinatra had good reason to sing anything but the blues with this recording; he was finally free of Capitol and able to immerse himself in his own two-year-old record company.)

Sinatra's petulance was plain to everyone in the studio that night, and the cause not merely Capitol Records. His anger over recording the song was actually mitigated by the presence of producer Dave Cavanaugh—one of the few people from his former label with whom he was still friendly.

But when the Capitol tune was dispensed with, Cavanaugh left, and Sinatra and May set out to record two songs by Cahn and Van Heusen: "The Boys' Night Out" and "Cathy." When Jimmy Van Heusen showed up in the control room, the singer's already touchy mood darkened.

A week earlier, Sinatra was to have played host to President John F. Kennedy, who had scheduled a visit to Sinatra's Palm Springs compound. The selection of his home as the unoffical "West Coast White House" was an unspoken reward for Sinatra's tremendous aid to Kennedy during his presidential campaign. Sinatra cherished his friendship with the president and viewed it as a public affirmation of his stature. He believed that Kennedy owed much to him for the success of his campaign—for reasons that extended well beyond his munificent fundraising efforts.

Robert Kennedy, the president's brother and U.S. attorney general, felt otherwise. As Jack Kennedy sought the exciting aura that accompanied a relationship with one of Hollywood's elite, Robert was making a valiant effort to distance the president from Sinatra and the undesirable mobsters he was believed to consort with.

Just prior to the president's departing for California, and after Sinatra had gone to the expense of adding a new building and other amenities to his property to accommodate the president and secret service, the White House, citing "security concerns," announced that the Kennedy entourage would not be staying at Sinatra's home: they would encamp at Bing Crosby's estate instead. Sinatra was furious. Worse, learning of the sudden change of plans, Sinatra's close friend Jimmy Van Heusen offered the president the use of his nearby home, in case additional rooms were needed. Sinatra, smelling disloyalty, now became incensed.

"There was a controversy between Sinatra and Van Heusen in the studio that night," Billy May recalls. "He was in a snit. We had done 'The

THE CAPITOL YEARS, 1953-1962

Boys' Night Out,' and all during the recording, Frank just glared at Jimmy in the control room. Then, it came time to do the second song, 'Cathy,' which was a pretty song—a waltz. Frank did a rehearsal, and then looked over at Van Heusen, and said 'Tell you what, Chester. Why don't you get Jack Kennedy to record this f—ing song, and then see how many records it sells?'"

"With that," May continues, "Sinatra tossed the music on the floor, and refused to sing it. But we made an orchestral track, and he stayed until that was done, and then dismissed the band. I re-member that we left before he did—he was still talking to somebody. He never did overdub a vo-cal on it."

The one Reprise song completed on the date, "The Boys' Night Out," is a throwaway that didn't see the light of day until 1995. And while the Capitol single, "I Got a Right to Sing the Blues," is pleasant enough, it lacks the sparkle Sinatra might have lavished upon it even a year earlier. With a simple "All right, that's all!" at the end of the final take, Sinatra bid adieu to Dave Cavanaugh and the weight of the Capitol Tower.

PHOTOGRAPH BY ED THRASHER, COURTESY OF MPTV ARCHIVE

PART 4

The Reprise Years

*T*aking full advantage of his parting with Capitol, Sinatra broke free of the Riddle, May, and Jenkins triumvirate that had dominated the last nine years of his recording life and, although he continued to utilize their talents on appropriate projects, began to produce a string of progressive, diverse recordings.

Between 1960 and 1967, there were full-blown swing outings with Johnny Mandel, Billy May, and Sy Oliver and three superior albums with Bill "Count" Basie (two studio efforts in 1962 and 1964, followed by a kickin', high-gear live set from the Sands Hotel in Las Vegas in 1966). Among the other unusual projects he completed were a collection of four albums titled the *Reprise Repertory Theater* series (1963), in which Frank and fellow label mates Bing Crosby, Sammy Davis, and Dean Martin joined a host of other celebrity vocalists for Rat Pack-esque versions of *Guys and Dolls*, *Kiss Me Kate*, *South Pacific*, and *Finian's Rainbow*. While the concept was interesting, the results were uneven, the Sinatra solo and duet recordings outshining the rest by a mile. On the easier side, there were ballad sessions with Jenkins, a gorgeous album of concert-style Broadway standards with Nelson Riddle, and a handful of albums and singles with Don Costa. The mid-1960s marked a foray into the snarly blues-rock scene with *That's Life*, charted by Ernie Freeman. Two superb pairings with Antonio Carlos Jobim and Duke Ellington came in 1967; as the decade ended, Sinatra found himself experimenting with Four Seasons producer Charles Callello and poet Rod McKuen in order to appeal to a more contemporary audience.

While still under contract to Capitol, Sinatra had recorded five full albums for Reprise: *Ring-A-Ding-Ding!*, *I Remember Tommy*, *Swing Along with Me* (later retitled *Sinatra Swings!* after yet another legal battle with Capitol, this time over Reprise's use of similar thematic album titles), *Sinatra and Strings*, and *All Alone*. Sprinkled among the LP recordings was a handful of pop-oriented singles, including three songs conducted by Felix Slatkin.

Sinatra had offered Slatkin the musical directorship of Reprise Records as soon as he formed the company. "My father was to be the chief A&R man, as well as Sinatra's producer and arranger," remembers Leonard Slatkin. "He stayed with Sinatra for a little while and then got an offer to go over to Liberty Records with a man named Simon Waronker. Liberty Records provided my father with a little more flexibility, and the chance to do more producing and conducting, plus, he retained part ownership in the company. Even during that time, though my father's focus had shifted to a different entity, Sinatra remained faithful." The bright young arranger Neal Hefti filled in for Slatkin when he left Sinatra's employ.

Reprise didn't maintain its own studios, as the major labels did, so Sinatra called upon ex-Columbia engineer Morty Palitz to direct its recording division. Palitz, who had suffered some personal setbacks, was ecstatic — but fate stepped in and dealt him a cruel hand before his work even started.

In a posthumous letter of tribute to the engineer, songwriter Alec Wilder described the high regard Sinatra had for him and reflected on the sadness of his tragic demise. "Sinatra had finally decided to open up a recording company, and you were his favorite recording man," Wilder wrote. "I remember your making a trip to Los Angeles to discuss the details with him. Everything was happily settled, and you came back to New York to wait for the job to start. Then that heart weakness grabbed you and totally unexpectedly, you died. Damn it, damn it, damn it! What a ball it would have been for you, working for Frank, who so truly respected and loved you! After all that long rejection and miserable series of disappointments, to get precisely what you'd always wanted — and then, death! Thank you for all you did for me and for all that glorious laughter!"

Palitz's death sent Sinatra scrambling. His search led him to the finest independent engineer

COURTESY OF ALLEN SIDES, OCEAN WAY STUDIOS

Nat Cole with engineer Bill Putnam in the control room at United Recording, Los Angeles.

in Los Angeles, Bill Putnam, who owned and operated two studios: United and Western Recording, on Sunset Boulevard. The pair quickly became friends, and for a while the Reprise offices were operated from the United Recording building.

So confident was Sinatra of Putnam's abilities that, when circumstances forced him to relocate for a session, his discomfort was sure to be reflected in his attitude on the date. Arranger Marty Paich, who recorded two songs with Sinatra in 1963, recalls their meeting at the RCA Victor studios in Hollywood. "He really wouldn't do a session without Bill, until he had to do our record. There was no studio available at United, so we brought him over to RCA Victor, and I got the feeling at the time that he was a little perturbed about it. Because Frank, at that time, pretty much got his own way, and it just felt to me that maybe he would rather have been over at United, with Bill Putnam."

"Bill Putnam had a great reputation, because he had recorded a lot of the classic Basie and Ellington records in the 1930s and 1940s," says Allen Sides, the current owner of Ocean Way Studios (formerly United Recording). "He had built Universal Studios in Chicago first, and was doing a lot of the Basie and Ellington recordings out there. As the music business moved west in the 1950s, he picked up and began United Recording, which next to Radio Recorders, was the second largest independent recording studio in L.A."

Putnam opened the original United Recording studio, located on the corner of the Columbia-Screen Gems lot at 6050 Sunset Boulevard, around 1952. "The building was the Douglas Fair-

COURTESY OF ALLEN SIDES, OCEAN WAY STUDIOS

United Recording's custom-built Studio A.

banks soundstage, which had been built around 1900," Sides explains.

"Bill designed both of the original United rooms, Studios A and B, contained in that building. What was different was that he presented a whole different type of studio: his rooms were much more dramatic . . . much more interesting than Radio Recorders, which was built in the 1940s, and looked like they hadn't changed. There was no comparison: the two studios that Bill built were astonishingly good—I mean *unbelievably* good. His concept of a recording room was that it should enhance the instruments within it, kind of like a concert hall. They were large rooms, and the biggest thing he would do in those two studios was maybe seventy-five pieces. The orchestra just sounded amazing in the room; the players could hear each other so well that it really helped them play well."

At approximately the same time that Sinatra began Reprise records, Putnam took over a second building on Sunset, just four hundred feet from the United studio. A 1920s edifice that had formerly been a radio theater, the Western building was promptly renamed "Western Recording," and soon became home to three more Putnam recording rooms: Studios 1, 2, and 3. Although the United and Western studios were located in different buildings, the new company became known as United-Western recording. Most of Sinatra's Reprise sessions took place in United's Studio A; on occasion, he would venture down the street to use Western's Studio 1.

"These studios were just incredible," Sides says. "They had big, live custom echo chambers that Bill designed himself. In fact, the one in Studio A is so good, my friend Bobby McFerrin would come up and just sit in the echo chamber and sing, because it is just so great sounding."

While he was known in the recording community as one of the most sensitive mixers in the business, Putnam was far more than a recording engineer. "Bill was a record producer (who worked on something like fifty gold records), he was an inventor who owned and operated UREI (which manufactured a lot of great gear that he developed). Bill tuned his own pianos . . . he did it all," says Sides.

"Bill Putnam also invented the concept of what we think of as a control room," Sides points out. "Before he built his control room in United's Studio A, they used to call them 'booths,' because they really were booths: little 10 by 12 rooms with a speaker in the corner! Bill's control room was quite a departure; he actually had room for a producer and A&R people . . . a few other people could actually be in the control room."

Phil Ramone, who would later establish himself as one of the most respected engineers and producers in contemporary pop music, best known for his outstanding work with Billy Joel, was already hanging around United-Western in the early 1960s. "My favorite engineer in the world was Bill Putnam," he says. "I wasn't supposed to be in the studio—Bill hid me in the back room, and let me be a tape operator so I could watch him work. He was, for all of us, probably

the greatest leader of the big-band style of recording, and having Frank's voice sound the way it did. The sound is immaculate! His work taught me a lesson about what immediacy is."

RING-A-DING-DING! AND SINATRA AND STRINGS

The ultra-relaxed atmosphere of the early Reprise years is evident from the looseness of Sinatra's premiere album for his label, *Ring-a-Ding-Ding!*, orchestrated by Johnny Mandel. The title track, written for the album by Cahn and Van Heusen, played off one of Sinatra's favorite phrases, "Ring-a-Ding-Ding," roughly translated as "Look out, we'll be having one mothery gasser of a time!" His unusual choice of arranger led to what is likely the jazziest of all the commercial Sinatra albums.

"He [Frank] was a big admirer of David Allyn," Mandel says. "I think that may have been part of it, of course. I did a lot of club acts, and one of them was Vic Damone. Vic used to come and play the Sands, and we had a real dynamite act at the time—I'd written a lot of hard swinging things. And Sinatra came in and heard it, and he came up to Vic and asked him, 'Who did those? Jesus Christ. . .' And Vic told him . . . I think that's where he got the idea for [me to do] the swingin' things."

As with his previous arrangers, Sinatra met with Mandel to discuss the fresh sound he was seeking. "I remember he was shooting *The Devil at Four O'Clock* on the Columbia Pictures ranch, and Bill Miller brought me out there," Mandel explains. "I'd known Bill for quite a long time. Frank started telling me about how he was finished with Capitol, and he was starting this new label, and the records were going to be colored vinyl . . . all that sort of thing. He had a lot of ideas, and I remember just watching his eyes as he was talking about the company, you know, and they were *sparkling*. It was like he was very proud of this thing. He had the most striking kind of blue eyes. Man, they drilled right through you! There were things here and there, like in "Ring-a Ding-Ding," where he said, 'I'd like to hear some bell sounds in that.' I said, 'OK,' and I wrote some bell sounds. Tubular chimes—you can hear them in there. In fact, I used them quite a bit in the album; not all the time, but just enough to make it sound a little different."

Unedited tapes reveal a remarkably jovial tone for these sessions. In the studio, there is electricity in the air; the atmosphere is light and fun. The musicians are warming up, joking, and laughing, as though the event weren't so much a recording session, but a real fun evening out with "the guys." One of the women—Eleanor Slatkin, or Sinatra's secretary, perhaps—is heard greeting a guest with a warm, sincere twinkle in her voice. "Thank you dear, thank you ever so much for coming . . . I certainly do appreciate it!" The conviviality is palpable—even infectious. Happy sounds come from the piano, the horns, the percussion, as they find their pitches.

Shuffling lead sheets at his music stand, Sinatra, anticipating one hell of a swingin' evening, addresses Mandel. "I'll tell you what we do, Johnny . . . let's do the title song, huh? Yeah, let's get into the mood with it!"

"Ring-a-Ding-Ding," Mandel calls out. "That's the name of the album, so let's get in the mood," Sinatra says, walking among the band, priming the musicians. He checks in with Felix Slatkin, who is producing from the booth. "Feel . . . ?"

Slatkin's voice comes back over the talkback system. "Ring-a-Ding?"

"Get everybody in the mood . . . ," Frank says. "Let's do about sixteen bars for balance, so we can get an idea of what we're doing. Then we'll do a test . . . run a test to see what we got."

As the musicians finish tuning up, Sinatra prepares for the recording test on the title track. To the soundtrack of Irv Cottler adjusting his snare drum and hi-hat cymbals, Sinatra begins singing and snapping his fingers sharply, trying to feel the groove that works best for the record.

> *Life is dull . . . it's nothin' but one big lull . . . and presto you do a skull . . . ba-da-ba-da-ba-bop . . . ba-da-ba-da-ba-beep . . . do-do-do-dee-do-doo . . . .do-de-do-do-do-de-do-do . . . do-de-do-do . . . do-de-do . . .* [speaking] *should be right . . . SNAP! . . . about . . . .SNAP! . . . in . . . SNAP! . . . there . . . SNAP! . . .*

The tempo now set, Sinatra continues to snap his fingers decisively, and Mandel, after taking a moment to match the pacing Sinatra has delineated, counts off to cue the band. "One, two, three, four!" The rollicking sound of one great big band blares forth. After the test take, it is clear that Sinatra has a winner on his hands, and the rhythm section breaks into a celebratory jazz-club style improvisation of the song.

As happy as he was with the title track, Sinatra had problems with two tunes scheduled for the album: "Zing Went the Strings of My Heart" and "Have You Met Miss Jones?" Neither made it to the final record.

"I loved the song 'Have You Met Miss Jones?' but it was a ballad, and it didn't seem to fit in the album," Mandel remembers. "It could have been done fast, but he wanted to do it as a ballad. It was one of those things that could have come off, but didn't. And there were a lot of copying mistakes in that, for some reason. You know, you don't have a chance to figure out why [certain things don't work] at the time. In those days, unlike today, you used to do three or four sides in three hours. That's how we did 'em."

"Have You Met Miss Jones?" is a pretty song: soft and light in the hands of Johnny Mandel. Even as the orchestral run-through of the song begins, though, problems crop up. Musicians, confused about what keys their parts have been written in, start to compare notes. "We've got B-flat." "We have A-flat." "Should there be a G in bar fifteen, or an F?" "It should be a G instead of an F."

All this ado prompts Sinatra to start making wisecracks. "You guys are in a lot of trouble tonight . . . A lot of trouble tonight. I think the copyist is drunk! Does Vern Yocum drink? *Jesus!*" he says.

One of the musicians, offering an opinion, confirms that Yocum is a teetotaler. Another guy in the band, clearly joking, quips back, "Well then he's a junkie!" "Maybe you got the wrong arrangement. You got the right arrangement up?" Sinatra jokes.

More notes are corrected, and moments later, Mandel counts off for another try at the tune.

The introduction is celestial: the winsome tones of Bud Shank's flute (Mandel's signature woodwind sound) are nestled among the soft sheen of a light bed of strings, to which both harp and bass have been discreetly added. After mere seconds, Sinatra comments on the difference of the arrangement's feel, as compared to the balance of the charts. "This sounds like a different album."

After another minute or so, the instrumental rehearsal breaks off, and more corrections are discussed. Sinatra's voice is not angry, but deliberate: you can sense that he is becoming impatient. "Jesus Christ, this is *brutal*," he says. He calls to an aide. "Eddie Shaw: call up Vern Yocum, and tell him that from here on in . . . from this minute, whatever he's copying, for Christ's sake to get the notes right! Jesus, this is murder!"

Slatkin, sensing Sinatra's concern, reassures him. "We'll run this down, Frank. Wanna put it on tape and listen to it?" The singer, perusing his lead sheet, is being thrown by the number of mistakes in the chart. "Are there A-flats in fifty-six? That's what it sounds like to me. Felix? Shouldn't there be A-flats in bar fifty-six? It sounds a little crazy." Mandel takes the orchestra from bar fifty-three and resolves the problem.

After some more tinkering, Slatkin asks if they should drop the tune. "Uh, whaddya think about this? What about this tune on the album?" Sinatra: "We'll try it and see what happens." Slatkin: "It's a lot different . . . unless we can pick up the tempo," he suggests. Sinatra: "We'll run it down first and see what happens . . . "

In the end, it didn't happen. After a full vocal run-through in which the tempo was increased to medium, it was obvious that the beauty of the chart as originally written was marred; after finding some additional problems with incorrectly transcribed notes, Sinatra simply calls for the next tune. "I've Got My Love to Keep Me Warm," he requests. "Pass this." (He must have admired the tune, because five months later, in May 1961, he made a striking recording of it with Billy May for *Swing Along with Me*).

Mandel, pressed for time, had engaged the services of two other arrangers to help complete the orchestrations. "I was a little rushed for time on a couple of them, and I may have taken more time on some of the arrangements than I should have. When you're writing a whole album, there's a lot of music to write, and I'm painfully slow. I'm still, to this day, slow. I'm sweatin' right now! And that's how I work. If I could be fast, I'd be fast. I can write fast, but it's gonna sound like I did, you know? Dick Reynolds wrote part of 'Easy to Love,' and he might have worked on 'When I Take My Sugar to Tea.' What I would do when I was in a hurry is write the intros and the ending, and they'd write the things in the middle. Skip Martin did one completely, 'Be Careful, It's My Heart.' I did not write that arrangement. Doesn't even sound like me."

A tune that is definitely Mandel's is a cookin' version of Gershwin's "A Foggy Day." Sinatra likes the bells, which set the stage for his Londonderry excursion. During the rehearsal, he jauntily hums along, at one point during the bridge calling across the studio to Mandel, "Good tempo, John."

When the run-through is complete, he offers some musical suggestions, both about the bells and some brass accents, to both Mandel and Slatkin. "Those brass notes you've got from fifty-one on . . . try not to rush those, it sounds like it's rushed. Don't jump at 'em . . . don't jump at 'em. *Pop, pop, pop, pop* . . . very relaxed." As the band plays through the particular section where the notes crop up, Sinatra points them out to Mandel. "Whoa . . . those notes . . . okay!"

Then, addressing Slatkin, he discusses the instrumental bridge: "Felix, beginning in bar fifty-five, I want to get a feeling of a concerted crescendo all the way up through sixty-five, sixty-six, sixty-seven, sixty-eight, sixty-nine, *boom!*—the cut-off." Slatkin agrees. "Yeah, that's great, Frank, but I tell ya, if they would do it out there, it would help a great deal," Slatkin says confidently. "That's what I'm talking about . . . but I want you to listen to it . . . ," Sinatra tells him. Slatkin clarifies who will be responsible for accomplishing the desired effect. "We won't build it in here too much: we'll hold it, and let you build it out there." Sinatra agrees. "No, no, no, no—not you," he says.

Mandel leads the band in a run-through, and at the end, Sinatra asks, "All right?" "Yeah, *good!*" Slatkin announces. "Really whack those chimes when we get in there," Sinatra tells percussionist Emil Richards, who nods. "Right."

"All right, let's try it, huh?" the singer says. Slatkin gets things underway. "Ready to go, John? We are rolling . . . this is M-103, Take Two."

Appropriately punchy, chimes thoroughly whacked in exactly the right spots, the performance emerges as one of the best of the lot. The conversations heard on these particular sessions underscore how Sinatra has honed his command of rhythm and musical nuance to perfection.

Having sharpened his rhythmic sense with Riddle and May at Capitol, he could now take bold control, easily communicating what he believed to be the appropriate, "in-the-pocket" groove to those responsible for executing it.

For example, as the group is about to begin a run-through of "Let's Face the Music and Dance," we find him characteristically humming, singing, and snapping, suggesting a tempo to the musicians. "In the first chorus, gentlemen, think of this thing in a fat 'two.' Just think of it that way. The rhythm's gonna play in a big, broad 'two.' Let's try it." The recording is made, a playback listened to.

Take one of the song, master M-104, is taken at a brighter tempo than subsequent takes. In the studio, Sinatra realized that maybe it was a bit too fast, and made the call to adjust the tempo. "I think it's gonna come down a little more," he says, humming the tune. His finger snaps begin to slow. "We've got another change. Irv, it's coming down a little more. Yeah, yeah . . . try it at this tempo," he instructs. His assessment of the proper tempo is uncanny; his judgment, right on the money.

"He made one change which was a very good change, and that was at the end of the verse of "Let's Fall in Love," Mandel recalls. "He stuck an empty bar in there before he went into the line, "Let's . . . [*pause*] fall in love . . . " That was his idea. Right on the date. But that's not a hard type of change to do."

The one-bar rest is very effective, sharpening the tension right at the top of the song. "You wonder, 'What's coming next?' 'Cause nobody's heard this verse before. It had never been done. As a result, nobody knew what was coming, so putting that bar in gave it extra dramatic impact," Mandel says.

As the band prepares to record the song, Sinatra, planning his attack, makes an inquiry about the introduction. "I've got seven beats tacit, John?" he asks Mandel, singing the end of the verse. "Why be shy . . . *two, three, four, one, two, three, four . . . "* he counts. After the last beat, he pauses, then practices, anticipating the rest between verse and chorus. Since his vocal would be coming in cold, he was concerned about whether he'd find the note easily. "What's the price I blow the first note?" he jokes. "I'll run it down once for ya," he tells Slatkin.

The band starts, and the verse flows along well. After the one-bar rest, Sinata indeed blows the first note, coming in flat. His self-deprecating humor takes over, and he laughs. "When I tune up, I gonna be great with that note!" he jokes, using his well-practiced Amos 'n Andy accent for effect. The balance of the take is fine, and after a minor adjustment of the vibraphone microphone, Sinatra proclaims the chart to be "cuckoo," and they go for the master takes.

Bill Putnam, running the technical side of the session in the control room, is cool, calm, and collected. On these sessions, he seems concerned with making sure that the sound of the bells and chimes are reproduced properly, and sets about checking and re-checking their assigned microphones. Not wanting the soft, mellow sound of the vibraphone on "Easy to Love" to be drowned out, Putnam double-checks the balance. "Larry, can I hear the vibes, please, just for a second?" he asks.

Quietly addressing Putnam from the studio floor, Sinatra makes a request, almost as an afterthought. "On the playbacks tonight, will you knock off a little of the gain when you play 'em back in here? About this much," he asks, demonstrating with his fingers.

The looseness of these sessions shows that Sinatra was definitely enjoying being the head of his own record company. But while the new recording outlet enabled him to maintain more artistic control and freedom than he had ever enjoyed before, Sinatra seems, at this point, to have begun losing interest in personally supervising the nitty-gritty details. As time wore on, he spent less and less time concerning himself with the particulars of the arrangements. With several ex-

ceptions, long planning sessions with his orchestrators became a thing of the past. "The routine of working tirelessly, and outlining every idea stayed the same in the earlier years, but in later years, Frank took less of a hand in it," recalls Bill Miller. "He'd say, 'Just have somebody write it. They know what they're doing.'"

Unfortunately, this casual attitude also extended to the post-production mixing that would result in the final records. As a result, when compared to the astonishingly beautiful and consistent sound quality of the Capitol recordings, many of Sinatra's Reprise efforts pale. The biggest problem with the singer's recordings from this period is their uneven sound quality: one album might be marred by mild distortion, excess reverb, an abundance of tape hiss, uneven mixing and balance; the next could be an audio delight. This first album, *Ring-a-Ding-Ding!*, was also the first weak link in a chain. The recent discovery of copies of master tapes, missing from the Reprise vaults for years, reveals some clues regarding the less than perfect sonics of this landmark recording, and underscores the importance of meticulous mixing and mastering.

Since its initial release in March 1961, *Ring-a-Ding-Ding!* has been plagued by a brittle, hissy, echoey sound. For many years, Sinatra aficionados believed that the original recordings were inferior, as these problems were noticeable in the first pressings of the album (both mono and stereo). A study of the aforementioned session tapes, however, contradicts this theory. (To date, two stereo compact disc versions have been released: the first, now out of print, retained the sonic deficiencies described above. The 20-bit digitally remastered version issued in 1998 is a marked improvement, but still lacks the crispness of the mono tapes in circulation.)

While the "lost" tape copies are mono, and therefore prevent any evaluation of the stereo mix, they are startlingly clear: essentially *dry* (no reverb), with very distinct separation among the instruments of the orchestra, and a remarkable presence or "liveness" that is noticeably absent on the original issues, indicating that all of the inferior sound arose during post-production mixing, after the original recordings were made.

"Of all the Reprise recordings, few sounded great," concurs Allen Sides. "The ones that sound the best are those that were mixed directly to two-track, like the original *Robin and the Seven Hoods* soundtrack album and *Strangers in the Night*. But if you go back to the original three tracks, they sound so good it can scare you! A lot of the problems *did* come with the mixdowns, and I know this because I have heard some of these three-tracks, and they are amazing."

How this occurred, and on Sinatra's own watch, is anyone's guess, but such inconsistencies were part and parcel of Sinatra's years at Reprise. Some explanation, and a sense that Sinatra was concerned about the sonic deficiencies of the final mixdowns, can be gleaned from a conversation that Bill Putnam had with Sides.

"Bill told me that he became so busy producing his own records for other artists that Sinatra couldn't get him, and Frank was really stressed out, because he sensed that there had been some sessions that weren't too happening. So Sinatra went to Bill, and said, 'Would you be willing to let me put you on a retainer?' They agreed on a figure of $200,000, which had no relation to what Bill would actually get paid for the sessions: he would get paid separately for the sessions. This retainer insured that if Frank needed Bill, he would be available to work on a session.

"He set Frank up with a little studio in the Palm Springs house, where he could play back all the tapes and listen to stuff, and it got to the point where Sinatra would call him at all hours of the night. He would be listening to a take, and call Bill and say, 'Hey Bill, what do you think about take four?' Bill was more than an engineer, he was a producer, and they were friends—so they relied on each other. But it finally got to the point where Bill couldn't do it anymore . . . he was burning the candle at both ends."

Putnam told Sides about a late-night call that was the last straw for the engineer.

Sinatra: Bill?
Putnam: Yeah. Who's this?
Sinatra: Frank.
Putnam: Frank who? (Then hangs up.)

"Frank called him back the next day . . . if you're his friend, you're his friend. He can take that—he can appreciate where you're coming from. They stayed friends for a long time."

Sinatra depended on Putnam because the engineer was a discerning mixer who appreciated and understood his style and method of recording. "The Olympic goal in being a great engineer, and then a great producer, is to find the immediacy. With Sinatra, there's no reason for a lot of takes past the second or third. Once you understand that, it puts you in another league," says Phil Ramone.

Ramone, probably more than any other producer who made his mark in the rock music era, can understand and make comparisons between the "Sinatra" method of recording (three tunes per session, an album completed in four days), and what has developed into an industry standard (albums taking months, even years, to be recorded and mastered), because he broke into the studios at a time when "live" recording was still the accepted practice.

"As a producer, I started great relationships with Paul Simon and Billy Joel and those people, because I constantly rolled tape. With subtle editing, sometimes you'd find the combination of a great take from a whole day's work, which was the total opposite of what I learned in the previous ten years of engineering: that if you weren't good enough to do four songs in three hours, you were an amateur. The key is, you have to understand the artist. Some people are very determined and slow, and that's okay," he says. "With Sinatra, it's so special. No matter how good you are, from a production and engineering point of view, it's the player—and the players play ten times better when he walks in the room than they did ten minutes before. It's a totally different uplift—there's nothing like it."

The immediacy that a thoughtful production team strives to achieve is brilliantly portrayed on Sinatra's first recording with arranger Don Costa, *Sinatra and Strings*. For this master, the producer and mixing engineer chose to enhance the flat session tapes with just the right shower of reverberation, resulting in an appealingly glossy, wet sound that perfectly underscores the plaintive feel of Sinatra classics like "Come Rain or Come Shine," "Yesterdays," "Prisoner of Love," and "That's All."

This combination of virtuoso performance and thoughtfully crafted sound expresses the late-night club ambiance that is the essence of Frank Sinatra. The album so moved its arranger that in the 1970s, he told British music historian and writer Stan Britt that "*Sinatra and Strings* was, and always will be, the hallmark of my existence."

Commenting on the recording in 1985 for his sister Nancy's first biography of her father, *Frank Sinatra, My Father*, Frank Sinatra, Jr., said "*Sinatra and Strings* opened up a whole new era. The orchestras were getting bigger, and Pop wanted that lush string sound."

Sinatra's son also recalled the very first session for the album. "They assembled the huge orchestra . . . and the old man walked in that night for the first take, 'Hey, hey: ring-a-ding-ding!' And he was playing with his hat and everything, and he saw the concertmaster, Felix Slatkin, slumped over in his chair. Felix had his violin still in its case, across his lap. He was sweating. He looked up and said, 'Frank, I don't feel good.' My old man turned around and looked at Costa with all the music, and the *fifty* musicians. But the concertmaster didn't feel well. So Dad turned to Hank Sanicola and he said, 'Hank, pay everybody off.' And he got up on the conductor's podium, [tapped on the stand] and said, 'Everybody, good

evening. Turn in your W-4 forms, we're not recording tonight. Come back tomorrow night at eight.' Pushed the whole album session back one day! Slatkin was not well, and he was not going to record without his concertmaster. Paid everybody off and sent them home. Got to do it right."

Don Costa, like Johnny Mandel and Sy Oliver, was originally part of Frank Sinatra's plan to diversify during the 1960s. Some, like Mandel and Oliver, never worked on another album with him. Except for two singles sessions (in 1963 and 1964), Sinatra did not call on Costa again until 1969, for the *My Way* album; these charts were as far removed from *Sinatra and Strings* as one could get.

Costa was a great pinch hitter. He was the guy you called in when you needed someone else's sound, but that someone else wasn't available. "Don Costa was a musician's musician; an arranger's arranger," says arranger-songwriter Mickey Leonard. "He was among the most emotional writers, and his orchestrations are very theatrical. He wrote with a great sense of drama."

Although only two songs he orchestrated for Sinatra in the 1970s ("What Are You Doing the Rest of Your Life?" and "Summer Me, Winter Me") come anywhere near the beauty of the arrangements for *Sinatra and Strings*, Costa is almost single-handedly responsible for the direction that Sinatra's post-retirement recording career took, often serving as arranger and producer for the singer's recording dates.

"What is remarkable is that Don didn't play piano, as most arrangers did," says Leonard. "His instrument was guitar, and that is what he used to work out his orchestrations—very unusual. He was anything but a formula writer: he never overpowered a song; he always delved deeper into the music. I would put him in the same league as the very best arrangers that ever lived, including Nelson Riddle, Eddie Sauter, Billy May, Ralph Burns, and Billy Byers. He had a good feel for the 'commercial' sound, too."

GREAT SONGS FROM GREAT BRITAIN: THE LONDON SESSIONS, 1962

PHOTOGRAPH BY DEZO HOFFMAN, COURTESY OF REX FEATURES LTD.

Despite an occasional technical miscue, the performances of the Reprise years were rarely dull-even in the unusual event the singer wasn't up to vocal par, as was the case when, in June of 1962, he arrived in England, weary from the rigors of a massive world tour, but determined to complete a scheduled recording date with admired British arranger Robert Farnon.

Interviews with Farnon (conducted by the author) and with the producer, the late Alan A. Freeman (courtesy of British music historian and writer Stan Britt) as well as unissued studio session outtakes allow us to paint a realistic picture of the events that occurred in a British studio over three nights in June of 1962.

The idea for the album was Sinatra's entirely. Word had come from his office in Los Angeles six months previously that he would be wrapping up an extensive charity tour in June and thought it might be nice to record an album in England. The specifications were simple: all the songs must be of British origin, with Robert Farnon creating the arrangements. The dates were scheduled for June 12, 13, and 14; the recording venue would be the CTS Bayswater Studios in London. The album (Sinatra's first and only studio album to be recorded outside the United States) would be titled *Great Songs from Great Britain*.

Those six months were hectic for Sinatra's British collaborators. Among their tasks was working with the singer to select dozens of appropriate tunes, which would eventually be narrowed down to the twelve that would be taped at the sessions. When word of the planned album hit the press, producer Alan A. Freeman found himself swamped with requests from songwriters to include their songs. "Eric Maschwitz, who wrote 'A Nightingale Sang in Berkeley Square,' called me up and drove me mad!" said Freeman. "He insisted that this would be the most important thing that could happen to his song, and career. And I said, 'I think it would stand a great chance [of being included],' and I sent it along to Frank. Personally, I think that's the song that came out best on the album."

"Frank picked out 'We'll Meet Again,' 'I'll Follow My Secret Heart,' and 'Garden in the Rain,' I believe. He also adored 'London by Night,' which was written by Carroll Coates, an Englishman who was living in the States," Freeman remembers. One song chosen personally by the singer, the lovely "Now Is the Hour," almost wasn't included, because it was not a British song. "It's near enough British!" Sinatra said, and the song remained.

"Don Costa, who was working closely with Sinatra, was a big champion of my work," remembers the record's orchestrater Robert Farnon, whose sweeping style is reminiscent of Stordahl's. "Perhaps it was Don, more than anyone, that suggested I arrange the album. I was sent the songs, and the keys by Frank's pianist, Bill Miller. And he just told me, 'Go ahead and write whatever you like,' which I did. They gave me carte blanche! It was a delight to work that way . . . to have that freedom. I met with Frank at the Savoy Hotel before the sessions, just to say hello and check the keys. Bill Miller was there to assist us as well."

A week before the sessions, Bill Putnam, Sinatra's engineer from Los Angeles, made a surprise visit to the studio, which was a relief to Alan Freeman. "I knew Bill was in Paris, and he phoned me, and said, 'I appreciate the state you've been in—I've been there!' I told Bill, 'It would be a godsend if you could get over to the studio and do a once-over, and give us some hints.' He came in, looked around, and said, 'This should be fine, he'll like this. Get him a screen, and surround him with rhythm,' Putnam told me, and that's exactly what we did."

Several hours before the first recording session, Freeman was visibly nervous. He'd been at the studio for hours to allow himself some time to relax and get the feel of the place. He was concerned about whether he'd have the luxury of a few minutes alone to acquaint himself with Frank. Freeman's function over the next three nights was to run the technical business and make sure the singer was comfortable in this strange environment. He refrained from imposing or enforcing his ideas on the vocalist. Sinatra, he knew, produced for himself.

Sinatra, nearing the end of a grueling world tour, was exhausted. Having been in the audience for the singer's rousing midnight show at Royal Festival Hall, Freeman understood that the famed voice was under a tremendous amount of stress. It was, in fact, nearly worn out. In addition to the many benefit concerts the world tour demanded, he was doing nightly club dates at the Mesmer Hall. The producer thought about this, as the call came that Sinatra was en route from his suite at the Savoy Hotel. "I just wanted to be able to talk to him alone, to have two minutes to sell myself to him, before we actually got into the studio," said Freeman.

"Twenty minutes after we got the call, he arrived, in the chocolate-brown Rolls he'd borrowed from Douglas Fairbanks, Jr. I was at the door, and I was really shaking . . . petrified! When he walked up, I was introduced to him, and he shook my hand and said, 'Hi, my boy, glad to know you.' And the way he said it, with a twinkle in his eye, led me to believe he knew the tremendous strain I was under. I said something like, 'Obviously, Frank, this is the greatest thrill that ever happened to me, as it would be any producer working with you . . . ,' to which he responded, 'Well, it's nice to be here.' As we entered the studio, all the musicians and guests started applauding, and I felt very proud walking in there with him"

The first tune-up that evening was a favorite of Sinatra, "If I Had You," which he had recorded twice before, in 1947 (Stordahl) and 1956 (Riddle). Freeman started the proceedings from the booth. "Take One, 'If I Had You.'" Then, "Okay, Bob," as Farnon counted off, cueing the orchestra. "One, two and three . . . " With the downbeat came immediate understanding of why Sinatra admired Robert Farnon. After tentatively negotiating himself through a series of hoarse, raspy lines, at three minutes and fifty-seconds into the first attempt, Sinatra aborted the take. "All right, hold it—cut it," he directed.

The orchestra worked out a few minor bugs, then played a few sections to give Sinatra a better sense of the timing of the melodic line. "He had great difficulty figuring out where to come in at the beginning of the song, because it had such a long intro, and he had no idea what the intro was," recalls Farnon. This affected the pacing of the rest of his vocal, which Sinatra was approaching with a bit of trepidation. "Frank is only human . . . this intro would have thrown any artist."

Then, Take Two. This time, twenty-seven seconds in, another vocal scrape, this time on the word *glad*. "One more, please," Frank requested. Takes Three and Four are broken down before the vocal begins, and remain incomplete false starts. Take Five is complete, but a bit rough vocally. Then, after a few more incomplete takes, a near calamity: "The most disastrous thing happened in the middle of recording this number—the piano broke down! The action on the piano went, and this had never happened to me before, and it never happened to me again. And the guy had been nursing that concert grand all day—tuning and retuning it. Well, can you imagine this on a Sinatra session, the first night, the first title . . . ? None of us were particularly at ease then, and I don't suppose Frank was either. He was in a strange studio; he had never recorded outside of the States before. He didn't know what the hell we were all about. So the piano breaks down, and he says, 'Have you got another piano?' We didn't, so I said, 'No, Frank . . . ,' and he said 'Okay, we'll do it on celeste.' I thought, 'Oh, thank God . . . you know, I thought we were going to have a tantrum there, first time out," says Freeman. For the eleventh and twelfth takes, pianist Bill Miller plinked on celeste, an unexpected and picturesque twist that added immeasurably to the album.

Patience tested and tension broken, the session continued.

"After the second title, 'The Very Thought of You,' we had a break," remembers Freeman. "I knew that Frank liked Jack Daniels, so I had three bottles of it waiting in the studio. As we broke, I asked, 'Would you like a drink, Frank?' He said,

PHOTOGRAPH BY TED ALLAN, COURTESY OF MPTV ARCHIVE

'What have you got?' So I said, 'This,' slapping it on the table. And he looked at me right in the eyes, and said, 'You've been doing your homework, haven't you?' So Frank had a drink, and asked me, 'Have you ever tried this stuff?' I said, 'No.' He said, 'Would you like one?' I responded, 'Love one.' 'Have you got a glass?' he asks. 'No, I haven't got one here.' Frank says, 'All right, share mine.' And Harold Davison took me aside, and said, 'You *must* be in, if he shared a glass with you . . .' And from that moment on, I couldn't go wrong. I felt great!"

"I was impressed with his musicality," says Farnon. "There was a bearded chap, a trombone player, that made one or two fluffs on one of the numbers. Sinatra, of course, caught it, and walked over during the orchestral interlude, and whispered to him, 'I'm afraid you got a little bit of whisker in there, mate.' That broke the orchestra up, and we had to stop playing. It was so lovely, because he heard this note even though the orchestra was playing. And it wasn't the first trombonist, it was Ray Primo, the bass trombonist!" Sinatra, who couldn't read a note of music, had neatly demonstrated his unerring facility for detecting a "clam" (his term) from within the deepest recess of the orchestra.

Throughout the taping, Sinatra constantly coughs and attempts to clear his throat, and the frayed edges cropping up on the ends of many notes remind one of the fragility of his instrument. Sinatra always had a self-deprecating way of joking about his vocal shortcomings on a record date. "I think I swallowed a shot glass," or "I got a busted reed," or "That was a Chesterfield, from oh, about 1947" were all typical tension-breakers, following blown notes or flubbed lines. In London, it was, at first, simply, "One more, please," or "Once more, Bob—for me." After feeling out the British contingency, he loosened up. Then, after a coughing spell, he wisecracked, "Man, we gotta sleep indoors!" eliciting laughs from the assembly. Freeman recalled that during one problematic song, Sinatra stopped the orchestra, looked up at the ceiling, and pleaded, "Don't just stand there, come down and help me!"

As in Hollywood, the sessions were an event—the venue filled to capacity, much to the consternation of the British recording team. "There were so many people in the studio that had nothing to do with the recording," Farnon recollects. "There were people sitting on my podium, under the piano, on the piano, all around us—the studio was absolutely crammed with people: the press, musicians, and fans who were privileged to gain admission. Frank loved it—he didn't mind at all." Freeman, who claims to have been a bit frightened by the unusual

number of onlookers, estimates that 120 people were jammed into the studio, in addition to the orchestra! "And thirty of those people were in the control room." Among the visitors was Nelson Riddle. "On one occasion, Frank went over to Nelson, and said, 'Listen to that woodwind writing . . . that's what I like!' and of course, my tail started to wag, 'cause it was quite a nice compliment."

Technically, this may have been the most well-covered Sinatra session ever. It was recorded simultaneously on four different tape machines, a task that engineer Eric Tomlinson handled beautifully. At the time, Reprise in the United States was recording all masters at 30 ips, and the CTS Studios were set up to record at 15 ips. Since Reprise had specifically requested that the masters be run at the superior 30 ips, an additional two tape machines were brought in. One Ampex and one Philips machine transcribed the tapes at 15 ips; a second Ampex and a second Philips operated at the required 30 ips. This plethora of tapes may account for the numerous "alternate" takes that have shown up on various commercial releases of the album through the years. Oddly enough, *Great Songs from Great Britain* was not released in the United States until nearly twenty-five years after its creation. Originally available only in England, the first British pressings are still among the most collectible Sinatra items on the market. (Today, the album is available domestically on compact disc.)

On the second night everyone, including Sinatra, was more at ease. The orchestra had been pared (the four trumpets weren't needed) and everything ran smoothly. Then, during Sinatra's performance of "The Gypsy," Freeman detected something unusual and began to worry. "He was doing some funny things in the middle. And Nelson Riddle was in the control room, so I said, 'Nelson, what he's doing is rather funny, isn't it?' And he replied, 'Well, this is a song that he doesn't know all that well. The phrases aren't quite right.' 'Would you like to tell him?' I ask.

Nelson said, 'No, you're the director of the session—you tell him.' 'Well, I can't tell him the phrase is wrong!,' I reply. 'Yes, you can,' he said. So, during the playback, we came up to the troublesome part, and I comment, 'Sounds like something's wrong with the phrasing there, Frank.' He tells me, "I'm trying to put a little syncopation in there.' 'I think it's wrong,' I say. And he said, 'Well, I like it . . .' He gave me one of those smiles, with a glint in his eye, and I replied, 'Okay! . . . that's fair enough—you're the boss.' And that little section worries me to this day!" Freeman noted.

While it was unusual for Sinatra to follow the accepted practice of editing multiple takes together to create a composite master (he remained insistent on performing each take live, as he always had, well into the tape era), he would occasionally allow an "intercut" to be made. If there were minor problems with a small section of a recording, the short passage would be rerecorded

With Alan Freeman and Robert Farnon.

and intercut (spliced) into the master take in the appropriate place.

"With 'A Nightingale Sang in Berkeley Square,' there were only two takes," recalls Freeman. "And that's the one we did an edit on, because Frank loved Harry Roche's trombone solo." The session tapes reveal Sinatra's instructions for making the cuts. "Intercut, using bar fifty-two on out for me . . . the trombone solo is excellent, so let's save that," he directed.

"This was the first time in the two nights' work that Frank actually came into the control room during the session," Freeman remembered. "He came in to tell the engineer to make the splice right there, on the spot . . . very frightening! And he stood over him while he did it. The guy was trembling, and I was having a thousand fits . . . what if the blade were to slip? The engineer making the cut was only nineteen years old, and I think this was his first multi-track session. Frank watched him do it, and it worked. We all breathed a sigh of relief!"

The true rarity to emerge from the London sessions was a song that Sinatra historian and author Will Friedwald cites as his personal favorite, the lovely "Roses of Picardy." Dropped from the final album, its obscurity became a topic of debate among Sinatra enthusiasts, and while the intervening decades have finally seen its official release, the story behind its exclusion bears repeating.

"On the last night, we were in the control room, having a drink and listening to all the playbacks," said Freeman. "Frank said, 'Scrub "Roses of Picardy," I don't like it.' I told him I thought it was rather nice, and he insisted, 'No, I didn't like it.' I tried to reason with him. I thought it was a beautiful Bob Farnon arrangement, and he put so much emotion into it; he sang it with tremendous feeling. I asked him, 'Is there anything we can do to get it right?' and he just said, 'No, no . . . just forget it, we'll go with eleven tracks.' He was quite definite about it. He was putting a lot of wisecracks in, as if maybe he'd already made up his mind he didn't want it—as if he was going through the motions of recording it, but not taking it seriously." (On the session out-takes, Sinatra can be heard, after muffing a take, "I don't think I'm gonna make the rest of that mother, I'll tell ya right now!" Later, obviously tired, he says, "My old man warned me about nights like these . . . but he was a drinking man! What did he know?")

After the sessions were completed and playbacks run on the third and final night, Sinatra seemed pleased with what he heard. "He was very happy with the musicians. He said, 'You know, I love the British strings—there's no strings in the world to touch them." Summing up the experience, Freeman described the atmosphere after Sinatra had gone: "I got my mother and father in on the last night, because they were dying to meet him, and I couldn't leave the studio when it was over. I just sat in that huge studio on my own, with my mother and father in the control room. I said, 'Just leave me alone,' and I sat and listened to the whole bloody lot of master takes. It must

have been one o'clock in the morning before I left that studio. I didn't want to leave it, because it was all over. It was gone."

FRANK AND SPLANK (SINATRA AND BASIE)

Back in the States, Sinatra commenced a project that was the fulfillment of a lifelong dream: to record with Bill "Count" Basie. Mickey Scrima, Sinatra's old roommate during the Harry James period, remembered that the singer always had an affinity for the Basie band. "Frank always said he wanted to be a singer with Count Basie. He just *loved* that band—he couldn't stop listening to them, and talking about them."

Twenty-three years later, his wish came true, when in October 1962 he recorded his first of three albums with Basie's swingin' aggregation. This album, scored by Neal Hefti, was rooted in the traditional ¼ time that was a hallmark of Basie's style.

As Hefti recalled, he completed the charts with no input from Sinatra. "I don't know how these ideas were shot back and forth . . . all I know is they said, 'This is what you're going to do next week.' I don't know who put it together . . . whose idea it was, who picked the tunes, or when they picked the

Recording with Count Basie, United Studio A, October 1962.

keys or any of those kind of things. I got a list of tunes and a list of keys, and a pile of sheet music with the key marked in pencil. I realized I could go up a half a tone or down a half a tone if I had any kind of an idea . . . ."

"I was always a reluctant writer; I don't really like to write, I never did. Or at least to write like that. I didn't mind writing a couple of tunes a year when I was with Woody Herman's band, when I could take six months to figure something out. But, if you're gonna say, 'Do this and have it tomorrow, and that's that,' to me it's like an order. 'You will do this.' I never liked that process, and I never wrote for another singer since that Basie-Sinatra album," Hefti said.

"But that wasn't *his* [Frank's] problem—he was very easy to work with. I would say he was the only guy I worked with who didn't squawk about anything that went on in the studio. I don't know what happened in his life outside of the studio, because I was never privileged to be part of that. But from a musical [standpoint], from the moment he walked in the studio to the moment he walked out, he just didn't do anything but sing."

Hefti was in a position to observe the overall picture, because in addition to arranging, he was then working as the head A&R man at Reprise. Emil Richards, the percussionist on many Sinatra dates, recalls Hefti's enthusiasm. "Frank's vocal booth was right next to the percussion section, and on one session, Frank had invited a bunch of people to watch. So Neal sticks his head out of the booth, and says, 'Frank—come on in, you're gonna cream in your pants when you hear this one!' And Frank looks at me, and says, 'Do you believe this guy, talkin' like that in front of all these people?' He was digging it!"

To Hefti, Sinatra seemed to be a bit distracted. It is entirely possible that the stress of the world tour, combined with the demands of the many other projects he was working on, were fatiguing the singer. "It's almost as if they were telling him what to do, and he couldn't wait for it to be over with, so he could get the hell out of

there. He very seldom would ask to do something more than two or three times, unless there was an obvious breakdown someplace."

Hefti's observation illustrates how Sinatra was becoming less interested and involved with the details that he once supervised like a hawk. "I very seldom had anything to do with him on these projects," Hefti says, offering the typical conversation that would occur:

> *Sinatra:* Did you get the songs the other day?
> *Hefti:* Yeah.
> *Sinatra:* You understand everything?
> *Hefti:* Yeah.
> *Sinatra:* You have any choices or anything?
> *Hefti:* No.
> *Sinatra:* Okay, next Friday, okay?
> *Hefti:* Okay.
> *Sinatra:* You need anything, here's my number.

When it was pointed out to him that Sinatra was noted for his scrupulous pre-session planning, Hefti seemed surprised. "I don't know that he ever acted any differently with anybody else, because I certainly wasn't getting any special treatment," he said.

Why Sinatra distanced himself from Hefti is somewhat perplexing, very different from his approach with Quincy Jones, who orchestrated the second Sinatra-Basie album, *It Might as Well Be Swing*, in 1964. The two had first met in 1958, when Jones conducted a Sinatra concert in Monte Carlo.

"The next time I talked to him, he called from Hawaii and asked me to do an album with him. That was Basie's album," Jones remembered. "This was right after he almost drowned, remember that? I went over there and he had a flag up over his bungalow in Hawaii. He was directing *None But the Brave*, and he had a flag up with his bottle of Jack Daniels on it. Huge flag! Instead of an American flag, he had a Jack

PHOTOGRAPH BY DAVID SUTTON, COURTESY OF MPTV ARCHIVE

Quincy Jones, Count Basie, and Frank Sinatra, 1964.

Daniels flag. And that's when we first got to know each other. He had one of the most complex personalities imaginable. We had a great, great chemistry."

Where Hefti's Sinatra-Basie album retained much of the legendary Basie sound, the record Jones scored had a much different feel—mainly tighter and jazzier. It also included more contemporary tunes than the first album, including "Fly Me to the Moon." As Sinatra sings in "I Believe in You," this one really *does* have the "slam, bang, tang" reminiscent of gin and vermouth.

"We started to talk about the tunes. And it's very funny the way songs come up. I'd suggest one, and he'd suggest a couple, and you keep thinking them up and you just come up with a real nice mix. He put 'I Can't Stop Loving You' in there because I had just gotten my first Grammy with Basie for an arrangement of 'I Can't Stop Loving You.' He didn't really talk to

me about the arrangements-he just kind of let me loose on that. We'd talk about a tempo and a key. And, because he was still busy with his picture, we came back to the States after Hawaii, and I moved in at Warner Brothers, into Dean Martin's dressing room. Frank was next door doing the picture every day, shooting interiors and editing and so forth. So, I used to stay there. I'd stayed straight through almost one weekend; I got locked in there and I stayed in the room and just kept writing and then fell asleep. On Monday morning, I looked up and there's Frank in a military outfit, asking me how I wanted my eggs. He was cooking breakfast!

"Later, after we'd finished the album, we went back in and added some strings to some of the tracks. Strings were so synonymous with Frank, and they worked well. You really can't submerge that Basie style! It was very exciting. I was absolutely in heaven because I had always wanted to write for Sinatra. I loved to write for singers, you know, because that was a challenge to create a palette. It really turns a singer on, and makes him want to sing the best he can. It's a great challenge, especially when you're talking about singers like Ray Charles. But I have been lucky from the early days to work with Dinah Washington and Sarah Vaughn and Billy Eckstine and Ray Charles, so I just love working with singers— the greatest singers in the world. And Sinatra? I just wish there were ten more of him. He's a very special human being."

TOUR DE FORCE: *THE CONCERT SINATRA*

*A*nother important Reprise album that is unimpeachable from a performance standpoint yet falls short of its sonic potential is a 1963 effort titled *The Concert Sinatra*. Counted among the very best of the Sinatra-Riddle ballad albums, the recording features eight tunes, including "Bewitched," "Soliloquy," "You'll Never Walk Alone," "Ol' Man River," and "This Nearly Was Mine": each a testament to Riddle's deft hand and ability to stir the soul.

As in a formal concert setting, the arrangements are lavish, utilizing a sweep of swirling strings, pretty woodwind countermelodies, and spine-tingling harp glissandi. The instrumental backings are surpassed only by Sinatra's vocal, which is as close to the *bel canto* style as a pop singer can get. The force of this recording, a rare combination of stately orchestral scoring and interpretation and superior vocal control, is exemplified by the majestic opening track, Rodgers

and Hammerstein's "I Have Dreamed" from *The King and I*. It may well be the most powerful performance of Sinatra's career.

Sinatra demonstrates an impressive range on several of the tunes presented here, especially on "Ol' Man River," which he sings wide open. But after the verse, which is sung with a fairly bright vocal inflection, Sinatra darkens the hue, instantly highlighting the seriousness of the song. Inspired by the powerful lyrics and Riddle's opulent textural setting, Sinatra ponders each syllable, searching to extract every gradation of color possible.

Here his acting skills serve him well. Near the finale he reaches the line:

You get a little drunk and you lands in jaiiiiiiiiiiiillllllllllllllllllll . . . ,

and without pause, slides into the next phrase:

Ohhhhhhhhhhhhhhhhhh . . . ,

then plummets way down, lower than you've ever heard him go, and then a half an octave lower than *that*. Finally, without the slightest trace of vibrato, he smooths it out, seemlessly flowing into the finale:

. . . ohhhhhhhhh . . . I gets weary, and sick of tryin' . . . I'm tired of livin', but I'm scared of dyin' . . . .

As Sinatra blazes across the final notes, the strings soar, the brass screams, and the percussion pounds, bringing the vocal and instrumental crescendoes to a dramatic close.

This ending powerfully captures the breadth of Sinatra's vocal range and the strength of his voice, as the following musical breakdown shows.

In the line "You get a little drunk and you lands in jail . . . ," Sinatra begins the word "jail" on a D, and dips down to a G.

With the line "Oh, I gets weary . . . " comes, in my opinion, the most riveting vocal moment of his entire recording career. On the word "Oh" Sinatra goes from G down to E-natural, then ever so fluidly glides up to G as he makes the transition from the word "Oh" to the word "I" at the beginning of the phrase "I gets weary . . . "

In the final line, "and Ol' Man River, he just keeps rolling along," Sinatra again dazzles us, approaching light operatic singing. In this line, he holds "along" for two measures, breaking the word into three separate notes: D, E, and C. This vocal trick approximates what an instrumentalist might do, and the glide between the three notes is buttery smooth. He holds the C to the end.

Here is an illustrative musical notation:

Sinatra's interpretation of "Ol' Man River" made an impression on percussionist Emil Richards, who recorded and toured with the singer during the 1950s and 1960s. "It used to freak me out when he used to sing 'Ol' Man River,' because what he'd do is hold his hands behind his back as if he were handcuffed, push his chest out, and pull his shoulders back. I think that gave him more air. Then, he would sing that last line, where he goes between those long notes without taking a breath . . . and he would get so

low and still be able to hold it. I tried myself to hold my breath while he was doing that on stage, and it was almost impossible! It was so effective that it gave me chills or made me cry every time he did it."

Another gorgeous song on the album is "Bewitched." Bill Miller once used it to explain to me how Sinatra executed the neat little key changes he sometimes used on song endings:

"The ability to make smooth key changes depends on how the arranger writes the key change, or how good the ears of the singer are. With Frank, his ears are pretty sharp. If he's holding a note on the fifth, he might change the key in the middle, like he did on the recording of 'I Get Along Without You Very Well.' To go up a half tone at any given point on the fifth of a tonic would be very simple for any singer. But you wouldn't want to go any further . . . .

On 'Bewitched,' the word "me" in the line, 'Although the laugh's on me . . . ' ends on a dominant note (the seventh). Now, as long as he's holding a long note like that for at least one bar, he has time to think about the next note being a half-tone higher, so there's no problem there. Also, on this arrangement and on that particular key change, Nelson laid the chord change in there for him, so he waits to hear it, and "then" falls in very sneakily so you don't notice it. He falls in like a sixteenth after the chord change, so he's actually changing (vocally) in the middle of "I'll [sing to her]."

Again, a musical notation helps illustrate the point:

Three songs on the album summarize Riddle's harmonic sensibilities. On "This Nearly Was Mine," the melodic harmonies within the strings allow them to shimmer beautifully; the ending of "You'll Never Walk Alone" is equally superb, the sustained tension resolved exquisitely through the blending of strings, woodwinds, and harp. (Listen to the way the horns are placed against the string crescendo at the end and to how their "stepping" up builds a counter both against and *with* the gradually climbing strings.)

At the close of "My Heart Stood Still," Riddle uses a similar technique, this time layering in individual instruments like oboe and horn against the swelling strings, building their intensity gradually to the song's finale. These techniques—the flourishing harp glissandos and the Gershwin-esque voicing of French horn against a throbbing string bed—are "Nelson-isms" that lend his music individuality and help distinguish it from that of other arrangers.

"[This] more robust, 'earthy' color I have used many times was lifted directly from Debussy's *La Mer*," Riddle explained. "Many years ago, I borrowed the score from the New York Public Library, and hidden in its pages, I discovered the structure of celli superimposed on open horns. I don't recall the balance of instruments on the original score, but I have had considerable success with eight celli and four horns, two celli to each horn."

This recording project sought to present these extended Sinatra performances in the richest, highest fidelity possible. Since virtually no other studio could accommodate the seventy-

PHOTOGRAPH BY TED ALLAN, COURTESY MPTV ARCHIVE

Session for The Concert Sinatra on Goldwyn's Soundstage 7.

three-piece symphony orchestra required for the sessions, the recordings were made on Stage Seven of the Samuel Goldwyn film studios in Hollywood, a hall noted for its reverberant qualities.

With the careful deployment of a battery of the finest microphones, the proceedings were preserved via the Westrex 35mm recording system: a sprocket-type multi-head magnetic recorder, utilizing 35mm recording film for the greatest possible signal-to-noise ratio.

The advantages of using this system were many. Since the transport film of magnetic film is ninety-six frames per minute (much faster than that of standard audio tape), it resulted in a better high-frequency response and lower noise levels. Also, the film stock was much wider than half-inch, three-track magnetic tape, which allowed for increased saturation and frequency response.

With such intense preparation and attention to detail, this should have been one of the most impressive recordings in history. In the album's liner notes Raymond V. Pepe, president of the Institute of High Fidelity, believed so: "Pages could be written about the technical details of the equipment employed and the techniques used in this recording . . . it could well serve as a guide to all recording companies to achieve the ultimate in a disc recording."

Unfortunately, their superior fidelity was lost in the transcription of the 35mm film recordings to the standard two-track, quarter-inch master that was used for production. Lee Herschberg, Bill Putnam's second engineer at United Recording, who would supervise Sinatra's recording activities in the late 1960s, describes the mixdown process. "I believe they had one eight-track, 35mm recorder running, and a whole bunch of separate 35mm tracks that could be synched together later, for a total of twenty-one tracks. Now, they were actually locking those twenty-one tracks together after the sessions at Goldwyn, and mixing them down to three-track tape. I was back at United, mixing the three-track tapes down to a final, two-track master."

The degradation occurred, it seems, after the original sessions. By the time the film stock session masters were twice mixed to regular tape (two generations removed from the originals), then pressed on vinyl, they had lost much of the spatial ambiance and sonic detail that made them unique.

"I would agree that the problem with those tapes is in the mixdowns," says Allen Sides. "At that time, the 35mm stock blew away any standard tape or tape recorder, because the oxide was so thick, and each channel was equivalent to full-track mono." "I have heard magnetic recordings, like the *Around the World in Eighty Days* score which was done on the old Charlie Chaplin stage, and the six-track stereo magnetic track of that is one of the most impressive recordings I've ever heard. It's just unbelievable. With *The Concert Sinatra*, the mixdown may have been a problem because the magnetic film recorders of that

time had unlimited bandwidth on the record side, but limited bandwidth on the playback side. When these magnetic tracks are played back on brand new reproducers with good heads, they have this incredible top end that you never heard! It was on the tape, but it wasn't coming through on the playback."

As of this writing, the original 35mm session tracks are presumed lost, and have not been utilized since the album's issue in 1963. It is not known if they were retained after the tracks were mixed to the three, then two-track tapes. The three-track mixdowns were preserved, and according to Warner-Reprise producer Greg Geller, have been used to create a newly restored compact disk version of the album (while the previous digital compact disc issues of the LP have been marred by excessive tape hiss, this latest remastering reduces this anomaly substantially, at the same time offering increased detail and more of the ambient characteristics of the original studio).

EARLY AUTUMN: THE SEPTEMBER OF HIS YEARS

By 1964, Sinatra had forged a friendship with Sonny Burke, an extraordinary musician-producer who ultimately guided Sinatra through a slew of albums, from that year's *America I Hear You Singing* (a group of patriotic songs featuring Fred Waring and his Pennsylvanians, and guest vocalist Bing Crosby) through his own personal brainchild, 1979's *Trilogy*. Of all the producers who worked with Sinatra, Burke was the one that he truly befriended and looked to for advice. Theirs was an unusual artist-producer relationship and probably thrived because Sinatra saw the need for a man of Burke's considerable talent at Reprise.

Allen Sides was a personal friend of Burke and had the opportunity to observe the pair at work in the studio. "My parents had met and befriended Sonny when I was a kid at *The Voices of Christmas* party they used to have here in Los Angeles every year. When I was ten years old, I was doing hi-fi installations for people like Sonny and Les Brown, and I became their friend and they invited me down to sessions. Frank and Sonny would sit down and go over the tunes, and Sonny would come up with different concepts for him. Frank was very much influenced by him; they were very tight, and while Frank would make changes out in the studio, Sonny carefully helped direct things from the control room."

Arguably, Burke's greatest triumph as a producer was his direction of Sinatra's autumnal masterpiece, *September of My Years*, recorded in celebration of the singer's fiftieth birthday.

One of the best Sinatra albums of the Reprise era, *September of My Years* is a reflective throwback to the concept records of the 1950s, and more than any of those collections, distills everything Frank Sinatra had ever learned or experienced as a vocalist. Where programs like *Only the Lonely* and *No One Cares* carry a common theme, they are as much about Sinatra the actor as Sinatra the singer; with *September of My Years*, he *is* the concept. Pairing a group of fine standards alongside contemporary songs, his ruminations on the ironies of age beautifully impart what Nancy Sinatra calls her father's "era of wisdom."

Jenkins counted this album among his favorites. "Frank's taste is so infallible . . . he knows what's right and wrong for him," he told Wink Martindale. "He knows it right down to the last sixteenth note, and I've never known him to be wrong."

"The songs all had a thing about age, and growing older," Jenkins said, "and I was exactly

the right age to do it, as he was. And we were talking about that on the date: that neither one of us could have made that album at any other time in our lives, except at that time."

Including "September of My Years," "How Old Am I?" "The Man in the Looking Glass," "Don't Wait Too Long," "It Gets Lonely Early," and Jenkins' own "This Is All I Ask," the tunes Sinatra selected are appropriately winsome and contemplative. The re-recording of "September Song" surpasses the stodgy version from 1961, and his readings of "I See It Now" and "Last Night When We Were Young" are confident and authoritative. "When the Wind Was Green" and "Once Upon a Time" are whimsical, folk-style songs, and Sinatra's charming interpretations turn them into the most endearing of tales.

Precious little film showing Frank Sinatra in the working environs of the recording studio exists, but footage shot on April 22, 1965, for a CBS Reports documentary called *Sinatra: An American Original* includes the session for Ervin Drake's "It Was a Very Good Year," the showstopper of the *September of My Years* album. This song, perhaps Sinatra's most personal, comes far closer to being an autobiographical statement than the impudent "My Way."

The tune had originally been written by Drake for the Kingston Trio. "I happened to stop in the office of a publisher I knew named Artie Mogull," the songwriter explained. "He took care of the trio's publishing, and he told me the boys were looking for a song to be done as a solo on their next album, titled *Going Places*. 'Do you have anything?' he asked."

"In the back of my diary I jot down new ideas for songs. So I looked through the diary, and saw a note I had made a while before. It read: 'Story of a guy's life . . . told in wine vintage terms . . . possible title, 'It Was A Very Good Year . . . neofolk.' I went to the piano, and started to fool around. The first thing I thought about was the nature of the group, which was a folk group, which was doing both genuine and neo (instant) folk songs. My initial idea was to use a minor key, because very often folk songs are written in minor keys. I suddenly had this idea, and the tune was written and notated practically simultaneously, all within an hour."

At the 1998 Frank Sinatra academic conference held at Hofstra University, Drake spoke at length about the song's composition:

"I took the liberty of making minor changes with the inner rhythm, which we would *never* do on 'Tin Pan Alley.' But, because of the circumstances, and the fact that I knew this group's songs (many of them were irregular), I gave myself that liberty. For example, when you say 'It was a very good year for blue-blooded girls of independent means,' the rhythm within the line is different than it is when you say, 'It was a very good year for small-town girls and soft summer nights.'"

"It worked, but I knew it would be dreadfully dull if it were not separated by some sort of instrumental break, since the main theme is in a minor key that always ends in a major I chord. For the little connecting pieces (or interlude), I returned to the minor feeling as a start, and ended it each time, as well as the very end, with an unresolved V7 chord. Then, I decided that in order to cover my behind, I'd better write something lyrically for that part, in case somebody wanted to sing it. But what do you write in a folk song? You go to the Elizabethan nonsense syllables! You're always safe there. So I wrote this:

Hi-lura-li,
hi-lura-lura-li,
hi-duri-doon-doon-doon

"Many performers kept that Elizabethan nonsense in—not Sinatra. One day, I said to him, 'I noticed that you skipped the option of those syllables that I wrote.' He said, 'What syllables are you talking about?' He wasn't even aware of them, because the Kingston Trio hadn't sung them. So I demonstrated it for him, and he just

looked at me, and said, 'You're lucky, buddy. If I would have sung that, it would have come out:

Hi-scooby-do,
hi-scooby-dooby-do,
hi-scooby-do-do-do!'"

The film is loaded with the charm and atmosphere that can be heard, but not seen, on existing studio tapes. It is among the most important documents showing how Frank Sinatra worked in the recording studio.

In United's Studio A, the orchestra is preparing to record. The tension will be just a bit higher tonight, owing to the CBS-TV cameras that are filming the session.

This evening's session is being recorded by Lowell Frank, one of the finest engineers on Bill Putnam's staff. His touch is expert, and he captures the soft sheen of the violins, and the rangy, colorful tone of Sinatra's mature voice.

Before the takes are made, Sinatra stands before his music, which rests on a metal stand in front of him. Behind him is a stool, on which sits a doubled-up paper cup filled with hot tea. He listens to the orchestra play the arrangement. At the end, he smiles broadly. "Yeah!" he says, obviously pleased with what he hears. He begins a dialog with Jenkins, who works out some incorrect notes. As Jenkins and Sinatra talk, Sonny Burke, in the control room, consults his score.

After a few moments, Sinatra is ready for a rehearsal. He lights a cigarette and picks up the cup of steaming tea. Pacing, smiling, he works the room like a prowling tiger. As the moment for his vocal entrance arrives, he approaches the stand. Collar unbuttoned, tie loosened, Sinatra alternately watches Jenkins and glances at the music laid out in front of him. He sings:

But now the days grow short . . . I'm in the
*   Autumn of the year . . . and now I think*
*   of my life as vintage wine from fine old*
*   kegs . . .*

A few feet away, Gordon Jenkins conducts from an elevated rostrum, the singer a stone's throw from his right elbow.

In the control room, Lowell Frank adjusts the balance as the tape reels on two recorders churn at a dizzying speed. Sinatra stops singing, and clears his throat. "I think I swallowed a shot glass!" He looks toward the control room and addresses the engineer. "Uh, listen, Lowell. Any popping of P's, let's stop, because there were too many P's popping on the past dates we did. Can you clear those up a little bit?" Giving the matter his undivided attention, Sinatra watches for the engineer's answer. Lowell responds from the booth. "Yeah, if they don't thump. If they're a real thump, I can't." Sinatra smiles. "Well, I don't thump, you know. I'm a sneaky P-popper!"

PHOTOGRAPH BY ED THRASHER, COURTESY OF MPTV ARCHIVE

In a moment, he is ready. "Can we make one?" He smoothes his jacket, and reaching down, adjusts the angle of his music stand. The orchestra is ready, and as they begin, the camera pans the studio, which is dotted with more than a dozen microphones attached to overhead stands. Then, a cut to Sinatra, who is framed behind the wide, sweeping gestures of conductor Jenkins, whose arms swing vertically and horizontally in approximate time with the music.

In a marked departure from standard operating procedure, the singer's trademark fedora rests not on his head, but on the end of the boom microphone stand, lending a relaxed touch to the studio's somewhat sterile atmosphere.

He grips the stand, closes his eyes, and begins:

> *When I was seventeen . . . it was a very good year . . .*

With each succeeding phrase, he massages the lyric, smiling in the direction of the conductor and the orchestra between choruses, nodding to friends in the small audience seated on metal chairs behind him. He steps back to survey the room, careful not to disturb anything.

As he sings, Sinatra nods affirmatively, and the twinkle in his eyes tells you he's really remembering what it was like to be seventeen, and twenty-one, and thirty-five. At a particularly sensitive passage, he cocks his head, leans in, and gently shrugs his shoulders. He is a study in motion, and somehow, the energy contained in the delicate gestures that accompany his coaxing of notes always manages to find its way into the sound of his records.

The song draws to a close, and Sinatra, spent, sags after singing the last note. Watching Jenkins, he raises his arms, palms outstretched, to remind everyone not to move until they get the okay from the booth. When the signal is given, he immediately asks a question.

"What's the time on that? 3:20?" When he's told the recording clocks in at 4:12, he responds, "4:12? That's longer than the first act of Hamlet! Can we hear it?"

As the tape is rewound, Sinatra strolls over to the rhythm section, which is isolated behind a small scrim. He begins talking to the bass player. After explaining some problems he's been having with his sinuses and congestion, he mentions the origins of the song. "I heard it on the car radio one day, by the Kingston Trio, and I said 'Gee, that'd be great for the album.'"

The orchestrations that Gordon Jenkins has fashioned for this album and "It Was a Very Good Year" in particular are melodically superior to any he has created for Sinatra in the past, going beyond his usual reliance on strings to demonstrate the complex harmonic voicings and instrumental textures and rhythms he was capable of. A gentle harp rhythm, pulsing quietly behind the haunting strains of the oboe, lends solemnity to the introduction. The harpist executes a glissando, and as Sinatra's vocal enters, a complement of delicately voiced woodwinds, gliding atop a layer of sustained strings, counters his lines with a simple melody. Between choruses, Jenkins varies the instrumentation, sometimes pairing strings and harp; at others, woodwinds and strings, each playing against the other.

The dainty rhythmic patterns he develops behind Sinatra's vocal in the choruses are equally imaginative and varied, featuring acoustic bass, bowed and pizzicato violin, horn, and percussion. In the chorus that begins "When I was thirty-five, it was a very good year . . . ," for instance, the violins play a series of short, repetitive notes in the background while flute, then horn, play a syncopated melodic figure against them. And in the second portion of the final chorus, as Sinatra sings, "And now I think of my life as vintage wine from fine old kegs . . . ," an impromptu folk dance is heard in the interplay between bass, pizzicato violins, and triangle. Throughout, the full string section that Jenkins is noted for is beau-

tifully harmonized with the lower winds, accentuating the vocal lines.

Jenkins once described a problem he encountered while scoring the song, and how much he appreciated Sinatra's musical sensibility. "In 'It Was a Very Good Year,' there's a line about halfway through that goes, '. . . their chauffeurs would drive—when I was thirty-five . . . .' When I made the arrangement, I put in what we call a 'Mickey Mouse' figure: a discord and comedy figure. And from the minute I wrote it down, I started to worry about it, so I asked my wife Beverly to listen to it. She did, and she laughed. And

PHOTOGRAPH BY ED THRASHER, COURTESY OF MPTV ARCHIVE

I said, 'Well, what do you think?' She said, 'Well, I don't know.' I said, 'I'll just leave it in and see what Frank says.'

"So I didn't say anything to him. We played it, and when we got to that point, he laughed. I thought, 'Oh.' But when the light went on to make it, he came over, and said, 'Take that thing out of there.' And he didn't even have to tell me what it was—I knew what it was. I was worried about it myself—he thought it was funny—but it didn't fit."

Back in the studio, the tape is ready, and the playback begins. Sinatra is seated on the base of Jenkins's podium, and as the music blares from the huge speakers inside the studio, he watches the floor, completely absorbed in what he is hearing. When the line "When I was thirty-five . . . it was a very good year" booms forth, Sinatra looks up at Jenkins, and breaks into a broad grin. He nods, and says, "Those were the swingin' years!" He smiles, shrugs, and in his own modest way, seems to be bursting with pride. When the recording concludes, the musicians and the audience break into applause. Sinatra stands, dusts off his fanny, and as he walks back to his stand, says simply, "Pretty song, isn't it?"

Most revealing about the scene is Sinatra's obvious pleasure in listening to the playback of a song he's just recorded; he seems to groove as much on the playback as he does on the actual performance. It's a rare glimpse of Sinatra digging *Sinatra*.

Ervin Drake was unaware that Sinatra had recorded his song until he was in London, and a British friend played it for him over the telephone. "I made him play it for me twice," Drake says. "As soon as we got home, I didn't run to the post office . . . I ran to the record store to get the album! And then I played nobody else's cut but my own. I must have played it thirty or forty times that first day, and I've *never* done that with any other song. Of course, the whole album is terrific, but I never get tired of the beautiful way that Gordon Jenkins and Frank Sinatra treated that song."

STRADDLING THE LINE: ROCK 'N' ROLL SINATRA

Motivated by the commercial success of daughter Nancy's 1966 smash hit "These Boots Are Made for Walking," Sinatra decided to update his image somewhat and turned to a young producer who'd been on staff at Reprise since 1963: Jimmy Bowen. A former rock and roller, Bowen was kicking around California, working for American Music as a demo writer. Through a mutual friend, Sinatra learned of Bowen and offered him a job. "My friend Murray had asked me if I'd be interested, and I said, 'Sure.' About five or six weeks later, I get a call one night, and Murray's talking soft. He says, 'Listen, you got the job . . . hang on, Frank wants to talk to you.' Sinatra came on, and said, 'James? Glad to have you aboard . . . *click*.' That was it!"

At Reprise, Bowen had one goal in mind: to work with Dean Martin. "I loved what he did on Capitol, and now I'm working for Reprise, and I told them 'He's the one act I want to produce—I know what to do with him.' And I just took the big orchestra, and did simple arrangements with him . . . we did quite a few country songs. And, you get lucky when you get [a song like] 'Everybody Loves Somebody,' which is a career record."

"Since I was making hits for his buddy, I think he [Frank] said, 'Well, I think I should give the kid a try.' He called me one day, and asked me if I'd come over for a meeting right across the street in Burbank. I grabbed out of my 'good song file' a number called 'Softly, as I Leave You,' that Frank just loved. We talked a bit, and he said, 'Listen, if you're going to produce some music for me, what would you do?' I said, 'Well, I wouldn't bastardize you . . . I'd change the music around *you*, to keep you who you are.' He said, 'Well, that makes sense . . . whaddya got?' Thank God I picked that song! I played him 'Softly . . . ,' and he said, 'Fine—let's do it.' So we went in like a week or two later, and recorded 'Softly, as I Leave You.'"

Following his success with Martin's "Everybody Loves Somebody," Bowen engaged arranger Ernie Freeman, a rhythm-and-blues veteran who was an ace at writing "rockabilly" charts, to provide a new and different sound for Frank Sinatra.

"I'd kind of get the guys who weren't your standard Martin or Sinatra kind of arrangers, 'cause that's not what I wanted," the producer said. "I used a whole different band, too. I wanted Frank (and Dean and Sammy when I worked with them) to feel like they were on stage, 'cause I'd watched them work in person, and they were knocking people out. But in the studio, the music was dated. So, I did two things: I changed the rhythm section, and I changed the concertmaster and about half the strings. Sid Sharp was the guy I liked to use . . . he knew to get me people who didn't mind bustin' their strings. I would tell Ernie not to write any rhythm parts; I'd get the band there a couple hours before, and work them out, 'cause I wanted them to do what I wanted them to do."

Manning the booth for many of these mid-1960s sessions was engineer Eddie Brackett, who had become a close associate of Bowen. "Ahh, he was so good," says Bowen. "Some of those records he did were cut and mixed at the same time, when you only had three tracks. There wasn't any fancy mixing." While Bowen relied on him, others viewed Brackett with a wary eye. "Eddie used to come in with these racks of stuff . . . custom stuff he'd plug in, and half the time it wasn't even hooked up! He used to dance behind the console . . . he was a real showman. He was just a line of sh—t that wouldn't quit! The schmooze was just too much for Bill [Putnam], and he never liked him," says Allen Sides.

"When Sinatra came to me, he wanted Top 40 radio . . . he wanted hits," Bowen recalls. "So he just sang the sh—t out of it for me. When I worked on his records, it was usually my idea of how I heard them in the marketplace at that time. I'd call Ernie, and say, 'Alright, Ernie, you've got twenty strings . . . six horns . . . eight voices . . . a rhythm section.' On 'Softly, as I Leave You,' I wanted the voices, because in those days I used a lot of eighth notes, a lot of 'on the head' stuff, 'cause the big orchestra gave it a pulse that made it more commercial. Basically, it's one of those things where you grasp the moment. I had a four- or five-year period where I had the feel of how to take these kinds of artists into the marketplace to Top 40 radio, at a time when the Top 40 radio DJs didn't want to play them."

Sprinkled among albums such as *September of My Years*, *Sinatra's Sinatra*, and *Moonlight Sinatra* are the Bowen-inspired albums *That's Life* and *The World We Knew*, and singles like "Forget Domani" and the smash hit "Strangers in the Night." Bowen was knocking his brains out trying to score some hits for someone who was quickly becoming an old-fashioned singer, whose main competition were four guys with mop-top hair from Britain.

"Every artist wants to have his music accepted," says Bowen. "After we cut 'Softly . . . ,' we were standing out in the studio listening to it, and Frank said, 'Well, James, what do you think?' And I said, 'Well, I think it's about a number 30 record, but it'll get us back on radio.' He looked at me like, 'Oh, okay.' It didn't please him too much, and he left . . . but we had a challenge to get Sinatra on Top 40 radio, when The Beatles were happening, so I was just dealing with it straight ahead, and he understood."

The singer allowed his young producer plenty of latitude and seemed to trust his instincts. "With 'Strangers in the Night,' which was the biggest thing I did with him, the publisher came by the house one day to play me a score Burt Kaempfert had done for the picture *A Man*

Could Get Killed," Bowen remembers. "A stiff picture, I think, but this one chunk of the score was the melody to 'Strangers in the Night,' and I said, 'Man, get me the lyric on that and I'll do it with Sinatra.' And I'd *never* said that to anybody, because obviously, nobody knows what Frank's going to do till he says he's going to do it! They sent me a couple of lyrics I didn't like, and finally, they got me one that I thought was right. And we went in and did that song . . . and got into a cover battle with Jack Jones."

The song had been given to two singers, and when the word that Jones had his version coming out on Kapp Records in just a few days, Reprise went on full alert.

"We went in and cut it on Monday, and I found out at dinner that Jack's record was supposed to land at radio the next Tuesday or Wednesday," Bowen remembers. "They had mailed it, just regular mail, on Friday . . . so it'd be there Tuesday or Wednesday. As soon as the guy said it, I said, 'I see . . . ' We cut it, and I had a mastering room booked in the same building. As soon as I got it mixed, I started cutting acetates, and I had half a dozen people working for me, and I had them running to the airport all night long and up until noon the next day, with twenty-dollar bills and an acetate with an address on it. I'd have our field rep ready to pick it up in each city, and the stewardess (who we'd paid the twenty bucks) would give it to the rep on the other end. By dark on Tuesday, we were nationwide . . . Jack's came regular mail, which doesn't get opened up too fast, but they open that sort of thing—special deal. So, it's not that they *wanted* to play Sinatra that much, but it just made it kind of special, and it just exploded."

When the song took off, it was placed at the head of an impending Sinatra-Riddle album, which was then renamed *Strangers in the Night.* No doubt to match the contemporary texture of the title track, Riddle made liberal use of the jazz organ and a more pop-oriented rhythm section in the blance of the album.

"'Strangers in the Night' is a great example of the difference between a competent engineer and a *great* engineer," says Allen Sides. "You can hear the difference on this album, because the song 'Strangers in the Night' was recorded by Eddie Brackett, and it sounds pretty lousy. The rest of the album was recorded by Lee Herschberg, who is an incredible engineer, and it sounds terrific!"

Sides, who by this time was hanging out with Putnam and Herschberg in the studio, remembers these sessions and Herschberg's recording philosophy very clearly. "Frank really didn't like being in any isolated area—he liked being right out in the middle of the room. You didn't need headphones or anything, because the whole thing was right there. Lee used to say to me 'When you balance these sessions up, first you begin with Frank's mike, and then figure out what you need to go along with it.' Because if you balance up the whole band and the orchestra, and then put Frank in, it would be all wrong, because of the leakage. But Bill's rooms sounded so spectacular that the leakage was a plus—not a minus. To be honest with you, walking around those studios, a lot of stuff didn't sound very good [in the room]. But when you walk in the control room, it just gives you chills, it sounds so good. That happened when Lee was recording *Summer of '42* with Michel Legrand. Lee was so exceptional."

Recording enthusiasts may have wondered about the microphone depicted on the cover of *Strangers in the Night*—a mike that looks curiously like a handheld Shure dynamic microphone. Next to the impressive looking Neumann U67 (the most common vocal mike of the mid to late 1960s) this instrument, sloppily taped to the head of the boom stand, looks anemic! It is, in fact, a Senheiser 405 condenser microphone, a crisp, snappy microphone which was a bit more directional than other condenser mikes.

The organ, tastefully provided by Michael Melvoin, also played a starring role in the next Sinatra album, the gritty, raucous *That's Life.*

Sinatra had found the song for an upcoming *Man and His Music* television special and approached Bowen with it. He liked it so much, they built an entire album around it.

"'That's Life' was a unique session," Bowen remembers. "It was a newly refurbished studio, and I walked into the engineer's booth, and he said, 'The only microphones getting in here to the tape machine are the rhythm section mikes.' That meant I had thirty strings, horns, the singers, and Frank . . . and the mikes weren't working. So I took the acoustic guitar's mike cord and hooked it into Sinatra's mike so he'd have one. 'Cause [his voice] wasn't getting into the control room . . . that mike wasn't there yet. I told the engineer, 'Don't you say a word to anybody, because out there and in the earphones he'll hear all this.' But somehow he couldn't get it to tape . . . he had just rebuilt this studio. Frank was next door in another studio warming up, and he came in and we ran it down. Then we made a tape. He came in, and I said, 'All you're going to hear is you and the rhythm section, 'cause the equipment's [not working] . . . and I'll put this other stuff on later.' He said, 'Oh, okay.' We listened."

Bowen then stepped mighty close to the edge. "Frank said to me, 'That's your hit, isn't it?' and I said, 'Well, no . . . if you want a hit, you're going to have to do it one more time . . . that just doesn't add up.' And everybody got real quiet, and he gave me the coldest look an artist ever gave me. But he went right out, and instead of singing it hip, he was pissed . . . so he bit it. That's when he sang 'That's Life!' He got to the end, and that's when he put in that, 'My, my!' It was me he was directing it to—you know, 'I'll show ya!' The echo died off, and I said, 'Got it!' and he just turned around and went out the back door. He was gone. As soon as he left, I took the mikes that worked, and ran them over the cords on the string mike, and we dubbed in the horns and the voices . . . piece by piece. I didn't plan it, I just didn't have any choice. The next day he called me, and he said he thought it was great."

Fleshing out the album are forgettable tunes like "Winchester Cathedral" and "Sand and Sea." Two major film hits, "Somewhere My Love" (*Dr. Zhivago*) and "The Impossible Dream" (*Man of La Mancha*, recorded piece by piece in more than a dozen separate takes) were also included. From a sonic standpoint, the album has an unconventional mix: Sinatra's vocals on one side, orchestra and/or chorus on the opposite side with little or no blending. Of all the Reprise albums Sinatra made, it is the oddest and least appealing, sound-wise.

"[We were] just trying to learn the technology that we had then, you know," says Bowen. "One day you had two tracks, then three, then four, then eight . . . that album was recorded on eight tracks—it was my first eight-track recording. Being able to do that gave me the opportunity to bring in Mike Melvoin, who played organ. He came in and played two tracks; before, you'd have to stack [tracks] in order to overdub somebody later. I recorded the chorus parts live at the session, and I overdubbed them later, as well. They'd be there live at the sessions, and then I'd bring them back later to get them clean, with no leakage."

The mid-1960s was a progressive time for sound recording. The multitrack tape machines that Bowen describes allowed producers and engineers to do far more manipulating and overdubbing than ever before. Moreover, because each added part was placed on its own "track" (or space) on the tape, the sound quality didn't suffer with each successive overdub.

Contemporary rock albums like The Beach Boys' *Pet Sounds* and The Beatles' *Sgt. Pepper's Lonely Hearts Club Band* demonstrated the medium's amazing potential: each was as much a product of technical wizardry as musical craftsmanship, and both heralded a completely new recording philosophy that was quickly embraced by both the studio and performing communities.

With improved multitrack recording, artists weren't pressured to achieve a perfect performance: if it wasn't happening for them creatively, they could save the portions of a recording that they liked, and return to the studio later to add in what needed to be corrected.

The increased flexibility also allowed individual soloists to come into the studio and add their part whenever they had time. To accomplish this, they would listen to what had been committed to tape by the previous instrumentalists, and play along to the pre-recorded track. If they made a mistake, they could keep re-recording their part until they were satisfied, without affecting the quality of the original recording.

This shift toward "modular" recording removed the spontaneity that accompanies a live performance, and older performers like Sinatra preferred to record the "old-fashioned" way, live in the studio, standing out in front of the band. Bowen attempted to strike a balance between exploiting the studio's technical potential and satisfying artists like Sinatra and Dean Martin. The producer made good use of the new freedom to experiment and add instrumentation to that of the original sessions.

How would Bowen compare Sinatra with his friend and label-mate, Dean Martin? "Sinatra was much more intense at sessions," says Bowen. "He'd be more curious about the process, and the new innovations . . . with Dean, nobody would ever know how serious he was about it or not. When we recorded [Dean], I made demos in his key so he could play them and sing along with them, driving back and forth to the golf course, or to and from the TV show. That's the way *he* worked. See, Dean was a *stylist*, and Sinatra was a *singer*. A great singer as opposed to a great stylist: you're going to have to approach it differently."

Bowen's touch certainly had the desired commercial effect: "Softly, as I Leave You" reached number 27 on the charts (eerily close to Bowen's prediction), and "That's Life" reached number 4. "Strangers in the Night" would reach number 1.

"SOMETHIN' STUPID"

One of the sexiest Sinatra collaborations of the Reprise years was with Brazilian guitarist Antonio Carlos Jobim, innovator of the ultra-chic bossa nova style that had swept the world in 1966, largely on the coattails of his famous "The Girl from Ipanema." The balmy, exotic rhythm of Jobim's sound caught Sinatra's attention, and in late 1966, he engaged German arranger Claus Ogerman to make some arrangements. In January '67, he and Jobim entered the studio to begin working on the album *Francis Albert Sinatra and Antonio Carlos Jobim*.

In the album's liner notes, writer Stan Cornyn (a brilliant sideline observer at many Sinatra sessions) quotes the singer as saying, "I haven't sung this softly since the [vocal] hemorrhage [in 1950]." He must have forgotten the sensitivity with which he approached the tenderest of vocals on *Close to You* in 1956.

"I was at the sessions, not to play guitar originally, but just to help out with some problems that might come up, because Jobim didn't speak English very well," remembers Al Viola. "And, sure enough, when they got to one of the songs [Irving Berlin's "Change Partners"], it just wasn't working out. Frank wanted a certain thing, and Jobim was having some difficulty with it. Frank said, 'Let Al play it.' So although I wasn't credited with it on the album, and most people don't know it, Jobim is *not* the only guitar player on the first Sinatra-Jobim album. I'm playing on there too!"

The final bossa nova session took place on the evening of February 1, 1967. A relaxed Sinatra arrived at Western Recording Studio 1 at a little past eight; within two hours, the last two songs for the Jobim album ("Once I Loved" and "How

Insensitive") had been put to bed, and a third number scored by Ogerman, "Drinking Again," was recorded for the upcoming album, *The World We Knew.*

PHOTOGRAPH BY RON JOY. USED BY PERMISSION.
SHEFFIELD ENTERPRISES, INC. AND NANCY SINATRA

At ten-thirty, the violinists and Sinatra's personal rhythm section moved out of the studio, and the Hollywood "wrecking crew" moved in. For the next hour and a half, another Sinatra, Nancy, Jr., would share the mike with her Dad. Their song, "Somethin' Stupid," became a number one hit—and Frank Sinatra's second gold record.

"Working with Nancy had to be the most fun I've ever had in a studio in my life," says arranger-conductor Billy Strange. "It was loose—all of us were very spontaneous. It never took much effort on anyone's part to get it done. Nancy was probably the most intuitive singer I ever worked with. Like her Dad, she knew from the first time she heard a song that it would be right for her. She had to love it, too. You couldn't just sell her a song."

"I just *knew* that this song would work," Nancy has told me. "I can't say exactly *why* you know something will be a hit, but when you hear

it, you just know. There were two songs that I had a strong feeling would be hits: 'Boots,' and 'Somethin' Stupid.' Sarge Weiss had brought the song to Dad's attention, and he said, 'Let's tack it on the end of the Jobim date.' So, after he finished his songs, what I like to call his 'A Team' stepped aside, and I came in with my little 'B Team,' and we recorded it. We did the song in two or three takes: we would have done it in one, except that Dad got silly, endlessly sounding his 'S's like Daffy Duck, which made me spoil the first take!"

"Lee Hazlewood and I co-produced it," recalls Jimmy Bowen, "because Lee was working with Nancy, and I was working with Frank. We had two microphones head up in the studio . . . they were out there side by side. It should have been filmed—it would have been a great TV thing!"

As always, the unedited session tapes are filled with priceless dialogue that put us inside Sinatra's musical head.

As Billy Strange preps the band for recording, Frank jokes, and does his first take à la Daffy. Nancy ribs him, feigning an admonishment. "Daddy!" "Sorry," he says. Frank begins singing softly to himself "And then I think I'll wait until the evening gets late and I'm alone with you . . ." Continuing, he talks his way through the next line: "There's a chance you won't be leaving with me . . ." He has some ideas, which he shares with the team.

> *Frank: (to Nancy)* I gotta sing a little louder, then. You too—you sing a little louder too, during that phrase.
> *Nancy:* Okay.
> *Frank:* I'll tell you what'll help us too: a little crescendo. Pretty good feeling up to there, huh?
> *Hazlewood:* Very good feeling up to there.
> *Strange:* Can we do a hold on that one note?
> *Frank:* No, no—no, no. If you stop I'll fall down! Keep right on going.

Strange: Crazy.

Nancy: (to Hazlewood) Is that better, Barton?

Hazlewood: Much, thank you.

Strange: (to Hazlewood) Do you wanna hear the guitars, just to make sure everything's cool?

Hazlewood: One real fast start, then we'll do it.

Strange cues the musicians. "Letter A," he calls out, and Strange's exotic guitar and rhythm intro begins. Both Nancy and Frank are pleased with what they hear.

Nancy: I *love* those guitars!

Frank: Pretty sound! Yeah, that's the whole trick of the record!

Bass player Carol Kaye, Nancy's trusted friend, remembers that "it didn't take long to get a hot performance." "The duet was poignant and sincere, different from the usual Hollywood glitter, they were both really happy, and we only did three or four takes." Later, during a playback in the booth, Nancy's beaming Dad proclaimed that the song would hit "Number 1." His prophecy landed him a financial windfall: earlier, Reprise President Mo Ostin had predicted that the song would fail. Upon its success, Frank joyfully told Nancy, "The silly bastard bet me two dollars it would be a bomb!" (The record not only charted: it stayed on the charts for thirteen weeks, four of them in the Number 1 spot—a first for a father-daughter duet. Nancy kept Mo Ostin's framed $2 bill, which is one of her most cherished mementos.)

PHOTOGRAPH BY RON JOY. USED BY PERMISSION.
SHEFFIELD ENTERPRISES, INC. AND NANCY SINATRA

PHOTOGRAPH BY RON JOY. USED BY PERMISSION.
SHEFFIELD ENTERPRISES, INC. AND NANCY SINATRA

While all three of Sinatra's children had the opportunity to work with him in the studio, Nancy was the first to record with him. Although their musical genres may have been worlds apart, Frank's influence was not lost on his eldest daughter. "My Dad had always said to me, 'Stay away from what I do, and you'll be better off.' He was really saying, 'Don't try to do what I do, because you'll be held up for too much criticism.' And he was right—he was always right," she says.

"Somethin' Stupid," issued on a single, was also included on the upcoming Sinatra "album," the artist's next step toward bridging the ever-widening generation gap. Far short of a classic concept album, *The World We Knew*, produced by Bowen, is an uneven smattering of contemporary singles with one of the most dreadful and bizarre arrangements ever made for the singer: an H.B. Barnum (H.B. Barnum?) orchestration of "Some Enchanted Evening." (It is quite possible that Sinatra recorded this version of the Rodgers and Hammerstein classic to annoy Richard Rodgers, who was critical of any artist who performed his songs in any fashion other than *exactly* as written. There is no other plausible explanation for this lapse in judgment on Sinatra's part.)

Several of the album's orchestrations are by Gordon Jenkins, and his attempts to update his sound with modern instrumentation are awkward at best. To make matters worse, the Jenkins charts are oddly juxtaposed with those of true contemporary arrangers like Billy Strange and Ernie Freeman, resulting in an oddly disjointed feel. Where Sinatra had been completely attuned to what Freeman and Bowen were doing with *That's Life*, some of the songs on *The World We Knew* sound like second-rate rehearsals. Sinatra may have known that this would be a throwaway.

Jimmy Bowen, the album's producer, disagrees. "We were just experimenting . . . if you listen to all those sessions, you can hear it," he says. "We tried to do stuff differently, which you've got to do if you're going to do something that you've done a lot [of times]. [Some Enchanted Evening] was just H.B. and me and Frank in there messing around. People took it as [a backhand slap to Rodgers] later. I remember people saying that to me, and I said, 'To tell you the truth, I didn't even know who wrote it.' That's not what I was thinking."

When he recorded *The World We Knew*, Sinatra had been in the spotlight for almost thirty years, and had created the major musical genres of the past two and a half decades. While he had diversified somewhat at Reprise in the early and mid 1960s, those albums basically extended what he had begun at Capitol in the 1950s. By June of

1967 he needed to refresh his place in contemporary music. He couldn't have asked for a better launch than his and Nancy's "Somethin' Stupid."

The World We Knew also marked the first time in nearly fifteen years that Sinatra recorded in New York. Except for the London sessions of 1962, from the time of his last Columbia session in September 1952 to the first full session for this album, every Frank Sinatra recording session took place in Hollywood.

"Frank decided, 'You know, I haven't recorded in New York . . . ,' and we needed a record, and he was going to be back there, so I set it up to do it back there," remembers Jimmy Bowen. "Oh, what a pain in the butt! I had to get the studio across the hall to put in closed circuit television, 'cause he hadn't been back there in years and everybody knew him, and he invited them all, *and they all came!* The control room was so packed, it would take me five minutes to get from the board out to the musicians. You know, the Bennett Cerfs were there, all those kind of people . . . the elite of New York."

This unusual New York session, at which three songs were recorded ("You Are There," "The World We Knew," and a version of "This Town" that remains unreleased), was done at the

COURTESY OF PHIL RAMONE

Phil Ramone at the board, A&R Studios, New York City.

old Columbia Records studios at 799 Seventh Avenue, which under new ownership had been renamed "A&R Studios." Producing the session was Bowen; Billy Strange conducted, and the engineer for the date was Phil Ramone, who was a partner in the studio. As an engineer and budding producer, Ramone's star was on the rise. "I guess my reputation, at that point, was really starting to grow. It was the beginning of the [industry] move toward what would be pretty big hit records. At that time, I'd been going back and forth between L.A. and New York, doing things for Pepsi-Cola and stuff like that. I was making records for so many people, like Burt Bacharach, that they wanted that kind of a sound . . . the L.A. sound was competing heavily with the New York sound then."

In the early 1960s, Ramone opened A&R, which was located on 45th Street. Several years later, someone told him that CBS was looking to sell the Columbia Records studio-office building, with the proviso that no other company could use it as a recording studio. "They were so afraid that somebody was going to come in and duplicate what they had been so successful doing there, that they were adamant about it.

"My partner and I worked through someone else, so they wouldn't know we were the ones buying it. And we didn't have a dime! We were banking on the money coming in from the sale of 45th Street to give us the down payment on 799, and somehow, it all worked out," Ramone says. "Boy, was Columbia pissed when they found out it was us that had bought the studio. They had actually turned Studio A into a miniature replica of 30th Street: if you looked at the building from the street, there was this weird looking metal dome that extended upward. When we came in, I just took my time and worked on making it a great acoustic room . . . I did little things, like adding splays up at the top. I didn't touch Studio B: I just left it exactly the way it had been."

A few years before, Sinatra had been booked to work with Bowen and Ramone at the old A&R

Studio on 45th Street, but the date was canceled, a major disappointment for the engineer. It wasn't until this 1967 date that Ramone's dream of working with Sinatra came true. "Jimmy Bowen is a wonderful producer, and I remember that I was basically piddling in my pants, wondering if I was going to get this right: not only for him [Jimmy], but for Sinatra. When Sinatra walks in the room, everybody *feels* it, and that first second, when that voice comes down through the speakers, is the most frightening moment in your life . . . *and* the most satisfying. 'Cause you know that you're competing on another level . . . you're above and beyond what you've been for years.

"It's a period in my life I'll never forget, because it flew by—it was so rapid. We had at least a hundred chairs set up on platforms in the studio . . . although the instructions were 'No audience.' I said, 'To hell with this . . . I'm putting up risers like it's a basketball court!' And, you look over, and there's Sarah Vaughan, or Ella Fitzgerald, or [on 1984's *L.A. Is My Lady*] Michael Jackson, and you say, 'Jesus! It's not just an audience—it's famous people!'"

The engineer went all out to make Sinatra comfortable. "I laid a red carpet between the control room and the studio, and a set of those velvet ropes they used to use for motion picture premieres, to give him a path. He actually came into the booth, too . . . sat down, listened to a playback, talked to us. I mean, he even called me 'Kid!' To me, that was the greatest moment of my life. And he's never stopped calling me that. Flattered to be a kid at my age," Ramone muses.

He describes his pre-session setup. "I took a lesson from other people that had worked with him, and we had rehearsed the band before Frank even got to the studio, so the sound check was done in advance. Everyone's earphones and all that sort of stuff had been figured out in advance. I went a couple of steps further, though, and put an actual sound mixer in the room, so that if he lifted his finger or anything, we knew what he wanted . . . you know, 'No waiting between tables here!' I set up two vocal microphones, and someone asked me why. I explained that I'd rather have a backup of Sinatra at the expense of an extra bass track . . . it was insurance. I couldn't rest until he had left the building, safety tapes had been made, and one set stored in another location . . . *then* you can relax and have a drink!"

"Jimmy hated New York. He had some interesting problems in the way that some of the players related to him, because he's kind of a tall country boy with a very hip L.A. groove, and he was using all New York players on this date. The playing is quite energetic . . . I don't know if what's on the record is my mix or theirs, but you'd wish you had the original mixes, because a lot of the stuff that goes on live is the best in the world. It gets tampered down, though . . . especially when they re-mix to reduce the leakage of the orchestra into his mike, because he's not a booth singer, you know."

Jazz bassist Milt Hinton, a veteran of hundreds upon hundreds of recording sessions with the greatest musicians of all time, shared his memories of recording "The World We Knew" with Ed Berger of the Rutgers Institute for Jazz Studies. "I remember a big date here in New York for Sinatra. It was just beautiful! I swear to you, there must have been seventy-five men on this date. The session started at ten o'clock at night, which meant we would go until one o'clock in the morning. And at ten o'clock, there was no Sinatra. About twelve midnight, he came in and ordered booze; had a guy wheel in a thing with booze for everybody. And they sat around and drank and talked and laughed. Gordon Jenkins had come in from California, and thay sat around and drank and had a ball, with this whole band going on overtime,

man. It's $40 an hour overtime, and he's got seventy men there, and maybe fifteen or twenty background singers. And nobody turned a hair! We finally recorded, and probably went until three o'clock in the morning."

FRANCIS A. AND EDWARD K.

Not quite ready to abandon the discriminating taste upon which his reputation had been built, Sinatra entered the studio in December 1967 to satisfy another desire: to record with Duke Ellington.

Far different than the sessions for *The World We Knew* of just a few months prior, Sinatra was completely focused for this album, although his collaborators seemed to be less so. The Ellington aggregation put a scare in him by not rehearsing the charts in a timely fashion. For a few

PHOTOGRAPH BY ED THRASHER, COURTESY OF MPTV ARCHIVE

Recording with Duke Ellington, 1967.

tense days, there was some concern that the group wouldn't be able to cut it on the scheduled recording dates, and Sinatra considered scrapping the project. Adding to the confusion was the fact that Ellington's close associate, Billy Strayhorn, who was supposed to write the charts, had died just before the album got under way.

By the time the album's arranger, Billy May, stepped in, the band was terribly short on rehearsal time. "I got the arrangements done, and they said, 'Fly up to Seattle and run them down with Duke's band,'" May recalls. "So Bill Miller and I went there, and we rehearsed them all afternoon. And Jesus, the rehearsal was *terrible*. That band, you know . . . they're terrible sightreaders. So we got it to where they ran them down, and they sounded okay, and Bill and I stayed that night, and they played the songs on the job: Duke played the vocal things on the piano, and everything was fine. So we took the plane home that night, and I thought, 'They only had two rehearsals . . . if only they'd had more rehearsal time.'"

May augmented the Ellington orchestra with a few of his most dependable studio musicians, including pianist Milt Raskin, who reportedly subbed for Ellington on a couple of tunes, and Al Porcino on trumpet. Miraculously, by the first session, everything had fallen into place, and the album survives as one of the finest pop-jazz crossover recordings of its time. Most attractive is the repertoire, which strayed from the Ellington "standards" one might expect.

A terrific, driving version of "Come Back to Me" opens the record, and is followed by the classy Styne-Sondheim tune "All I Need Is the Girl," a song from *Gypsy* that Sinatra had begun to work into some of his concert dates. Renditions of "Follow Me" and "Poor Butterfly" are authoritative; "Yellow Days" and "Sunny," sassy. An arrangement of "I Like the Sunrise" (the one tune with a direct Ellington-Strayhorn association on the album) beautifully contrasts Sinatra's voice with a muted trumpet. The real treasure,

though, is the recording that Nelson Riddle once called his all-time favorite Sinatra performance: "Indian Summer," a tune whose contemplative mood is heightened by a Johnny Hodges alto sax solo that will bring a tear to your eye.

It is sad that the pair never produced a follow-up album, where they might have addressed classic Ellington tunes like "Take the 'A' Train" and "Sophisticated Lady," which could easily have become Sinatra staples. Instead, the outing with Ellington was the last "traditional" album the singer made for twelve years, until 1979's *Trilogy*.

MIDDLE OF THE ROAD

Between December 1967 and November 1970, Frank Sinatra recorded seven albums. The three years marked a time of great change for him as he tailored his art to the meet the whims and fancies of the contemporary music market.

Cycles, arranged by Don Costa, is proof that Frank Sinatra belonged on the contemporary music scene. While the songs may not have been his first choices ten years prior, he could interpret them with conviction and give them his own personal mark.

Listen to "By the Time I Get to Phoenix," or "Wandering," or "Little Green Apples," and you'll appreciate how Sinatra has been able to peel away the superficiality of their original interpretations to unmask their real beauty. Our ears perk up, and we acknowledge their quality, simply because Sinatra's poignant renditions demand that we do so. The opener, the pounding "Rain in My Heart," is a terrific example of how

Sinatra's classic style enhances the most modern musical genres.

In February 1969, Sinatra completed *My Way*, a smattering of introspective ballads (the beautiful Costa arrangements of "Didn't We" and "If You Go Away" and a superior remake of the Cahn–Van Heusen classic "All My Tomorrows" are the standouts) taking their place among some raucous contemporary tunes including "For Once in My Life" and Simon and Garfunkel's "Mrs. Robinson."

While some of the choices don't emerge as the best vehicles for Sinatra's crossover to the contemporary market, one must admire his effort to attract an older audience to some of the biggest pop tunes of the day. (Easy-listening giants like Bert Kaempfert, Andre Kostelanetz, and Percy Faith, further out of their realm than Sinatra was, enjoyed tremendous success with this older demographic as they churned out nauseating instrumental versions of every hit Beatles and Simon and Garfunkel tune known to man.)

The send-up version of "Mrs. Robinson," in which Sinatra throws caution to the wind, singing "How's your bird, Mrs. Robinson? Mine's as fine as wine, and I should know . . ." and "Jilly loves you more than you will know . . .," attracted the attention of its writer, one very young Paul Simon, as producer Phil Ramone remembers. "Paul told me many years later that he was quite upset that Sinatra had changed his lyrics, and that he had every intention of suing him over it. And when he told me the story, he was kind of saying, 'Boy, was that naive, or what?'"

The title track, with English lyrics by Paul Anka, had been recorded in December 1968. It marks a tragedy that struck one of Sinatra's closest musical friends, his longtime pianist Bill Miller. Injured in a mudslide that destroyed his Los Angeles home and claimed his wife's life, Miller was not able to play on the session. Lou Levy, an extraordinary jazz pianist, filled in during Miller's absence. The tune, which would become one of the singer's signature songs, was inserted at the head of the album when it became apparent that it would be the smash single Sinatra was looking for.

Two experimental albums, one set to the poetry of Rod McKuen (*A Man Alone*) and one produced by Four Seasons guru Charles Callello (*Watertown*: Sinatra's modern-day *Manhattan Tower*) were in the can by July 1969, and should be admired for the courage it took to attempt them. Their musical high points (and there are many) are a bonus.

On November 2, 1970, Frank Sinatra made his last recording session . . . or so he thought. A few months after this session (which included two duets with daughter Nancy, "Feelin' Kinda Sunday" and "Life's a Trippy Thing" and a solo single, "The Game Is Over"), he announced that he would retire from performing. "I've had a handful, and maybe the public's had enough too," he told *LIFE* reporter Thomas Thompson. "I've got things to do, like the first thing is not to do *anything* at all for eight months . . . maybe a year."

The 1971 retirement was short-lived, and by April 1973 he had returned to the recording studio to make a "comeback" album that would signal the birth of his career as a touring concert artist, playing to sold-out arena crowds on every corner of the earth. By this time, there were probably few people on Earth who didn't know the voice of Frank Sinatra.

ELDER STATESMAN

*A*lthough the 1970s saw his recorded output diminish dramatically (at his peak in the 1950s, as many as three Sinatra albums were released each year), several of his post-retirement recordings are noteworthy, if not always for content, then for their value as technical and historical recording milestones.

Ol' Blue Eyes Is Back marked his return to the recording studio. At Sinatra's request, the tapes from the first session held at Goldwyn Studios on April 30, 1973 (the twentieth anniversary of his first recording session with Nelson Riddle), were destroyed.

He returned to the studio almost two months later with a cache of new tunes, and began recording in earnest. Several fine recordings would come from these sessions, including "You Will Be My Music," "Winners," "Dream Away," and Joe Raposo's "There Used to Be a Ballpark." But the most important recording born of the album was Stephen Sondheim's "Send in the Clowns," with a dark, pensive Gordon Jenkins orchestration.

"I was at his home in Palm Springs when he received the song in the mail," remembers sculptor Bob Berks, whom Sinatra commissioned to sculpt his bust. "We were sitting around the pool, and I was working away, and he sat down and opened the envelope. He smiled, and asked if I'd like to hear a new song. He then proceeded to sing it to me. I was the first person to hear Sinatra sing that wonderful song!"

Of course, Sinatra took a stab at some numbers that would have been better off unrecorded. Of all the *real* dogs in the Sinatra repertoire (discounting 1951's "Mama Will Bark"), many come from 1974 and the album *Some Nice Things I've Missed*. "Bad, Bad Leroy Brown," "I'm Gonna

PHOTOGRAPH BY ED THRASHER, COURTESY OF MPTV ARCHIVE

At the Goldwyn Studios, Los Angeles for the Ol' Blue Eyes Is Back sessions, 1973.

Make It All the Way," "You Are the Sunshine of My Life," and "Tie a Yellow Ribbon Round the Old Oak Tree" are reminiscent of "Mrs. Robinson" just a few years before.

But amongst them are some outstanding examples of how much quality the older Sinatra had left to his voice. "What Are You Doing the Rest of Your Life" could easily take a place alongside of anything on *Sinatra and Strings*. Two sorrowful recordings with Gordon Jenkins ("Just as Though You Were Here" and "Everything Happens to Me") demonstrate the pathos that Sinatra could still project.

By 1976, Allen Sides had taken over Studio B at United Recording; eventually, he bought Studio A and purchased the Western Studio as well. Sides renamed the California studios, plus a studio in Nashville, "Ocean Way," after the street his first garage studio was located on. Bill Putnam, who died in the early 1990s, had become less and less involved in the business as time went on. "He was very together, he had three triple bypasses," Sides explains. "He lived such a hard life: I can imagine the drugs and booze that they did, to keep it all rolling. And Bill had an accident that was as bad as Quincy Jones's aneurysm—he fell down a stairway at United, and he had to relearn how to speak and everything. But he recovered completely. He was totally on, he was completely brilliant, and an extremely funny, humorous guy. The day before he died, you'd never know that anything was wrong. He was quite a guy."

As United Western changed, Sinatra began seeking other places to record. While he still frequented that studio, he also began using studios in Burbank, and returned more often to New York, where some of the best recordings of his later years would be made.

Several songs for a proposed album with Nelson Riddle, *Here's to the Ladies*, were recorded in the Burbank Studios in 1976 and 1977; the best of them is his irresistible reading of Cy Coleman and Michael Stewart's "I Love My Wife." Only a few of the songs chosen for the album were

recorded by Sinatra: "Emily," "Nancy," "Sweet Lorraine," "Linda," and a new tune written by Jimmy Van Heusen and Mack David as a tribute for Sinatra's wife, "Barbara." Several other orchestral tracks, including "Stella by Starlight" were laid down, but no vocal overdubs were ever made.

The session of March 14, 1977 (at which "Linda," "Sweet Lorraine" and "Barbara" were recorded), marked the last time that Frank Sinatra and Nelson Riddle would work in a recording studio.

The most ambitious Sinatra recording in years, a three-record set entitled *Trilogy*, was produced in 1979. It was the last recording to be created in collaboration with his longtime producer, Sonny Burke.

The Past, a collection of older songs that had either escaped the singer's attention or merited re-recording, was taped at United Western's Los Angeles studio in July, with Billy May handling the orchestrations. (Sinatra wasn't happy with the results, and almost all of the songs were redone in September). *The Present*, featuring contemporary numbers, including his signature "Theme from New York, New York," arranged by Don Costa, saw the singer's return to New York and the Columbia 30th Street studio, in August. (Some songs for this portion would be re-recorded in September and December, in Los Angeles.) The original inspiration for the project, an extended Gordon Jenkins suite called *The Future*, was completed over two days in December.

Trilogy was the first Sinatra recording in which the singer's touring pianist, Vinnie Falcone, was involved. The late 1970s found Sinatra and his longtime pianist-conductor Bill Miller going their separate ways, and Falcone had been engaged to take his place.

"I had been playing piano for Mr. Sinatra since 1976, and I got a call one day from Don [Costa]. He said, 'Mr. Sinatra called me, and he wants you to come to L.A. to do a record date, and he wants you to conduct.' I thought that I had not heard him properly, and I said, 'Would you say that again?' And Don repeated, 'Yeah, he wants you to conduct. I'm going to be in the control room.'"

"Don preferred to sit in the booth," Falcone explains. "He didn't want the strain that drummer Irv Cottler put on everybody that stood in front of the band. Don's heart wasn't the greatest even then; he'd suffered a heart attack in Japan, where he was conducting concerts for Frank. Irv was hard on people, for whatever reason . . . he would do whatever was necessary to keep the attention on him, and not the conductor."

The date for the session was set for July 17, 1978. "I flew out to Burbank, and Don's brother Leo picked me up and took me to Warner Brothers," Falcone remembers. "I was wondering, 'What the hell's going to happen here?' I walked in, and went over to the dressing room that they had put aside for Mr. Sinatra, and he was going over what he wanted to do. Of course, he [Sinatra] later told me that the whole recording session was bogus: he just set it up to test me out! He told me this years later. At the session, he was very cold to me—you know, he never said, 'How ya doing?' or 'Everything's going to be okay . . . don't worry about a thing . . . relax.' Nothing! He kept the tension up there intentionally, I imagine, to see how well I'd be able to withstand the pressure."

"He told Don to take me out and introduce me to the orchestra, and I walked into the room, which is an enormous sound stage at Warner's Studio in Burbank. Hell, there must have been a fifty- or sixty-piece orchestra sitting there, and in every single chair were people that I'd admired all my life: Gerald Vinci was the concertmaster, Dick Nash and Gus Bivona were there . . . I mean, I'm supposed to conduct these guys! We did 'You and Me (We Wanted It All),' and 'That's What God Looks Like to Me,' I believe, although my memories of that night are vague, because I was under such pressure." "The air-conditioning broke down, and it was hot, and I was perspiring so heavily that the drips of perspiration were blot-

PHOTOGRAPH BY ED THRASHER, COURTESY OF MPTV ARCHIVE

(Left to right) Billy May, Don Costa, Frank Sinatra, and Gordon Jenkins announce the Trilogy *album, 1979.*

ting the music on the podium! But I got through it. He [Sinatra] said *nothing* to me. He went into the control room, listened to the takes with Don, discussed a few things. I stood behind him. When we were done, I said, 'Goodnight, thank you very much.'"

"*Trilogy* was Sonny Burke's idea from the beginning," says Falcone. "It was a total package from its inception; it didn't develop into a three-record package—that's what Sonny Burke brought to him. We were, as a matter of fact, in a recording studio, when Sonny came. He had apparently called Frank, and wanted a meeting with him, so he came to the recording studio and showed the old man the project. He explained it to him—he had it all laid out. And at that point, if my memory serves me correctly, Sinatra ended the recording session right then. He said, 'We will not do another thing until we do this.' He was so taken by Sonny's project."

Gordon Jenkins, excited about collaborating with his friend on one of his epic musical tales, flew to Las Vegas, where Sinatra was appearing. He carried with him small reels of tape containing the entire score he had written for *The Future*, and he played it for Sinatra, who was impressed by what he heard. He and Jenkins apparently spent time planning for the upcoming sessions. Later, both Billy May and Don Costa met the pair, and the project was announced at a joint press conference.

One might have expected that Nelson Riddle would get the first crack at writing the sentimental orchestrations for *The Past*. During the two years preceding *Trilogy*, though, he and Sinatra had grown apart. From all accounts, the rift was caused by Sinatra's failure to appear as master of ceremonies at a dinner held in Nelson's honor. The organizers, and Riddle himself, had postponed and rearranged the event to accommodate Sinatra's touring schedule. On very short notice, after all the tables had been filled and programs planned, Sinatra backed out—leaving Nelson embarrassed and deeply hurt.

Falcone recalls, "Nelson was bitter to the point where one time Sinatra and I were in the dressing room in the suite at Caesars, and we were talking about Nelson, and I was shouting his praises. Frank turned to me, and said, 'Call him on the phone, and ask him if he'll write a chart for me.' And I said, 'Wow, man—this is like *history*!' So I picked up the phone and called Nelson. I said, 'Nelson, Mr. Sinatra asked me to call you. He would like to know if you would write an arrangement on . . .' And there was just dead silence on the other end of the phone for a good ten or fifteen seconds, and then Nelson said, 'Tell him I'm busy,' and hung up."

Billy May, who had dinner with Riddle and a German recording executive in Beverly Hills around the time of the incident, remembers Nelson being upset at even the mention of Sinatra's name. "In the course of our conversation, the German guy started asking Nelson about Sinatra, and Nelson got very angry . . . I'd never heard him talk that way before! He was very vehement about how he didn't like Sinatra anymore, and how he felt that he'd been taken advantage of, so

I just kept quiet about it. Then I asked Nelson one day what happened. And he told me about the dinner. He said that he just felt that Frank was too egotistical to be a decent guy."

So Billy May was called to arrange *The Past*. "Right after that is when they started doing the *Trilogy* album, and I saw Nelson somewhere else," May explained. "He said, 'Did they call you to do the album?' I said, 'Yeah, I'm going to do it.' He said, 'Good, because that's what I was supposed to do, but you're getting it on account of me!' I told him, 'Well then, I owe you one.' But we'd been doing that for a long time, you know. It's too bad, because they worked so well together."

Of the album's three volumes, *The Past* is the best. Much of the disc contains standards that Sinatra had never recorded: "I Had the Craziest Dream," "But Not for Me," "My Shining Hour," "It Had to Be You," "More than You Know," "They All Laughed" and "All of You." Three chestnuts, "The Song Is You," "Street of Dreams," and "Let's Face the Music and Dance" were familiar Sinatra records from the past. The ballad numbers are especially noteworthy, as they are enhanced by the most supple of Billy May's string charts, his first for Sinatra since the 1957 *Come Fly with Me* album.

Don Costa was selected to do *The Present*, featuring the tune that was fast becoming Sinatra's signature closer, "New York, New York," which Sinatra first sang at his Radio City Music Hall opening in the fall of 1978.

"We were up at NBC rehearsing, in October of 1978, when he brought the sheet music to 'New York, New York' in to me," Falcone recalls. "He put it on the piano, and said, 'Here, play this for me.' I played it, and he told me that he wanted a new overture of all New York songs for that particular engagement, and he wanted it to end with 'New York, New York.' So Don wrote the overture: 'Autumn in New York,' 'Sidewalks of New York,' and so forth. When it ended with 'New York, New York,' he would walk on stage with the vamp going: 'Dat-da-da-da-da . . . ,' and then open with the song [as a vocal]."

"After we had done it for that engagement, he said to me, 'Man! This thing is getting big— we've got to take it out. Can you take it out of the overture?' So I did, and then he just used it as the opening for the show. Then, he said 'Nah, we've gotta put this further down in the show.' And it went about halfway down, because 'My Way' was still closing the show. And the song just kept getting bigger! Well, all during this period of about a year, he started to grow with the song, and he began to put it into the shape that it eventually became. It didn't start out being as dramatic at as it is now, with the much slower tempo at the end. That's not the way he originally sang it: he *developed* it, which is why he likes to do a song on stage for several months before he records it."

At some point, the number became the most requested song of Sinatra's live concert performances, and it moved from the middle to the coveted "closing" spot. "Eventually the song got so powerful," says Falcone, "that Frank said, 'Let's take "My Way" out of the show. I'm sick and tired of singing the song. I've been trying to find something to replace it for years, and we've finally gotten it.' For several years during that period, we didn't even do 'My Way' in the show-it was only performed when we went to Europe, or some other place abroad. 'New York, New York' became the closer, and nothing has ever come along [to supplant it], and nothing ever will, as I see it."

Appropriately, "New York, New York" was recorded in the Big Apple, at the August 1979 sessions for *The Present* held at Columbia's 30th Street Studio. A month later, though, it was redone in Los Angeles, as Sinatra felt he hadn't quite nailed it down the first time. "The old man didn't like the way it came off in New York," says Vinnie Falcone. "He had been growing with the song, and between the time we recorded it in New York and the time we recorded it in Hollywood, it had grown that much more, and he said,

'I want to do it over again.' Don Costa said, 'The hell with it—leave it the way it is.' I guess they talked, and Don said, 'Let Vinnie do it.' So for the Hollywood session [the released version], I conducted it, and Pete Jolly played piano."

Frank Laico recorded *The Present* at the venerable 30th Street studio. "It was a big thrill for me, because it was the first time I worked with Frank and Don, and Don could have been my brother, I loved him. We were good friends, and this was the first and only time we disagreed. He had prepped me . . . he said, 'Frank, I don't want you to open your mouth,' because in a session, when someone asks questions, I answer truthfully. I said, 'What's the matter?' Don said, 'Promise me. I don't want you to open your mouth—I take care of Sinatra. Whatever I want him to know I'll tell him—don't you say a word.'"

"That was the first time I was ever told something like that, and from Don, I thought, 'Okay, there's got to be something in there that he's not telling me, and I'm not going to pry,'" Laico says. "I said, 'Fine . . . but, if there's something wrong, and you don't call it to his attention, then I'm going to. I have to—I can't sit there and be a dud.'"

"I got the whole studio set up, and Frank shows up. He came in and said to Don, 'Everything okay? Charts?' Don said, 'Fine.' He looks at me, and we were introduced. 'My name's Frank,' I say. He looks at me, and says, 'Italians call Frank *Cheech*. Y'all set, Cheech?' I say, 'I'm all set.'

"He went out in the studio, and he made a take, and all through the take I'm saying to myself, 'We're in trouble . . . *I'm* in trouble.' Frank came in after the take, and heard it. He looked at Don. 'What do you think?' 'Great—one more take and we got it,' Don tells him. Frank is in front of me, by the console facing me and Don. 'Cheech, how are you? You happy?' I looked at Don, and I looked at Frank, and I said, 'I'm going to make *him* [Don] very unhappy, because I'm going to tell *you* that I'm not happy with the sound of your voice.'"

" 'Oh?' Sinatra says. 'Yes,' I said. 'You've just come off the road, and you use those hand mikes, and you're inside this microphone and you shouldn't be . . . it's not your voice. That's not the Sinatra sound I know . . . ' 'All right,' he said. 'What are we going to do?' 'Well, I'd like to go out and re-set you . . . I want to put the microphone where it should be. And, I'd like you to stay there, and not walk in and out on it. I think you'll hear a good difference.' "

"Sinatra said, 'That all right with you, Don?' 'Yeah.' We go out into the studio, and I said, 'I think we need air between you and the microphone.' 'Okay, I'll do it,' he says. 'Give me eight bars at least,' I tell Don. 'Have him sing because now I have to make some adjustments in here.' So we did that, and made a take, and Sinatra came back in, and we played it back. Gentleman that he is, about half-way through, he looks at me, gives me a thumbs-up, and says, 'I like that. I like that!' The playback finished, and he said to Don, 'How do you feel?' 'Sounds great!' Sinatra said to me, 'Thank you. I appreciate that. That was great. I hear the difference now. Let's go.' And we went on from there and didn't have any trouble at all."

A complex work, *Reflections on the Future in Three Tenses*, the third part of *Trilogy*, involved not only the undivided attention of Frank Sinatra, but the 154-member Los Angeles Philharmonic Symphony Orchestra and Mixed Chorus as well. So large was the ensemble that in order to accommodate them for recording, the sessions were held at the Shrine Auditorium in Los Angeles. "That was the first digital recording we did with Sinatra," recalls engineer Lee Herschberg. "It was thirty-two-track digital, but we ended up using the analog tapes for the album, because digital editing was so new, we couldn't possibly edit that number of tracks.

We spent weeks working on it," recalls Vinnie Falcone. "Not only on the road: I spent a great deal of time with him up at the house in Beverly Hills. We used to go down to the projection room where the piano was, and we spent hours down

there! I had to teach him, by rote, all of that material, because it was all original."

The structure of the individual songs, and how they relate not just to each other, but to the overall concept, is much different than for a standard four-part song. This added to the time and effort that it took for each of the participants to perfect his performance. "It was difficult for *me* to learn it . . . and I had to *remember* it all too," said Falcone. "When we went to the recording sessions, there were no piano parts written, so it was my job to make sure he [Sinatra] 'toed the line,' so to speak. After several of the takes, I went to him, and said, 'You'd better listen to this, because you're not going to be happy with it,' or 'You'd better do that again . . . ' Things other people were afraid to do, I would do."

Although this portion of the album was the one that intrigued Sinatra the most (he adored Jenkins, and was a great fan of his thematic musical epics like "Manhattan Tower"), it was misunderstood by both the critics and the public, and is probably the least remembered work that Frank Sinatra ever did. "Gordon never got over the criticism that he got for that," Falcone remarked.

"The feeling was that it came off as too much of an ego thing for Sinatra . . . but they missed the whole point entirely. But, what did people expect? *Trilogy: The Past, The Present, and The Future*. It was conceived as being the culmination of a great career! And yet, he wasn't old enough to hang it up, so there was a 'future,' and *The Future*, as Gordon saw it. In this respect, it was saying 'thank you' to all his friends, and reminiscing, as he was still in the business. It's like a retirement without being retired! It was a work of love, and musically, it's terrific. It may not have been classic Sinatra, but it wasn't intended to be. I think that in time, it will be recognized as a major work."

When the last session for *The Future* was completed, Falcone accompanied Sinatra to the parking lot outside The Shrine. "He had driven himself to the session, and we walked over to our cars," Falcone says. "He was about to get into his Jaguar, and suddenly, he turned to me, and simply said, 'Thank you for everything.' That affirmation was more important than anything else he could have said or done."

Another series of New York outings held between July and September of 1981 yielded *She Shot Me Down*, perhaps the finest Sinatra album to emerge from the singer's "late" period, nearly rivaling Billie Holiday's 1958 chilling masterpiece *Lady in Satin*, recorded in the same studio (Columbia's 30th Street) by the same recording engineer, twenty-three years before.

He'd talked about doing the album for years, even planning way in advance to call it *She Shot Me Down*, after a line from "Bang, Bang"—one of daughter Nancy's songs that he greatly admired, and one that is captivatingly effective on this recording. "He told me many times that he wanted this album to be a tribute to Gordon Jenkins, that he wanted to honor Gordon," said Vinnie Falcone. He was very specific about that, because Gordon, by this time was already sick . . . his health was failing, and the Old Man figured that this would be the last album that Gordon would ever do."

"Gordon came out from L.A., but because he was so sick, I conducted the sessions. He became a close friend to me . . . he was so wonderful in the studio. He'd come up to me after the takes, and pat me on the back . . . he was so supportive and complimentary. Even though he was not feeling well and had to put up with a lot physically, he was a busybody at those sessions! He was such a kind, wonderful man," Falcone remembers.

Sinatra envisioned this as the quintessential torch album—his sage advice on living with the despair of the "gal that got away" reflected in the husky, deep-voiced musings of one who has trod a darkened path. Not since *Only the Lonely* or *Sinatra and Strings* has the gloomy, bittersweet atmosphere of a late-night saloon permeated a record as palpably as on *She Shot Me Down*.

When Sinatra sings, "I've tasted the 90-proof gin, and chased it away with the blues . . ." in the Loonis McGlohan song "A Long Night," you almost feel the pitifully ravaged Lady Day standing in the same studio decades before, drowning her sorrows and masking *her* pain with the bottle of gin that was as much a part of her recording studio persona as her voice itself.

Gordon Jenkins made the trip with Sinatra from Los Angeles to supervise the sessions in the studio. "Jenkins just loved the studio . . . he loved the sound, and he was very happy. He was such an easy person to get along with. I'd really admired him for years on record, having never met him until then, and I was pleased that he showed up," says engineer Frank Laico.

"The only song on the album that wasn't Gordon's was 'The Gal That Got Away/It Never Entered My Mind,' which Don Costa had melded together from Nelson's original arrangements," Falcone explains. The Old Man wanted to include it because we were doing it, and we didn't have anyplace else to put it! I conducted that, and we did it separate from the rest of the recordings with Gordon's arrangements. Because I couldn't conduct and play piano at the same time, we recorded it in two sections: first we taped the parts with the vocal and orchestra (straight through, live), and then I dismissed the orchestra, and Frank and I went into the booth where the piano was, and did 'It Never Entered My Mind.'"

The mood and tone achieved are certainly a credit to Laico's hand in the studio, and Jenkins's piercing orchestrations are some of his most outstanding efforts ever on behalf of the vocalist. "It just happened . . . the charts were written that way," Laico says. "It was just so beautiful. Most people think engineers don't listen, but we do. And when I heard what was happening, I thought, 'This is going to be a nice time. Everybody's going to be happy.'"

"What separates Sinatra from everybody else is that as he aged, his approach to the material

PHOTOGRAPH BY ED THRASHER, COURTESY OF MPTV ARCHIVE

Recording "L.A. Is My Lady" at A & R Studios, New York City, 1984.

changed, and he developed a whole different way of performing his music. As he matured into the poet he eventually became, the songs became a narrative dialogue set to music, instead of just music with lyrics," says Vinnie Falcone.

Frank Sinatra taped his very last "live to tape" album, the slick *L.A. Is My Lady*, in New York's A&R Studios over three nights in April 1984. Videotapes of the sessions show Sinatra in top form, working along with producer-arranger Quincy Jones and Phil Ramone, who made a rare return to the engineering booth to aid Sinatra in recording both newly written songs as well as a group of older tunes that he'd never done before.

"I'd been friends with Quincy for a long time, and he called me and said, 'Would you like to be involved in it?' I said, 'You know, if you want me to fix microphones, sweep the studio floor— that's where I'll be . . . I just want to be a part of it,'" Ramone told him. "When Q called, he said, 'You know how to make a band holler on tape!' and I said, 'Yeah, I'm ready! I hope my chops are there.' It was a side step, and was a different kind of responsibility for me. We ran some experimental digital tape . . . I had an F1 tape recorder, which is one of the early PCM beta recorders, and those were just live mixes . . . direct to two-track."

Sensing that this would be a momentous occasion, Jones planned to have the entire run of sessions filmed for posterity. "We had cameras set up to catch him from every angle: even as his car came up to the curb and he walked in to the studio . . . there was a camera to catch that way up at the top of the building," Ramone remembers.

Before Sinatra set one foot in the studio, the principals realized that the lighting apparatus required for the handheld, 16mm film cameras might cause a problem for the singer. "Quincy and I had discussed that, and they had set up a key light right over the top of the vocal booth, above where Frank would be standing," says Ramone. "Q said to me, 'He's gonna flip out when he sees that!' It was pretty bright—this was film, not videotape, and the cameras weren't as sensitive as they are today. Sure enough, as soon as he came in, he told us to kill the lights. Even though we had backup lights already in place, they weren't really bright enough for those handheld cameras, and consequently, the best stuff—a lot of the rehearsal footage where he's laughing and having a good time, when he was learning the songs and flubbing the lyrics, wasn't usable."

"His personality really hit me when Michael Jackson came into the studio to visit," Ramone remembers. "Frank saw him standing over on the other side of the room talking to Quincy, and he said to me, 'If I don't get his autograph for my granddaughter I'm gonna be in real trouble! Do you think he'll mind giving me an autograph?' I mean, that was it! Here is Frank Sinatra, and he's in awe of Michael Jackson . . . and concerned about getting an autograph!"

Ramone describes the vocal booth at A&R, much of which was built for Sinatra's first return there to record in 1967. "It was like a sound stage, about forty feet long . . . like a big platform. There was some soft, woven cloth behind it, so the reflection was pretty cool. It was an open booth, and had these huge doors which were slid back, so he had lots of room. He had a piano in there, and a stool . . . a little couch for him to sit on. It was kind

of like a living room. But, when you stand there, you can hear the band, and you could be heard when you said, 'Hello.' Everybody could hear you. We designed it in 1967, and it was the same booth—everything was the same. He made a little comment, something like 'I've been in this joint before,' which was really nice."

From these sessions came "After You've Gone," "Teach Me Tonight," and the lovely "How Do You Keep the Music Playing?" A highly charged "Mack the Knife" would remain a Sinatra favorite for years. He knew it was a great recording in the studio, for as soon as the overring died down, he twirled his finger in the air, signaling Ramone in the booth. "Play it back right away!" he instructed, grinning from ear to ear. The post-session party, with Lionel Hampton, Frank Foster, The Brecker Brothers, George Benson, and the rest of the band, was loaded with excitement. Although the repertoire selected for the album is uneven, Sinatra was in top form, lucid, relevant after nearly fifty years.

The mood became nostalgic when Jones, who'd worked with Sinatra since the early 1960s, brought out a photo of the singer and Mitch Miller at a 1952 Columbia session, standing in the same studio, in nearly the very same spot. Shortly after these sessions, A&R was sold and the historic building razed. "Boy, that was tough. Losing that studio was like losing one of your children," says Ramone.

One of the New York sessions was a disaster: the air-conditioning in the building broke down, and an electrical short caused a power failure in the studio. While it is generally believed that Sinatra and Jones were unhappy with the key for "Stormy Weather" and re-recorded just that one tune back in Los Angeles, Ocean Way Studio engineer Allen Sides remembers differently.

"There were some problems with that album, and they wanted to re-do some of the songs here in L.A.," he says. "Frank came in, and began to sing, and then about halfway through, he stopped. They worked something out with the band, and then everybody thought that he would do a re-take, from the top. Instead, he said 'Let's take it from bar so-and-so and intercut it.' He didn't want to do a whole new take. Knowing that I had to get good vocals on the rest of the tracks, I just rolled them one after the other—I think there were five songs—and instead of stopping, he just sang them one right after the other. I know that one of the songs we recorded wasn't used on the album."

On the first session, Sinatra had completed two takes of "Body and Soul," which he hadn't sung since the original Columbia recording of 1947. The videotaped documentation shows an edgy Sinatra doing a few perfunctory runthroughs, which are ragged at best. Then, looking at his watch and remarking that he was concerned about being late for an appointment after the session, he begs off making any further attempts to record the song. It is unclear whether this was the song Sides remembers Sinatra re-recording in L.A., or if they might have attempted a different tune than what was done in New York.

Sources close to the singer who wish to remain anonymous have said that in the end, Frank was not entirely pleased with *L.A. Is My Lady*, feeling it was far more commercial and less spontaneous than originally planned. The mix of songs is disjointed, and the entire affair would have benefited from a more consistent repertoire.

Between 1984 and 1993, there would be only a handful of singles sessions, most remaining unissued until a recent twenty-CD compilation of Sinatra's complete Reprise recordings. Veering away from the studio, he chose to increase his already frenetic concert schedule, adding enough live appearances to keep him on the road for more than two-thirds of every year. The audiences seemed to be getting younger and younger by the day, and that inspired the singer. The demand to see this legend was tremendous, and rarely, through the mid-1980s, did he fail to deliver.

One positive event occured in January of 1985: Nelson Riddle and Frank Sinatra met, and patched up their differences. After a dinner honoring Ronald Reagan, the pair struck up a conversation, and inevitably, the conversation turned to music. Sinatra told Riddle that he was thinking of returning to the studio, to record some songs he had missed along the way. Would Nelson consider scoring the album for him?

By this time, the arranger was gravely ill. He had recently completed two albums of standards with Linda Ronstadt, and a third was almost done. He was also working with Australian opera singer Kiri Te Kanawa, who sought to record with him as well. While he was enjoying renewed popularity among a much younger group of fans, his progressing illness (a chronic liver ailment) was wearing him down.

Riddle accepted Sinatra's invitation, and told his son that he was excited about the prospect of working with his old friend again. Sadly, they never got the chance, for Riddle died that October.

"The day after Dad died, we went down to his office on Sunset Boulevard to take a look around, and maybe pick up a picture or two. There were things there that we had made him when we were in school, and we wanted to have some of them," says Rosemary Riddle-Acerra. "We saw what was in the office, we saw what he was working on. There were charts for the new album they were going to work on, sitting right there on the drafting table. They were marked, 'Frank Sinatra.'"

As the decade turned, one could see a steady decline in Sinatra's ability to focus. In 1991, at seventy-five, he was plagued by a number of ailments: cataracts, loss of hearing, and problems associated with the partial removal of his colon several years before. And, as one close associate who toured regularly with the singer told me, "He can't drink after he takes his medicine. If he has even one drink, it throws him completely off." The huge screens that dotted the stage to prompt him with the words to the oldest of songs in his repertoire were a reminder that he wasn't working with his full concentration: maybe, at times, instinct was taking over, and he was working on a personal auto-pilot. More and more, Frank Sinatra, Jr., working as his father's conductor and protector, would prompt him, cover for him, to keep him focused, to avoid embarrassment.

Even when he faltered (losing his musical train of thought mid-phrase at some points), the audience sympathized with him, encouraging him on with standing ovations and loud cheers of support. These gestures must have assured the singer that all was well. They were cheering! And he thrived on that. Many years from the pandemonium of The Paramount Theater, the magical bond between the man and his audience was tighter and warmer than ever. Those closest to him must have realized that the adoration Sinatra received from the audience and the palpable embrace they cocooned him in were keeping him alive.

PHOTOGRAPH BY HARRY LANGDON, COURTESY OF CAPITOL RECORDS/HARRY LANGDON

PART 5

Capitol Revisited

DUETS

Sinatra's last foray into a formal studio setting would take place at Capitol Records, the site of some of his greatest recording achievements, for what remain the most hotly debated sessions of his career: those for *Duets I* and *Duets II*. Initially, the *Duets* recordings seemed to be a bizarre combination of fractured artistry: glossy, technology-driven albums pitting Sinatra's highly edited, time-worn voice against those of an array of contemporary performers many years his junior—their genres ranging from rock to country to rhythm and soul. At first, some critics and Sinatra devotees eschewed the idea, even abhorred it. Sinatra with Chrissie Hynde? Sinatra with Gloria Estefan? Sinatra with *Bono*? Preposterous, absurd. Or so it was thought.

Time and Sinatra's death have afforded us the opportunity to reexamine and rethink the two *Duets* albums, not so much in terms of performance, but as a *concept*. When you consider the motivation for the recordings, and the fact that they are, on several levels, major milestones in Sinatra's recording history, you cannot help but understand (or at least be intrigued by) their brilliance. The albums remain, after all, the greatest *selling* records of Sinatra's career, coming at a time when the contemporary music industry might well have chewed up and spit out any *other* seventy-eight-year-old singer who dared attempt what Frank Sinatra did.

Lengthy discussions with producer Phil Ramone, arranger Patrick Williams, and recording engineer Al Schmitt aid us in placing the performances on these albums in perspective.

"*Duets* is a part of the passion that I have for Mr. Sinatra, and the reasons I did the albums are not selfish ones, although they probably could be considered as such," Ramone says. "In 1992, I approached Elliot Weisman, and said, 'I have this idea for an album: I would love to see Frank at The Rainbow Room, with a beautiful string section, the hottest rhythm section, and some of the great soloists, like Phil Woods. Or, maybe doing a duets album.' My idea was for him to do an album along the lines of what Tony Bennett was doing with the Ralph Sharon Trio . . . something like that. Elliott said, 'Maybe we should approach him with the *Duets* idea first, because I doubt you'll ever get him in the studio to do a live album.'"

"It took a year before Sinatra would even listen to this concept. I was given the job of pitching the project, and we were sitting down in a house he had rented in Palm Beach (where he was performing). He said to me, 'Kid, why would I want to do this?' Now, a guy as active and as bright as he's been all his life, there's no way to talk to him about something that he doesn't want to do. I just looked at him, and said, 'You know, I went to see you play, Francis. For two nights I've watched you work, and if there's something that I can ask you to do, it would be for us to hear you sing this music the way you're performing it now.'"

"For any of the fans that have been out there, and heard him sing in this period—the early

1990s—it was some other kind of experience. Frank asked me, 'Well, what are you talking about? Why would I do it again?' I said, 'You know, Laurence Olivier did Shakespeare when he was probably in his twenties . . . but in his seventies, it was another reading.' He said, 'Well, that's interesting. But why would we do duets?' I said, 'Because there's a generation of artists, from twenty or thirty years ago to this present moment, who would give *anything* in their life to be able to stand next to you, sing next to you, or be a part of this album.' After a little talking, a little coaxing, he got very enthusiastic. I thought, 'Well, we're halfway started,' and then the next step was to continue inviting him into this process of how we would do it."

One of Ramone's first moves was to bring arranger Patrick Williams to the project. Williams, best known for his television themes and film scores (*The Mary Tyler Moore Show* and *The Bob Newhart Show* among them), had been a longtime friend of the producer. Williams first spoke publicly about his work at Hofstra University's 1998 Frank Sinatra academic conference.

"It really was a *process*," Williams explains. "When we started, we didn't have any idea at all that he would do it, and there was a great fear that at any point along the process, he would just blow it off—which would be understandable, actually. But the intensity and the passion that Phil and I both felt was incredible. We said, 'We are *going* to make this work. We are *definitely* going to make this work . . . and neither one of us is going to be the reason why it *doesn't* work.' I think we took everything we ever knew about music and recording, and tried to make it through this experience with Sinatra, at this point in his life, and in ours."

"I had too great a respect for not only Sinatra and his musical legacy," Williams says, "but the arrangers and the music itself, to go in there and not do anything that I didn't feel was of the highest musical caliber. I felt that I was a musical caretaker, in a sense, for Nelson and Billy and

Neal and Quincy and everyone else that wrote for him, because he had the best arrangers that ever lived."

Ramone's next task was locating the best recording engineer for the project. Everyone in Los Angeles pointed him in Al Schmitt's direction. Schmitt, an independent engineer and producer, had worked at Radio Recorders in the early 1950s, and eventually became a staff engineer-producer at RCA Victor in Hollywood, where he recorded all the classic Henry Mancini albums like *Pink Panther* and *Peter Gunn*.

"People would ask me, 'Do you have any regrets about your career?' And I would always tell them, 'I only have one regret: I never got to work with Frank Sinatra.' Then, all of a sudden, the phone rang, and it was Phil, asking me to do Sinatra. So it was a big thrill for me,'" Schmitt says. "It wasn't the easiest project to do, but it certainly was the most fun."

The collaborators treated Sinatra with the greatest respect. "I assured him he wouldn't have to be around a lot of the production end of it, but that he would be involved in all the choices of songs and selection of artists," Ramone explains. "You know, the first question out of his mouth was, 'How's Ella doing?' I said, 'You know, she's not in great health, and if I can get her to agree to it, obviously she'll be there.'"

"We started off with a very simple meeting, and I said to Bill Miller, 'Do you think we can pull this off?' And he said, 'I think if we do it fairly quickly, we can.' So I called Terry Woodson, who handles the Sinatra music library, and asked him to send me the library. So I got about thirty-five arrangements, which came by messenger, and I was totally unprepared for the next thing that happened to me," Williams says.

"I opened the package and put them on the desk, and I was going to very professionally and clinically go through them, and see, 'Okay, how many ballads do we have here . . . ,' and so on. And what I was totally unprepared for, was that on the very top of the pile was "I've Got You Under My Skin." It says, 'Arranged by Nelson Riddle.' And I started to cry. Jesus. And the next song, and the next . . . one right after the other, thirty-five of them — all these songs had been such a part of my life. I thought, 'My *God*! This is unbelievable. . . .' I had no idea that I was going to get hit this way, with this music . . . what it meant to me. I mean, I'd heard Frank Sinatra sing when I was six years old, so just the power of all of that, and being a part of it, just being able to dip into that well — even though he was seventy-eight years old — was just an incredible feeling."

"So Bill Miller and I picked the tunes, and when we were ready to go into the studio, I wanted him to feel as comfortable as possible, so we had Bill Miller and the guys who were on the road with him: Greg Fields, Chuck Berghoffer, Ron Anthony . . . and I hired Conte Candoli, George Roberts, and some of the guys that had played with him on some of the Capitol dates. And I added a dynamite trumpet section. Then, for a week, I did nothing but rehearse: every day, two sessions a day. No Frank — we didn't know when he was coming, if he was coming . . . whatever. We were rehearsing on tape — all thirty-five charts.

"About the third day, the weirdest thing happened. At the end of the day, I see this limo pull up to Capitol, and they took a tape of what we'd been doing out to the limo. That limo was going out to Palm Springs so he could hear what I was doing! He was checking up on me! I thought, 'Isn't that beautiful?' I felt very comfortable with the way the band was sounding, everybody was loving doing this. . . . If he wanted to do this, we were ready to do it."

With the arrangements completed and the technical details worked out, session time was booked at Studio A on Vine Street. Ramone, remembering the red-carpet treatment that had been afforded Sinatra on their first record date together back at A&R in 1967, went all out to welcome the singer to his old home in the Capitol Tower. "I had built a beautiful, huge vocal booth with television monitors and sound monitors. . . ."

"I've never seen a vocal booth in my entire recording career like this," says Patrick Williams. "It had furniture in it . . . it had his microphone . . . it looked like something at the Mariott! I was told it cost thirty or thirty-five thousand just to build the vocal booth. Speaking of money, we were up to about two hundred thousand dollars in rehearsal time, and he hasn't sung anything yet. . . ."

The first session was a disaster. The man whose presence once intimidated now eyed the vocal shed cautiously. He entered it to face the professional microphone, mounted on the music stand before him. Panic-stricken, he turned to walk away. At age seventy-eight, Frank Sinatra was afraid.

Phil Ramone explains: "He was so uncomfortable. I had carefully designed the booth so that he could see his teleprompters, he had speakers, he had his choice of microphones . . . it was all hyperventilation, and a lot of him saying, 'You know, I don't need this . . .' We talked to him, and he said, 'Well, let me see if I can sing to those tracks . . .'

"It was awful. Nothing worked. I looked at Patrick, and he's like, 'Oh my God, what are we gonna do?' When Frank gave you that stare, it was either in, or out—and I knew it was out! And I know the greatest lie of the century is if he says, 'You know, why don't you just lay a good track down and I'll do this tomorrow?' which really means 'Goodbye, folks . . . I'll see you some other time.' He didn't quite slough us off: he said to me, 'I'm not comfortable in this room . . . I don't feel right.' So I said to him, 'Why don't we try it differently tomorrow?'"

On the second night, Sinatra entered the studio, and complained of a sore throat. "I've got some problems with my reed," he told Ramone. Stepping back into the booth, he again felt uncomfortable.

"I was standing there with Bill Miller, right outside the door," Williams remembers. "Frank checks it out, walks right out the door, and says,

'I'm not singin' in there.' With that, three executives' jaws dropped . . . their eyes were like saucers. Sinatra said, 'I'm singin' out there with the band.' Bill Miller grabs my arm. It was a very emotional moment, because it was not that he wasn't going to sing in the booth, it was that he *was* going to sing with the band.

"With that, we were now very excited, except we had no 'Plan B.' There was no place for him to sing, other than the booth. Nobody had thought, 'What if he doesn't want to sing in the booth?' With that, he sits down right next to me, next to the podium, on a riser. And I'm thinking, 'Oh no . . . no, no, no . . . ,' and the technicians are running around with mikes and cords . . . and he's just sitting there looking at this. That went on for maybe five minutes, and he walked out. It was like, 'I'm not gonna stick around for this . . . get it together, and maybe I'll come back.' He was gone. And once again, we're sitting there, looking at each other."

"Hank Cattaneo (Sinatra's friend and concert sound director) and I built a little stage, creating the environment of his live performances, around the orchestra," Ramone explains. A third session was scheduled for July 1, 1993. Williams picks up the story. "We didn't know if he was coming the next night or not. I'd rehearsed all the arrangements, and the band was called at three or four in the afternoon . . . if we were going to record with him it was going to be at six o'clock. But, by this point, I figured, 'Well, we'll be there, but somehow or other I don't think this is going to happen.'"

"The bets were on or off: most of them, I can tell you, were off," Ramone explains. "This was my sense, from people calling me and saying, 'I'm sorry it didn't work.' Then the people who had put up the money for the record started asking me, 'Well how much are we in the hole?' I said, 'Well, we'll probably be in the hole for no worse than some rock-and-roll band you spent this money for . . . , but, if we do it, we'll be way ahead of the world.'"

The studio had been set, then struck, at least twice before. Once again, every detail had been tended to. The musicians had been summoned, the studio readied, and producer Phil Ramone hoped that this, the final attempt to nudge Frank Sinatra back into the arena which he once dominated so comfortably, would work.

"Suddenly, Frank came in, and sat down. The control room was dead quiet . . . the studio, for the first time in as many years as I could remember, seemed to be awfully quiet; worse than I ever remembered. No musicians talking to each other—nobody tuning up. He motioned for me to come over to him, and I knew what I was in for. He gave me hell for about ten minutes. He just kept asking me why we were exposing ourselves to this kind of possible ridicule. His whispered dialogue to me was, 'Why am I doing this?' And I said, 'Francis, we need to do this record because we promised each other that we would make a record that is *of this time*.

"He said to me, 'I'm not sure—I did this forty years ago. Why would I want to do this again?' And I said, 'It's the legacy of *you*. I want my children and my grandchildren to know who Sinatra is at this most important moment . . .' He said, 'All right, well, we'll give it a try.'" Ramone provided Sinatra with a reassuring out. "I told him, 'If it doesn't work, no one will ever find these tapes . . . I promise you no bootlegger in the world will find these, 'cause I will personally destroy them.' He said, 'Okay,' and I said 'It's gonna be great!' As I walked ten feet away, he turned, and said, 'It better be!'"

"When he walked in at about ten of six," Williams recalls, "the band was on a break! So, everybody's scurrying around. 'He's here! He's here! Get the band in here!' And I was sitting on the podium, and he walks over in my direction. Now I had never met him. He did not know me . . . he knew *of* me, I think; otherwise he wouldn't have called me. He came up, and I said hello and all that stuff, and he said to me, 'Where do you want me to go?'

"I direct him to where his chair is, and he goes up to the music stand, sits down, and starts thumbing through a pile of lead sheets. They were all there—maybe twenty-five tunes. Now it's five minutes to six, and the musicians are getting settled. By one minute to six, all of the musicians were there in place, and I have never been in a recording studio with fifty-five musicians and fifteen guys in the booth that was that quiet!" Williams says. Ramone had given Sinatra a hand mike, which along with the small stage, essentially replicated the setting that Sinatra had been working in night after night for years.

"I looked up at Frank, and he's got a sports jacket on—he looks great! It's Frank Sinatra! He says to me, 'Whaddya want me to sing?' I completely lost it. I stumbled, and said, 'Ahh, ahh, uhh . . . ,' so Hank Cattaneo says, 'How about "Come Fly with Me," Frank?' 'Okay, we'll give that a try.'

"Now, we had turned two forty-eight-track machines on, and they never went off for the next four hours. Two forty-eight-track machines on the entire time. There was no stopping: I kicked the band off, and he roared into 'Come Fly with Me,' and he was singing, and giving it everything he had. The courage of this guy is just incredible! He was doing everything he could do to make it come off . . . the band sounded great, and he recorded nine tunes that night, in about three and a half hours," the arranger remembers.

"Frank stood right out in front of the brass section. It was an engineer's nightmare!" says Schmitt. "But what we got from Frank was so spontaneous. He sounded great. The night we hit it, we got almost everything for *Duets* and *Duets II*—all in one night. He just clicked it off, one right after the other. Some of the orchestral tracks for *Duets II* were done in New York, and we added the vocals in later."

"After the session, about six of us went to dinner, and he was in wonderful spirits . . . he was telling stories . . . and that started the process of the next few days, where we actually got his tracks

for the *Duets* albums . . . none of the duets themselves—these sessions were strictly for his vocals
. . . just getting Frank Sinatra in the studio, one
last time. And I'll never forget it," Williams says.
With a tear in his eye, Williams told the audience
at Hofstra University: "For all the times I've been
in studios (and it's in the thousands, I can assure
you), I've never walked out of a studio feeling
what I felt the nights we recorded with Frank
Sinatra."

Now that Sinatra's vocal tracks were in
the can, Ramone set about solidifying the list of
guest artists whose vocals would be paired with
his. "I gave him what I call a 'wish list,'" the
producer said. "Between me, Don Rubin, and
Hank Cattaneo, we came up with the greatest
fifteen or twenty artists you could think of. There
were so many people that were a generation
or two younger than him, like Gloria Estefan,
who had grown up with his music as kids in
the '60s understanding what Sinatra meant.
And then there's a few Tony Bennetts, and Liza
Minnelli's . . ."

Each of those chosen was thrilled to be involved; many have mentioned their participation
on *Duets I* and *II* as a major event in their professional lives, and while the recordings may lack
the spark of two superstars working side-by-side
on a real duet in the studio, they retain more
spontaneity than one might expect.

Sinatra's duet partners were added via a
miraculous fiber optic system called EDnet, a
fiber optic link between various parts of the entertainment community. Developed at Skywalker
Sound, system allows high quality audio, com-
pressed video, and multimedia data to be sent via
phone line from studio to studio throughout the
world.

"The first 'duet' we did was Luther [Van-
dross], and he came into the Capitol studio," says
Schmitt. "Phil had worked out who would sing
what line, where we would drop Frank out, and
that sort of stuff. Then, once the artists began
working on their parts, they added things of their

own . . . they made suggestions, and in many
cases, we followed them."

Information has circulated about the substi-
tution of concert performances and backstage re-
records to smooth out Sinatra's vocals. To some
extent, this was necessary. To insure that all the
elements would be available in case anything
needed adjusting, Hank Cattaneo taped several
shows. Individual words or phrases could be
edited in digitally if there turned out to be a problem with a studio master take. "The little tag,
where Frank sings 'I have got a crush, my Barbra,
on you . . . ,'" in the Streisand duet was done backstage," Schmitt says. "Hank just had Frank sing
into a DAT machine, and we cut it in during the
mixing."

Cattaneo, who directed the sound at Sinatra concerts for decades, was a major asset,
since Sinatra felt comfortable with him and
trusted his instincts. "Hank was a tremendous
help to us: he was there at the sessions, at the mixdowns . . . he was able to get Frank to do things
on the road. He really made it happen," says
Schmitt.

Working with the most advanced digital
recording and editing equipment available, the
production team had unlimited enhancement
tools at its disposal. These could be used to add
and remove vibrato, adjust pitch, and perform
other sonic miracles, enabling them to edit in
Frank's "duet" partners in the most unobtrusive
ways.

*B*y the late 1970s, the computer revolution
had spawned a new method of recording sound: digital recording. The first digital recorders were extremely expensive, and in
the late 1970s and early 1980s the technique was
still largely experimental. It wasn't until the mid-
1980s, when the compact disc began to supplant
the LP as the superior playback medium, that
digital recording spread to mainstream recording
studios.

Digital recording opened up yet another world of sonic possibilities, including that of "near perfect" sound. This not only affected new recordings: the digital era brought a renewed interest in the back catalogs held in record company vaults and paved the way for restoration projects involving all types of music.

Standard or "analog" recording consists of an electronic signal whose wave forms replicate that of the original sound. Analog signals may be on the grooves of a disc (an original lacquer disc or a finished LP pressing), or on a tape, where magnetic particles have been arranged and preserved. Both of these analog mediums use physical force for playback (the stylus traces the groove of a record; tape passes over the heads of a recorder), and are susceptible to noise, distortion, and other anomalies that are added to the original signal during recording or playback.

In digital recording, the signal to be recorded is converted to computer-readable binary (digital) form. The computer "samples" or reads the signal thousands of times per second, and generates chains of pulses or numbers, each corresponding to the analog signal. On playback, the computer converts the pulses back to the signals originally sampled, and a special filter converts them to an analog signal that recreates the audible sound.

The advantages of digital recording are many. First, in theory a digital recording will preserve all of the characteristics of the original analog signal, without adding hiss or distortion. Also, the digital recording is infinitely reproducable without the addition of extraneous noise or distortion: a tenth generation tape will sound exactly like the first generation master tape. Analog copies suffer a deterioration of sound with each successive copy.

For consumers, the compact disc is the primary format for digital recordings. Introduced by Philips and Sony in 1983, CDs store digital information as a series of numbers: zeroes and ones. This binary code is burned into the shiny aluminum surface of a CD at the pressing plant, and is read in the CD player by laser beam. A microprocessor then converts the binary code back to an analog signal, which is what we hear upon playback.

The main advantage of CD recordings is their high quality reproduction, free of the clicks and pops attendant to even the finest vinyl record pressings. Compact discs are far more durable than their analog counterparts, and with reasonable handling, will not wear or deteriorate the way vinyl does.

FULL CIRCLE

*W*ith *Duets*, Frank Sinatra stepped fully into the digital age, completing an audio adventure that began in 1979 with the experimental digital recording of *The Future* for *Trilogy*.

Musical flashes of the old Sinatra shine through. A piano and vocal rendition of "One for My Baby" is a profound reminder of the power in his simplest of interpretations, and why he kept Bill Miller on his team for so long. Other knockout performances include "For Once in My Life" (Gladys Knight and Stevie Wonder), "I've Got a Crush on You" (Barbra Streisand), "My Funny Valentine/How Do You Keep the Music Playing?" (Lorrie Morgan), "Come Rain or Come Shine" (Gloria Estefan) and "New York, New York" (Tony Bennett). A rousing "My Kind of Town" is especially interesting, as it pairs Sinatra vocally with his talented son, Frank Jr.

A revelation to Sinatra buffs was a tape of his solo performances from the *Duets* sessions. Remarkably, the unedited, non-duet performances are excellent and could stand with the two exist-ing *Duets* albums as a fitting companion disc. These solos support Ramone and Williams's claim that once he got started, Sinatra was smokin' on those final sessions at Capitol.

Much of my personal resistance to even the concept of *Duets* was rooted in the theme of this book. Frank Sinatra had spent fifty-four years es-tablishing a reputation as the ultimate pro in the recording studio, fastidiously tending to every last detail of his sessions. He had built that reputation on one word: quality. He rejected most modern recording techniques, such as overdubbing, that would have made his job far easier and less com-plicated. He felt, in his heart, that performances were evanescent, and needed to be captured and preserved for what they were—fleeting moments in time. It was for this reason that virtually his en-tire recording career was predicated on *live* per-formance. To make a 180-degree turn at this late stage in the game seemed to me the antithesis of what he, as a recording artist, always stood for.

Yet this nearly eighty-year-old man, who be-gan recording at a time when sounds were im-pressed on crude wax discs, was able to bridge yet another generation of recording technology and make use of the most advanced digital and fiber-optic technology available in the world. As he al-ways had, Sinatra was trusting those around him, taking advantage of the benefits that state-of-the-art technology afforded him, in much the same way as he made the transition from disc to tape recording, from mono to stereo, and from ana-log to digital.

What if he had decided to never record again because he didn't believe in stereo? What if he had pooh-poohed tape, and insisted on record-ing on lacquer discs? His capacity to flow with whatever was in vogue at the time helped to build his recording career, and is also what wrought *Duets*. The technology behind *Duets*, however different from the traditional "Sinatra" style of recording, simply reflects the changing way that music is created and preserved.

After carefully auditioning these records again and speaking with the men who worked so hard to create both *Duets* albums, I am con-vinced that these are recordings of substance that deserve appreciation not for just the idea, but for the emotional quality of the performances as well. Not every duet partner is appropriate, not every performance great, yet the albums allow us to examine Sinatra at the most fragile point in his life, and they introduced him to a whole new gen-eration of young listeners.

The brash young vocalist who allowed no barrier to stop him, the kid who made his first recordings on wax back in 1939 with the James band, had now conquered every technical record-ing marvel of his lifetime. From wax impressions to compact disc, Frank Sinatra has left his mark, and as of this writing (one year after his death at age eighty-two), is one of only a handful of per-forming artists to have recorded in each of the last seven decades. His recordings are a chronicle of every revolutionary technical advance that oc-curred within this period.

History has no recorded documentation of the way Mozart, Beethoven, or Bach intended their compositions to sound. We have no chance to experience these composers playing or con-ducting their own work, and thus, no opportunity to enjoy the spirit of the original dynamics they desired, and the tempos that they dreamed their music in. Instead, we must settle for close ap-proximations, transcribed and revised to accom-modate the changing orchestras, and the whims of their conductors in subsequent centuries. Were such recordings available, their artistic value alone would make them priceless. Fortunately, we do have the recordings of Sinatra.

Frank Sinatra has left an indelible impres-sion on the landscape of pop culture. The record-ings he bequeathed to us are part of a rich communal tapestry that, while an indispensable link to our past, simultaneously binds us to the next century, and future generations. Unfettered by the ravages of time or space, the precious musings of one man remain both musical and technological triumphs, a combination of ideals resulting in the perfection of an art form that is unlikely to become passé.

Frank Sinatra had few lapses of judgment when it came to his work in the recording studio, and invested unprecedented effort in extracting the very best performance from himself, from his musical partners, and from the recording technology that marked his travel through time. He approached each performance with unmatched equanimity, which is reflected in the veracity of the individual recordings that comprise his canon. Sinatra possessed aesthetic values of the highest order, and used his talent to enrich our understanding of the literature of modern music through his patient and nurturing role as a singer, musician, and producer. Moreover, he brought unparalleled attention to a body of work that we must all consider a national treasure: the popular music born of the great songwriters of the twentieth century. His superior interpretations of these tunes ensure that his legacy—the more than one thousand recordings he made during his career—will continue to shine as the jewels in the crown of the "Great American Songbook."

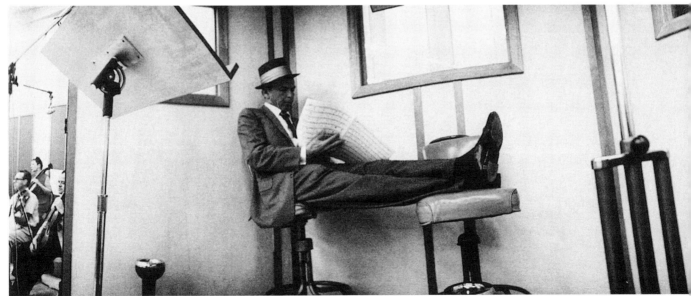

PHOTOGRAPH BY TED ALLAN, COURTESY OF MPTV ARCHIVES

Afterword

*E*xplaining all that my Dad's recordings represent for me is not an easy task, because almost every song has personal meaning for me. Each one takes me to a particular time and place in which I can relive my own history.

Moments frozen in time are forever etched on my soul. Driving to his recording sessions at Capitol when I first got my license, watching and listening intently as he created masterful works of art, and the feelings of pride and admiration that washed over me in the hush of the studio. Carefully storing the acetates he would give me or send me if I couldn't be present at a

session. His little scribbles on the sleeve: "For you, Chicken," or "Play it loud!" or "Mine is better than his" (meaning Dad felt his version of "I'm Walking Behind You" edged Eddie Fisher's). My high school girlfriend and her boyfriend choosing "You, My Love" as "their song."

Dad's gifts as a performer were such that scholars will continue to study his work in perpetuity. They will be forced to ask what it was about him that separated him from the others who, though they may have had technically equal or even superior voices, just couldn't meet the challenge set by the greatest entertainer of nearly six decades—"the voice of the century."

And what indeed was it? I think that if I had to use one word to describe him it would be *honest*. A painfully honest man who recognizes the sadness and joy of others *has* to feel the pain and joy himself. These feelings fueled the interpretations of the songs he made his.

It's this honesty, and his passion for his craft that propelled his recording sessions, which we are now able to study and understand, thanks to the memories of some very special people who worked closely with Dad to help him realize his vision.

Reading through the conversations and "backstage" dialogue that occurred at some of Dad's greatest recording sessions and hearing the reminiscences of some of his best friends (the musicians) have brought back many wonderful memories for me. Although I must admit that I don't remember all of the details of each session that I attended (and there were many), I have special, warm recollections of the hours—the big clocks on the studio walls clicking off the minutes 10 P.M., 11:46 P.M., 12:15 A.M., 1:00 A.M.—and wanting the magic to never end. I watched him work at United, Western, Capitol, Goldwyn, RCA, Columbia in Los Angeles and New York, never tiring of the experience—always hungry for more of the magic, always learning from him.

My father always had a genius for picking the right songs, and when you consider the relationship between the tunes he selected, and the remarkably different themes that come with each passing decade, you can see that his music tells a story that parallels his life and ours. Those songs, and their changing themes, represent Dad's most passionate dream—the one he talked about on dates with my mother—and the realization of that dream, which brought him almost insurmountable pain along with irrepressible joy as he experienced it, and as he lived it. Although he never gave us his autobiography, he told us about

himself using a very precise and powerful tool: his music.

I have always thought of my Dad's music as having four distinctly different themes that guided him. His earliest recordings with Harry and Tommy were "The Dream." When he went to Columbia and began recording under his own name, that dream became "The Reality." The magnificent recordings he made at Capitol with Nelson and Billy and Gordon build on what he gleaned from his earliest lessons, and thus reflect "The Experience." Later, after creating his own record label, he summed up the experiences, in retrospect, of a life lived at full tilt with "The Wisdom."

My own favorite recordings are those from the Columbia period. The up-tempo numbers are great, but if given the chance, I'd listen to only ballads from this era. Once I get started listening to Axel and Pop, I don't want anything interfering with those sweet, beautiful classic songs! We were fortunate that Dad was a part of a time that was undoubtedly the best period in American music, and without those records, he wouldn't have become known.

His strength is something that was communicated loudly and clearly during the Capitol years, when he really was in top form. His need to have constant change—to continually drive himself in the hardest and fastest of ways—was an inherent part of his restless and inquisitive nature, and was one of his many complexities. He was driven by passion and ambition; by ego; by inextinguishable talent; and by gentleness, a force that can be almost violent, a love that is surpassing. His passions were great, and so was his pain. Both emotions found their outlet in the dynamic energy of his music.

In his sixties, he was able to really understand what he had experienced, measure the triumphs and disasters (and how to deal with both), and pass along the resulting wisdom to others. What he had learned was important to him, and he felt it might help younger people, so he sang to us of summer winds and rolling dice and getting sentimental and concentrating on one love and having children, to guide us along our own paths of loving and losing and taking a chance. In the end, I can't help thinking that even though he may have gotten "sick of tryin'," my father, not unlike the mighty Mississippi River of which he sang, just "keeps rolling along," even now that he is gone from us. Frank Sinatra is timely and timeless—there will always be a place for him, and his music.

Each generation has its own music, and its own identity—each group of kids that comes along needs something new. I experienced this with my own career, and I've seen it with my own daughters, A.J. and Amanda. Listening to their music, I've learned that you can have an appreciation for *all* of it—there's always somebody that does something in the new genre that you can identify with.

Dad just took *his* whole generation, and swept it away—literally swept it way up into this wonderful cloud of lyrics and violins. He's transcended every musical trend during these last fifty years because every generation finds something in Sinatra to like: something it can identify with. Each generation understands and appreciates the truth, and there's no one more truthful than Frank Sinatra.

One thing I have always recognized as being important (especially in the past few years) is how great the correlation was between him and recording technology. Dad was a pioneer who concerned himself with not only the intricacies of the music, but those of the technology that would preserve it as well. Tracking his career, one has to track the changes in technology that occurred in this century—from the megaphone to fiber optics. Amazing!

The role of "singer as producer" was one that few pop artists willingly accepted in those years, and my Dad really enjoyed this part of his work. I got the chance to experience the satisfaction that came with that responsibility when he recorded the song "Cycles" at a New York session in 1968: he asked me to go into the booth and produce, so Don Costa could be out in the studio working with him. What an honor—it was thrilling! I must admit I was nervous when I had to stop a take because of a mistake. I had always tried to never criticize anyone—especially my father! I mean he was Frank Sinatra, for heaven's sake!

I always had the overwhelming sense that when Dad walked into a session, the respect for him was unequaled. There was always a tangible and audible collective inhaled breath—a pause in the life of those present, a quick flash of "Oh my God! There he is." He had *earned* the esteem of everyone in the room, because he was part of the team. His voice was an instrument in the orchestra, and knew the ensemble inside and out. His love of and respect for the music knew no bounds, and could actually be felt in the intensity of his concentration while working in the studio—an inexplicable force that is echoed in the remarkably vivid descriptions that for the first time, our respected friend, Sinatra historian Chuck Granata, has lovingly and sensibly recounted on these pages.

Words can't describe the pride I have for Dad's work, and my understanding of the magnitude of what these sessions represent. Preserving the very essence of what transpired in those fleeting moments, and the perfection my father painstakingly worked to achieve, is of vital importance to me. Nothing could ever dilute the power of his legendary body of work, or the quality of what dad and the arrangers and producers accomplished in the recording studio.

The music of Frank Sinatra sings our joys, our sorrows, and our silences. He sang of love and loneliness, of exultant life and of still, small hours of sadness. He sang as he lived, with spirit not fear; with energy not ennui. His amazing mountain of work is a testament to his incredible talent and speaks volumes about him—in his own voice. In his soul, way down deep, was a force that motivated him, guided him, and separated him from himself, making him and his work bigger than his life. It was this force that enabled him to find a measure of eternity before his body tired of the journey.

Leo Rosten once said that "The purpose of life is to matter, to count, to have it make some difference that we lived at all." I have always admired those words, and have quoted them often because they describe so eloquently the way I feel about my Dad and his life.

The recordings are irrefutable proof that it did indeed matter that Frank Sinatra lived. A book that documents his studio methodology is precious, for it insures that musicians, vocalists, and historians that come along in the future will be able to understand the care and thoughtfulness that accompanied the creation of these very special records, and perhaps learn from the wisdom imparted by my Dad through the previously undocumented words with which he guided his sessions.

Dad and I were always as close as could be, having lived our lives in the relentless presence of the end of things. It is said that the way to love anyone is to realize he could be lost to you. That is a painful way to love, but it is how I loved my father, and although he is gone, I am comforted by the realization that I'll still carry his blood in my veins and his life's music in my heart and see his immortal soul in the bright, loving eyes of my children.

He was, and always will be, my hero.

—Nancy Sinatra Lambert
Beverly Hills, April 1999

Appendixes

Companion Recordings

The stories and information contained in the body of this volume should, at the very least, inspire you to seek out and listen to the recordings cited herein. As I explained at the outset, I highly recommend having at least some of the following music available to you while perusing the book.

With these recorded samples at your disposal, you'll be able to experience maximum understanding of the musical and technical explanations I have provided, and will undoubtedly gain a solid appreciation for the craftsmanship and beauty of the music.

Since many songs and albums have been mentioned in the book, I have limited this list to the recordings that have been treated exhaustively in the body of the book. Some legwork and the use of the listings in the appendixes that follow will lead you to the balance of the recordings.

1. **The Popular Frank Sinatra, Volume 1**
    (RCA/BMG 68711)
    Contains the most popular Sinatra-Dorsey recordings, including "Say It."

2. **Swing and Dance with Frank Sinatra**
    (Columbia/Legacy CK 64852)
    A reincarnation of the 1950 10-inch LP classic with George Siravo. Retains the original eight Sing and Dance album tunes and eleven other Siravo charts including the original full-length version of "It All Depends On You" and the slow tempo alternate of "Bye Bye Baby."

3. **Sinatra Sings His Greatest Hits**
    (Columbia/Legacy CK 65240)
    Contains many of the Columbia recordings cited, the most important of which are "Body and Soul," the original version of "April in Paris," "I Could Write a Book," and "I'm a Fool to Want You." (See note*.)

4. **The Capitol Years**
    (Capitol 94777)
    Includes "I've Got the World on a String," the classic version of "I've Got You Under My Skin" (with Milt Bernhart on trombone), "In the Wee Small Hours of the Morning," "The Tender Trap," "Guess I'll Hang My Tears Out to Dry" (with Al Viola on guitar), "Almost Like Being in Love" and "Nice 'n Easy." The versions of "Close to You" and "Only the Lonely" contain bits of session chatter that precede the musical performance.

5. **Close to You**
    (Capitol 46572)
    Wallow in the classic beauty of the entire album, featuring The Hollywood String Quar-

tet (see note**), and some of Nelson Riddle's most sensitive arrangements.

6. *Come Fly with Me*

(Capitol 96087)

The first Sinatra-Billy May collaboration contains the 1957 version of "April in Paris," and the original (superior) recording of the Cahn–Van Heusen title song.

7. *Only the Lonely*

(Capitol 94756)

Quintessential renditions of "What's New?" "Gone with the Wind," "Willow Weep for Me," "Angel Eyes," and "One for My Baby" are included on this melancholy classic, which both Sinatra and Riddle called their personal best.

8. *Sinatra's Swingin' Session!!!*

(Capitol 46573)

The intensity of "Should I," "My Blue Heaven," and "I Concentrate on You" build to a feverish pitch that leads to "River, Stay 'Way From My Door," which is a fitting bonus cut that is well worth the price of the album.

9. *Point of No Return*

(Capitol 48334)

Sinatra and Stordahl's final uneven and controversial album. As a bonus, the four songs from Frank's first Capitol session (4/2/53) are included.

10. *Great Songs from Great Britain*

(Warner/Reprise 42519)

Highlights form Sinatra's first European recording include "A Nightingale Sang in Berkeley Square," "If I Had You," "A Garden in the Rain," and "Roses of Picaroy."

11. *The Concert Sinatra*

(Warner/Reprise 9-47244)

Featuring "I Have Dreamed," "Ol' Man River," "Bewitched, Bothered, and Bewildered," "You'll Never Walk Alone," "This Nearly Was Mine," and three other electrifying performances. The most current compact disc edition (under the banner "Entertainer of the Century") has been restored and remastered from the original three-track tapes, and is the preferred version.

12. *September of My Years*

(Warner/Reprise 46946)

Frank's fiftieth birthday classic that wrought "It Was a Very Good Year." Check out the CBS News documentary "Sinatra," which offers a firsthand look at the "Very Good Year" session. (Available on home video.)

13. *For My Dad*

(DCC DZS-165)

Nancy Sinatra's tribute to her Dad. Includes two of their three duets: "Feelin' Kinda Sunday" and "Somethin' Stupid," which contains some fabulous pre-recording session chatter.

Endnotes

*   The analysis of "Body and Soul" herein discusses the evolution of the performance as Sinatra works through various takes. The take contained on this CD is the PB3 take. The other two takes discussed are available on the following CD issues: First take: **Portrait of Sinatra** (Columbia/Legacy C2K 65244) and second take: **Best of the Columbia Years** (Columbia/Legacy C4K 64681) and *The Complete Recordings* (Columbia/Legacy CXK 48673).

** As of this writing, **Close to You** has been deleted from Capitol's current CD catalog. It is expected to be remastered and restored in the near future, but may still be available in some outlets. The search for either the original CD or a vinyl LP copy is a worthwhile venture.

The Basic Collection

With any luck, this book will inspire you to delve deeper into the mystery and intrigue of the Sinatra legacy that enriches our musical heritage. I would be remiss if I did not offer to newcomers some suggestions for building a basic Sinatra record library.

Fortunately, each of the four major labels he recorded for has compiled complete, all-inclusive compact disc packages, and/or comprehensive retrospectives that include most of his essential recordings. All of the packages recommended have been assembled with meticulous care, and feature extensive liner notes, photos, and art that are sure to enhance your listening experience.

If you desire to have a solid, complete overview of Frank Sinatra's entire recording history, a collection of the following compilations will be indispensable.

1. *Harry James and His Orchestra, Featuring Frank Sinatra*
   (Columbia/Legacy CK 66377)
   Contains all ten Sinatra-James master recordings, plus two alternate takes and seven of their earliest rare radio airchecks from The Roseland Ballroom and Atlantic City's Steel Pier.

2. *Tommy Dorsey and Frank Sinatra: The Song Is You*
   (RCA/BMG 66353-2)
   This five-CD set contains the complete Sinatra-Dorsey master recordings (eighty-three songs), plus six alternate takes, Sinatra's first four solo sides with Axel Stordahl, and twenty-four ultra rare radio transcription performances. This is a fine collection that accurately captures Sinatra's burgeoning vocal style.

3. *Frank Sinatra: The Best of the Columbia Years, 1943–1952*
   (Columbia/Legacy C4K 64681)
   A well-balanced, ninety-four-song collection that encompasses the wide range of musical styles that bespeak Sinatra's Columbia years. Includes samplings of the early a cappella recordings, the great romantic "standards" that are so closely identified with the singer, and a generous offering of songs from the controversial late (Mitch Miller) period.

4. *Frank Sinatra: The Capitol Years*
   (Capitol 94777)
   By far the finest compilation of recordings from Sinatra's best period, blending an almost per-

fect mix of songs from his great Capitol concept albums and singles. All of the hits are here, and the sonics are superb. These three CDs will surely leave you pining for more Sinatra from this incredibly fertile period!

5. *Frank Sinatra: The Complete Capitol Singles Collection*
   (Capitol 38039)
   The rich suppleness of Sinatra's voice and the exquisite repertoire contained on this four CD set will surely garner a place on your CD shelf and in your heart. Program all of the ballads in sequential order, and revel in the breathtaking beauty of Sinatra's vocal peak, as demonstrated through the fine vocal coloration and shading and superb control that this "sweet" period is noted for. The inherent quality of these performances is exceeded only by that of their counterparts, the sixteen original Capitol concept albums.

6. *Frank Sinatra: The Reprise Collection*
   (Warner/Reprise 26340)
   A four-CD set that combines the hits and rarities from Sinatra's very own Reprise label, spanning the years 1960 to 1986. Includes samples from the London session, dates with May, Riddle, Costa, and Jenkins, and collaborations with Count Basie, Duke Ellington, and Antonio Carlos Jobim.

7. *Duets*
   (Capitol 89611)
   The blockbuster original, featuring the legendary duets with Barbra Streisand, Aretha Franklin, Tony Bennett, and Gloria Estefan, as well as his haunting final version of "One for My Baby."

Once you have sought out and explored the seven packages above, move on to the individual Capitol and Reprise concept albums (Capitol first, Reprise second), as listed in Appendix C. Then, and only then, should you tackle the two major "complete" multi-disc collections: *Frank Sinatra: The Columbia Years/The Complete Recordings 1943–1952* (Columbia/Legacy CXK 48673 — 12 CDs), and *The Complete Reprise Studio Recordings* (Warner/Reprise 46013 — 20 CDs).

Concept Albums

*T*hrough the years, hundreds of Frank Sinatra albums have been issued by all of the four major labels he recorded for: RCA Victor, Columbia, Capitol, and Reprise. Of greatest value are the true "concept" albums, which are all listed below. I have not included the proliferation of uneven singles collections that were created (primarily at RCA Victor and Columbia) to compete directly with his Capitol and Reprise products in the 1950s and 1960s. Also excluded are the film soundtrack albums, live albums, and the Capitol and Reprise albums consisting of singles.

COLUMBIA RECORDS

Although most people view Frank Sinatra's earliest Capitol efforts as his first concept albums, Columbia was assembling cohesively packaged theme albums as early as 1946. Originally, the 78 rpm album sets consisted of four 10-inch shellac discs (eight songs), which translated easily to the time constraints of the 10-inch LPs, which were issued from 1948 on. Here is a complete list of his pre-1953 Columbia concept albums.

The songs have been listed here for reference, as these original sets are much more elusive than the later Capitol and Reprise albums:

The Voice of Frank Sinatra
Orchestra under the direction of Axel Stordahl
78 rpm album set C-112 released March 1946
10-inch LP CL-6001 released June 1948

> *You Go to My Head*
> *Someone to Watch Over Me*
> *These Foolish Things*
> *Why Shouldn't I?*
> *I Don't Know Why*
> *Try a Little Tenderness*
> *A Ghost of a Chance*
> *Paradise*

Songs by Sinatra, *Volume One*
Orchestra under the direction of Axel Stordahl
78 rpm album set C-124 released April 1947
10-inch LP CL-6087 released January 1950

> *I'm Sorry I Made You Cry*
> *How Deep Is the Ocean?*
> *Over the Rainbow*
> *She's Funny That Way*
> *Embraceable You*
> *All the Things You Are*
> *That Old Black Magic*
> *I Concentrate on You*

Christmas Songs by Sinatra
Orchestra under the direction of Axel Stordahl
78 rpm album set C-167 and 10-inch LP CL-6019
    released October 1948

White Christmas
Jingle Bells
Silent Night
Adeste Fideles
O Little Town Of Bethlehem
It Came Upon a Midnight Clear
Have Yourself a Merry Little Christmas
Santa Claus Is Coming to Town

Frankly Sentimental

Quintet accompaniment and orchestra under the
    direction of Axel Stordahl
78 rpm album set C-185 released June 1949
10-inch LP CL-6059 released July 1949

> Body and Soul
> Laura
> Fools Rush In
> Spring Is Here
> One for My Baby (and One More for the Road)
> Guess I'll Hang My Tears Out to Dry
> When You Awake
> It Never Entered My Mind

Dedicated To You

Orchestra under the direction of Axel Stordahl
78 rpm album set and 10-inch LP CL-6096
    released March 1950

> The Music Stopped
> The Moon Was Yellow
> I Love You
> Strange Music
> Where or When
> None But the Lonely Heart
> Always
> Why Was I Born?

Sing and Dance with Frank Sinatra

Orchestra under the direction of George Siravo
78 rpm album set C-218 and 10-inch LP released
    October 1950

> Lover
> It's Only a Paper Moon
> My Blue Heaven

It All Depends on You
You Do Something to Me
Should I?
The Continental
When You're Smiling

CAPITOL RECORDS

With the exception of his last Capitol album, *Point of No Return*, each of Frank Sinatra's Capitol albums is a model of perfection, and represents the ultimate musical experience. All are essential components of any well-rounded pop music library. Since these recordings are commonly available in one form or another, I have limited their listing to album title, primary arranger-conductor, and date of release:

Songs for Young Lovers 10-inch LP (Nelson Riddle, January 1954)

Swing Easy 10-inch LP (Nelson Riddle, August 1954)

In the Wee Small Hours 10- and 12-inch LP (Nelson Riddle, April 1955)

Songs for Swingin' Lovers (Nelson Riddle, March 1956)

Close to You (Nelson Riddle, January 1957)

A Swingin' Affair! (Nelson Riddle, May 1957)

Where Are You? (Gordon Jenkins, September 1957)

A Jolly Christmas from Frank Sinatra (Gordon Jenkins, September 1957)

Come Fly with Me (Billy May, January 1958)

Only the Lonely (Nelson Riddle, September 1958)

Come Dance with Me (Billy May, January 1959)

No One Cares (Gordon Jenkins, July 1959)

Nice 'n Easy (Nelson Riddle, July 1960)

Sinatra's Swingin' Session!!! (Nelson Riddle, January 1961)

Come Swing with Me (Billy May, July 1961)

Point of No Return (Axel Stordahl, March 1962)

REPRISE RECORDS

If Sinatra's Capitol albums represent perfection, his Reprise efforts represent versatility. This period finds Sinatra working in an amazing variety of settings, as the records indicate:

Ring-a-Ding-Ding (Johnny Mandel, March 1961)

Sinatra Swings (Billy May, July 1961)

I Remember Tommy . . . (Sy Oliver, October 1961)

Sinatra and Strings (Don Costa, February 1962)

Sinatra and Swingin' Brass (Neal Hefti, July 1962)

Great Songs from Great Britain (Robert Farnon, recorded 1962, released on LP in Great Britain 1965—no U.S. LP release until 1993)

Sinatra-Basie (with Count Basie) (Neal Hefti, January 1963)

The Concert Sinatra (Nelson Riddle, May 1963)

Sinatra's Sinatra (Nelson Riddle, August 1963)

Academy Award Winners (Nelson Riddle, March 1964)

It Might as Well Be Swing (with Count Basie) (Quincy Jones, August 1964)

September of My Years (Gordon Jenkins, August 1965)

Stranger in the Night (Nelson Riddle and Ernie Freeman, May 1966)

Moonlight Sinatra (Nelson Riddle, March 1966)

That's Life (Ernie Freeman, November 1966)

Francis Albert Sinatra and Antonio Carlos Jobim (Claus Ogerman, March 1967)

Francis A. and Edward K. (with Duke Ellington) (Billy May, January 1968)

The Sinatra Family Wish You a Merry Christmas (Nelson Riddle and Don Costa, September 1968)

Cycles (Don Costa, November 1968)

My Way (Don Costa, August 1969)

A Man Alone (Don Costa, August 1969)

Watertown (Charles Callelo, March 1970)

Ol' Blue Eyes Is Back (Gordon Jenkins and Don Costa, September 1973)

Some Nice Things I've Missed (Don Costa, July 1974)

Trilogy (Billy May, Don Costa, and Gordon Jenkins, March 1980)

She Shot Me Down (Gordon Jenkins and Nelson Riddle, November 1981)

QWEST RECORDS

L.A. Is My Lady (with Quincy Jones) (Various arrangers, August 1984)

CAPITOL RECORDS

Duets I (Patrick Williams, November 1993)

Duets II (Patrick Williams, October 1994)

Fifty Songs That Define the Essence of Sinatra

There are fifty recordings that I believe epitomize the very essence of what the music of Frank Sinatra is all about. Within this small cache of performances, one can experience the breadth of what this book endeavors to impart: the uniqueness of his vocal style, his impeccable approach to music and recording, and his highly developed flair for the dramatic.

You might note the absence of most of the "hits" that are commonly associated with Frank Sinatra. The following recordings have been chosen not for their commercial success, but for their exceptional musical value. Of course, everyone's opinion will differ and some people may disagree with my personal selections.

1. *Say It* (Tommy Dorsey, 1940, Victor)

2. *East of the Sun* (Tommy Dorsey, 1940, Victor)

3. *Night and Day* (Axel Stordahl, 1942, Victor Bluebird)

4. *All the Things You Are* (Axel Stordahl, 1945, Columbia)

5. *These Foolish Things* (Axel Stordahl, 1945, Columbia)

6. *Sweet Lorraine* (Sy Oliver, 1946, Columbia)

7. *Body and Soul* (Axel Stordahl, 1947, Columbia)

8. *American Beauty Rose* (Norman Leyden, 1950, Columbia)

9. *Hello Young Lovers* (Axel Stordahl, 1951, Columbia)

10. *I'm a Fool to Want You* (Axel Stordahl, 1951, Columbia)

11. *My Girl* (Axel Stordahl, 1952, Columbia)

12. *The Birth of the Blues* (Heinie Beau, 1952, Columbia)

13. *I've Got the World on a String* (Nelson Riddle, 1953, Capitol)

14. *My One and Only Love* (Nelson Riddle, 1953, Capitol)

15. *Rain* (Nelson Riddle, 1953, Capitol)

16. *Someone to Watch Over Me* (Nelson Riddle, 1954, Capitol)

17. *Last Night When We Were Young* (Nelson Riddle, 1954, Capitol)

18. *In the Wee Small Hours of the Morning* (Nelson Riddle, 1955, Capitol)

19. *Weep They Will* (Nelson Riddle, 1955, Capitol)

20. *I've Got You Under My Skin* (Nelson Riddle, 1956, Capitol)

21. *With Every Breath I Take* (Nelson Riddle, 1956, Capitol)

22. *From This Moment On* (Nelson Riddle, 1956, Capitol)

23. *April in Paris* (Billy May, 1957, Capitol)

24. *Brazil* (Billy May, 1957, Capitol)

25. *Guess I'll Hang My Tears Out to Dry* (Nelson Riddle, 1958, Capitol)

26. *Willow Weep for Me* (Nelson Riddle, 1958, Capitol)

27. *I Could Have Danced All Night* (Billy May, 1958, Capitol)

28. *Here's That Rainy Day* (Gordon Jenkins, 1959, Capitol)

29. *Embraceable You* (Nelson Riddle, 1960, Capitol)

30. *When the World Was Young* (Axel Stordahl, 1961, Capitol)

31. *In the Still of the Night* (Johnny Mandel, 1960, Reprise)

32. *That's All* (Don Costa, 1961, Reprise)

33. *Come Rain or Come Shine* (Don Costa, 1961, Reprise)

34. *A Nightingale Sang in Berkeley Square* (Robert Farnon, 1962, Reprise)

35. *I Have Dreamed* (Nelson Riddle, 1963, Reprise)

36. *Ol' Man River* (Nelson Riddle, 1963, Reprise)

37. *Luck Be a Lady* (Billy May, 1963, Reprise)

38. *Emily* (Nelson Riddle, 1964, Reprise)

39. *It Was a Very Good Year* (Gordon Jenkins, 1965, Reprise)

40. *Indian Summer* (with Duke Ellington, 1967, Reprise)

41. *Whatever Happened to Christmas* (Don Costa, 1968, Reprise)

42. *Wandering* (Don Costa, 1968, Reprise)

43. *The Song of the Sabia* (Eumir Deodato, 1969, Reprise)

44. *Send in the Clowns* (Gordon Jenkins, 1973, Reprise)

45. *What Are You Doing the Rest of Your Life?* (Don Costa, 1974, Reprise)

46. *I Love My Wife* (Nelson Riddle, 1976, Reprise)

47. *Summer Me, Winter Me* (Don Costa, 1981, Reprise)

48. *Everything Happens to Me* (Gordon Jenkins, 1981, Reprise)

49. *A Long Night* (Gordon Jenkins, 1981, Reprise)

50. *One for My Baby* (Nelson Riddle, 1993, Capitol)

Acknowledgments

I am particularly indebted to the talented men and women who had the good fortune to assist Frank Sinatra in transferring the musical ideas in his head to the grooves of his phonograph records. It is satisfying to think that in some way, this volume containing their words will serve to highlight their vastly underrated contributions, and preserve their recollections for future generations of historians and music enthusiasts.

In 1990, author Will Friedwald and I embarked on a mission to seek out and interview as many of Mr. Sinatra's key collaborators as possible. Along the way, we befriended many people who enriched our knowledge and understanding of all music, and I am grateful for the cooperation of these exceptional musical figures:

Tony Bennett, Alan Bergman, Milt Bernhart, Johnny Blowers, Jimmy Bowen, Joe Bushkin, Sammy Cahn, Rosemary Clooney, Buddy Collette, Matt Dennis, Ervin Drake, Harry "Sweets" Edison, Vincent Falcone, Robert Farnon, Frank Flynn, Stan Freeman, David Frisina, Bert Hall (Harry Zinquist), Lee Hazlewood, Neal Hefti, Lyle "Skitch" Henderson, Carol Kaye, Jack Lawrence, Quincy Jones, Mickey Leonard, Mitchell Lurie, Johnny Mandel, Dave Mann, Frank Mane, Billy May, Bill Miller, Mitch Miller, Lillian Clark Oliver, Jack Palmer, Les Paul, Emil Richards, Christopher Riddle, George Roberts, Mickey Scrima, Paul C. Shure, Nancy Sinatra, George Siravo, Eleanor Slatkin, Leonard Slatkin, Marshall Sosson, Jo Stafford, Billy Strange, Alvin Stoller, George van Eps, Al Viola, David Vogel, Warren "Champ" Webb, Paul Weston, Patrick Williams, and Fred Zlotkin.

And to these executives, producers, recording engineers and technical experts: George Avakian, Bill Cook, Matt Cavaluzzo, Hugh Davies, Michael Frondelli, William Gottlieb, Bud Graham, Fred Grimes, Lee Herschberg, Larry Keyes, Frank Laico, Alan Livingston, John Palladino, Jack Pfeiffer, Phil Ramone, Bill Savory, Al Schmitt, Howard Scott, Arthur Shimkin, Allen Sides, George T. Simon, Carson Taylor, Jim Webb, and Pete Welding.

I am also grateful to the following individuals for providing access to their archival interviews: Stan Britt (Alan Freeman and Nelson Riddle interviews), Jack Ellsworth (Frank Sinatra interview), Bruce Jenkins (Wink Martindale's Gordon Jenkins interview), Sid Mark (Frank Sinatra interviews), Jonathan Schwartz (Nelson Riddle interviews), and Sidney Zion (Frank Sinatra Yale interview).

A project of this size and scope requires the aid of many people, whose thoughtful contribution, small or large, is of immeasurable value to this writer/researcher. I am most appreciative for the kind efforts of: Michael Anthony, Bill Auerbach, Irmgard Bambrick, Christopher Barling, Jenny Barthwick (Landseer Productions), Bob Berks, Adam Block, Stan Britt, Michael Brooks, Ken Carley, Nancy Collins-Castellanos, Janet Cohen, Larry Cohn, Joe D'Ambrosio and Nina DiCecco (assistants to Phil Ramone), Natalie Datloff, Dustin and Mary Doctor, Robert Finkelstein, Joel Friedman, Sonny Golden, Joyce Gore,

Marty Halperin, Beverly Harris (assistant to Leonard Slatkin), Sheila Hart, Ken Howard (Landseer Productions), Bob Irwin, Charlotte and Toni Janak, Jeff Jones, Eric Kohler, Greg Lake, Peter Levinson, Hal Lifson, Heather Lomax, Robyn Lomax, Mary Mane, Randall Martin, Robert McNally, Patrick Milligan, Amy Oringel, Robert Oringel, Gary Pacheco, Tina Petillo, Kerry and Bernie Pranica, Al Quaglieri, Tom Rednour, Katherine Reinhardt, Rosemary Riddle-Acerra, Samantha Rosenman, Richard Schuller, Kerry Rasp, Eric Schmertz, Jonathan Schwartz, David Scott, Tina Sinatra, Paul Stefany, Steve Sussmann, Bob Waldmann, and Alan Wright.

The dedication and perseverance of the following individuals helped pull the illustrative portion of this book together: Corey Anderson (Sony Music Entertainment), Helen Ashford (Michael Ochs Archive), Sid Avery (MPTV Archive), Nat Brewster (Sony Music Archives), Stewart Brown (Testament Records), William Gottlieb, Michael Gray, Nat Johnson (RCA Records), Loanne Rios Kong and Jarrett T. Seals (Sony Music Photo Library), James Lum, Nancy Marcus (Sony Music Entertainment), Chuck Musse (REX USA), David Scott, Douglas Tarr (Edison National Historic Site), Tom Tierney (BMG Photo Archive), Doug Tinney (Ampex Corporation), Warren Wernick (Sony Classical), Karl Winkler (Neumann USA), Terry Woodson (Frank Sinatra Music Library), Ernie Woody and Jack Woltz (Ocean Way Recording), Monika Wright (Warner-Chappell Music), and Eric Young (Archive Photos).

I am grateful to the friends and family members who went "above and beyond" to help me realize my goal. This work could never have been completed without their tireless support and encouragement: Linda Austin, Karen and Russel Barling, Gerald Campanella, Al and Dorothea Corona, Adrienne and Guido Granata, John Granata, Marion and Tom Kosman, Sid Mark, Frank Military, Leonard Mustazza, Deborah Paull, and Jude Spatola.

I have been fortunate to spend time with producer Phil Ramone, both at his home and as co-conversants on the music of Frank Sinatra at Hofstra University and the Museum of Radio and Television in New York. I am genuinely appreciative of his sensitive and heartfelt words that open this book.

As well, I am grateful to the wonderful staff at A Cappella Books, including associate managing editor Gerilee Hundt, project editor Lisa Rosenthal, and my editor, Yuval Taylor, whose patience and linguistic sensibilities are reflected in these pages.

Very special thanks to my good friend Linda Corona, Public Services Librarian at the Mountainside, New Jersey, Public Library, who functioned as the research assistant for this book. I have the utmost respect and admiration for her tireless dedication to the accuracy of this project, and the value of the printed word.

Two close and respected friends, Steve Albin and Michael Kraus, read and re-read dozens of incarnations of the manuscript, and their meticulous corrections and suggestions have added tremendously to the final product.

There are three very special musical compatriots, whose friendship and constant encouragement I cherish: Didier C. Deutsch, Will Friedwald, and Nancy Sinatra. Thank you for being there—always.

Last, but not least, are three very important people in my life: my wife Barbara and beautiful daughters, Kate and Alex. Their endless reserve of patience and understanding while I was "otherwise occupied" during the hundreds of hours spent researching and writing this book mean more to me than words could ever express.

Bibliography

BOOKS

Burt, Leah Brodbeck Stenzel and Walter L. Welch. *From Tinfoil to Stereo: The Acoustic Years of the Recording Industry 1877–1929*. Gainesville, Fla.: The University Press of Florida, 1994.

Cahn, Sammy. *I Should Care*. New York: Arbor House Publishing, 1974.

Clifford, Martin. *Microphones: How They Work and How to Use Them*. Blue Ridge Summit, Penn.: TAB Books, 1977.

Dearling, Robert and Celia, with Brian Rust. *The Guinness Book of Recorded Sound*. London: Guinness Superlatives Inc., 1984.

Douglas-Home, Robin. *Sinatra*. New York: Grosset & Dunlap, 1962.

Friedwald, Will. *Sinatra! The Song Is You: A Singer's Art*. New York: Scribner's, 1995.

Gellatt, Roland. *The Fabulous Phonograph*. New York: J. B. Lippincott Company, 1954.

Grein, Paul. *Capitol Records Fiftieth Anniversary 1942–1992*. Hollywood, Calif.: Capitol Records Inc., 1992.

Karolyi, Otto. *Introducing Music*. New York: Viking Penguin, Inc., 1989.

Marco, Guy. *Encyclopedia of Recorded Sound in the United States*. New York: Garland Publishing, Inc., 1993.

Millard, Andre. *America on Record: A History of Recorded Sound*. New York: Cambridge University Press, 1990.

Mustazza, Leonard. *Sinatra: An Annotated Bibliography, 1939–1998*. Westport, Conn.: Greenwood Press, 1999.

Oringel, Robert. *Audio Control Handbook for Radio and TV Broadcasting*. New York: Hastings House Publishers, 1956.

Paper, Lewis J. *Empire: William S. Paley and the Making of CBS*. New York: St. Martin's Press, 1987.

Petkov, Steven and Leonard Mustazza. *The Frank Sinatra Reader*. New York: Oxford University Press, 1995.

Pleasants, Henry. *The Great American Popular Singers*. New York: Simon and Schuster, 1974.

Rednour, Tom. *Songs by Sinatra: A Unique Frank Sinatra Songography*. Beacon, New York: Wordcrafters, 1998.

Riddle, Nelson. *Arranged by Nelson Riddle*. Secaucus, New Jersey: Warner Bros. Publications Inc., 1985.

Rust, Brian. *The American Record Label Book*. New York: Da Capo Press, 1984.

Sinatra, Nancy. *Frank Sinatra: An American Legend*. Santa Monica, Calif.: General Publishing Group, 1995.

Slater, Robert. *This . . . Is CBS: A Chronicle of 60 Years*. Englewood, New Jersey: Prentice Hall, 1988.

Shaugnessy, Mary Alice. *Les Paul: An American Original*. New York: William Morrow & Co., Inc., 1993.

Valin, Jonathan. *The RCA Bible: A Compendium of Opinion on RCA Living Stereo Records*. Cincinnati, Ohio: The Music Lovers Press, 1993.

Yarwood, Guy. *Sinatra in His Own Words*. London: Omnibus Press, 1982.

PERIODICALS

Berger, Myron. "The Hundredth Anniversary of Stereo—Sort Of." *Stereo Review*, December 1981, pp. 62–63.

Canby, Edward Tatnall. "Audio Etc." *Audio*, April 1980, pp. 13–14.

Degraaf, Leonard. "Thomas Edison and the Origins of the Entertainment Phonograph." *NARAS Journal*. Winter/Spring 1997/98. Volume 8, Number 1, pp. 43–69.

Elliott, Susan. "The Audio Interview: Jack Pfeiffer." *Audio*, November 1992.

Gray, Michael. "The Winged Champion: Mercury Records and the Birth of High Fidelity." *The Absolute Sound*, Issue 60, pp. 47–57.

Gray, Michael. "The Winged Champion: Mercury Records and the Birth of High Fidelity Part 2." *The Absolute Sound*, Issue 61, pp. 47–57.

Lubin, Tom. "The Sounds of Science: The development of the recording studio as instrument." *NARAS Journal*. Summer/Fall 1996, Volume 7, Number 1, pp. 41–99.

Reed, Peter Hugh. "Records to Meet War Usage." *The Etude*, March 1943, pp. 155; 216.

Sinatra, Frank. "Back on Top." *Time*. 10 May 1954, pp. 72–74.

Sinatra, Frank. "Me And My Music." *Life*. 23 April 1965, pp. 86–87, 99–104.

Thompson, Thomas. "Frank Sinatra's Swan Song," *Life*. 25 June 1971, pp. 70–74.

INTERNET SITES

Beaupre, Walter J. "Music Electrically Transcribed!" users.aol.com/edwardelec/artwb006.html (29 December 1997).

Bensman, Marvin R. "A History of Radio Program Collecting." www.people.memphis.edu/~mbensman/collectingarticle.html (21 December 1997).

Biel, Michael. "A History of Radio Broadcast Recordings." www.kemetro.cc.mo.us/pennvalley/biology/lewis/crosby/transcrib.htm (30 December 1997).

Classic Records. "Jack Pfeiffer's Corner." www.classicrecs.com/jack.htm (20 December 1998).

George Neumann Gmbh/Berlin: "Historical Collection." www.neumann.com/history/welcome.htm (29 December 1998).

INTERVIEWS

Except where noted, all interviews conducted by Charles L. Granata and/or Will Friedwald. Dates are for formal interviews pertaining specifically to Frank Sinatra and his work in the recording studio.

Acerra, Rosemary Riddle. 7 February 1999; personal conversations 1998–1999.

Avakian, George. December 1991; 28 December 1998.

Bennett, Tony. Formal interviews and personal conversations, 1992–1998.

Bergman, Alan. 15 July 1994.

Berks, Robert. October 1998.

Bernhart, Milt. Formal interviews and personal conversations, 1990–1999.

Blowers, John. December 1991.

Bowen, Jimmy. 1994.

Bushkin, Joe. June 1992.

Cahn, Sammy. 7 December 1991; personal conversations 1991–1992.

Clooney, Rosemary. 25 and 27 February 1992.

Collette, Buddy. February 1993.

Cook, Bill. 7 and 8 November 1998.

Davies, Hugh. August 1992.

Drake, Ervin. Formal interviews and personal conversations, 1992–1999.

Edison, Harry. December 1991.

Falcone, Vinnie. May 1994 and December 1998.

Farnon, Robert. 14 November 1992.

Flynn, Frank. December 1991.

Freeman, Alan. Interviewed by Stan Britt, circa 1970s.

Freeman, Stan. November 1991.

Friedman, Joel. 12 February 1999.

Frisina, David. December 1991.

Frondelli, Michael. November 1998.

Gottlieb, William. 30 July 1998.

Gray, Michael. 1992–1994.

Grimes, Fred. August 1998.

Hazlewood, Lee. July 1996.

Hefti, Neal. March 1992.

Henderson, Skitch. February 1992.

Herschberg, Lee. October 1993.

Jenkins, Gordon. Interviewed by Wink Martindale, circa 1970s.

Jones, Quincy. October 1993; 5 November 1998.

Kaye, Carol. Formal interviews and personal conversations, 1997–1999.

Laico, Frank. January 1992; June 1998.

Lawrence, Jack. May 1995.

Leonard, Michael (Mickey). Personal conversations, 1995–1999.

Livingston, Alan. 14 June 1992.

Lurie, Mitchell. 4 September 1998.

Mandel, John. April 1993.

Mane, Frank. July, 1998.

Mann, David. 1 October, 1996.

May, Billy. Formal interviews and personal conversations 1992–1998.

Military, Frank. Formal interviews and personal conversations 1992–1999.

Miller, Bill. Formal interviews and personal conversations 1992–1998.

Miller, Mitch. 27 January 1992 and April 1998.

Paich, Marty. December 1991.

Palladino, John. July–August 1992, September–December 1998.

Palmer, Jack. 29 December 1998.

Pfeiffer, Jack. Personal conversations, 1993–1994.

Raskin, David. 1996.

Ramone, Phil. Formal interviews and personal conversations, 1993–1999.

Richards, Emil. January 1993.

Riddle, Christopher. January 1994.

Riddle, Nelson. Interviewed by Jonathan Schwartz/WNEW Radio 1983; Robert Windeler/KCRW Radio, 1985.

Roberts, George. December 1991.

Savory, Bill. Formal interviews and personal conversations. 1994–1997.

Schuller, Richard. November 1998.

Scott, Howard. 28 December 1998.

Scrima, Mickey. 28 December 1998.

Shimkin, Arthur. September–December 1998.

Shure, Paul C. October 1991; 2 and 3 September 1998.

Sides, Allen. 12 February 1999.

Simon, George. Formal interviews and personal conversations. 1993–1996.

Sinatra, Frank. Interviewed by Sid Mark/Orange Productions, 1980–1988.

Sinatra, Nancy. Formal interviews and personal conversations, 1993–1999.

Siravo, George. September 1992; 4 March 1997.

Slatkin, Eleanor. October 1991.

Slatkin, Leonard. Interviewed by Ken Howard/Landseer Productions. London, July 1998.

Sosson, Marshall. July 1998.

Stafford, Jo. October 1991; April 1995.

Stoller, Alvin. July 1992.

Strange, Billy. July 1996.

Taylor, Carson. 28 December 1998.

Van Eps, George. March 1992.

Viola, Al. Formal interviews and personal conversations, 1990–1999.

Vogel, David. December 1998.

Webb, James. December 1998.

Webb, Warren. February 1993.

Weston, Paul. October 1991; April 1995.

Williams, Patrick. 5 November 1998.

Zinquist, Harry (aka Bert Hall). 4 February 1992.

Zlotkin, Fred. April 1999.

ADDITIONAL SINATRA AUDIO INTERVIEWS

Sinatra, Frank. Interviewed by Walter Cronkite, CBS News, 1965.

Sinatra, Frank. Interviewed by Jack Ellsworth, New York, 1949.

Sinatra, Frank. Interviewed by Ben Heller, Atlantic City, New Jersey, 1950.

Sinatra, Frank, Interviewed by Sidney Zion, Yale University, 1986.

Index